Early Exits

The Premature Endings of Baseball Careers

Brian McKenna

The Scarecrow Press, Inc.
Lanham, Maryland • Toronto • Plymouth, UK
2007

SCARECROW PRESS, INC.

Published in the United States of America
by Scarecrow Press, Inc.
A wholly owned subsidiary of
The Rowman & Littlefield Publishing Group, Inc.
4501 Forbes Boulevard, Suite 200, Lanham, Maryland 20706
www.scarecrowpress.com

Estover Road
Plymouth PL6 7PY
United Kingdom

British Library Cataloguing in Publication Information Available

Library of Congress Cataloging-in-Publication Data

McKenna, Brian, 1966–
   Early exits : the premature endings of baseball careers / Brian McKenna.
     p. cm.
   Includes bibliographical references and index.
   ISBN-13: 978-0-8108-5858-9 (hardcover : alk. paper)
   ISBN-10: 0-8108-5858-4 (hardcover : alk. paper)
   1. Baseball–Miscellanea.   2. Baseball players–Miscellanea.   3. Baseball–History.   I. Title.
GV873.M375   2007
796.357–dc22   2006013804

♾ ™ The paper used in this publication meets the minimum requirements of American National
Standard for Information Sciences—Permanence of Paper for Printed Library Materials, ANSI/
NISO Z39.48-1992. Manufactured in the United States of America.

For my little buddies,
Brian and Rachel

Contents

~

Introduction

Like many of you, I've had a lifelong obsession with baseball. I started collecting base-ball cards when I was eight years old in 1974, read the newspapers and as many maga-zines and books that I could get ahold of and happily watched my local club, the Orioles, whenever I got the chance. One of my earliest memories is of my father taking my brother and me to Memorial Stadium. Because I was the one so gung ho, he'd asked me where I wanted to sit. Of course, it had to be on the third base side, near Brooks Robinson.

As I passed through my teenage years, my interest never waned. The most glori-ous event of my youth happened in eighth grade; I broke my arm. It was great, not the pain but the cure. My mother gave me a Christmas present two months early, my first *MacMillan Baseball Encyclopedia*. I had it all now.

Then, something wonderful happened at my household around 1981; we got cable. Games were now on all the time and, can you believe it, one station was actu-ally dedicated to sports. I still read whatever I could find and eventually I started to piece things together in my mind. The game was coming into focus.

You might think that's funny but the history of baseball is so immense it can be overwhelming. Just the study of the major leagues is formidable. By now, I was fin-ished with college, so I was free to read on my own terms. I decided that I was, to a point, wasting my energy. I needed to focus and develop a deeper understanding of the various topics. In short, research was required. Not heavy research—after all this was just a hobby—but I needed to consult more than one source on each topic and I needed to separate myth from reality. The game is steeped in both.

In the back of my mind, I always thought I should pick a topic, research it, and write my own book. I could never settle on that topic. Years passed but the thought was always there, though nothing concrete came of it. I wanted to do what I hadn't seen before. Then, one day it came to me. Why not write about baseball men whose careers were shortened for reasons other than the common sports injury? I originally thought that would include just illness, accidents, and death. It didn't take long to realize that Pete Rose's career and the playing days of the Black Sox were abruptly cut short. Now, I was onto something.

I decided the best way to start was with the large reference books. I read *The Ballplayers* and *Baseball: The Biographical Encyclopedia*, both great for biographical content. Suddenly, I had tons of notes. I just kept bouncing from source to source collecting everything I could. The story came into focus. It would also include those that were blacklisted or forced out of the game for a wide array of reasons—sought other jobs, chose other professional sports, went into politics, dedicated themselves to military service or participated in a wide range of gambling and game-fixing activities. I also thought it appropriate to highlight those that were seriously injured on the field by a beaning or similar tragedy.

I began to see that my view of the game was narrow. Baseball is more than just the major leagues. It takes a lot of work but one can come to a basic understanding of the Negro leagues, minor leagues, women's baseball, and the international game, particularly in Latin American and Japan. And do not omit the 19th century. The genesis of the game demands our attention. Too many dismiss it by focusing only on the modern game, usually quoted as 1901 onward. I did, however, center solely on those men and women who were paid to play the game.

I knew little of these topics when I started. If nothing else, I am immensely grateful for this process that led to a better understanding of the entire spectrum of the national pastime. I also learned a great deal about sports history in general. I didn't know much but now I can at least hold a conversation about the professional origins and growth of golf, boxing, auto racing, basketball, hockey, and football.

After my original draft of *Early Exits*, I suddenly had a coming of age, so to speak. I discovered the Internet. It is all there. More than you can soak in. There are encyclopedias and biographical websites. It's all free. Just click and the information pops up.

I could never have included as much information as I did about Japanese baseball without the Internet. Also, my membership in the *Society for American Baseball Research* provides me with Internet access to Atlanta, Boston, New York, Los Angeles, Chicago, Washington, D.C., and other periodicals dating to the genesis of the majors. I can get it all right at my desk in seconds.

The Internet is also a great place for fact-checking. So many of our beliefs of the game come from oral stories or conversations with others. This is great, but the facts are often a little off or twisted entirely. Just run a search on a topic and you'll be able to compare the data. I also joined several forums, one each on baseball, football, and boxing. These fans have really saved me. I throw ideas out there and they tell me whether I'm full of it or not. The also pick apart my misconceptions and errors. I am eternally grateful for their help and they don't even know it.

There is a great deal of information on major league history on the 'net. What we really need is men and women who are willing to dedicate themselves to providing us all with more in-depth statistics, biographical and other information on Japanese baseball, Latin ball, the Negro leagues, minor leagues, and professional football. These are the big topics for me. I hope many take up the task.

My greatest hope is that just one fan will read my material and think, "Wow, that was a fun journey." You might not want to read every little story but I could omit none. Some names may be unknown or foreign, for that matter, but in the end they are all a part of our great game. They all tell a piece of the story.

CHAPTER ONE

Gambling and Game-Fixing Scandals

Sports and gambling go hand-in-hand. Contest-fixing can be traced back to wrestling matches in ancient Greece. Baseball has proven to be no exception. In fact, during the days of purported amateurism, men had a stake in the final score. In 1860, $1,000 went to the winners of a Unions of Medway and Upton Excelsiors contest. It is only because of apathetic reporting and lost whispers in the stands that today we don't know the specifics of what were surely numerous other occurrences.

Gambling was so entrenched that at the Union Grounds in Brooklyn a facility was erected to handle the betting action. And a special seating section was created for gamblers behind third base in Boston. This interplay was immortalized in the 1895 stage show *Runaway Colt*.

1877 Louisville Grays Scandal

A defining moment in National League history occurred with the expulsion of the "Louisville Four" after the 1877 season for game-fixing. First, a review of the players is necessary.

Jim Devlin, from the Bechtel affair, was one of the top two pitchers in the National League at the time. In the league's first two campaigns, Devlin led in games, starts, complete games, losses, and innings pitched. He also won 65 games while accumulating an ERA of 1.89. In 1877, Devlin became the only major league pitcher to work every inning of every game for his team. Devlin was also one of the heaviest drinking men of the era, a talent he shared with Bill Craver.

Civil War veteran Bill Craver was the team's shortstop. While with the Chicago White Stockings in August 1870 in the old NABBP, he had been expelled for gambling and general disobedience, usually a synonym for drunken and disorderly conduct. Craver later signed with the Troy Haymakers in the National Association and continued his questionable play. His team tried unsuccessfully to have him banned by National Association officials for bribing an umpire. Craver holds the distinction of being suspected of fraud in three different leagues and convicted in two. He was also the team captain for Troy in 1869 who pulled his team off the field with the game tied against the undefeated Cincinnati Red Stockings at the behest of gamblers and team owner Big John Morrissey, a corrupt New York politician in the mold of Boss Tweed.

One of the better hitters in early baseball history, team captain and outfielder George Hall batted .301 over a five-year span in the National Association. He continued slugging the ball in the National League, hitting .366 in 1876 to finish second to Ross Barnes for the title. Hall also finished second in triples, total bases, on-base percentage, and slugging average. Hitting .323 in 1877, Hall led the league in home runs with five. That year, he finished among the leaders in runs scored, doubles, triples, total bases, walks, and slugging average.

Utility player Al Nichols was picked up in midseason by the Grays on Hall's recommendation. Nichols was needed to replace injured third baseman Bill Hague. Perhaps what impressed Hall the most was Nichols' friendship with gamblers. Soon after his arrival, the team began to fade in the standings.

With three-quarters of the season over, Louisville needed to go only .500 down the stretch to clinch the pennant. They began losing at an alarming rate because of untimely strikeouts, pickoffs, costly errors, and poor pitching. Devlin, the everyday pitcher, lost 13 of his last 20 games.

Eventually, Louisville blew the lead altogether, at one point losing eight straight, and finished second to Boston. *Louisville Courier-Journal* sports reporter John Haldeman smelled a rat. Suspiciously, Devlin just happened to be pitching much better in post-season exhibition contests and sporting flashy jewelry.

Louisville vice president Charles Chase also noticed that Nichols was receiving a lot of telegrams. The players were confronted. Hall confessed on October 27th and outlined the details. He stated that his brother-in-law Frank Powell had been after him for some time to supplement his income by throwing games. Finally relenting, Hall approached Devlin with the idea. Coincidentally, Devlin had already been approached by a New York gambler named McCloud for the same reason. Together, the players conspired to lose games in which they were favored and split part of McCloud's gain. Hall named Nichols as the ringleader; however, it appears that Hall and Devlin were the leaders and that Nichols was the go-between with the gamblers.

Chase called a team meeting and demanded to see everyone's telegrams. Craver was the only one who refused. He was promptly suspended. Hall, Devlin, and Nichols were expelled after they confessed. Their telegrams had implicated them anyway. No actual evidence was ever presented implicating Craver other than a mention by one of the conspirators. Craver never actually said he wouldn't let his telegrams be read. He merely linked their release to payment of his back salary. Craver continually maintained his innocence, at least in this affair.

Nevertheless, all four players were expelled from the National League. It is interesting that the NABBP, the National Association, and the National League were not able to respond to such issues in a timely manner. League business was usually conducted at an annual meeting that could have been 9, 10, or 11 months after a crisis arose. Rarely were matters adjudicated promptly.

Subsequent requests for reinstatement by the four went unrequited. Devlin went so far as to literally cry and beg National League president William Hulbert for re-admittance in a humiliating scene witnessed by Spalding and others. Hulbert personally slapped $50 into the destitute's hand but maintained that there was no place in baseball for a game-fixer.

The banishments gutted the Louisville franchise. It disbanded. Hulbert's permanent banning of the Louisville Four was a major turning point in the history of major league baseball. It was the first highly publicized case in which baseball took a stern view of gambling. The tone was set for the rest of the century. After only two years, the National League and Hulbert had built a stronger foundation than either the NABBP or the National Association.

1903 World Series
The first modern World Series took place in 1903, more a result of an agreement between the Boston and Pittsburgh franchises than the two leagues. The credit here belongs to owners Henry Killilea and Barney Dreyfuss with a lot of persuasion by American League president Ban Johnson, who sought to further legitimize his league.

Officially, the majors did not mandate postseason play until 1905, permitting the pennant-winning Giants owner John Brush and manager John McGraw to decline competition against, in their eyes, the inferior American League at the end of the 1904 season.

On the eve of the series, Boston catcher Lou Criger, Cy Young's personal catcher even back in the National League with Cleveland and St. Louis, later reported to Ban Johnson that he was approached by a gambler named Anderson to throw the games. Anderson had offered him a $12,000 bribe to enlist Young and ensure a Pittsburgh victory. Criger refused.

The story's importance lies not in Lou Criger or the attempted bride but in the handling of the affair. In an attempt to avoid public scrutiny, many such events were hushed up and ignored. In fact, the incident was never even disclosed until 1924 when Johnson attempt to further implicate John McGraw in the O'Connell–Dolan affair. Per Criger's disclosure, McGraw had been seen in the company of Anderson back in 1903.

It was the typical hear no evil, see no evil, and speak no evil mentality. This led, in part, to a mushrooming of the problem. Others saw certain players getting away with cheating, so they felt punishments were lax. In turn, they sought the extra cash as well. This directly led to the blow-up involving the 1919 World Series.

1910 American League Batting Race
The race for the 1910 American League batting title came down to the last day of the season between Napoleon Lajoie and Ty Cobb. Both would eventually enter the Hall of Fame. Lajoie was well-liked and admired throughout the league and had already won three batting titles and the Triple Crown in 1901. His 1901 batting average was 0.086 better than his nearest competitor, a still-standing record. His team was even nicknamed the Naps in his honor. Cobb, though only 23, had copped the last three batting titles and would go on to win every one through 1919 except 1916. He was also as despised as Lajoie was adored.

The problem occurred on October 9 as the Browns attempted to deprive Cobb of the batting title and the automobile that the Chalmers Motor Company had promised the winner. In a doubleheader versus the Browns, Lajoie in nine plate appearances compiled a triple, six bunt singles, a sacrifice bunt, and a shot to shortstop

Bobby Wallace that was ruled a hit on an errant throw. He went 8 for 8 and had apparently won the title.

Uproar ensued in Detroit and Ban Johnson investigated. Young Browns third baseman Red Corriden admitted that team manager Jack O'Connor had ordered him to play deep whenever Lajoie came to the plate, thus allowing bunts to roll for hits.

"Rowdy Jack" O'Connor was a hard-living, hard-drinking 21-year major league catcher and long-time battery mate of Cy Young. He had been expelled by the American Association back in 1892 for habitual drunkenness, disorderly conduct, and insubordination. The heart of his career was spent with the aggressive National League Cleveland Spiders of the 1890s, a team that rivaled the Baltimore Orioles of the era for hard-nosed tactics. Once, O'Connor broke the jaw of umpire Jack McNulty.

Johnson further learned that Browns pitcher-coach-scout Harry Howell wrote a note promising the official scorer a suit of clothes if he ruled close plays in the favor of Lajoie. He was also seen popping in and out of the scorer's box throughout the game, possibly trying to influence his decisions. Howell was one of baseball's first spitballers, winning 134 games in 13 major league seasons. He had been arrested back in 1906 for book making.

Johnson questioned O'Connor and Howell to no avail. They were officially cleared but Johnson forced their dismissal and sought to exclude them from organized baseball. No action was taken against Corriden, who would spend over 50 years in baseball, or Lajoie. When the official statistics were issued, Cobb was declared the winner anyway. Seeking to capitalize on the publicity, Chalmers gave each player an automobile.

A *Sporting News* researcher in 1981 found an error in the official calculations that mathematically gives Lajoie a higher batting average for the 1910 season. A Bowie Kuhn ruling chose to ignore the discrepancy; consequently, Major League Baseball still recognizes Cobb as the winner.

O'Connor never again appeared in organized baseball, though he did find a job with the Federal League. The manager was in the middle of a two-year contract when dismissed from the Browns. He sued and recovered $5,000. In his only season as a major league manager he had lost 107 games. Despite Johnson's efforts to exclude him, Howell found employment as an umpire in the minors and, later, in the Federal League.

1919 Chicago White Sox

October 1919 was a singular month for defrauding the American public. First, in the White House President Woodrow Wilson suffered a massive stroke. To this day, historians are unsure of the extent of the damage to his mental acumen. For the rest of his presidency (17 months), Wilson was hidden from all except his doctors and wife. All matters of state were transacted through the First Lady. In all likelihood, Mrs. Wilson unlawfully administered the affairs of the nation. Significantly, the president's incapacitation probably kept the United States out of the League of Nations, which in turn may have exacerbated the depths of World War II.

Then, eight ballplayers conspired to throw the hallowed World Series. Though they derived their nickname from an earlier laundry dispute, the Black Sox gave new meaning to the term. The 1919 Black Sox Scandal is the single darkest event in the history of American sports. It threatened the very core of the game—the public's confidence in its matches. The power structure of the game would be completely replaced by the fallout. 1919 also marked the end of the dead ball era. Out of the ashes of scandal, a new, more exhilarating product emerged.

Precipitating Factors

Everyone knows that certain elements on the Chicago White Sox set out to throw the 1919 World Series and succeeded. Obviously, they did it for money. It is doubtful that eight players would collude to defraud based solely on financial gains. Contributing factors played a role in their decision. Each had personal reasons, as well. The following is a partial list of possible contributing factors.

1) The fact that Hal Chase routinely fixed games and got away with it had to add to a feeling of invincibility among the players. To boot, league officials routinely cleared Chase of any wrongdoings, often praised his sterling reputation and still others sought his presence on their rosters. In essence, many knew Chase was making additional cash with questionable play and saw that little was being done about it.

2) Some other players, a few even independent of Chase, had in one form or another benefited financially by appeasing gamblers. A lot of ballplayers spent their off-hours in company with questionable characters either in a saloon, pool hall, or elsewhere. Certainly, clean ballplayers knew this and drew their own conclusions. Rumors abounded. Even if a player didn't know what was going on or how to get in on it, surely, it led at least to curiosity. Some even saw it as an opportunity to enhance their income. The temptation was present. In fact, notorious owner Harry Frazee openly permitted gambling at Fenway and gamblers even mobbed the field during a game in June 1917 trying to force a forfeit and victory for the opponent.

3) Baseball had an unwritten policy that it wanted to avoid negative press concerning these issues. Considering this, a player could have easily inferred that there was a well-established "don't ask, don't tell" policy. If the corruption was present and no one brought it to light, why not take part and cash in?

4) White Sox owner Charles Comiskey, like most magnates, was a tightwad. Only second baseman Eddie Collins was paid his fair market value, as part of a multi-year contract. The team had won two pennants in the last three years, but raises were not forthcoming. Chicago had been among the leaders in attendance since 1916; however, the players were not reaping the benefits. Collins and catcher Ray Schalk were two of the higher-paid players and were resented as such. Chick Gandil exploited these ill feelings to draft others into the fold.

Many have exaggerated this point. The fact is a reserve clause existed for all players, not just those on the Chicago American League roster. Owners routinely stood firm against demands for more money especially after the Federal League folded. Comiskey was universally admired by his peers for his business acumen but he was not the only tight-fisted negotiator.

Then, as today, major leaguers earned a great deal more than ordinary workers.

The work was less arduous plus their salary could be supplemented during the considerable off-season.

Also weakening this argument is the fact that all major leaguers faced the same predicament. Why excuse eight men who acted in concert to throw the World Series? Why mitigate their offense and supply a justification for their actions? At least they had received a World Series check two years prior. Most major leaguers do not similarly cash in.

5) The players had asked their manager Kid Gleason to speak to Mr. Comiskey on their behalf, but he was rebuffed. Comiskey refused to even sit down and listen to the manager. Players of the day had virtually no recourse. If the owner did not acquiesce on a matter, a player could appeal only to the league president. Seldom did this work in the player's favor. Later, the players did have the ear of Judge Landis and other commissioners to some extent. Often, a player's fear of Landis quashed an appeal even before it started. It would be many decades before Marvin Miller successfully spoke for the players.

6) To add insult, Comiskey promised the players a bonus after winning the 1917 pennant and world championship. He merely delivered a case of champagne for their celebration. This must have left an indelible impression on the players, who had an entire off-season to digest it.

7) At one point, Comiskey refused to launder the team uniforms. Thus, the nickname "Black Sox" was born as the players were forced to wear dirty outfits. Here, not only does Comiskey's cheapness smack you in the face but the players undoubtedly surmised Comiskey's level of respect for them as people was relatively little.

8) During World War I, Comiskey publicly embarrassed players who sought war-related work instead of enlisting in the armed forces. Repeatedly, he called such men "slackers" and questioned their manhood. Joe Jackson and Lefty Williams, two of the famed eight, were particularly ridiculed. Comiskey reviled his players not only in private conversations but sought the newspapers to air his opinions.

9) World War I also caused the shortening of the 1918 and 1919 seasons, adding to the fiscal crunch of each player. The White Sox played only 124 games in 1918 and 140 in '19 during the regular season. That's a loss of 44 games from the normal 154-game schedule. What particularly irked all players was that the owners limited the 1919 season unilaterally and unnecessarily.

More importantly to the players, it meant a loss of six weeks' pay. In contrast, just a few years before, salaries had skyrocketed as a result of the tug-of-war between the Federal League and the American and National Leagues. Some suggest that the sharp decline in salaries after the Federal League folded led to many tainted contests between 1916 and Judge Landis' verdict against the eight.

10) World War I forced the closing of racetracks. Gamblers sought other avenues of income. Ballplayers are notorious carousers and, as such, would often find themselves in the company of like-minded individuals. It was only a matter of time before the two elements linked up. Gamblers have always befriended sports figures. With the tracks closed, they would have more time and devoted interest to do so. Similarly, with the doors shut after the Black Sox scandal, gamblers would find their way to the upstart National Football League.

11) Major League Baseball had a long history of incorporating gamblers and questionable politicians into its ownership ranks. In New York, Tammany Hall had financed or otherwise gained influence in club operations from the beginning of the old National Association. As recently as 1914, the Yankees were owned by famed gambler Frank Farrell. Oddly, or suspiciously, he shared ownership with former corrupt New York City police commissioner William Devery. Together, Devery and Ferrell, with Tim Sullivan (future partner of Arnold Rothstein) controlled gambling in Manhattan during the 1890s. Also, the Boston Braves were purchased by Tammany cronies James Gaffney and John Carroll in 1912.

Known gamblers, such as Arnold Rothstein, were frequent guests of management at the ballparks and often sat in the highly visible owners' boxes. Braves owner Emil Fuchs was Rothstein's attorney and Giants owner Charles Stoneham was a long-time business partner with the gambler. In turn, Rothstein was more than friendly with Giants manager John McGraw. In fact, it was at McGraw's pool joint that Rothstein first gained fame after a marathon billiards contest in 1908.

This was a problem that particularly plagued Judge Landis in the early part of his tenure. Over the years, gamblers had cultivated many strong relationships within the baseball industry, particularly in New York and Chicago. Al Capone could often be found shaking hands and joking with the players and officials in Chicago ballparks, even posing for a picture with Gabby Hartnett. It was only Landis' zero-tolerance of associating with gamblers and the fear of his wrath that would break the cycle. Along these lines, baseball had found the perfect individual to lead it out of crisis.

12) Whispers of questionable conduct had been heard throughout baseball history. Even National Commission chairman Garry Herrmann, the Cincinnati Reds president, wagered $6,000 that rival Pittsburgh would not win the pennant in 1906. To help his cause, Herrmann shipped outfielder Cy Seymour to the Giants. The previous summer Seymour had led the league in hits, doubles, triples, RBIs, batting average, and slugging average.

13) It was often acceptable for one team's players to pay an inducement to another team's players for future or past victories over a pennant rival. Many variations of this took place and were uncovered by Judge Landis' investigations of the 1920s, particularly in the Cobb/Speaker Affair. This practice personified the era. Players, en masse, thought nothing of the implications. Similar "incentives" can be traced as far back as an 1893 contest between Baltimore and Pittsburgh. Officially, inducements were not disallowed until Landis' ruling after an investigation of a 1917 case involving the Tigers and White Sox. Then, the commissioner expressed his reluctance to look into any further matters that occurred before his hiring, in essence, giving amnesty for previous misdeeds.

14) Much of what we know about gambling and game-fixing scandals comes from players who were accused of malfeasance. When someone is charged, it sets off a chain reaction of accusations. The large majority of players would never speak on the issue. No one wants to be a rat. You have to live and travel with your peers day in and day out. Hence, no one turned another player in. Only the fear of Landis would change that in the future.

Whatever the precipitating factors, any of the Chicago Eight could have said no. Hod Eller did. The Cincinnati pitcher was offered $5,000 to toss games as well. He immediately reported the incident to his manager Pat Moran.

The Team

The 1919 Chicago White Sox were impressive. They won 88 games for a .629 winning percentage and took the pennant by 3.5 games. Remember, they only played 140 games. The Sox led the league in runs, hits, batting average, and stolen bases. The club boasted three future Hall of Famers in 2B Eddie Collins, C Ray Schalk, and RHP Red Faber. Very likely, LF Joe Jackson and possibly RHP Eddie Cicotte were headed for Cooperstown. Field manager Kid Gleason was a 30-year major league veteran.

The core of the team had played together for years. 3B Buck Weaver, Cicotte, and Schalk joined the team in 1912. Faber joined in 1914. Jackson, Collins, RF Nemo Leibold, and CF Happy Felsch were introduced in 1915. LHP Lefty Williams and UT Fred McMullian were added in 1916. 1B Chick Gandil and SS Swede Risberg came over in 1917. RHP Dickie Kerr was a rookie in 1919.

The team had won the pennant in 1917 by nine games but slipped in '18 when war call-ups depleted the roster. Chicago was on the verge of a dynasty. Not only did they win two of the last three pennants, but they were even better in 1920. Winning 96 games, the White Sox only lost the pennant in the final days of the season after the remaining players were suspended. It would have been a public relations nightmare if the Sox won the pennant with a make-shift team. The 1920 team boasted four 20+ game winners in Kerr, Faber, Williams, and Cicotte. Only one other team in the 20th century, the 1971 Baltimore Orioles, can say the same. The brilliant pitching combined with probably the best hitting in the league could have formed a powerful combination for years to come and maybe even delayed the rise of the Yankees.

The Principals

Knuckleball pitcher Eddie Cicotte's 14-year major league career ended with 209 wins and a 2.38 ERA. He was also partial to the spitball or any pitch that was deceptive and kept him in control. In the 1917 championship campaign, Cicotte led the league with 28 wins, 346 innings pitched, a .248 opponent on-base percentage, and a 1.53 ERA. He also won the opening game of the World Series giving up one run on seven hits. In 1919, he led the league with 29 wins, 306 innings pitched, 30 complete games and a .806 winning percentage. He finished second to Walter Johnson with a 1.82 ERA, a .228 opponent batting average and a .261 opponent on-base percentage. Enlisting the staff ace in the fix, the gamblers could feel confident about the outcome. Later in hiding, the Cicotte family, residing in Detroit, would live under an assumed name.

Lefty Williams compiled an 82-48 record over a seven-year career. Winning 45 games his last two seasons, the control pitcher's future seemed bright. In 1919, he finished third in the league with 23 wins, a .676 winning percentage, 297 innings pitched, 125 strikeouts, and a .289 opponent on-base percentage. The southpaw also finished second to Cicotte with 27 complete games. The pair produced a powerful one-two punch any manager would relish.

Chick Gandil was a steady player with otherwise no star potential. He hit .290 with 60 RBIs in 1919. The slick fielder led the league four times in fielding average. He, Risberg, and Weaver were good friends who all resented the higher-educated and higher-paid Collins and Schalk. The resentment and the cliques fueled the fix. Gandil became the ringleader.

Buck Weaver was a solid third baseman whose skill kept Ty Cobb from bunting against him, no small testimony to his talent. He was also a consistent hitter, batting .296 with 75 RBIs in 1919. He finished fourth in the league with 89 runs. His downfall is linked to his friendship with Gandil and Risberg.

Swede Risberg was a weak-hitting shortstop who didn't produce his finest year until 1920. He proved to be quite useful to Gandil as an enlister and intimidator of the others. Risberg was also Gandil's main confidant and conspirator. Together, they would see that the plan was carried out.

Shoeless Joe Jackson was the hitting star of the franchise, one of the best in baseball history. His career-.356 batting average rests below only Ty Cobb and Rogers Hornsby on the all-time list. Babe Ruth so admired Jackson's stance and poise in the batter's box that he adopted it. Ruth even copied the fearsome "Black Betsy" Jackson wielded at the plate.

Shoeless Joe was brought to the major leagues by Connie Mack in 1908. His impoverished and illiterate background proved an ill fit for a major U.S. city. He repeatedly jumped the club and three years later had only appeared in thirty games. Mack traded him to Cleveland.

In his rookie year in 1911, he hit .408 but lost the batting title to Cobb's .420. Cleveland became strapped financially, partially because of the Federal League competition, and traded Jackson to Chicago for three players and cash. During the 1917 pennant drive, he batted a below-par .301 but finished fifth in the league in RBIs and slugging average and fourth in runs. Jackson had another impressive season in 1919. The left fielder placed third in the league with 181 hits, 96 RBIs and a .422 on-base percentage. He finished fourth with 14 triples, 261 total bases, and a .351 batting average. His .506 slugging average was the fifth highest in the league. In 1920, Jackson pulled off an extremely rare feat by accruing more triples than strikeouts, 20 to 14.

Happy Felsch possessed an intimidating arm in center field. He led the league at least once in putouts, assists, double plays, range, and fielding average. Felsch would not reach his finest hitting performance until 1920 but his production during the 1917 pennant drive impressed peers. He batted a solid .308 with 102 RBI. His production during the 1920 season ranks as one of the franchise's best for the 20th century. Felsch placed fourth in the league in home runs and fifth with a .540 slugging average. He also batted .338 with 300 total bases and 115 RBI.

Fred McMullin was a utility player who wouldn't elicit much conversation today if not for his involvement in throwing the World Series. He overheard a conversation between Gandil and Risberg, which forced the pair to include him. There would have been no tactical reason otherwise.

The Fix

Anyone who believes the rhetoric that the White Sox were assured of winning a legitimate series doesn't understand the importance of competition and execution in professional sports. It had already been shown that strong teams could lose the national championship and would be repeatedly proved in the future.

The Cincinnati Reds were a fine team that won the pennant by nine games over John McGraw's Giants. The scandal has tainted the reputation of Cincinnati's first National League pennant winner (Cincinnati did win the title in the first season of the American Association in 1882). They led the league in walks and on-base percentage and finished second in batting average. The pitching staff was even more impressive, giving up the fewest runs in the league. Reds pitchers also led in shutouts, fewest hits, opponent batting average, and opponent on-base percentage. On defense, the team led handily in fielding average and committed the fewest errors. Clearly, the two best teams in the majors would be facing each other for the title.

The series began with Cicotte plunking the first batter as a signal to the gamblers that the fix was on. The game was lost in the fourth because of the shoddy pitching of Cicotte and questionable plays by Risberg. Game 2 was lost in the fourth inning on three walks by the *control* pitcher Williams. The White Sox won Game 3 on a shutout pitched by Dickie Kerr. Cicotte tanked Game 4 with two errors in the fifth inning. Game 5 was lost in the sixth inning as Williams conceded four runs. Dickie Kerr won again in Game 6 and, in rebellion, Cicotte was the victor in Game 7.

With the series 4-3 in favor of the Reds, the gamblers became very anxious. Some of the gamblers were betting heavily from game to game. On the other hand, Arnold Rothstein bet on the series as a whole. Rothstein wanted the series over and quickly. As if directed for television, a man was dispatched to have a conversation with Game 8 starter Lefty Williams.

Williams was told in no uncertain terms that he would lose the following day or face repercussions against him and his wife. Furthermore, there was to be no drama. He would tank it in the first inning. Williams went to the mound and pitched nothing but fastballs ignoring the signals of catcher Schalk. The Reds scored four runs in the inning and Williams was removed after retiring only one batter. The Reds went on to win the game and the tainted championship.

It is apparent that Cicotte and Williams determined the outcome of the fix. They were aided by the weak performances of Felsch, Risberg, and non-conspirators Leibold, RHP Bill James, RHP Grover Lowdermilk, and Collins. Surprisingly, Gandil, Jackson, and Weaver performed solidly. McMullin was not a factor.

Roles of the Principals

Getting to the truth through the rumors, lies, false testimonies, contradictory statements, stolen confessions, witness tampering, false identities, webs of deceit, and double crosses is nearly impossible. All the principals and gamblers had good reason to keep quiet and mislead. None survive today. It is possible, though, to piece together information and arrive at some conclusions.

The plan to throw the World Series was hatched by Chick Gandil and constructed in consultation with Swede Risberg and Ed Cicotte. The thought occurred to Gandil early in the 1919 season. He realized that the plan would only be successful if he added Cicotte and Williams to the fold. The rest of the conspirators were the men on good terms with Gandil. To find financing for the deal, Gandil began discussions with gamblers Bill Burns and Sport Sullivan. Gandil received all the incoming monies and conducted the meetings with the gamblers. He also kept the players in line, before and during the fix. It is estimated that he received $35,000 for his role.

Risberg was all for the idea when it was proposed. He acted as Gandil's lieutenant, running messages to and from the players and gamblers. Risberg also played a key role in recruiting the other players and keeping them focused. For his efforts, Risberg pocketed over $10,000.

Eddie Cicotte was approached by Gandil in August. After some persuasion, he agreed to participate for $10,000 up front. Cicotte was approaching the end of his career and had recently purchased a farm. The payoff more than covered the financial burden of the mortgage. Cicotte was responsible for introducing friend Bill Burns to Gandil, thus setting the wheels in motion. Cicotte probably had a bigger role in the conspiracy than many think, including but not limited to recruiting other teammates, organizing the plot, and entertaining potential moneymen like Sport Sullivan. Cicotte and Gandil likely planned it all, celebrated when things went well, and ultimately anguished when they didn't. After all, the success or failure of the plan rested with Cicotte's right arm.

Shortly before the series began Cicotte found $10,000 under his pillow. As a prearranged signal to the gamblers, the pitcher pelted the first batter. The fix was on. Cicotte would later be the first to confess to Comiskey and the grand jury.

Lefty Williams at first resisted Gandil's overtures but enlisted when he found out Cicotte was involved. The plan's success rested with those two pitchers. Williams was threatened prior to Game 8 and proceeded to tank it in the first inning. He might not have received very much money.

Happy Felsch played a limited role before and during the fix. Afterward, he was sought out by the press, who viewed him as the dimmest of the bunch and, as such, probably the easiest target. He freely confessed. Felsch probably did not receive a great deal of money.

Fred McMullin backed into the deal based on his friendship with Risberg. He was not a necessary component until he caught Gandil and Risberg in conversation. McMullin is thought to have received $5,000.

Buck Weaver's downfall lies with his close friendship with Gandil and Risberg. He attended a couple meetings but received no financial benefits nor acted improperly during the series. Judge Landis expelled him based on his prior knowledge of the fix and failure to report it.

Joe Jackson hit .375 in the series with 6 RBIs and 5 runs. However, he had prior knowledge of the fix and accepted $5,000. Later, he became the second player to confess to the grand jury. His legend grows even today but it doesn't diminish his complicity in the affair.

Role of Auxiliary Characters

Bill Burns was a former major league pitcher who was then in the oil business and loved to gamble. He heard rumors of the fix and approached his friend Eddie Cicotte to confirm. Realizing the profit potential of the scam and being unable to personally finance the deal, Burns sought investors to get the ballplayers the $80,000 or $100,000 they requested. He enlisted friend and ex-pro boxer Bill Maharg.

Maharg had appeared briefly in the majors, most notable as a replacement in the Tigers one-day strike on May 18, 1912, protesting a Ty Cobb suspension. His real name was Graham, Maharg spelled backwards.

The two set out to find financial backers. Burns went to Montreal and Maharg to Philadelphia to talk with gamblers. Both came back empty-handed but they did learn that the man to talk to was New York gambler Arnold Rothstein. Preparing to talk with Rothstein, Burns and Maharg sought counsel from gamblers David Zelser (identified only as Bennett), Abe Attell, as well as the infamous Hal Chase. All three to some extent held Rothstein's confidence. The key, though, was that Rothstein knew all about the fix and had for some time.

Rothstein, known as "The Big Bankroll," had strong ties to Tammany Hall. He met with Burns and Maharg and publicly blasted them and their plans. In reality, Burns and Maharg could only mess up what Rothstein was already brewing. He sent crony Abe Attel to keep an eye on the two. Meanwhile, Rothstein dispatched fellow gambler Nat Evans, using the alias "Brown," to hold a meeting directly with Sullivan and the players to determine if the plot could be carried out. After being convinced that it could, Rothstein gave Sullivan $40,000 to ensure the players' involvement.

Sport Sullivan, a Boston gambler, was approached by Gandil, Burns, and Maharg after Rothstein rejected them. Sullivan didn't have that kind of money so he decided to intervene with Rothstein. Sullivan gave the players $10,000 of the $40,000 he was given by Rothstein and placed bets with the rest. The initial $10,000 had to go to Cicotte who demanded his money up front. All this is rather murky. Reports also suggest that David Zelser was the money dispenser.

Meanwhile, Abe Attell kept his foot in the door and, bluffing, maintained the interest of the ballplayers by constantly leading Burns and Maharg to believe that cash was forthcoming. Attell was a former boxer who held the featherweight championship from 1901–12 and is a member of the International Boxing Hall of Fame. Though he never dished out a cent, Attell's continued contact was enough in the beginning to entice the players even though they hadn't received much money.

David Zelzer, a Des Moines, Iowa, gambler; colleague Carl Zork from St. Louis; and other Midwestern cohorts initiated the plot and brought it eastward to the lap of The Big Bankroll. The first stirrings of the fix were probably made long before either league championship was determined. And Rothstein was there from the beginning.

The players dumped the first two games but Dickie Kerr won Game 3. Burns lost all his winnings in Game 3 and couldn't coax more out of Attell. He confronted the players who were now ready to drop the fix. This scared Sullivan who didn't want to run counter to Rothstein. Sullivan immediately gave the players $20,000 and promised another $20,000 prior to Game 5. It never came.

After the White Sox won Game 7, Rothstein became concerned. He contacted

Sullivan and insisted that the series end the following day in the first inning. Sullivan contacted a Chicago thug who visited Lefty Williams and settled the matter. The series ended and at some point the players received another $40,000 of which Gandil kept $25,000.

The Aftermath

So many people were aware of the fix or noticed the shoddy play that rumors abounded. No one wanted to believe it was possible. *Chicago Herald and Examiner* sportswriter Hugh Fullerton was among the first to investigate. He printed a fairly accurate accounting of the events but it was ignored by the baseball community and even ridiculed.

White Sox owner Charles Comiskey had a hand in the cover-up. He had heard the rumors before, during, and after the fix. Rightfully, he had alerted both the American League and National League presidents but was basically rebuffed. He hired attorney Alfred Austrian, who urged Comiskey to protect his investment. Austrian argued that because past scandals had been whitewashed, repercussions might be minimal. Nevertheless, Comiskey had to protect his own reputation.

The owner placed a newspaper ad offering a $20,000 reward for any information concerning a fix and hired John Hunter, a private investigator. This was all for show, as Comiskey rebuffed those who came forth with information seeking to claim the money. He also refused to meet with Joe Jackson who had planned to confess. The owner even failed to reply to a letter Jackson dictated to his wife concerning the affair.

Hunter turned up much of the fix but that information was never disclosed by Comiskey. Much of what is known in this area is due to Bill Veeck who discovered Comiskey's secretary's notes on Hunter's report in the White Sox offices after he bought the franchise in 1959.

An unrelated Chicago game-fixing scandal occurred in 1920 involving the Cubs and a grand jury was convened. The focus quickly shifted to the Black Sox Scandal. Comiskey had no choice but to suspend the eight players after Cicotte and Jackson confessed. The trial jury found the players not guilty in August 1921. Regardless, Judge Landis issued the following statement:

> Regardless of the verdict of juries no player who throws a ball game, no player who undertakes or promises to throw a ball game, no player who sits in a conference with a bunch of crooked players and gamblers, where the ways and means of throwing a ball game are planned and discussed and does not promptly tell his club about it, will ever play professional baseball.

The eight were banned.

The Consequences

The most significant consequence of the Black Sox Scandal was the hiring of Judge Kenesaw Mountain Landis as baseball's first commissioner. The idea of a single commissioner was not new. Johnson foes Harry Frazee and Comiskey had supported the idea for some time. Frazee had previously suggested that the owners hire former U.S. President William Howard Taft but he was seeking another title: Chief Justice of the United States.

The National Commission had obviously failed to belie outside corruptible influences. The Landis hiring proved to be a public relations coup for baseball. The judge himself proved to be the ideal candidate to correct these ills. His 24-year reign would prove to be eventful. Many would come to regret his hiring and the comprehensive powers he was bestowed.

The ones who regretted it the most were Ban Johnson and his cronies. Garry Herrmann had resigned in January 1920 as the third member of the National Commission. Johnson was working feverishly to replace him with another ally. He was supporting his friend and old hunting partner Judge Charles MacDonald in this effort. Wishing to promote MacDonald and at the same time embarrass if not eliminate Comiskey, Johnson saw his opportunity when the Chicago Cubs scandal hit in August 1920. MacDonald managed to get a grand jury convened to investigate. Quickly, he switched the focus to the 1919 World Series and other baseball scandals.

Johnson was backing the wrong horse or, more accurately, MacDonald was backed by the wrong horse. In July 1919, Johnson had blocked the transfer of Carl Mays to the Yankees. New York owners Colonels Huston and Ruppert countered Johnson's tactics by gaining approval for the deal from the courts. Meanwhile, rumors arose that Johnson, scandalously, was trying to divert Mays to the Indians. The colonels filed a half-million dollar suit claiming that the American League president was trying to force them from the league. Fellow owners were stunned. Usually, league matters were handled internally. A closed-door meeting/melee/settlement resulted in the stripping of much of Johnson's power.

Johnson's influence was waning and he could only count on five teams to back him. The other eleven supported Landis and threatened to secede. The Johnson loyalists folded and Landis was chosen, not as a member of the National Commission but as the commission itself. Landis would later push Johnson out at the end of the Ty Cobb/Tris Speaker affair.

Though rarely discussed, many honest men and women in the White Sox organization, both on and off the field, were disillusioned. Many individuals work a lifetime to get to the postseason. To have teammates sell it off is frustrating beyond words. Chicago fans and fans of the game in general were let down. The events gave baseball a questionable reputation, similar to boxing.

Finally, the White Sox franchise was decimated, though Comiskey would keep the team. They would not finish higher than fifth until 1936 nor match 1920's attendance level until after World War II. Baseball itself was primed for a major boom. The hiring of Landis and the stiff penalties for game-fixers did a lot to restore the public's faith in the game. The home run did more.

1920 Chicago Cubs

On August 31, 1920, before an unimportant game between the sixth-place Cubs and the last-place Phillies, Cubs president Bill Veeck Sr. received a telegram claiming that today's upcoming game was fixed. Manager Fred Mitchell benched starter Claude

Hendrix in favor of Pete Alexander. Then, Veeck launched a public investigation and at the same time called for a review of the 1919 World Series. A grand jury was convened.

Suspicion fell on four players: RHP Hendrix, 1B Fred Merkle, IF Buck Herzog, and RHP Paul Carter. Hendrix was an accomplished pitcher who won 20 + games on three occasions. He compiled a 20-7 record with a 2.78 ERA for the National League champion Cubs in 1918. Amassing 144 wins and a 2.65 ERA in his career, Hendrix was perhaps the best pitcher in the Federal League's short history, winning 45 games over its two-year existence.

Merkle had a solid 16-year major league career, notching 733 RBIs and a .273 batting average. He is best known today for his "boner" during the 1908 pennant drive. Herzog was a long-time National Leaguer who appeared in four World Series for John McGraw. He has the distinction of being traded for future Hall of Famers Christy Mathewson, Bill McKechnie, and Edd Roush on July 20, 1916. Carter's only distinction is being involved in this affair.

It was alleged that Hendrix sent a telegram to Kansas City gambler Frog Thompson, placing a $5,000 bet against the Cubs. No proof was ever offered before the grand jury switched its focus to the Black Sox Scandal. Nevertheless, the suspected ballplayers were released by the Cubs. Merkle was the only one to return to the majors, as a player–coach five years later.

1920 Pacific Coast League
On October 15, 1920, a Los Angeles deputy district attorney filed bribery charges against individuals allegedly involved in a game-fixing scandal involving the Vernon and Salt Lake City clubs during the 1919 season.

In the fallout, four players were suspended in November for conspiracy to throw games by PCL president William McCarthy:

Babe Borton	Vernon first baseman
Harl Maggert	Salt Lake City outfielder
Bill Rumler	Salt Lake City outfielder
Gene Dale	Salt Lake City pitcher

Pitchers Tom Seaton and Casey Smith were previously released from San Francisco for questionable activities. All six were eventually blacklist from organized baseball. Borton, Dale, Rumler, and Maggert were former major leaguers. Hal Chase was also expelled by McCarthy. In the end, players from five teams were implicated. Rumler reappeared eight years later to man right field for the Hollywood Stars.

Similar to the majors, this incident was a wake-up call for McCarthy and the Pacific Coast League. He would have players followed and continuously waged a battle to keep gamblers away from the parks and players.

1924 New York Giants
This incident was never fully explained and leaves a lot to the imagination concerning just how many individuals were involved. On September 27, 1924, 23-year-old,

sophomore Giants outfielder Jimmy O'Connell approached Phillies shortstop Heinie Sand and offered him a bribe. Specifically, Sand was offered $500 to tank games to the Giants who were in a close pennant race with the Dodgers and Pirates. All three teams finished within three games of the flag.

The Giants had just paid $75,000 to acquire O'Connell from San Francisco of the Pacific Coast League two years prior. Landis investigated and O'Connell confessed, naming coach Cozy Dolan as the instigator, along with several other teammates, including future Hall of Famers George Kelly, Ross Youngs, and Frankie Frisch. Dolan was evasive under questioning. Landis banned both Dolan and O'Connell on the eve of the World Series. The others were cleared.

A cry erupted throughout the baseball community calling for the removal of the Giants from the World Series or the canceling of it. Ban Johnson, as part of a running feud with John McGraw, among others supported the cancellation. The situation seemed odd, considering that Dolan was one of McGraw's right-hand men. With whom did the scheme originate? Further questions arose as Dolan sued, using gambler Arnold Rothstein's lawyer paid for by Giants management.

1946 Evangeline League

Outgoing National Association president William Bramham formally banned five Class-D Evangeline League players on January 25, 1947, for alleged gambling and game-fixing activities involving the playoffs between Houma and Abbeville, both from Louisiana, the previous fall. The champion Houma team lost its manager–first baseman Paul Fugit and Al Kaiser, Leonard Pecou, and pitcher Bill Thomas. Abbeville player Don Vetorel was the fifth. Supposedly, payoffs were even distributed in the dugout.

Thomas had won 35 games that year at the age of 41, plus another five in the postseason. In all, the control artist won 383 games in the minor leagues but never cracked the show because he lacked a major league fastball. He ended up atop the minor league career leader board in victories, losses, games pitched, runs allowed, and hits allowed. Happy Chandler upheld the bans in April but Thomas and Pecou were reinstated two years later. Thomas pitched in the minors until age 47.

1959 Southern Association

On July 3, 1959, the Chattanooga Lookouts of the Southern Association suspended first baseman Jesse Levan, a 33-year-old former major leaguer, and 24-year-old shortstop Waldo Gonzalez indefinitely for failing to report a bribe. They had been approached by gamblers to tip off opposing batters about pitch selection.

The National Association, the ruling body of the minor leagues, investigated and placed Levan on the permanently ineligible list and gave Gonzalez a one-year suspension. Levan allegedly had approached teammates to participate in game-fixing schemes involving some sort of "foul-ball hitting" scandal. Further investigation turned up widespread corruption throughout the Southern Association. Levan had been in the minors since 1944.

Former major league catcher Joe Tipton was also expelled due to a foul-ball hitting scheme. Tipton had been the backup catcher on the 1948 World Champion Cleveland Indians. He admitted to intentionally fouling off pitches at the behest of a gambler. The gambler would bet people in the stands that the next pitch would be a foul ball. Seems strange, but it did affect on-field performance.

1969 Black Mist Scandal

Nishitetsu Lions pitcher Masayuki Nagayasu was permanently expelled from Japanese professional baseball in October 1969. He had accepted bribes to throw easy pitches to the opposition. Furthermore, he encouraged teammates to participate in game-fixing schemes. Teammates Masaaki Ikenega, Akio Masuda, Yoshinobu Yoda, Kazuhide Funada, and Kimiyasu Wada were also expelled, though Funada and Wada were reprieved after six months. Broadcaster and recently retired Lion Futoshi Nakanishi also resigned, claiming responsibility in the affair. Ultimately, twenty men received punitive measures for game-fixing, gambling, and/or organized crime actions. Similar to an American scandal in 2005, baseball officials were summons to appear before the Diet.

Pitching star Ikenega admitted to accepting cash (million yen) from former teammate Tsutomu Tanaka but insisted that it did not affect his performance. In five seasons in the league, Ikenega had amassed 99 wins and a 2.36 ERA. He would be expelled after winning four more in 1970.

1970 Auto Racing Scandal

Kentaro Ogawa joined the Toei Flyers out of high school in 1954, then left a year later to work in the private sector. Nine years later, he joined Chunichi at age 30. The submariner won 93 games between 1964–69, including winning the Sawamura (Cy Young) Award (Japanese equivalent of U.S. Cy Young Award) with a 29-12 record and a 2.51 ERA in 1967. Arrested in May 1970, the righthander was forced to retire after participating in a scheme to fix auto races. Ogawa was also implicated in the Black Mist Scandal.

Third baseman Takeshi Kuwata was a leading hitter for the Taiyo Whales during the 1960s, notching 222 home runs and over 600 RBIs from 1959–67. He won the Rookie of the Year award in 1959 with a league-leading 31 homers. He was also forced to retire in the auto racing scandal.

2005 Taiwanese Professional Baseball

La New Bears catcher Chen Zhaoying and minor league manager Cai Shengfeng were arrested in July 2005 in a gambling-related scandal. They were both expelled from their clubs but were released from jail in August after confessing. Also implicated were a translator for the Sinon Bulls, seven bookmakers, and gang members.

In 1997, the league almost folded after three China Times Eagle members were accused of game-fixing. In all, 32 men were implicated. The incident spurred the formation of a rival league. The two ultimately merged in 2003.

In 1996, four members of the Brother Elephants were kidnapped and beaten by gamblers who apparently lost $125,000 on a game.

George Bechtel

One of the first scandals in National League history occurred on May 30, 1876, when Louisville Grays George Bechtel's shoddy play drew suspicions from the press and fans in attendance. Three of Louisville's nine errors were attributed to the right fielder in a loss to the New York Mutuals. In the seventh inning, a ball rolled through his legs, allowing two runs to score. Many onlookers believed he could have easily stopped it, as well as two others that went past his grasp.

Bechtel had brought a shady reputation with him from his National Association days. The Grays immediately suspended the outfielder. Bechtel further implicated himself in dirty deeds by sending a telegram to teammate Jim Devlin who was in Boston for a series with the Red Caps on June 10th. It read:

> We can make $500.00 if you lose game today. Tell John [manager John Chapman] and let me know at once. Bechtel

Devlin turned the document over to Louisville management. Bechtel was expelled by the team. Possibly owing him a favor, the Mutuals quickly signed Bechtel. Once again, the Tammany-led New York Mutuals were involved in a seedy affair. Bechtel, though, only lasted two games before his major league career ended.

His case wasn't reviewed by National League officials until after the 1877 season. The player was then formally banned and all subsequent requests for reinstatement were denied. Bechtel was only one of five Grays blacklisted at that meeting.

Rube Benton

Rube Benton was a lefthanded pitcher who amassed 154 wins and a 3.09 ERA in fifteen seasons with the Giants and Reds. At the grand jury hearings in the Black Sox affair, Benton claimed that Buck Herzog and Hal Chase had offered him an $800 bribe in September 1917 to throw games to the Cubs. He also claimed that John McGraw had been in on it. Herzog countered with affidavits declaring Benton's boasting of winning $1,500 on the tainted World Series.

Benton denied claims that he had prior knowledge of the World Series fix. When faced with the affidavits by Boston Braves Norman Boeckel and Art Wilson to the contrary, Benton recanted. In fact, he admitted that he had been tipped off about the fix by Hal Chase.

Benton also testified to being witness to a telegram Jean Dubuc had been sent from Cincinnati gambler Hahn concerning the fix. Moreover, Benton claimed that Hal Chase won $40,000 betting on the World Series but denied any personal profit despite charges to the contrary. His testimony was a key element of the prosecution's case. McGraw released Benton on August 1, 1921, for being "undesirable;" thus, the player was forced out of the majors.

Benton had a big year in the American Association in 1922, winning 22 games. Cincinnati Reds president Garry Herrmann noticed and signed him for 1923. McGraw tried to block the move claiming that Benton had been blacklisted. National League president John Heydler and American League president Ban Johnson agreed, as did a vote by the National League owners. They argued that even if Benton wasn't formally blacklisted, he should be, based on his prior knowledge of the World Series fix, admissions that he was offered a bride but did not report it, and for his unsupported claims against Herzog and McGraw.

Undeterred, Herrmann wanted the pitcher's reinstatement and sought redress from Landis. Heydler bitterly refused to permit Benton's admission to the National League. Landis in a truly paradoxical and ridiculous ruling found Benton to be a member in good standing of Major League Baseball. He openly defied two league presidents and several owners. Landis further criticized Herzog, Heydler, and several sportswriters. The judge presented Benton as a martyr who was "as clean as any man in baseball." It would not be the last time he sided with Herrmann.

Landis' probable intention was to exert his authority over the leagues and their presidents. The Benton case was merely a vehicle to do so. However, in the process, Landis tainted his own reign and drew serious questions about his judgment.

Joe Blong

Another prominent case involved the St. Louis Brown Stockings in early 1875. Pitcher Joe Blong and utility player Trick McSorley were expelled by the team for suspicion of crooked play. The pair then found jobs with the independent Stars of Covington, Kentucky. In September, the Stars ousted Blong for throwing a game against a Cincinnati club which, ridiculously, only made him available for St. Louis to re-sign. These difficulties and others centering on player revolving—that is, ignoring their contract to jump from one team to another in search of the best deal—led to the downfall of the short-lived National Association.

Julio Bonetti

Righthander Julio Bonetti won six games for the St. Louis Browns from 1937–38, then was sold to The Los Angeles in the Pacific Coast League. Over the next two and a half seasons with the Angels, the ace won 41 contests and even appeared in a game for the Cubs. He last pitched on June 22, 1941.

Shortly after that game, National Association president William Bramham declared Bonetti ineligible for suspicious association with gamblers. Private detectives had witnessed a gambler paying the pitcher a large sum of money. Like many ballplayers, Bonetti enjoyed going to the race track. The payoff may have been for a horse bet; no game-fixing was alleged. Nevertheless, he never gained re-admittance.

Babe Borton

See 1920 Pacific Coast League

Paul Carter

See 1920 Chicago Cubs

Prince Hal Chase

Hal Chase was the most corrupt player of the 20th century outside the eight men who threw the 1919 World Series. He was openly accused by three major league managers and suspected by countless others of game-fixing. Chase is considered the master of the "indifferent play" for his ability to swing the score while making it look like another's error or misplay.

Ironically, he is often credited as being perhaps the finest fielding first baseman of his era. This is despite the fact that he led the league in errors seven times and committed an incredible 402 errors in a 15-year career, an average of 27 errors a year, at first base yet. Quite a testament to his fielding skills—or, more appropriately, a testament to his fraud! *The Sporting News* in 1913 wrote, "That he can play first base as it never was and perhaps never will be played is a well-known truth. That he will is a different matter."

In the minors, Chase gained a reputation for great defensive play. He quickly became a fan favorite after joining New York in the American League. The Highlanders were ecstatic about the future after Chase finished third in the batting race in only his sophomore season in 1906 with a mark of .323. The first baseman quickly dashed those hopes after he began jumping the team, once to seek extra cash and once after he was spurned for the manager's job.

In 1910, New York manager George Stallings accused Chase of throwing games. Ban Johnson investigated and issued a statement praising the "sterling" character of Chase. Later, Stallings was fired and replaced by Chase. Chase was himself replaced as manager after the 1911 season. In '13, another New York manager, Frank Chance, accused Chase of throwing games and traded him to the White Sox in May.

In 1914, Chase jumped the White Sox for the Federal League. The Federal League was a third major league that challenged organized baseball from 1914–15. After the Federal League folded, Chase caught on with the Reds. Cincinnati manager Christy Mathewson suspended Chase for "indifferent play" in August 1918.

The National League initiated an investigation into Chase's conduct and, in January 1919, met with Mathewson, Giants pitcher Pol Perritt, the Reds Jimmy Ring, Greasy Neale, and Mike Regan, and Giants manager John McGraw testifying as Chase's accusers. Nevertheless, National League president John Heydler cleared Chase, citing lack of evidence. It was an obvious whitewash (or at least apathy) and a precursor to that year's World Series difficulties. Ridiculously, John McGraw had stated prior to the hearing that if Chase was cleared, he wanted to sign him, a point that makes one question why so many game-fixing scandals involved the Giants during McGraw's reign.

The inability (or indifference) of the National Commission to stymie Chase reminded many of similar circumstances surrounding pitcher Jack Taylor the previous decade (interestingly, just as Chase joined the majors). Repeatedly, Taylor was charged with and even openly admitted to fixing games and just as repeatedly he escaped sanction. Not only was this a foreshadowing to some in the game, especially an outspoken Barney Dreyfuss, but it was certainly fodder for subsequent indiscretions.

Though disclosed later, Cincinnati Reds second baseman Lee Magee charged Chase with bribing him to lose games in 1918. Chase, Magee, and Heine Zimmerman were all forced out of the major leagues at the end of 1919 for suspected crooked play. They were never officially expelled but were unwelcome nonetheless.

In August 1920, Chase was banned from Pacific Coast League ballparks for trying to bribe Salt Lake City pitcher Sider Baum and various other players and umpires. He was also expelled from the Mission League and the outlaw San Joaquin Valley League.

Later, Chase joined the outlaw Copper League in Arizona and Northern San

Joaquin Valley League and played with fellow expelled players Buck Weaver, Chick Gandil, Lefty Williams, Jimmy O'Connell, Harl Maggert, and Tom Seaton. In 1931, Chase wrote a note to Judge Landis inquiring about his status in organized baseball and apologizing for his past indiscretions. Landis replied that Chase was in good standing with organized baseball but, coyly, asked Chase to describe these indiscretions. Chase's lawyers prevented him from replying.

Chase's name popped up early in the grand jury investigation of the throwing of the 1919 World Series. He had heard early on about a possible scam and contacted various parties to confirm the rumors. Nothing delighted him more. What his role was is still unclear; it was reported, though, that he won money betting on the Reds, possibly $40,000.

Just the fact that Chase was able to work the system and profit from it for so long surely led, in part, to the 1919 Black Sox Scandal. The entire industry knew of Chase and what he was doing. Certainly, unnamed others prospered in undisclosed fixes. Major League Baseball had refused to confront its flaws and, as such, fed the greatest scandal of all. The National Commission would soon lose its job.

Eddie Cicotte
See 1919 Chicago White Sox

Ty Cobb/Tris Speaker Affair
Out of the blue, Tigers player-manager Ty Cobb and Indians player–manager Tris Speaker turned in their resignations in late 1926. They were two of the finest players of the dead ball era and two of the biggest names in the game. The sporting public was shocked and reporters suspected an underlying scandal.

In June 1926, Ban Johnson had paid $20,000 to former pitcher Dutch Leonard for two letters penned by Ty Cobb and Smokey Joe Wood. Supposedly, they implicated Cobb, Speaker, Wood, and Leonard in a gambling scandal back in 1919. In consultation with other league officials, Johnson set about to push the two out of the game. Leonard and Wood were already retired.

Leonard claimed that the four players met under the stands at Navin Field in Detroit on September 24, 1919. They made plans to bet on the Tigers for the following day's game against the Indians. At the time, Leonard and Cobb played for the Tigers and Wood and Speaker donned an Indians uniform. Back then, it was not against any official rules to bet on a game.

Detroit won 9-5. Speaker had a good game but Cobb did not. Wood and Leonard did not play. Also, Speaker fielded his best team that day. All the regulars played, except for shortstop Ray Chapman, who went home to prepare for his upcoming wedding. The importance of the game lies in the standings. The top three teams in the league at the end of the season would receive a share of the World Series money, a practice that began the previous year. Cleveland had already clinched second while Detroit was vying with New York for third.

The implication here is that the Indians sat down to ensure a Tigers victory. A review of the box score cannot confirm this. In fact, it could be argued that if the fix was in, Speaker probably wouldn't have done so well nor Cobb so poorly.

Cobb penned the following note:

Augusta, Ga., October 23, '19
Dear Dutch:

Well, old boy, guess you are out in old California by this time and enjoying life. I arrived home and found Mrs. Cobb only fair, but the baby girl was fine, and at this time Mrs. Cobb is very well, but I have been very busy getting acquainted with my family and have not tried to do any correspondence, hence my delay.

Wood and myself are considerably disappointed in our business proposition, as we had $2,000 to put into it and the other side quoted us $1,400, and then we finally secured that much money it was about 2 o'clock and they refused to deal with us, as they had men in Chicago to take the matter up with and they had no time, so we completely fell down and of course we felt badly over it.

Everything was open to Wood and he can tell you about it when we get together. It was quite a responsibility and I don't care for it again, I can assure you.

Well, I hope you found everything in fine shape at home and all your troubles will be little ones. I made this year's winner's share of World's Series on cotton since I came home, and expect to make more.

I thought the White Sox should have won, but am satisfied they were too confident. Well, old scout, drop me a line when you can.

We have had fine weather here, in fact, quite warm, and have had some dandy fishing since I arrived home.

With kindest regards to Mrs. Leonard, I remain, sincerely

TY

Wood followed up with this letter:

Cleveland, O., Friday
Enclosed please find certified check for sixteen hundred and thirty dollars ($1,630).

Dear Friend "Dutch":

The only bet West [clubhouse man Fred West] could get up was $600 against $420 (10 to 7). Cobb did not get up a cent. He told us that and I believe him. Cobb would have put some at 5 to 2 on Detroit, but did not, as that would make us put up $1,000 to win $400.

We won the $420. I gave West $30, leaving us $390, or $130 for each of us. Would not have cashed your check at all, but West thought he could get it up to 10-7, and I was going to put it all up at these odds. We would have won $1,750 for the $2,500 if we could have placed it.

If we ever have another chance like this we will know enough to try to get it down early.

Let me hear from you, "Dutch."

With all good wishes to yourself and Mrs. Leonard, I am always

JOE WOOD

Leonard's relationship with Cobb had deteriorated by the mid-1920s. In 1925, Cobb sold him to a minor league team in the Pacific Coast League. No other major league team claimed him, even after a plea to Speaker, Cleveland's manager. Leonard was bitter. In September 1926, he turned the letters over to Johnson to get his "revenge" and $20,000, of course. Leonard used the money to purchase farmland in the San Joaquin Valley. At his death, he owned one of the largest grape-growing businesses in California and an estate worth more than $2,000,000.

Johnson must have been having a flashback to the old days when his word was the law if he believed that he could unilaterally make these decisions without the judge's consent. Landis investigated. First, he went to Leonard's home in Sanger, California, because the ex-pitcher would not come to Landis in Chicago. He obviously feared Cobb. Leonard quipped, "They got guys in Chicago who bump people off for a price." In November, the squire interviewed Cobb, Speaker, and Wood. Cobb and Speaker demanded to confront their accuser. Leonard refused to appear.

In the interim, Landis released information for the press to mull over. Cobb and Speaker hired heavy-hitting lawyers. Public opinion was beginning to weigh in favor of the superstars. In fact, Landis was vilified for publicizing the information. Cobb and Speaker were highly respected among the baseball public.

Landis delayed his decision, in part, to test the patience of Johnson. Another gambling case arose and Landis poured his full attention into conducting an investigation and interviewing witnesses.

Meanwhile, Johnson was stewing. It was the beginning of the end for the American League president. Landis was very publicly usurping his power and humiliating him. Johnson mouthed off to the press that no matter what, Cobb and Speaker would never be allowed in the American League again. Landis hit the roof and called a meeting of the American League owners. Frustrated, Johnson felt the walls closing in. He went into an angry diatribe condemning Landis for everything since he took office in 1920. Johnson even called for federal control of the game. He was forcing a showdown with Landis.

He did not have the votes to do so. The owners called another meeting on January 23, 1927. Johnson came under immediate attack. Ultimately, they forced Johnson to take time off for "health reasons." He didn't return until opening day. On January 27, Landis issued the ruling clearing the ballplayers. He made a point of assuring that they re-signed with teams in the American League. Cobb went to Philadelphia to join Connie Mack and Speaker signed with Washington.

On July 8, the American League owners called a meeting under the pretext of discussing rule changes. Johnson must have known what was coming. He refused to attend but stayed nearby in the hotel. A debate ensued with Phil Ball of St. Louis the only real ally of Johnson. Three times the meeting broke up and the owners asked for his resignation. Finally, Johnson slid it under the door. He would leave at the end of the season.

In retrospect, it's hard to determine exactly what the betting was all about. Why? Was it a common practice? Were the Indians induced to lose? Cobb's letter is so generic that he could have been betting on roller hockey for all we know. Clearly, it's an interesting story with numerous implications. The debate continues.

William Cox

The National League purchased the bankrupt Philadelphia Phillies in 1942 from owner Gerald Nugent and sought a buyer. Bill Veeck offered to purchase the club but claims that he was rebuffed because of his plan to stock the team with African-American players. The sale was quickly routed to Bill Cox who had built his fortune in the lumber business. Cox also owned the Brooklyn Dodgers in the professional All-America Football Conference.

Further controversy erupted as National League president Ford Frick allegedly dodged inquiries to purchase the franchise from sports promoter and Negro league executive Ed Gottlieb. Gottlieb, acting as an agent for a wealthy Philadelphia radio station owner, wanted to know if Major League Baseball would accept a Jewish bidder.

In their haste to find a buyer or maybe just accepting the lesser of evils, Landis and Frick failed to note the extent of Cox's involvement in gambling. Landis later forced Cox to sell a racehorse and pressured him to turn down the commissionership of New York State racing. After 92 games in 1943, Cox fired popular manager Bucky Harris. The two traded barbs in the newspapers. Harris snapped to the press that he didn't want to play for a man that gambled on his own team anyway.

Landis investigated. Cox initially denied the charge but later admitted to placing "some small sentimental bets" on the Phillies. Cox smelled an expulsion coming and resigned. Landis expelled him anyway on November 23, 1943. Cox was forced to divest from the club. Interestingly, only two owners have been barred from baseball and both controlled the Phillies.

Bill Craver

See 1877 Louisville Grays Scandal

Joseph Creamer

Three teams finished within one game of the National League pennant in 1908. Highlighting the year is the September 23rd game at the Polo Grounds between the Giants and Cubs. Two of the best pitchers of the era, Christy Mathewson and Miner Brown, dueled to a 1-1 tie with two outs in the ninth when the Giants Al Bridwell singled to knock in the winning run.

Fans flooded onto the field as Harry McCormick crossed the plate with what was thought to be the winning tally. However, first base runner Fred Merkle, a 19-year-old rookie filling in for injured Fred Tenney, seeing McCormick score, ran to the clubhouse under the center field bleachers. Noting that Merkle never touched second base, alert Cubs second baseman Johnny Evers grabbed a ball and tagged the base. In all the excitement the ball may or may not have been the actual one in play. In fact, Giants pitcher Joe McGinnity, noticing Evers' excitement, claimed to have thrown the true ball out of the playing area.

Base umpire Hank O'Day, who in his playing days pitched to battery mates Fleet Walker and Connie Mack, failed to notice Merkle's departure. Nevertheless, that evening, hours after the game, he ruled Merkle out on a force play and the game a tie. National League president Harry Pulliam supported his umpire and confirmed that the game was indeed a tie. A week later, both the Giants and Cubs finished the season with identical 98-55 records; the Pirates posted a 98-56 mark. A one-game playoff between the Giants and Cubs was set for October 8th. It's hard to imagine a more exciting pennant race.

Prior to the playoff game, Hall of Fame umpire Bill Klem reported that Giants team physician Joseph Creamer offered him a $2,500 bribe to "call close plays the Giants' way." Creamer's motives were unnamed in the matter, as were any co-conspirators among the Giants, though it is known he was tight with manager John McGraw. The National League expelled Creamer from its ballparks for life. The Cubs won that day and went on to defeat Hughie Jennings' Tigers in the World Series.

Interestingly, Detroit edged the Cleveland Naps by a mere half game and the White Sox by 1.5 games to win the American League flag. Because of a rainout, the Tigers played one less game than the Naps. After 1908, clubs would be required to make up lost games if they had a bearing on the pennant race.

Gene Dale
See 1920 Pacific Coast League

Barney DeForge and Ed Weingarten
The National Association expelled Carolina League manager–pitcher Barney DeForge of Reidsville and minor league executive Ed Weingarten on June 1, 1948, for bribery, gambling, and game-fixing charges.

The plot was hatched in a hotel room on May 10 between the two and used car dealer W.C. McWaters. On the 14th, DeForge pulled his pitcher and took the mound. He walked three and bounced a pitch past the catcher, allowing three runs to score. Reidsville lost 5-0 to Winston-Salem. McWaters paid the manager $300. DeForge confessed and was later sentence to a year in jail.

Weingarten was an official in the Tri-State and Blue Ridge Leagues. He escaped any lasting punishment by passing away a month later.

Jim Devlin
See 1877 Louisville Grays Scandal

Cozy Donlan
See 1924 New York Giants

Shufflin' Phil Douglas
RHP Phil Douglas won 94 games in his nine-year career. He came up with the White Sox in 1912. Under the guidance of Hall of Famer Big Ed Walsh, he developed a spitball. His career highlight came in 1921 as his two wins helped the Giants defeat the Yankees in the World Series. The pitcher's career would end within a year.

Douglas was a heavy drinker who continually broke training rules, not unlike many of his time. He was a difficult player to manage and would constantly disappear on self-declared "vacations." He joined the Giants in 1919, thus, coming under the thumb of disciplinarian John McGraw. It was a hard three years for Douglas, as he frequently faced the ire of his no-nonsense manager.

McGraw hired private detectives, a common practice of the era, to follow Douglas. In June 1922, McGraw fired a private detective, Jim O'Brien, who had become too chummy with Douglas, and assigned dour coach Jesse Burkett as Douglas' keeper. Douglas and O'Brien had been carousing together. The loss of his friend enraged Douglas.

In July, McGraw stepped up his verbal abuse of Douglas after a couple losses. Fed up, Douglas declared to Les Mann and Rogers Hornsby his desire to join the Cardinals. After another loss, McGraw verbally abused Douglas in front of the team, something that was not uncommon in the Giants dugout. Douglas snapped back that he wanted to be traded. That night, he eluded Burkett, got drunk and disappeared for 24 hours. The police finally tracked him down and the Giants forced him into a sanitarium to dry out.

After his stay, McGraw handed Douglas a $200 bill for the sanitarium plus fined the player $100 in addition to five days' pay. The still woozy ballplayer wrote a letter to Mann stating that he hated to see McGraw win the pennant and he didn't want to help him do so. Douglas requested a gift to entice him to jump the team and "go fishing." Fearful of being implicated, Mann turned the letter over to Cardinals general manager Branch Rickey. Landis investigated and gained Douglas' confession. The Giants banned him.

Unfortunately, Douglas was just mad at his manager and was merely trying to force a trade, though his methods were questionable. Douglas threatened a lawsuit and sought reinstatement from Landis. The commissioner rejected all pleas. In happier times, Douglas would toss baseballs to women in the stands with his name and phone number inscribed.

Jean Dubuc

Jean Dubuc was a relief pitcher for the New York Giants who had advanced knowledge of the Black Sox scandal. Testifying at the trial, Rube Benton claimed that Dubuc had received a telegram informing him of the fix. Dubuc won money betting on the Reds. Previously, he was also involved with Hal Chase and Heine Zimmerman in game-fixing scandals. Landis banned him along with the eight White Sox members.

Happy Felsch

See 1919 Chicago White Sox

Horace Fogel

Horace Fogel was a Philadelphia sportswriter who formally managed for parts of two seasons in the National League and as such would be famous for trying to convert Christy Mathewson to a first baseman. In 1909, he bought into the Phillies and became the club's president. By 1912, he had developed a running feud with National League President Tom Lynch based mostly on Fogel's constant bickering about umpire bias against his team.

Near the end of the season, Fogel publicly criticized Cardinals manager Roger Bresnahan for "taking it easy" against his mentor John McGraw. Specifically, Fogel alleged that Bresnahan did not play his best team against the Giants and, as a consequence, the Giants won the pennant. Taking it one step further, Fogel published an article in the *Chicago Post* with the above accusations, plus he charged Lynch and the umpires of conspiring against his Phillies. The accusations must have seemed particularly absurd since the Giants won the pennant by 10 games and the Phillies finished fifth, 30.5 games out.

Lynch became irate. In October, the National League directors met and forced Fogel to divest from the club. Fogel later took part in the Federal League but was deemed a liability there as well.

Back in 1898, Fogel was a co-founder and president of the first professional basketball league, the National Basketball League. The league was represented by mainly Philadelphia and New Jersey interests. It lasted five years.

Paul Fugit
See 1946 Evangeline League

Kazuhide Funada
See 1969 Black Mist Scandal

Chick Gandil
See 1919 Chicago White Sox

Barbaro Garbey
Barbaro Garbey was one of eighteen players expelled for life in 1978 by Cuban baseball for throwing games. He openly admitted to taking money. Later, he signed with the Detroit Tigers and reached the majors in 1984. Garbey hit .287 with 52 RBIs for the world champions, though he went hitless in twelve at-bats in the World Series. It was probably imprudent that the majors freely added a confessed game-fixer.

Joe Gedeon
Joe Gedeon was a good-field, no-hit second baseman for the St. Louis Browns, leading the league in fielding percentage twice. The 48 sacrifice hits that he placed in 1920 also led the league. Unfortunately for him, he was a friend of Swede Risberg. Risberg had Gedeon place bets for him during the 1919 World Series. Gedeon capitalized as well and acted as an intermediary with players, gamblers, and other money men.

Gedeon offered to tell all to Comiskey for the $20,000 "reward." Commissioner Landis banned him for his "guilty knowledge" of the fix.

Waldo Gonzalez
See 1959 Southern Association

George Hall
See 1877 Louisville Grays Scandal

Claude Hendrix
See 1920 Chicago Cubs

Buck Herzog
See 1920 Chicago Cubs

Dick Higham
Perhaps the dirtiest man of 19th-century baseball, Dick Higham is the only umpire ever banned for game-fixing in major league history. His checkered past extends back to his early playing days.

Higham had been a decent hitter in the National Association, amassing a .302 batting average over its five-year existence. It was his fielding that was particularly questionable. Higham's shoddy play was implicated in game-fixing scandals in July 1874, August 1874, June 1875, and August 1875, in all likelihood an incomplete list. He was suspended at least twice.

His reputation never seemed to derail future employment opportunities as a player, manager, or umpire. In the National League, Higham led the league in doubles and outfield assists in 1876 and runs scored and doubles in '78.

After retiring from playing, Higham became a National League umpire in 1881. In '82, he began the season assigned to the Detroit Wolverines. Back then, it was not uncommon for an umpire to travel with one team for an extended period of time to limit expenses. He oversaw 26 of the team's first 29 games. Detroit's mayor and Wolverines team president William Thompson became increasingly irritated at his club's losing streak. He began to question all the close calls being made against his team. Thompson hired a private detective who intercepted the following letter written by Higham:

> Friend Todd [gambler James Todd]:
> I just got word we leave for the East on the 3 p.m. train, so I will not have a chance to see you. If you don't hear from me, play the Providence Tuesday, and if I want you to play the Detroits Wednesday I will telegraph you in this way, "Buy all the lumber you can." If you do not hear from me, don't play the Detroits but buy Providence sure, that is the first game. I think this will do for the Eastern series. I will write you from Boston. You can write me at any time in care of the Detroit BB Club. When you send me money, you can send a check to me in care of the Detroit BB Club, and it will be all right. You will see by the book I gave you the other day what city I will be in.
>
> Yours truly,
> Dick

With the letter in hand, Thompson called a meeting of major league club owners in Detroit on June 24th. Thompson had procured several other letters from Higham but only the above incriminated him. Higham immediately denied writing the incriminating letter but claimed ownership of the other letters. At which time Thompson produced three handwriting experts who all affirmed that the incriminating letter was indeed penned by Higham. The umpire was banned. Naturally, he later became a bookie in Chicago.

Harry Howell
See 1910 American League Batting Race

Masaaki Ikenega
See 1969 Black Mist Scandal

Joe Jackson
See 1919 Chicago White Sox

Al Kaiser
See 1946 Evangeline League

Takeshi Kuwata
See 1970 Auto Racing Scandal

Jesse Levan
See 1959 Southern Association

Lee Magee
Player–manager Lee Magee hit .323 for the Federal League's Brooklyn team in 1915. His nine-year career saw him in seven different uniforms in three leagues. Magee confessed to throwing games with Hal Chase while with Cincinnati in 1918. The plot was exposed when Magee stopped payment on a $500 check he had given gambler Jim Costello as good faith in placing bets. The check ended up in the hands of National League president John Heydler. Magee confessed to Heydler and Cubs president William Veeck and implicated Hal Chase and Heinie Zimmerman. All three ballplayers were forced out after the 1919 season. Magee sued for reinstatement into the league but was rebuffed by the courts.

Harl Maggert
See 1920 Pacific Coast League

Akio Masuda
See 1969 Black Mist Scandal

Marion McElreath
Incoming National Association president George Trautman expelled Muskogee, Oklahoma, of the Western Association outfielder Marion McElreath on June 5, 1947, for attempting to bribe a teammate in an effort to throw a game on May 4.

He was also accused of betting on games and failure to perform at his highest level. Specifically, it was alleged that McElreath muffed a fly ball resulting in a triple and three runs and, while at bat, he called for a hit-and-run but didn't swing, resulting in the runner being tagged out at second. Strangely, the 32-year-old was not new to the game. He had entered organized baseball back in 1931.

Fred McMullin
See 1919 Chicago White Sox

Trick McSorley
See Joe Blong

Fred Merkle
See 1920 Chicago Cubs

Masayuki Nagayasu
See 1969 Black Mist Scandal

Al Nichols
See 1877 Louisville Grays Scandal

Jimmy O'Connell
See 1924 New York Giants

Jack O'Connor
See 1910 American League Batting Race

Kentaro Ogawa
See 1969 Black Mist Scandal

Gene Paulette
Gene Paulette was the Phillies first baseman in 1920 who had once been the backup of future Hall of Famer George Sisler in St. Louis. The story broke in early 1921 that Paulette had accepted gifts from St. Louis gamblers Elmer Farrar and Carl Zork while he was with the Browns in 1919. Specifically, he had accepted a loan without repaying from Zork who was also implicated in the Black Sox affair.

A letter Paulette penned stating his willingness to throw games for remuneration ended up in Landis' hands. Paulette refused to confront Landis and he was expelled, becoming the first ousted by the jurist.

Leonard Pecou
See 1946 Evangeline League

Bill Phyle
Bill Phyle, a Lakota Indian, pitched in the National League with Chicago from 1898–99 and with New York in 1901, posting a 10-19 record. He appeared in a game at shortstop the latter year, becoming the first Native American to do so.

On one of his many stops through the minors Phyle found himself with Memphis in the Southern League in 1903. There he gained a reputation as a heavy drinker and all-around bad actor. After the season, he claimed that members of the Montgomery and Atlanta teams were paid to throw games during the stretch run to Memphis. Plus, he claimed that Little Rock did the same in the postseason. When Phyle failed to appear before the league directors to substantiate the charges, he was blacklisted by the Southern League.

Phyle simply headed West and joined a Pacific Coast League franchise. In 1906, he was traded from the American Association to the St. Louis Cardinals, appearing in 22 games at third base. Phyle later worked as an umpire in the PCL from 1913–31. He was reinstated by the Southern Association in 1905.

Lipman Pike

Lip Pike was the Worcester Ruby Legs center fielder who had once led the league in home runs. He was accused of "selling" the game of September 3, 1881, in which he committed three errors. Pike was immediately suspended by the team, though no evidence was ever presented other than his shoddy fielding. At season's end, he appeared on the league's formal blacklist with eight others: Mike Dorgan, Buttercup Dickerson, Emil Gross, Sadie Houck, The Only Nolan, Bill Crowley, John Fox, and Blower Brown. All but The Only Nolan were later reinstated.

Pike's career was nearly over at age 37 anyway, so he left without a fight. He was officially removed from the blacklist in 1882. It is interesting to note that he had also been blacklisted in 1878 and did not play at all for two years. Pike played one more game in the majors of no consequence. Some believe that Pike was the first professional Jewish player back in the 1860s.

John Radcliff

John Radcliff was a utility player for the Philadelphia Athletics in the National Association. Prior to a game of August 20, 1874, versus the Chicago White Stockings, Radcliff allegedly approached umpire Bill McLean and offered him $175 to make sure that Chicago came out the victor that day. McLean promptly reported the incident. Radcliff claimed that he was not the only one behind the fix and the league investigated. The charges were eventually dropped against the others due to lack of evidence but Radcliff was expelled. The punishment was meaningless because he was reinstated by the National Association at their March 1875 convention, just in time to open the season with the Philadelphia Centennials.

Swede Risberg

See 1919 Chicago White Sox

Angel Rodriguez

Angel Rodriguez was a catcher assigned by the Pirates to the Carolina League. The 20-year-old was suspended for tipping off batters to upcoming pitches on August 19, 1981. Six of the league's umpires testified to his actions. The National Association later imposed a one-year suspension. Rodriguez never reached the majors.

Pete Rose

Pete Rose was a baseball original. Just seeing him play inspired a generation of fans. He popularized the headfirst slide and exhibited his intensity by sprinting to first on walks and hit-by-pitches. Symbolizing his versatility and dedication to the game, Rose performed as a regular at five positions throughout his career: first base, second base, third base, left field, and right field. Rose was given the nickname "Charlie Hustle" by Whitey Ford, and it suited him.

In 1963, Rose came to the Reds after two strong minor league seasons. He promptly won the National League Rookie of the Year award with a .273 average, 170 hits, and 101 runs. Two years later, Rose had the first of his record ten 200-hit seasons. Fourteen times the battler hit over .300. Seven times he led the league in hits, four times in runs, three times in batting average, and twice in on-base percentage.

Coming down to the last day of the season in 1969, Rose and Roberto Clemente were in a virtual tie for the batting title. In his last at-bat, Rose bunted for a single to win the crown.

A defining moment in Rose's career occurred at the 1970 All-Star Game. In a collision at the plate, Rose took out Indians catcher Ray Fosse, separating his shoulder. The injury led to a premature ending of Fosse's career. In the 1973 National League Championship Series, Rose slid hard into Mets shortstop Bud Harrelson, trying to break up a double play. A melee ensued. Manager Sparky Anderson pulled his Reds off the field until New York fans calmed down and stopped throwing objects from the stands.

Rose won the National League MVP award that year with 115 runs and a league-leading .338 batting average and 230 hits. In 1975, he won the World Series MVP in the classic battle against the Red Sox. He placed 10 hits for a .370 average. In seven National League Championship Series, Rose hit .381. In six World Series, he posted a .269 average with 12 runs and 9 RBI.

1978 was a banner year for Charlie Hustle. The 37-year-old electrified the baseball public with a 44-game hitting streak, the longest in the National League during the century. He was eleven years older than Joe DiMaggio was in 1941. On May 5, Rose notched his 3,000th hit. At the end of the season, he gained free agency and signed an impressive $800,000 contract with the Phillies.

Two more World Series followed in 1980 and '83. With his best years behind him, Rose still managed to scatter over 1,000 hits after the age of 38. He collected his 4,000th for the Montreal Expos. At the end of 1984, he re-joined Cincinnati as player-manager. His proudest moment came in 1985 when he surpassed Ty Cobb for the most hits in baseball history. Rose ended his active career in 1986 with an impressive array of records, all of which he could name by heart:

		RANK
Games	3,562	first
At-bats	14,053	first
Hits	4,256	first
Singles	3,215	first
Doubles	746	second

Runs scored	2,165	third
Total bases	5,752	sixth
Base on balls	1,566	tenth

As a manager, Rose guided the Reds to four consecutive second-place finishes in the National League West from 1985–88. His won-loss record stood at 412–373. But life went downhill in '89 for Charlie Hustle.

Pete was a compulsive gambler. It had started as early as his rookie season in 1963. He could be found spending countless hours at the track. Soon, he began betting illegally through bookmakers. In 1971, Commissioner Bowie Kuhn had baseball's head of security, Henry Fitzgibbon, launch an investigation of Rose. According to Fitzgibbon, the investigation was active through his retirement in 1981. Fitzgibbon would regularly question Rose about his activities and often scold him; however, neither Kuhn, the Reds, nor the Phillies ever took action against the superstar.

On February 20, 1989, Rose was called before Commissioner Peter Ueberroth, Commissioner-elect Bart Giamatti, and Deputy Commissioner-elect Fay Vincent to account for his actions. He denied any betting on baseball. The next day, baseball launched a full investigation. For this purpose, John Dowd, a Washington, DC, lawyer, was employed. Dowd was formerly with the U.S. Justice Department, where he led the Strike Force 18 unit that was charged with prosecuting mob-related cases.

Dowd found that indeed Rose had bet on baseball in 1985, '86, and '87. He was also convinced that Rose was betting on the Reds. On May 9, Dowd issued his report. Rose had allegedly used his friend Tommy Gioiosa, a gym manager, to run bets for him on pro football, college basketball, and baseball, including the Reds, since 1984 with bookmaker Ron Peters. Peters confirmed this. Supposedly, Rose also used Paul Janszen to run bets since 1986 on basketball, hockey, and baseball. As evidence, Dowd turned up:

- Betting sheets written by Rose with his fingerprints
- Janszen's betting notebook
- Peters' betting records
- Telephone records from the Reds' dugout and Rose's home
- Numerous eyewitness accounts
- Bank account records, including cancelled checks

To preempt a *Sports Illustrated* story, Major League Baseball revealed the Rose investigation on March 20, 2006 during spring training. The *SI* article hit the newsstands the next day. An array of legal jockeying followed.

The entire time, Rose maintained his innocence. His legal strategy was to attack the motives of Dowd's witnesses and to highlight an alleged bias by now Commissioner Giamatti. On June 19, Rose filed suit against Giamatti. By this time, Rose had supposedly admitted to reporters that the information was pretty much accurate, except for his betting on baseball.

In August, the parties met to negotiate a settlement. The agreement was announced on the 23rd. Pete Rose—Charlie Hustle—inspiration to a generation of baseball fans, agreed to be placed on the permanently ineligible list with the under-standing that there would be no conclusive finding that he bet on baseball. In doing so, Rose had rejected Giamatti's offers of a 7-year or 10-year ban.

At the news conference, Giamatti unequivocally stated that he personally believed that Rose had bet on baseball. Unrepentant, Rose went on air to hawk base-ball merchandise that evening.

In 1990, Rose pled guilty to filing false income-tax returns in 1985 and '87. He had omitted income earned from baseball card shows. Rose was sentenced to five months imprisonment, which he began in August at a federal facility in Marion, Illinois.

With his eligibility for Cooperstown coming after the 1991 season, Hall of Fame administrators ruled in February that any player on baseball's ineligible list is similarly ineligible to the placed on the Hall of Fame ballot.

Happier times came in 1997 when his son Pete Jr. played 11 games for the Reds.

In 2004, after 14 years, the previously remorseless Rose finally copped to betting on baseball and the Reds. But, as usual, he did so for profit (to push a book venture) and personal gain (possible inclusion in the Hall of Fame). Highlighting the latter, Rose timed his book release during the week of Hall of Fame induction announcements. His self-promotion gained heavy fire from those who felt his explanations and sincerity fell short.

Bill Rumler
See 1920 Pacific Coast League

Tom Seaton
See 1920 Pacific Coast League

Cai Shengfeng
See 2005 Taiwanese Professional Baseball

Casey Smith
See 1920 Pacific Coast League

Tris Speaker
See Ty Cobb/Tris Speaker Affair

Bob Tarleton
Bob Tarleton was the general manager for two different Texas minor league teams from 1937–39. In December 1938, he was selected by Louis Comiskey to oversee minor league operations for the White Sox. It was discovered that Tarleton employed a known bookmaker to scout for him. Landis banned Tarleton from organized base-ball. This was just one of many minor league cases the judge oversaw.

Bill Thomas
See 1946 Evangeline League

Hooper Triplett
The Class-A South Atlantic League fined Columbus outfielder Hooper Triplett $500 and suspended him on August 11, 1946, for placing a $20 bet against his club eight days earlier versus Columbia. On the 21st, National Association president William Bramham made the ban permanent.

The 26-year-old had previously won the South Atlantic League batting title in 1940 with a .369 average before the league closed down during the war. Triplett, brother of ex-major leaguer Coaker, signed with a Mexican League franchise. Then league president Jorge Pasquel stepped in and voided it.

On his way out the door as National Association president after 14 years, Bramham blasted the "roaches" that were tainting the game. He specifically cited game-fixing scandals involving Hooper Triplett and the Evangeline League and gamblers who hung out at ballparks. Bramham warned of the widespread influence of these men.

Don Vetorel
See 1946 Evangeline League

Kimiyasu Wada
See 1969 Black Mist Scandal

William Wansley
One reason for the downfall of the National Association of Base Ball Players was its inability to police itself. The fallout from what has come to be called the Wansley Affair is *the* example. It was baseball's first significant game-fixing scandal.

On the evening of September 27, 1865, gambler Kane McLoughlin gave New York Mutuals catcher William Wansley $100 for the purpose of ensuring a Brooklyn Eckfords' victory the following day. Wansley quickly enlisted teammates Tom Devyr, shortstop, and third baseman Ed Duffy, giving them $30 each. These details were later confessed by Devyr.

A crowd of 3,500 saw the Mutuals leading 5-4 after the fourth inning. The Eckfords scored 11 times in the fifth. After his sixth passed ball, Wansley was moved to right field. The infielders also dropped easy fly balls and threw erratically. Not surprisingly, the Eckfords won 23-11.

Attendees became highly suspicious. The Mutuals president John Wildey, a Tammany man and city coroner, accused Wansley of improper conduct and called for a team meeting to review each player's conduct. At the hearing, Wansley confessed and implicated Devyr and Duffy. The three were expelled from the club and later by the NABBP. The situation deteriorated from there.

The following year, the Mutuals found themselves in need of a shortstop, so they unilaterally reinstated Devyr. At the same time, Wansley was hired by the Fulton club. The other clubs protested and the case was argued at the NABBP convention in early 1867. The Mutuals argued that Devyr was only 18 years old at the time of the incident and should be given a second chance. The convention reaffirmed the bans. Nevertheless, New York continued to play Devyr and he was eventually reinstated by the meek NABBP officials. Likewise, in 1868, the Mutuals began playing Duffy. He was officially reinstated the following year.

Wansley was ushered back in by the New York Baseball Association at the following year's convention. Among other rulings that day, African-Americans were formally banned.

The weak-kneed NABBP officials proved to be incapable of firmly administering the league. The very light punishments cast a shadow over the association, as well as baseball itself.

Buck Weaver
See 1919 Chicago White Sox

Ed Weingarten
See Barney DeForge

Lefty Williams
See 1919 Chicago White Sox

Yoshinobu Yoda
See 1969 Black Mist Scandal

Chen Zhaoying
See 2005 Taiwanese Professional Baseball

Heinie Zimmerman
Heinie Zimmerman won the Triple Crown in 1912 with the Cubs while also leading the league in hits, doubles, total bases, and slugging average. It's hard to image a finer year, though researchers later took away his RBI crown. He also led the league in RBIs in 1916 and 1917. The questionable John McGraw picked up Zimmerman in 1916 while he was serving a suspension by Cubs manager Joe Tinker for "laying down on the job."

The self-proclaimed "Great Zim" was a well-known bad actor, a problem player. McGraw always thought he could bring in troubled players, turn them around, and win. No denying that McGraw usually won but he had much less success at curing a player's evils. Often, their disruption in the clubhouse worked counter to the team's goals. In this case and others, McGraw showed poor judgment and would later pay for it with the stink of a scandal.

In late 1919, Zimmerman was suspended by McGraw for allegedly offering teammates OF Benny Kauff and RHP Fred Toney a bribe to throw games. Somehow, Lee Magee, Rube Benton, and Jean Dubuc were also involved.

McGraw offered both Zimmerman and Hal Chase extremely low salaries for

1920, knowing that they would not accept and would be bound by the reserve clause. In short, McGraw forced them out of the majors and they became persona non grata. Their only alternative was to play in outlaw leagues.

Later, Zimmerman and his brother-in-law Joe Noe would be linked to illegal activities with famed gangster Dutch Schultz. Noe would be slain by machine gun fire.

CHAPTER TWO

~

Forced Out

Gambling and game-fixing were not the only reasons for expelling a player. Players, managers, umpires, and even executives have been forced out of their jobs for a variety of reasons, some just for running counter to the club owners. Even whole teams have been ousted. Moreover, countless individuals have been excluded due to their race, height, or sex gender. Some couldn't adjust to new rules and regulations. Others caused their own demise.

Babe Adams

Babe Adams' 19-year major league career was spent entirely, save one game, with the Pittsburgh Pirates from 1906–26. Above all, Adams was known as a control artist. He walked only 430 batters in his long career. Virtually unheard of today for a starter, he barely allowed more than one base runner per inning, hits plus walks per inning pitched. On May 17, 1914, Adams pitched and won a 21-inning game over Rube Marquard without allowing a single walk, a record that probably will never be broken.

Adams' reputation was made in 1909 when he went 12-3 with a dazzling 1.11 ERA during Pittsburgh's pennant drive. In the World Series, he pitched three complete game victories, including a shutout in the final game. By 1926, Adams had won 194 games and a 2.76 ERA.

Hall of Famer Fred Clarke had been the team's manager from 1897–1915, winning four pennants. He had recently been brought back by owner Barney Dreyfuss as the Pirates vice-president. For some reason, field manager Bill McKechnie permitted Clarke to sit on the bench every day in full uniform and openly criticize the players. One day in August 1926, Clarke remarked that the batboy could hit better than future Hall of Famer Max Carey. Several players revolted and requested Clarke's removal from the bench.

To exasperate the bumbling, Clarke insisted that the players be reprimanded. Pittsburgh ownership suspended Carey and then shipped him to Brooklyn. Adams and OF Carson Bigbee were released and never again appeared in the majors. McKechnie was fired at the end of the season and Clarke soon followed. The players' appeal to National League president John Heydler fell on deaf ears. The events became known as the ABC Incident for Adams, Bigbee, and Carey. Dreyfuss, often hailed as a players' owner, proved to be no clubhouse hero, at least in this case.

Sadly, the Pirates were the defending world champions and finished a mere four and a half games out of first. The dissention and dismantling of the team surely played a factor. They rebounded, though, and took the pennant in 1927 only to be crushed by the mighty Yankees in October.

American League Umpires

Two American League umpires, eight-year veteran Al Salerno and six-year man Bill Valentine, attended a meeting of the National League Umpires Association on September 13, 1968. At the time, unionizing efforts were much further advanced in the National League. The umps hoped to join in the cause.

Three days later, American League president Joe Cronin told the pair that their contracts were not being renewed for the following year due to "incompetence." Essentially, they were fired.

Back in 1964, National League umpires formed the first successful umpires' association. American League arbiters attempted the same the following year; however, they were not as close-knit as their counterparts. Meeting organizer Bill McKinley, a 20-year employee, was quickly ushered into retirement. American League administrators simply changed the retirement age of 55 from optional to mandatory.

Emmett Ashford

Emmett Ashford became the first African-American umpire in organized baseball in 1951, working for the Southwest International League. By '54, he was toiling in Triple-A, spending the first of eleven seasons in the Pacific Coast League. In 1966, Ashford was given a shot, joining the American League at the advanced age of 51 as the first African-American umpire in the majors.

Ashford was ushered out four years later after calling the 1970 World Series because the mandatory retirement was 55. Art Williams became the first African-American ump in the National League in 1972.

Banning of African-American Players

The birth of the National Association of Base Ball Players in 1858 highlighted the growth of baseball from a backyard game to a formal, organized sport. The key word here is *association*. It signifies a private club. Not only did the organizers wish to dictate the future of the game and how it was played, they wanted to control who could join. The sporting contests were the attraction but the highpoint of the day was the dinner party after the game. Organizers were more concerned with who was a member than with playing the best contests.

This was an amateur association, which means that the players had to have leisure time to play. This excluded much of the labor class. The also formally barred black clubs in 1867 after Octavius Catto requested admission of his Pythians from Philadelphia, stating:

> If colored clubs were admitted, there would be in all probability some division of feeling, whereas, by excluding them no injury could result to anyone.

In actuality, the NABBP was courting Southern teams. The admission of clubs with African-American players was contradictory to this objective.

Later, 1887 proved to be the pivotal year in the exclusion of African-Americans from organized baseball. The International League formally barred any additional signing of African-American players on July 14. Specifically, a vote taken by the club owners directed the league secretary to "approve of no more contracts with colored men." The International League at the time was considered only one step below the majors. Officials were reacting to white players' grumblings and derogatory comments by the press suggesting that they change their classification to "colored league."

Another reason may have been the irrefutable, thus unacceptable, success of black players, such as George Stovey and Frank Grant. That year, Stovey won 34 games and Grant led the circuit with a .366 batting average. Also, the increased practice of black teams barnstorming against, and even defeating, white teams became too much for many in society to digest.

Concurrently, Chicago White Stockings team captain Cap Anson refused to take the field in an exhibition game against Newark of the International League unless pitcher George Stovey did not play. Fleet Walker, Stovey's battery mate, was not scheduled to play that day. Anson had tried a similar tactic unsuccessfully against Walker in 1884. This time, Anson and his club stood firm and Stovey backed out of the game feigning illness.

In late July, Monte Ward of the New York Giants tried to sign Stovey to a National League contract. Anson protested again, in part, prompting the National League to formally ban African-Americans from its rosters. The official ban was later rescinded allowing major league executives to ludicrously deny the exclusion of African-Americans for decades to come. Officially, this was Judge Landis' response whenever the question was brought up in public. Behind closed doors, he had other things to say.

Previously, the Philadelphia Athletics of the American Association offered a contract to Arthur Thomas of the New York Cuban Giants in June 1886 but were turned down by the Negro league rookie.

In October, the Tri-State League sought to formally prohibit African-Americans. Though they reconsidered, no other African-American appeared in the league. By the late 1890s, no African-Americans could be found in organized baseball.

It is much too easy to blame the exclusion of African-American players on Cap Anson. The fact is it was a defect in society, though baseball did not distinguish itself. The monopoly power wielded by organized baseball ensured complete segregation. Like today, the road to the majors went through the minors. If African-Americans were not permitted in the minors, how could they make the senior circuit?

In January 1893, the Cuban Giants, probably the best black team of the 19th century, applied for admission to the newly proposed Middle States League. By then, segregation was nearly entrenched. Their request was denied.

For the most part, African-American players found work where they could, often switching uniforms as teams literally rose and fell in existence. Barnstorming was the only way to survive financially. The players lived on the road for minimal monetary gains. This would not change until the formation of the Negro National League in 1920.

Red Barber

Red Barber was a highly acclaimed pioneer broadcaster. He defined the baseball broadcasting style and its non-biased approach. In 1934, general manager Larry Mac-Phail plucked Barber from a college radio station to broadcast games for the Reds with Al Helfer. He announced home games and re-created away games from Teletype reports with sound effects to enhance the broadcast.

Barber followed MacPhail to Brooklyn and began a long, storied New York broadcasting career. "The Old Redhead" was selected to announce the first live television broadcast with NBC in 1939. Ernie Harwell and Vin Scully later joined him in Brooklyn. A salary dispute led Barber to sign with the Yankees in 1954 and pair with Mel Allen, Jim Woods and, later, Phil Rizzuto.

In 1966, the Yankees finished in last place for the first time since 1912. One September afternoon, a mere 413 fans showed. Barber asked the cameraman to pan to all the empty seats and made a fuss, declaring the story of the day was not the game but rather the crowd. Barber was unceremoniously fired. His 33-year play-by-play career was over.

The Yankees had been on top for a long time, appearing in the World Series 29 times since 1921. Many factors had contributed to their sustained success, especially, the development of the finest farm system in baseball. A distinction they lost well before the mid-1960s for the simple fact that they failed to sign, develop, and promote black players. Much of the American League shared this affliction. It would be another decade before the Yankees would reach the postseason again.

Clete Boyer

Clete Boyer batted eighth and played third base for the great New York Yankees teams of the early 1960s. He played top-notch defense at the hot corner, leading his league five times in range, three times in assists, and twice in double plays and fielding percentage, though it wasn't until he went to the National League that he won a Gold Glove. Brooks Robinson of the Baltimore Orioles monopolized the award in the American League for sixteen years, from 1960–75.

Boyer's best year at the plate was 1962 when he hit .272 with 18 home runs and 68 RBI. In the World Series that year versus the San Francisco Giants, he batted .318 with 4 RBI. The infielder was traded to Atlanta in November 1966.

Boyer didn't get along with the Braves vice-president of baseball operations Paul Richards, publicly criticizing his boss in May 1971. Richards offered the ballplayer his release if he would return the 60-day severance pay that the team would be obligated to shell out. Boyer, arguably, bought his release. The players union filed a grievance and Commissioner Bowie Kuhn forced the team to return the money.

Around the same time, Kuhn also fined Boyer $1,000 for betting on football and basketball after the player admitted the wrongdoing. In fact, betting pools could be found in every clubhouse. Boyer was merely made the example.

After the affair, Boyer found no interest from other major league teams. He joined Hawaii of the Pacific Coast League. There, he was traded to the Tokyo Whales of Nippon Professional Baseball for John Werhas, where he wowed the country with his glove. It is thought to be the first East–West trade.

Jim Brosnan

Like Jim Bouton's *Ball Four*, Jim Brosnan's two books shook up the baseball establishment. In 1959, with the Cardinals and Reds, Brosnan started a diary. *The Long Season* was published the following year from his notes. It became a bestseller. He repeated the process and published *Pennant Race* about Cincinnati's 1961 championship drive.

Some in the sport did not want to see a bunch of tell-all books about the inner workings of the game and its personalities, so executives tried to pressure him to censor his writings. When Brosnan refused, he was shipped to the White Sox. Once again, management tried to curtail his writing. He rebuffed their efforts and found himself without a job. No one else was interested, either. With the ice broken, many other sports personalities published "insider" chronicles.

Nixey Callahan

Jimmy Callahan anchored the Chicago Colts pitching staff with Clark Griffith during the late 1890s. He jumped across town with Griffith to the American League in 1901 and succeeded him as manager in 1903. Callahan also left the mound that year to man third base for the White Sox. After 1905, he was banned for playing in an outlaw league and was relegated to semi-pro ball until Charles Comiskey brokered his reinstatement in 1911.

Al Campanis

Al Campanis had a cup of coffee in the show with Brooklyn during World War II. In 1946 with Jackie Robinson at second, they formed the double-play combination for the Montreal Royals of the International League. By 1987, Campanis had spent more than 45 years with the Dodgers as a player, scout and, at that time, vice-president of player personnel. As a scout, Campanis had originally signed Roberto Clemente.

Ted Koppel for ABC's *Nightline* interviewed the 70-year-old on April 5 for a 40th anniversary tribute to Jackie Robinson. When asked if there was prejudice in baseball, Campanis relied, "No. It's just that they (African-Americans) may not have some of the necessities to be, let's say, a field manager or perhaps a general manager." The national audience was outraged. Campanis apologized but, nevertheless, the Dodgers asked for his resignation.

Canadians

The Alien Exemption Act of 1894 temporarily made it illegal for Canadians to be employed in the United States. It was passed in the wake of the Panic of 1893. By May 1894, the unemployment rate hit an all-time high at 18%.

An immigration inspector named De Barry asked clarification from the Treasury Department if baseball was indeed a "recognized profession." If it was, a minor league Buffalo franchise had violated the alien contract labor laws by signing two men from the north. Buffalo officials quickly released the players before De Barry got his reply. At least a half dozen other Canadians simply altered their birth certificate to skirt the law.

Hal Carlson
See Spitballers

Billy Clingman
See Washington Senators

Sam Crane
Sam Crane was the second baseman for the National League New York Giants in 1890. He was arrested in 1889 for running away with the wife of a Scranton fruit dealer and her husband's $1,500. The couple was living in hiding in New York under the name Morrison. Crane ultimately became a sportswriter with the *New York Evening Journal* for more than 25 years.

Shag Crawford
Shag Crawford was a National League umpire for 20 years, from 1956–75. He was one of the founders of the umpires union. In 1975, he was asked to work the World Series by the umpire supervisor. He refused, stating that it had already been agreed that all umpires would do so on a rotational basis. Crawford claims that he was secretly forced out for his refusal.

Jerry Dale
Over his strong objections, 15-year National League umpire Jerry Dale was dismissed in 1984 due to his lack of mobility as a result of a knee injury.

John Davidson
John Davidson was the owner of the AA Louisville Colonels in 1889. It seems that he had been having financial trouble and this was being compounded by a poor 27-111 season. So naturally, he began fining his players to make up for his losses.

Things came to a head on May 22, when he fined six players for poor play after a loss. By then, a few players had accrued fines approaching the total of their income for the season. The six staged a two-day strike in Baltimore. An investigation led to refunds of the fines; however, Davidson just wrote the checks on a closed account. The magnate was forced to divest from the club at the end of the year.

Dizzy Dean
Dizzy Dean ran afoul of Commissioner Landis on numerous occasions. In 1944, the judge prohibited Dean from broadcasting the World Series. It didn't seem to matter that Dean was named Broadcaster of the Year by *The Sporting News* and was extremely popular with the fans. Landis omitted him because of his "oral atrocities" and grammar that was "unfit" for a national audience.

Mike DiMuro

Mike DiMuro was the first American to umpire in Nippon Professional Baseball. He left in June 1997 after being poked by a player and surrounded by a mob of teammates, not an uncommon occurrence. DiMuro was ordered to return to the States by the American League, which held his contract, after complaining of the unsafe work conditions.

Herm Doscher

Herm Doscher was expelled from the National League in 1882 for "embezzlement and obtaining money under false pretenses." As the third baseman for the Cleveland Blues, he was cashing checks from both the Blues and the Detroit Wolverines. Strangely, Doscher was scouting for Detroit and stocking their roster with prospects and former teammates.

He was eventually reinstated four years later and began to umpiring the following season, 1887. When his son, Jack, took the field for the Cubs in 1903, they became the first father–son duo to make the majors.

Sam Dungan
See Washington Senators

Leo "The Lip" Durocher

Controversy followed wherever Leo Durocher traveled. He gained a reputation as a battler way back in the 1920s with the Yankees. Babe Ruth and others had the bruises to prove it. Even though he was a good-field, no-hit shortstop, Durocher was a team leader with the Gas House Gang in the '30s. By 1939, Brooklyn hired him as their manager. Many battles with Branch Rickey and Larry MacPhail followed. In fact, he was fired and rehired more times than Billy Martin, though usually only overnight.

Durocher also established himself as a premier manager and umpire baiter. Few won more than his 2,008 games. The Lip copped three pennants and a world championship in New York. Problems arose in 1946. Durocher had always been a flashy guy with addictions to the ponies, poker, and Hollywood starlets. He had also kept company with gamblers and other questionable characters. Perennially, Durocher was in hock to club officials, his players, friends, or a host of acquaintances.

Rickey convinced Commissioner Happy Chandler to have a talk with Durocher. Chandler advised him to stay away from gamblers. Durocher's highly publicized relationship with a divorcee also concerned the pious Rickey. Durocher smelled problems and toed the line. The hammer still hung above his head in 1947. Spring training was held in Havana that year in an effort to defray difficulties because of the introduction of Jackie Robinson to the major leagues. Along those lines, Durocher quashed a player insurrection over Robinson's presence.

To Durocher, winning was everything. It didn't matter who got him there. He couldn't understand how others saw it differently. In fact, the manager had openly declared his desire to sign black players back during Landis' reign if it ". . . weren't barred by the owners." The comment and Landis' reaction renewed the controversy, especially in light of African-American participation during World War II.

Unfortunately, Chandler suspended the manager for the entire season for a still undisclosed reason. Durocher returned in '48 but lasted only 73 games in Brooklyn. All of baseball was shocked when he immediately took over the Giants. The most-hated Dodger was now the cross-town boss. He went on to take pennants in 1951 and '54. The Lip was still managing in 1973.

Durocher's battles with baseball's establishment extended his entire life. Sadly, he was denied inclusion in the Hall of Fame until after his death. Never think that Hall of Fame voting is devoid of personal politics.

Eleanor Engle

Eleanor Engle, a softball star, was signed by the Harrisburg Senators of the Interstate League on June 21, 1952. The next day, the 24-year-old infielder delighted the crowd during pre-game drills, but failed to play in the game.

National Association president George Trautman stepped in and immediately voided her contract. He further prohibited the future signing of women to minor league contracts. Commissioner Ford Frick then formally barred all women from organized baseball. The ruling still stands.

Female Managers

During the 1946 season, Thelma Eisen, one of the All-American Girls Professional Baseball League's top hitters, managed her Peoria team briefly. Canadian Bonnie Baker became the only fulltime manager with Kalamazoo in 1950. The following winter, league officials formally banned female field managers—in a women's circuit!

Ray Fisher

Ray Fisher, a 10-year major league veteran, compiled 100 wins and a 2.82 ERA from 1910–20. The righthander proved to be a consistent pitcher for the Yankees in the 1910s. With the Reds in 1919, he was credited with the loss in Game 3 of the World Series to straight arrow Dickie Kerr. After the season, Cincinnati president Garry Herrmann sent Fisher a contract for 1921 with a $1,000 pay cut. Instead, the pitcher asked for his release when he was offered the baseball coach's position at the University of Michigan for $5,000 a year.

Herrmann supposedly countered with a raise but Fisher now wanted a two-year deal. Herrmann balked, so Fisher took the coaching job. Officially, Herrmann was to place Fisher on the voluntarily retired list but instead classified him as ineligible. Meanwhile, Branch Rickey of the Cardinals and an outlaw league contacted Fisher to inquire about his willingness to play for them. Fisher sought redress about his status in organized baseball from Commissioner Landis but the judge barred him permanently.

Landis did not even give Fisher the courtesy of a hearing. There seems to be no basis for the ruling other than Landis' appeasement of Herrmann and accusations that he had caught Fisher in a lie. The commissioner had the power and wielded it as he saw fit with little concern for formalities: the need for a trial, presentation of facts, collaboration of evidence, and an appropriate verdict. No wonder so many of his rulings on the bench were overturned on appeal. However, there was no appeals process in baseball.

Herrmann was obviously getting back at Fisher for the snub. Years later, the incident file was discovered and found to contain a multitude of inaccuracies, exaggerations, and false claims by Herrmann. A thorough investigation by Landis would have discovered the truth.

The pitcher went on to coach at Michigan for 38 years. Forty years after the blacklisting, Fisher was formally reinstated by Bowie Kuhn and found work as a spring training instructor for Atlanta and Detroit.

Curt Flood

Curt Flood became the Cardinals everyday center fielder when Johnny Keane took over the team in mid-1961. He posted by far his best year with a batting average of .322, the first of six .300+ seasons. For the '64 world champions, he collected 211 hits, 97 runs, and batted .311. The three-time All-Star also won seven Gold Gloves.

Flood soon became known as the best center fielder in the game, as Willie Mays was aging gracefully. He led the league five times in range, four times in putouts and twice in fielding percentage. For 226 consecutive games, from September 1965 to June '67, Flood failed to commit an error, a National League record. He handled 568 chances flawlessly, a major league record. Obviously, his 1966 fielding percentage equaled 1.000. On June 19, 1967, Flood completed the first unassisted double play by a National League outfielder since 1933 and the first in the majors in 22 years.

The Cardinals co-captain, with Tim McCarver, helped lead St. Louis to pennants in 1964 and 1967–68. In '69, Flood publicly criticized club officials for throwing in the towel while the season was in progress. He was traded to Philadelphia on October 7, learning about it from a reporter. Flood did not particularly care for the Phillies franchise and had questions about the treatment of African-Americans in Philadelphia. Unhappy, he threatened retirement.

Flood had, after all, built a life for himself in St. Louis over the previous decade. The Cardinals were also a racially harmonious team, especially after copping three National League pennants together. Gussie Busch had purchased the franchise back in 1953. His fortune had been derived from Budweiser beer, a product that owed much of its success to African-American consumers. The Cardinals of the 1960s, in contrast to such teams as the Yankees, showcased an array of black and Latin talent, which not surprisingly spurred them to championships: Bill White, Flood, Lou Brock, Julian Javier, Orlando Cepeda, and the great Bob Gibson.

Flood decided to discuss his options with Marvin Miller, executive director of the Major League Baseball Players Association. Together with former U.S. Supreme Court Justice Arthur Goldberg, they drafted a letter to Commissioner Bowie Kuhn on December 24. It read,

> After twelve years in the major leagues, I do not feel I am a piece of property to be bought and sold irrespective of my wishes. I believe that any system which produces that result violates my basic rights as a citizen and is inconsistent with the laws of the United States and of the several States.

> It is my desire to play baseball in 1970, and I am capable of playing. I have received a contract offer from the Philadelphia club, but I believe I have the right to consider offers from other clubs before making any decision. I, therefore, request that you make known to all Major League clubs my feelings in this matter, and advise them of my availability for the 1970 season.

Flood was questioning the legality of the reserve clause that bound players to their team, potentially forever. Kuhn had no choice by to reaffirm the reserve clause and the player's 1969 contract.

On January 16, 1970, Flood, backed by the Players Association's financial resources, filed suit in U.S. District Court in New York against Kuhn and MLB. At the trial in May, Bill Veeck, Jackie Robinson, Hank Greenberg, and Jim Brosnan testified on the outfielder's behalf. No active players testified or even showed up, a failure by Miller, who could not convince the shortsighted players otherwise. Flood was an outcast. No active player stood beside him. Let none claim otherwise. Meanwhile, Flood sat out the entire season, forfeiting his salary.

In August, a ruling upholding the 1922 U.S. Supreme Court's decision that exempted organized baseball from antitrust laws was rendered against Flood. Similarly, the U.S. Supreme Court found 5-3 against the ballplayer on June 12, 1972.

Though Flood lost, his cause focused the Players' Association on the reserve clause and free agency issues. Major League Baseball itself was concerned by the process and, eventually, modified the reserve clause. In 1976, arbitrator Peter Seitz established free agency. Union chief Marvin Miller would arguably become the most powerful man in the sport.

Flood, however, gained no benefits. He incurred only grief, legal costs, and lost salary. In 1971, he joined the Washington Senators but left after only 13 games and retired with a .293 average. Flood moved to Europe but eventually returned as a broadcaster for the Oakland A's in 1978.

Curry Foley

NL Buffalo Bison outfielder Curry Foley was injured early in 1883. He went without pay for one year and incurred extensive medical expenses. After recovery, he was offered positions on several independent and minor league clubs. However, invoking the reserve clause, Buffalo would not release him from his contract nor would they pay him, even through 1884. Fellow ballplayers eventually threw a benefit to raise money for his family; however, Foley never played in the majors again.

Andrew Freedman

Andrew Freedman purchased control of the debt-ridden New York Giants in 1895 for $50,000. He was another New York owner with ties to the corrupt Tammany Hall political organization. Freedman would accrue a long list of offenses against the game before he was finally ousted in 1903. For example, if a sportswriter offended him, Freedman barred him from the grounds—even if the journalist presented a ticket. He went as far as to punch a young *New York Times* reporter. Freedman attorneys could often be found filing lawsuits against journalists.

Like a New York magnate a century later, Freedman employed 12 managers in eight years. *The Sporting News* exclaimed, "He had an arbitrary disposition, a violent temper, and an ungovernable tongue in anger which was easily provoked and he is disposed to be arbitrary to the point of tyranny with subordinates." Freedman often did as he pleased as weak-kneed National League president Nick Young stayed out of his way. He once pulled his team off the field after an opposing player insulted him. He still felt justified in the face of forfeiture, refunding of the gate receipts and a $1,000 fine.

Freedman was a big proponent of the National League slimming to eight teams after the 1899 season. The abandoned cities joined with Ban Johnson to pave the way for the development of the American League as a major circuit. Freedman later used his Tammany influence to keep the American League out of New York. One of his most unpopular stances was a salary dispute with star pitcher Amos Rusie. Here, Freedman incurred the wrath of fans, players, and fellow executives.

Moose Fuller
See Spitballers

Carl Furillo
"The Reading Rifle" Carl Furillo led the National League in outfield assists in 1950 and '51; then, runners stopped testing the right fielder's powerful arm. He could hit as well, posting 192 home runs, 1,058 RBIs, and a .299 batting average over 15 major league seasons spent with the Brooklyn–Los Angeles Dodgers from 1946–60.

Five times he hit over .300 and six times exceeded 90 RBIs. In 1952, Furillo slumped to .247, then underwent an operation for cataracts. He rebounded to lead the league in batting the following season with a .344 mark. His season ended on September 6 with a broken finger obtained in a melee after being hit by a pitch. Instead of going after the pitcher, Furillo attacked Giants manager Leo Durocher.

Furillo was released by L.A. on May 17, 1960. The player claimed that he was injured and should have been placed on the disabled list. The shunned employee sued and won a year's pay, $21,000. However, after the settlement, Furillo could not land a job, leading him to claim that he was informally blacklisted. Furillo exclaimed, "I won. I got my money. Then, all of a sudden, I was blackballed. Nobody wanted me to coach, to pinch hit, not even in the minors."

Eddie Gaedel
Everyone knows that St. Louis Browns owner Bill Veeck slipped a midget into the lineup in the 1950s. Shocking as it was, people would come to expect the unusual from Veeck, one of the premier showmen in major league history. It has become the most heralded stunt in baseball history.

Between games of a doubleheader on August 19, 1951, 3'7", 65-pound, stage performer Eddie Gaedel popped out of a cake, wearing a Browns uniform and elf slippers, and announced his signing of a major league baseball contract with St. Louis in front of a Sunday crowd of 18,000 +. He had been distributed the uniform number "1/8" and was to be paid $100 per game.

Veeck wasted no time. Gaedel pinch-hit for the leadoff batter. Home plate umpire Ed Hurley objected to his insertion but manager Zack Taylor presented the signed contract with the proper league notification. Veeck had filed his papers with the American League at the last possible moment before the weekend to ensure that it would not be reviewed until Monday morning.

Gaedel took his place in the batter's box and, as instructed, crouched low and did not swing. He walked on four pitches by Tigers lefthander Bob Cain who could barely contain himself. Gaedel was immediately removed for a pinch runner to the roar of the crowd who gave him a standing ovation.

American League president William Harridge was not amused. That night, he issued a statement declaring the contract void because it was not in the best interests of baseball and blasted Veeck for conduct detrimental to the game. Happy Chandler had recently been fired as commissioner and the position was still vacant. Harridge had the final say and banned future stunts. In his fury, Harridge even tried, unsuccessfully, to have Gaedel stricken from the record books. Veeck had plans to sign the nine-foot tall Ted Evans as well but that, too, was nixed.

At age 26, Gaedel was banned from the game. He would use his notoriety to make a decent living until his death 10 years later. Veeck would even use him in future promotions. Upon Veeck's returning to baseball as owner of the Chicago White Sox in 1959, he had a helicopter land on the field at Comiskey Park. Several midgets jumped out dressed as Martians and mock-kidnapped the diminutive keystone combination of Nellie Fox and Luis Aparicio. Gaedel was one of the Martians.

Back in 1938, Red Sox manager Joe Cronin tried a similar stunt with batboy Donald Davidson on the last day of the season. Umpire Bill Sommers quickly quashed the idea. The four-foot Davidson was a mainstay in Boston for the Sox and Braves for nearly 40 years. For a time, he served as traveling secretary for the Braves.

Mazio Gamiz

Mazio Gamiz pitched for the Cuban Stars of the Eastern Colored League from 1925 until he ran afoul of immigration authorities in August 1929. He was arrested and deported, never appearing on a U.S. club again.

Al Hall

Al Hall was the Cleveland Blues left fielder on May 13, 1880. A collision with the center fielder broke Hall's leg in a contest in Cincinnati. Cleveland president Ford Evans immediately released Hall to avoid the expenses. Not only was Hall responsible for his medical costs, but he had to find his way home to Cleveland as well. Fortunately, the Cincinnati fans passed the hat and raised money for Hall. He never played in the majors again.

Club owners had little regard for their players. They viewed themselves as businessmen who had to attend to the bottom line, regardless of employee squabbles. They saw the players as toughs who possessed little education or business savvy. This was a common management perception of labor during the 19th century. Eventually, this led to unionizing, as laborers sought to protect themselves.

For their part, many ballplayers were hardened young men who drank excessively, lacked self-discipline, and expressed themselves through profanity. To symbolize this, as many as 80% of the ballplayers of the era became saloonkeepers after retiring from the game. Few owners felt the need to minister to such men.

Bill Haller
Bill Haller had previously umpired in the American League for 21 years. He was the assistant supervisor of the American League arbiters in 1985. He allegedly was fired as part of the fallout of the 1984 umpires strike.

Joe Harris
Cleveland Indians first baseman Joe Harris was disqualified for the 1920–21 seasons by Ban Johnson for playing in an outlaw league. He would return to bat .317 his next season, and eight times over .300, during a 10-year career.

An outlaw league is one that did not sign the National Agreement and, consequently, operated outside "organized baseball." Major League Baseball was a monopoly and it was further strengthened by incorporating the minors in this concept of organized baseball. The potential for abuse of the laborers was abundant. In Harris' case, the majors expelled a worker because he had the audacity to seek income outside its purview.

Burt Hart
Baltimore Orioles first baseman Burt Hart was suspended by American League president Ban Johnson in 1901 for punching an umpire. He was batting .311 after 58 games in his rookie season. Hart never again appeared on a major league diamond.

Havana Sugar Kings
Cuban interests fielded a team, the Havana Sugar Kings, in the Triple-A International League from 1954–60 as part of the Cincinnati Reds organization. Much of the roster was filled with local talent, such as longtime major league pitchers Orlando Pena and Mike Cuellar and infielders Leo Cardenas and Cookie Rojas.

With the communist revolution on the island in 1959, political pressure mounted on the International League. In July, bullets were fired in political celebration outside the stadium that nicked a coach and player on the field as the bullets landed. The visiting club left the country as soon as possible and league officials forced the relocation of most of the club's remaining home games to the road.

Finally, the International League abruptly relocated the franchise to New Jersey with an edict on July 8, 1960. The club was on the road in Miami at the time. Several Cuban players and the manager immediately resigned and returned home. Others, like Pena, stayed in the United States to pursue their careers.

Mike Hines
At his contract signing in 1885, NL Providence Grays catcher Mike Hines objected to the standard reserved clause in his contract. Providence would not relent. Hines sat out and, meanwhile, the club folded. The league still viewed him as reserved to

the defunct franchise. He was not signed again by another National League club until 1888. After only four games, Hines' career was over.

Tim Hurst

Tim Hurst was a rough and tough umpire. In an era that wasn't kind to arbiters, Hurst gave better than he got. The redhead from Ashland, Pennsylvania, was always amid controversy, arguing and fighting players, managers, and fans alike. If a player particularly irked him, Hurst would later track him down at his hotel and give him a beating. To keep players in line on the field, he would pinch them hard and whack them upside the head with his mask.

On August 4, 1897, in Cincinnati, a fan threw a beer stein onto the field, landing just inches from Hurst. The umpire picked it up and hurled it back into the stands. Unfortunately, he hit the wrong person—a firefighter—in the nose. The fans came after the umpire and police were forced to escort him from the field. The National League released Hurst at the end of the season.

St. Louis Browns owner Chris Von der Ahe, always willing to buck the system, immediately hired Hurst to manage his club. The former arbiter became one of the fiercest umpire baiters and despised managers; however, a last-place finish ensured his firing at season's end.

Hurst's hard-nosed reputation did not keep Ban Johnson from employing him as an umpire in the American League's inaugural season in 1900. Hurst was not even fired when he followed New York Highlander manager Clark Griffith to the dugout after an argument and knocked him cold. Griffith had made the mistake of dirtying the umpire's shoes.

In 1909, 12 years to the day after the Cincinnati beer stein incident, Hurst was fired for spitting in the eye of Philadelphia Athletics fan-favorite Eddie Collins. A riot ensued. To compound the problem, the umpire failed to submit an incident report. Hurst holds the distinction of being the only man in blue fired by both the American and National Leagues.

Hurst was also a longtime boxing referee and promoter. He officiated between 1894–1906, including three fights of future heavyweight champ Marvin Hart and a world middleweight title match.

Ted Husing

Until 1960, the commissioner's office held the right to select each postseason broadcaster. In 1935, Judge Landis prohibited broadcaster Ted Husing from obtaining a job in organized baseball. His crime? On the air the previous World Series, a heated battle ensued between the Tigers and Cardinals; for CBS, Husing had decried the umpiring as ". . . some of the worst I've seen."

Bill Hutchison

From 1890–92, Chicago Colts pitcher Bill Hutchison won 120 games, struck out 862 batters, and compiled a 2.73 ERA. The righthander led the National League each year in starts, innings pitched, and victories. In 1892 alone, he fanned 312 men.

Hutchison lost his effectiveness when the mound was pushed back to 60′6″ from

50 feet in 1893. His ERA ballooned to 4.75 then to 6.06 in '94. Over the next four seasons, Hutchison lost 62 games against only 44 wins. The rule change affected "Wild Bill" more than most.

Sig Jakucki

RHP Sig Jakucki appeared in seven games in 1936 but couldn't stick in the majors until World War II. In 1944, he won 13 games to help the Browns win the only pennant in their 50-year history. His 5-2 victory over the Yankees on the final day of the season clinched the title. However, Jakucki's heavy drinking prompted a suspension the following year. He never pitched in the majors again.

Charley Jones

Charley Jones was the first man to hit two home runs in an inning, on June 10, 1880. In 1879, he led the National League in homers, runs scored, and RBIs. In 1880, Jones complained to Boston Red Caps owner Arthur Soden that he hadn't seen a paycheck in three weeks. On a road trip at the time, Soden told Jones that they would take up the matter back in Boston. Jones put in a claim for $378 and Soden accused the player of wanting cash so that he could desert the club. Soden suspended Jones and stranded him in Cleveland and fined the player $100.

Jones sued for back pay and won, even attaching gate receipts in May 1881. However, he remained blackballed. It was not until the formation of the American Association that he found another major league job.

Jones discovered future Hall of Famer Bid McPhee while roaming Ohio in search of prospects for the Cincinnati Red Stockings. Jones also umpired during the final season of the American Association.

Dorothy Kamenshek

First baseman Dorothy Kamenshek of the All-American Girls Professional Baseball League was offered a contract by Fort Lauderdale of the Florida International League in August 1951. AAGPBL officials nixed the deal.

Benny Kauff

Benny Kauff got a second lease on his career when the Federal League opened in 1914. Acquiring the nickname "Ty Cobb of the Federal League," Kauff led the league in hits, doubles, triples, runs, stolen bases, batting average, on-base percentage, and slugging average. The following year, he copped the league's only other batting crown. When the Federal League folded after the 1915 season, Kauff was sold to the Giants for $35,000. Twice he topped .300 in the next five seasons and finished with a career .311 batting average.

Kauff testified before the Black Sox grand jury in 1920 that Hal Chase and Heinie Zimmerman were involved in game-fixing while teammates. Zimmerman countercharged the same. Ban Johnson further reported to the *Chicago Tribune* that Kauff, with a gambler named Henderson, had approached Arnold Rothstein seeking $50,000 to fix the 1919 World Series. Also, Billy Maharg had previously linked Kauff to the scandal.

Kauff was a loud guy who wore expensive suits and jewelry and toted a huge bankroll, as much as $6,000, a year's salary. He was also part owner of an automobile business with his brother. In February 1920, he was arrested in New York for auto theft. Two of his employees had implicated him in stealing, repainting, and selling a Cadillac.

Prior to the 1921 season, Landis summoned Kauff to Chicago to account for himself. The meeting would prove unsuccessful for Kauff. He was banned by Landis from baseball before his trial started. Kauff called John McGraw, pitcher Jesse Barnes, former National League president John Tenor, and Giants outfielder George Burns as character witnesses at his trial. Kauff, defended by future Boston Braves owner Emil Fuchs, was acquitted.

Nonetheless, Landis denied reinstatement. Though the case against Kauff seemed to be weak, Landis read the transcripts and came to his own conclusions, as the czar was apt to do. Kauff sued and received an injunction from the courts preventing the denial of his job. It was overturned on appeal. He never again played in organized baseball.

Ray Keating
See Spitballers

Dickie Kerr
Dickie Kerr, winner of two games for the White Sox in the famed 1919 World Series, sat out the entire 1922 season in a salary dispute with Charles Comiskey. The 5'7" lefthander expected a $500 raise after coming off two successful seasons in which he won a combined 40 games. Comiskey, now at the helm of a decimated and dwindling franchise, disagreed.

Kerr played semi-pro ball in Texas with a few of the banned Black Sox. Landis suspended him for it. Not reinstated until August 1925, Kerr pitched in only 12 more major league games. Later as a minor league manager, he switched Stan Musial from pitcher to outfielder.

Stan Landes
Stan Landes was a National League umpire from 1955–72. His weight ballooned to 360 pounds and he was fired. The league also had concerns about his indebtedness, making him a potential target of gamblers.

Harry Lord
Immobile third baseman Harry Lord played nine years in the majors, mostly with the Red Sox and White Sox, at one time captaining Chicago. Like many in 1914, he jumped the Sox for the Federal League but backtracked and attempted to negotiate with owner Charles Comiskey. After being turned down and only appearing in 21 games that year, Lord was named player–manager of the Buffalo Feds for 1915.

After the new league folded, major league executives began to cut wages. Lord refused to sign and sat out 1916, trying to get Comiskey to relent but he didn't realize who he was dealing with. Lord never did find another job in the majors and continually claimed that he was blackballed.

Larry MacPhail

Larry MacPhail was another battler. As a 28-year-old captain in the Army, he participated in a non-sanctioned attempt to kidnap Germany's exiled ruler, Kaiser Wilhelm. Over the rest of his life, he jumped in and out of baseball, becoming perhaps the game's foremost innovator. His highlights include these firsts: airplane travel, batting helmets, the broadcasting of all home and away games in New York, night games, old timers' games, pension funds for front-office personnel, player pension funds, regularly scheduled doubleheaders, season ticket plans, stadium clubs, and televised games.

Despite this list, MacPhail may be best known for turning the hapless Dodgers around and building a dynasty. He also developed pennant winners with the Reds and Yankees. In 1947, MacPhail left for the last time. At the World Series victory party, he got drunk, unleashed a hail of insults, slugged a sportswriter, and announced his retirement. Co-owners Dan Topping and Del Webb made him keep his word, quickly buying MacPhail out.

Mickey Mantle and Willie Mays

Commissioner Bowie Kuhn forced two of the top names in the game out of the sport. In 1979, it became apparent that Willie Mays was about to sign a contract to do public relations work for Bally's Casino in Atlantic City. He would greet and entertain potential and existing clients.

It presented a problem for Bowie Kuhn. First, Mays was extremely popular and, in fact, had joined the Hall of Fame over the summer. Second, Kuhn had already set a precedent by forcing Charlie O. Finley, among others, to divest from the parent company of several Las Vegas casinos. Also, he had kept former Yankee owner Del Webb from purchasing the White Sox unless he sold his casino interests. Actually, the precedent was set much earlier when Judge Landis forced Giants owners Horace Stoneham and John McGraw to divest from a Havana racetrack and casino.

Kuhn did not want to be seen as playing favorites and buckling under to the player's popularity. At no time did anyone question Mays's integrity in the game. Mays was offered a deal that was much more lucrative than his front office position with the New York Mets. But on October 26, Kuhn forced Mays to disassociate himself from the Mets.

Mickey Mantle signed in a similar capacity with the Claridge Hotel in Atlantic City in 1983. Kuhn continued his unpopular rulings by forcing Mantle to remove himself from his baseball interests. Capitalizing on the potential popularity windfall, new commissioner Peter Ueberroth reinstated the pair in 1986.

Willie Mays

See Mickey Mantle and Willie Mays

Jim McCormick

Pitcher Jim McCormick won 265 games in a 10-year career. In 1880 and '82, he had led the league in games, starts, complete games, innings pitched, and victories. He won more than 35 games three times, capping at 45 in 1880. His ERA dipped below 2.00 on three occasions and the righthander exceeded 200 strikeouts three times. This didn't matter in 1888, following a below-par season because McCormick was offered a contract with a pay cut by the NL Pittsburgh Alleghenys.

McCormick sat out the entire season, hoping to sign with another club. Pittsburgh kept him reserved and, as such, he was off-limits to other league teams. His productive major league career ended at age 32.

Bill McKinley
See American League Umpires

Larry McLean
Giants backup catcher Larry McLean, another perennial bad actor, got drunk early in the 1915 season and staggered up to John McGraw and his coaches in front of a St. Louis hotel. Accusing McGraw of welching on a $1,000 bonus for good behavior, which he had surely earned, McLean challenged the manager to a fight. The catcher had to be restrained. Scout Dick Kinsella threatened to break a chair over his head and McLean fled. The manager suspended the player indefinitely. He never appeared in the majors again. Later, at age 39 in 1921 McLean was shot and killed in a fight by a bartender in Boston.

Heinie Meine
See Spitballers

Marty Murphy
San Francisco first baseman Marty Murphy was expelled from the Pacific Coast League on May 17, 1905, after attacking umpire Fred Perrine. On April 30, Murphy started punching Perrine and continued until a policeman arrested the ballplayer. The tough umpire dressed his cuts and continued the game.

Negro League Owners
An unfortunate side effect of major league baseball's acceptance of African-American players was the demise of the Negro leagues. Club owners lost their players and ability to compete, often without compensation. The major leagues now had a slew of well-trained talent to pick from that cost next to nothing.

Though Newark Eagles owner Effa Manley was the only vocal opponent against integration of the leagues, she summed up the other owners' attitude. They knew that the day major league baseball accepted African-Americans would be the beginning of the end for their league and, hence, their investment.

The Only Nolan
The Only Nolan was a pitcher for the Indianapolis Hoosiers in 1878 during the franchise's short tenure in the National League. He won 13 games for the team, tossing 347 innings.

Nolan was suspended by team owner William Perritt twice that season. First on suspicion of game-fixing and then for faking a family crisis to spend the day at a brothel. Nolan left the team and joined a minor league club. He was blacklisted for deserting the club and did not reappear in the major leagues until 1881.

Harry Overbeck

Harry Overbeck was enticed by St. Louis owner Chris Von der Ahe to jump his minor league club in the Northwestern League. Von der Ahe was the man who supposedly introduced the hot dog to baseball. Without ever appearing in a game, Overbeck was released from St. Louis. He was unemployed and had already been barred from the Northwestern League for desertion. Overbeck had no other recourse but to sue. He won $400 in relief.

Dave Pallone

Dave Pallone was a National League umpire for 10 years when he got into a shoving match with Pete Rose in 1988. Rose was suspended for 30 days and fined $10,000 by National League president Bart Giamatti. Many believe that Pallone was also at fault.

Giamatti fired Pallone at the end of the season without a hearing. Pallone claimed in his book *Behind the Mask* that he was actually fired because he was gay. Many other umpires held a grudge against Pallone because he was first hired as a scab back in 1979.

A. T. Pearsall

Organization in baseball began with social clubs. Men would be asked to join an organization and participate in its gatherings. Naturally with young males, sporting contests and bravado would be at the core of their kinship. One such group, the Excelsior Club of Brooklyn, became quite adept at playing the New York version of the game, the basic rules of which we still follow today.

As the Excelsiors and similar clubs traveled from community to community challenging local nines, the New York version gained wider acceptance throughout the Northeast. In the 1860s, many men enlisted in the Army and further spread their rules for the bat and ball game as they traveled. Eventually, the New York version became universally adopted over the Massachusetts form and countless other local variations.

Ninety-one members of the Excelsior club joined the Union Army. One of the first-string nine, A. T. Pearsall, a physician, defected to the Confederacy in the winter of 1862–63. Upon hearing the news, the Excelsiors expelled the traitor.

Fred Pfeffer

Chicago Brotherhood leader Fred Pfeffer was one of the premier fielding second baseman of his day. He was a key member of Cap Anson's "Stonewall Infield." Pfeffer led 26 times in key fielding statistics, possessing perhaps the strongest arm in the league. In his 16-year career, Pfeffer accrued more than 1,000 RBIs, knocking in 70+ ten times. Interestingly, all 25 of his home runs in 1884 came at home.

Pfeffer negotiated his release from Louisville in 1895 and joined an unsuccessful attempt to revive the old American Association. In response, the National League threatened to blacklist all rebels. The other players caved and re-joined their old teams. Pfeffer claimed that because he had been released, he could do whatever he wanted; in essence, he was a free agent. The owners didn't see it that way. Pfeffer was blacklisted. He regained admittance, however, after presenting a 10,000-signature fan petition, paying a $500 reinstatement fee, and signing a loyalty oath.

He joined Andrew Freedman's New York Giants but was quickly suspended and released for being "played out." Freedman, one of the most despised owners in major league history, refused to dole out the customary two-week severance pay. Pfeffer retained lawyer John Montgomery Ward and sued for his full salary. Ward won the case after humiliating Freedman on the witness stand. The player won interest as well because the case was not settled until 1907. Pfeffer would later administer the nation's first baseball instructional camp.

Pfeffer's troubles with management probably stemmed from his union activities. Many would face similar struggles. Few would boast a legal victory, though.

Pam Postema

Pam Postema entered an umpiring school in Florida and finished 17th in a class of 130. Her minor league career began in the rookie leagues in 1977. As expected, she endured endless sexual harassment. Postema slowly worked her way up the ladder. The last five seasons of her 13-year career were spent at the Triple-A level in the Pacific Coast League. She worked the 1988 Hall of Fame game and several major league spring training games in 1988 and '89 but never made the bigs. Despite generally good marks, she was released in 1989. Postema sued and later settled a sexual harassment case against organized baseball.

Jim Price

New York Giants manager Jim Price was fired near the end of the 1884 season while on the road in Detroit for embezzling club funds. He had previously been caught at the beginning of the year and forgiven. Monte Ward saw the team through its final 14 games. Price, a New York native, stayed away from his hometown for fear of prosecution.

Bugs Raymond

Bugs Raymond was a hard-living, hard-drinking pitcher who amassed a 2.49 ERA over six seasons. By 1908, his drinking was out of control. Manager John McGraw picked him up as part of his continuing plan to heal the wayward. Raymond spent the next three years with the Giants; however, his appearances were cut in half after 1909. McGraw tried to keep tabs on the player with roommates and detectives, but nothing could keep Raymond out of the saloons. The Giants even footed the bill for Raymond's family to travel with the team, hoping to keep the pitcher in line.

McGraw went as far as to lock him in the clubhouse during the first game of a doubleheader when he was due to pitch the second game. Raymond merely lowered a bucket out the window and fans filled it with beers. The manager would even remit

Raymond's paycheck directly to his wife. Bugs, not one to be curtailed, would just trade baseballs for beers at local taverns.

A trip to a sanitarium in 1910 had little effect on the alcoholic. Finally, McGraw had enough and threw Raymond off the team the following year. The next day, Bugs was tending bar across the street from the Polo Grounds. A year later, he was killed by a kick to the head in a barroom brawl.

Charles Ridgeway

On July 19, 1952, Class-D Fitzgerald manager Charlie Ridgeway permitted 12-year-old African-American batboy Joe Relford to bat and take the field during an official game. League officials fired Relford and Ridgeway plus the umpire for allowing it to happen.

Amos Rusie

Hall of Famer Amos "The Hoosier Thunderbolt" Rusie was an outstanding pitcher of the late 1800s. Some say his speed was the primary reason for the pitcher's mound being moved back to 60'6″ from 50 feet in 1893 because the fireballer struck out 982 batters the previous three seasons. Actually, pitchers, as a whole, were throwing much harder since the legalization of the overhand delivery.

Rusie led the league in strikeouts in 1890–91 and again after the mound was pulled back from 1893–95. In his 10-year career Rusie won 248 games, 164 of them from 1890–94, and amassed 1,950 Ks and 30 shutouts. Three times he struck out 300+ batters, though it was his wildness that scared batters the most. Five times he led the league in walks, averaging 170 passes a year over the span of his career.

However, in 1895, he ran contrary to one of the most oppressive and loathed moguls in baseball history, New York Giants owner Andrew Freedman. After winning 24 games, Rusie found $200 in fines deducted from his last paycheck for a reason he could not determine.

Rusie insisted that the money be restored to him in his 1896 contract. Freedman refused and Rusie sat out the entire season. New York fans were going nuts, losing the services of one of the best pitchers in baseball. Freedman's name became a four-letter word throughout the industry. Rusie hired Monte Ward to defend him but lost his case in front of league officials. Ward decided to seek remedy from the courts and take the opportunity to challenge the reserve clause as well. The last thing National League officials wanted was a challenge to the reserve clause to be overseen by the judicial system.

The case was still in the courts in the spring of 1897. Freedman stood firm even after the other owners begged him to capitulate. Shortly after, though, Rusie signed. The other league owners had paid all his lost salary. In turn, Rusie agreed to drop the lawsuit. Even after Rusie reported, Freedman refused to use the pitcher until a fan uprising demanded it.

Rusie sat out 1899, as well, in another salary dispute and 1900 because of marital problems. Cincinnati sought his services and traded a young Christy Mathewson for him on December 15, 1900. Rusie never won a game for Cincinnati but Mathewson went on to notch 373 for the Giants.

Al Salerno
See American League Umpires

Marge Schott
The cause for female participation in major league baseball was set back 100 years when Marge Schott assumed control of the Cincinnati Reds in 1985. Schott will forever be remembered for her ethnic slurs against African-Americans, Asians, homosexuals, Italians, Jews, working mothers, and for other insensitivities.

In 1993, Schott was suspended for one year after making racial slurs towards star outfielder Eric Davis and questioning his manhood. On Opening Day 1996 when umpire John McSherry passed away, causing the game to be postponed, Schott was quoted as saying, "I feel cheated."

A particularly low point came in '96 when she was quoted as saying "Hitler was good at the beginning . . . He just went too far," in an ESPN interview. Fellow owners forced her from the team's daily activities. Finally, to the delight of the politically correct everywhere, Schott sold the team in 1999.

Frank Shellenback
See Spitballers

Commissioner Matsutaro Shoriki
Yomiuri Giants owner Matsutaro Shoriki was named commissioner of Japanese baseball in February 1949. He was forced to resign in June because the American occupation authorities had him listed among the purged individuals for his actions during WWII.

Frank Shugart
Frank Shugart was the starting shortstop for Clark Griffith's Chicago White Sox in 1901. The American League's arrival gave him, among others, a second chance at a major league career. His last appearance had been in 1897. In August, Jack Katoll threw a baseball at umpire John Haskell and Shugart punched the arbiter, causing a riot that necessitated police intervention. American League President Ban Johnson suspended the players. The decision began the rift between Johnson and White Sox owner Charles Comiskey. Shugart never again appeared in a major league game.

Spitballers
In February 1920, major league owners voted to outlaw the spitball but, as a concession to men making their living by its use, permitted each team to grandfather two legal spitballers. The following season saw a soiled ball kill Ray Chapman. In response, the Rules Committee further voted to prohibit the application of any foreign substance to a ball in play. Seventeen men were grandfathered to use the pitch legally because it was already their primary weapon. They were:

Doc Ayers (1921)	Ray Caldwell (1921)	Stan Coveleski (1928)
Bill Doak (1929)	Phil Douglas (1922)	Red Faber (1933)
Dana Fillingim (1925)	Ray Fisher (1920)	Marvin Goodwin (1925)
Burleigh Grimes (1934)	Dutch Leonard (1925)	Clarence Mitchell (1932)
Jack Quinn (1933)	Dick Rudolph (1927)	Alan Russell (1925)
Urban Shocker (1928)	Allen Sothoron (1926)	

Grimes lasted the longest, until 1934. That year, he threw the last legal spitball in the National League, with Pittsburgh, and the American League, with New York.

The Boston Braves also designated Ray Keating to continue throwing the spitter but he was released prior to the 1920 campaign. The righthander pitched in the Pacific Coast League through 1932. He had first joined the Yankees at age 20 in 1912. In all, Keating posted a 30-51 record in the majors.

Spitball pitcher Heinie Meine was not one of the hurlers permitted to use the pitch legally. He was in the minors at the time and had to develop a new repertoire of pitches. Appearing in only one major league game, Meine retired from baseball in 1927. Running a tavern, he still worked on his pitching skills. Meine finally made it back to the majors as a junkballer in 1929 at age 33. He went on to lead the league in wins, starts, and innings pitched in '31 with Pittsburgh. The righthander notched 46 wins from 1931–33.

White Sox hurler Frank Shellenback was farmed out to fine-tune his game in 1919. Chicago management forgot to include him on the list grandfathering established spitballers. Legally permitted to throw the pitch in the minors, he never returned to the bigs. Instead, the righthander racked up 315 wins in 22 minor league seasons. In the mild weather and extended seasons of the Pacific Coast League, Shellenback is the circuit's all-time leader with a 295-178 record, a .624 winning percentage. He also started and completed 361 contests. White Sox owner Charles Comiskey could have used an effective starter after aces Eddie Cicotte and Lefty Williams were barred for their participation in the 1919 World Series fix.

Hal Carlson was not grandfathered for the use of the spitball in 1920 because Pittsburgh owner Barney Dreyfuss distained the delivery and had, for years, campaigned for its eradication. Dreyfuss refused to list the pitcher as a registered spitballer. It took five years for Carlson to reinvent his game. While with the Cubs in 1930, Carlson died of a stomach hemorrhage shortly after the season began. He had just celebrated his 38th birthday.

Righthander Moose Fuller won 230 games in the minors from 1913–29 but none in the majors because his main pitching weapon, the spitball, was outlawed shortly after he returned from military service in WWI.

Ernie Stewart

Ernie Stewart umpired in the American League from 1941–45 during World War II. He was forced off the job after writing a letter at the behest of Commissioner Happy Chandler regarding possible improvements to the working conditions of arbiters. The project was one of Chandler's numerous failings in the eyes of many baseball executives, that is, his employers. Apparently, it was one conviction he was unwilling to back up.

Harry Swacina

Harry Swacina was a defensive whiz at first base for Pittsburgh. In 1908, he wrote an ill-advised, abrasive letter to club owner Barney Dreyfuss expressing his discontent with club policies. As a result, he was banished and didn't reappear in the majors until the formation of the Federal League in 1914.

Charlie Sweeney

Charlie Sweeney played nearly every position in his five-year major league career split between the National League, American Association, and Union Association. With the NL Providence Grays and the UA St. Louis Maroons in 1884, Sweeney won 41 games, helping both teams win a pennant. After winning his 17th game for Providence that year, the hung-over pitcher was expelled for leaving the field in the middle of a game. He just walked off the mound and left. Because the Union Association did not honor the blacklist, they immediately signed the hurler. The Grays other pitcher, Hoss Radbourn, would go on to finish the team's season virtually alone on the mound.

Sweeney struck out 19 men in a game against Boston in June before he jumped the Grays, a record that stood for 102 years. However, the hard-drinker was washed up by the age of 24. In 1894, Sweeney killed a man in a San Francisco bar fight. His own death came shortly after his release from prison eight years later.

Kazuhito Tadano

Top college pitcher Kazuhito Tadano should have been a high draft choice in 2002. However, he was shunned by Japanese professional baseball after tabloid publicity exposed his participation in a gay porn video. Tadano had to leave the country to find a job. In 2003, he signed a minor league deal with the Cleveland Indians and eventually made it to the majors.

Tadakatsu Takayama

Tadakatsu Takayama played outfield for Yakult from 1963–70. He was sold to Hanshin for the 1971 season. Takayama jumped the club at midseason without a word to his family or the Tigers. He was permanently suspended by the commissioner on August 4th.

Umpires, 1999

In a contract negotiation ploy developed by Major League Baseball Umpires Association chief Richie Phillips, 22 umpires voluntarily gave their notice on July 14, 1999. The plan fell through when the rest of the union failed to back the 22. Commissioner Bud Selig merely accepted their resignations and showed them the door in September. A legal battle followed but nevertheless their paychecks were halted at the end of the year. Many lost an occupation that paid them in excess of $200,000 a year with numerous perks.

As usual, few had sympathy or spoke out on the plight of the umpires—not players, not fans and certainly not baseball's officials. 25 new hires were ushered in, the umpires union disbanded and reformed and Phillips lost the backing of his charges. The 22 are:

Drew Coble	Gary Darling	Bob Davidson
Bruce Dreckman	Jim Evans	Dale Ford
Rich Garcia	Eric Gregg	Tom Hallion
Ed Hickox	Bill Hohn	Sam Holbrook
Mark Johnson	Ken Kaiser	Greg Kosc
Larry McCoy	Paul Nauert	Larry Poncino
Frank Pulli	Terry Tata	Larry Vanover
Joe West		

Bill Valentine
See American League Umpires

Hippo Vaughn
Southpaw Hippo Vaughn is best remembered for the double no-hit game on May 2, 1917. Pitching for the Cubs at Weeghman Park, he squared off against the Reds Fred Toney. Both sustained no-hitters through nine innings, the only time in major league history. Vaughn lost in the tenth on a hit by Olympic standout Jim Thorpe.

Vaughn experienced his best season the following year when he won the pitching Triple Crown with 22 wins, 148 strikeouts, and a 1.74 ERA. He also led all National League hurlers in starts, innings pitched, shutouts, and opponent batting average. In the World Series, Vaughn recorded a meager 1.00 ERA in three complete games: 1-0 loss to Babe Ruth in Game 1, 2-1 loss to Carl Mays in Game 3, and a 3-0 victory over Sad Sam Jones in Game 5.

Vaughn posted five 20 + -win seasons and three years with an ERA under 2.00. He finished with 178 wins and a scant 2.49 ERA. He ranks among the best lefthanded pitchers of the dead-ball era.

In 1921, Cubs manager Johnny Evers suspended him for breaking training rules; his weight was beginning to balloon. Vaughn jumped to a semi-pro club under an alias. Landis stepped in and barred the pitcher. Hearing this, Vaughn signed a three-year contract with an outlaw nine. He pitched outside organized baseball until he was 42 years old. The following year, Vaughn applied for reinstatement and was accepted; however, his pitching days were over.

Irv Waldron
See Washington Senators

Washington Senators
The Washington Senators finished in sixth place in the American League's inaugural season. The team did have a few highlights, though.

Shortstop Billy Clingman, 31, led the league in assists and fielding percentage.

He was known from his days in the National League as the circuit's fastest infielder and for possessing the most accurate arm.

Rookie center fielder Irv Waldron, 25, hit .322 in the last half of the season. Also playing for Milwaukee in 1901, he led the league in games and at-bats while scoring 102 times.

Right fielder Sam Dungan, 35, batted .320 and led the team with 73 RBI. He had previously played four seasons in the National League and won the AL batting title in 1900 while with the Kansas City Blues.

None of the trio appeared on a major league roster in 1902. One must wonder the circumstances that led to three of a team's stars' disappearance. Only Clingman reappeared in the majors, for 21 games with Cleveland in 1903.

Phil Weinert

Lefty Weinert jumped the Philadelphia Phillies in 1921. Landis promptly banned him for five years. He applied for reinstatement in 1922 and was accepted, rejoining the Phillies. The case is particularly curious in that Ray Fisher got a *lifetime* ban for a similar offense. Weinert had first joined the majors at age 17 in 1919.

Gus Weyhing

Gus Weyhing won 177 games from 1887–92 but only 87 more in a major league career that lasted until 1901. Like Hutchison, his career took a nosedive after the mound was pushed back. Weyhing is the only ballplayer to win 30 games in a season in three different major leagues: American Association (twice), Players League, and the National League.

CHAPTER THREE

~

Criminal Activity

Hi Bithorn

Hi Bithorn, the first Puerto Rican in the majors, won 18 games for the Cubs in 1943 with a 2.60 ERA and a league-leading seven shutouts. A sore arm forced the right-hander out of the majors after only two games in 1947. Attempting a comeback in the Mexican League, he was shot and killed at age 35 on January 1, 1952, fleeing from the police in El Mante.

Lyman Bostock

Lyman Bostock was drafted by the Minnesota Twins out of California State University in 1972. He broke the parent club's lineup in 1975 after three successful minor league seasons, hitting .282 as a rookie. The lefthander upped the ante as a sophomore, batting .323.

Teammate Rod Carew was the only American Leaguer to top Bostock's .336-batting average in '77. The center fielder also set the putout record with 12 in a game. Posting career highs with 90 RBIs, 36 doubles, 104 runs scored, an impressive .508 slugging average completed his breakthrough.

The emerging superstar attained free agency and joined the California Angels for a multi-million dollar contract. The following summer started with a batting slump; however, Bostock was able to push his average up to .296 during a heated divisional race with Kansas City and Texas.

On September 23, 1978, he was sitting in the back seat of his uncle's car in Gary, Indiana, with two women he had just met, when a man pulled up and fired a shotgun into the vehicle. Bostock, age 27, died three hours later. Police later arrested Leonard Smith, the estranged husband of one of the women.

Bostock's death sealed a tragic decade for the Angels who also mourned young ballplayers Chico Ruiz, Minnie Rojas, Mike Miley, and Bruce Heinbechner during the 1970s.

James Bray

Backup catcher James Bray played his entire Negro league career, 1922–31, for three Chicago teams. A drunken tussle with teammate Johnny Hines resulted in Bray's death in 1931.

Art Brown

26-year-old Art Brown, a first baseman for Albany in the New York State League, was shot to death by a jealous husband on June 15, 1911. John McStea, a local actor, found his wife sitting on Brown's knee and shot the ballplayer five times in the chest. McStea was later acquitted.

Dave Brown

Dave Brown is widely reputed to be the best southpaw pitcher in early Negro league history. His arsenal included a rocket fastball and an above-average curve. In 1918, Rube Foster posted a $20,000 bond to gain Brown's parole after a conviction for highway robbery in Texas. He became the ace of the staff for the Chicago American Giants in the upstart Negro National League.

During the player war of 1923, Brown jumped to the Lincoln Giants of the rival Eastern Colored League. He later disappeared after killing a man in New York in a fight over cocaine in 1925, initiating a FBI fugitive search. Stories were told during the remainder of the decade of Brown popping up with various clubs under an assumed name. Some reports suggest that Brown's throat was slit sometime in the early 1930s.

Octavius Catto

Octavius Catto owned and managed the leading black team in Philadelphia, the Pythians. His request for admission to the NABBP resulted in the formal banning of black teams in that organization.

Catto, a school teacher and principal at the local Institute for Colored Youth, was also a vocal advocate of black voting rights and a popular political figure in his community. For this, Catto had incurred the ire of white Philadelphians who considered his cause and tactics as a militant slap at society itself. He had originally come to the forefront by leading a crusade to eliminate streetcar segregation in 1867.

After leaving the institute on October 10, 1871, and heading to vote on Election Day, Catto was gunned down by a white man who was egged on by Democratic politicians disgruntled with the new voting rights of African-Americans. In other words, he was killed in a race riot designed to keep blacks from voting on Election Day. Catto was 31 years old. Reflecting the tone of the day and of the city itself, the killer was freed shortly thereafter. Within a year, the once-mighty Pythians disbanded.

Rube Chambers

Negro league pitcher Rube Chambers' involvement with gamblers and bootleggers during Prohibition led to his early death in February 1928. He was found shot and killed in a boxcar in Florida.

Al Clark

American League umpire Al Clark was terminated in June 2003 after 26 years for alleged improper use of league-supplied plane tickets. Previously, he had been questioned in a memorabilia investigation in 1998 centering on David Wells signed balls.

In 2004, Clark pled guilty to conspiracy to commit mail fraud and was jailed for four months. The ex-umpire was peddling balls that he falsely claimed were used in historically significant games.

Lefty Craig
George Craig, a pitcher for Indianapolis in the American Association, was shot in the abdomen and killed by two burglars. The incident occurred at the club's spring training facility on April 22, 1911, at 1:00 a.m. He was 23 years old. Apparently, the robbers learned that Craig was expecting cash from home.

Sam Crane
Sam Crane was a light-hitting shortstop who played in only 174 games in seven years. He killed his girlfriend Della Lyter and her date in a hotel bar in 1929. Serving 13 years for second-degree murder, Crane did continue playing baseball—for the prison team.

Steel-Arm Davis
Starting left fielder in the inaugural East–West game in 1933, Walt Davis was killed in a bar fight two years later at a Chicago hotel at age 33. He had first appeared with the Detroit Stars in 1923.

Steel-Arm Dickey
Just getting started in his Negro league career, John Dickey was stabbed to death trying to break up a fight in March 1923.

John Dillinger
It is often reported that Public Enemy #1 John Dillinger played minor league baseball. More likely, he only played local town ball.

Jim Egan
Heavy-drinker Jim Egan was blacklisted as a rookie from the NL Troy Trojans in 1882 for excessive drunkenness. Reinstated in '84, Egan was arrested for theft before he could re-take the field. The 26-year-old died in prison that September of brain fever.

Mike Flood
Minor leaguer Mike Flood was shot and killed in a bar fight on July 24, 1905, in New Mexico.

Howie Fox
Righthander Howie Fox spent nine years in the big leagues for three teams. Back in the minors in 1955, he was stabbed to death after tossing three men out of his tavern near San Antonio, Texas. Fox was 34 years old.

Mickey Fuentes
Miguel Fuentes pitched in eight games for the expansion Seattle Pilots in 1969. Unfortunately, the 20-year-old didn't make the trip east to Milwaukee when the fran-

chise was purchased by Bud Selig. He was killed in a barroom scuffle in his native Puerto Rico on January 29, 1970.

Don Gallagos
Ft. Worth pitcher Don Gallagos of the Texas League was shot to death in a fight in January 1908.

Mazio Gamiz
Cuban Mazio Gamiz entered the United States to play ball with the Cuban Stars in the Eastern Colored League in 1925. In a contract dispute with the pitcher, Havana Red Sox owner Syd Pollock reported immigration violations by Gamiz and had the player deported.

Eloy Gutierrez
Catcher for the Vera Cruz Aguila of the Triple-A Mexican League, Eloy Gutierrez was shot and killed in a fight in 1967.

Shigeo Hasegawa
Japanese slugger Shigeo Hasegawa of the Nankai Hawks was found murdered in June 1966. The outfielder had become deeply indebted to mobsters, at one time commenting to friends that he feared for his life. The 33-year-old hit .269 for Nankai, Chunichi, and Kintetsu from 1956–63.

Lem Hawkins
First baseman Lem Hawkins had a hard time staying out of trouble. After serving in World War I and playing eight years in the Negro leagues, he ran afoul of the law and was arrested for armed robbery. Released, he held up a beer truck in Chicago in 1934 only to be mistakenly killed by his partner in the foray.

John Hines
Negro league player John Hines killed his teammate James Bray in a drunken fight in 1931. He was subsequently sentenced to life in prison.

Pat Hynes
Former Cardinals and Browns outfielder Pat Hynes was shot in the head and killed by a St. Louis bartender on March 12, 1907. He was 23 years old. Hynes was planning to join Milwaukee in the American Association.

Frank Jackson
Pirates farmhand Frank Jackson, a pitcher, was accidentally shot and killed at age 21 on January 2, 1961, in Los Angeles. He was innocently watching a parking lot fight from the doorway of a restaurant. The shot entered his back and he died within minutes.

Ora Jennings

Ora Jennings was killed in Indiana in 1901 after being hit in the head with a bat by a ballplayer.

Koji Kobayashi

Koji Kobayashi played the outfield from 1972–74 for the Taiyo Whales, hitting .087 in 23 at bats. In December 1974, he was arrested for breaking and entering and attempted assault. He was banned from Nippon Professional Baseball.

Len Koenecke

Casey Stengel released Brooklyn outfielder Len Koenecke in 1935 after the player refused to limit his carousing. Unrecognized then, he was displaying traits many today would identify as signs of mental illness.

On September 17, he was flying in a commercial airline headed for Chicago. The crew expelled him in Detroit for being drunk and disorderly. Not to be deterred, he chartered a small plane.

In flight, Koenecke attempted to seize control of the aircraft by attacking the pilot and copilot. A 15-minute fight ensued. It ended when pilot William Mul-queeney killed the 31-year-old ballplayer with a fire extinguisher to the head. It may have been one of the first attempted hijackings in American aviation history.

Terry Larkin

Righthanded pitcher Terry Larkin accumulated 89 wins between 1877–79 in the National League for Hartford and Chicago. The 1,500 innings he pitched during that span destroyed his arm. He later attempted to come back as an infielder.

During batting practice in 1879, Larkin was struck in the head by a line drive off Cap Anson's bat, virtually ending his baseball career. Some reports suggest that the blow caused the player to become deranged.

In 1883, Larkin came home drunk one night, shot his wife, and attempted suicide. Both survived; however, the player continued to drink heavily and to find himself on the wrong side of the law until his death, by suicide (slashing his throat with a razor), in 1894.

Ron LeFlore

Ron LeFlore grew up in a Detroit ghetto. As a child, he continually skipped school. Eventually, he was committing burglaries and selling drugs. On April 28, 1970, the 21-year-old was convicted of armed robbery. There, in a maximum-security prison in southern Michigan, he picked up a baseball for the first time in May 1971.

A fellow inmate knew a bar owner who surprisingly knew Tigers manager Billy Martin. A tryout was arranged. LeFlore was granted a 48-hour furlough in June 1973 to perform for the manager at Tigers Stadium. The Tigers were impressed with his power, speed, and arm strength. LeFlore was paroled a month later and sent to an affiliate in the Midwest League.

LeFlore joined the parent club in '74 and quickly filled the center field gap. In 1976, he led the club with a .316 average, stole 58 bases, and scored 93 times. He maintained a 30-game hit streak, the longest in the majors since Joe DiMaggio's 34 in '49. LeFlore also played in his only All-Star Game that summer.

In 1979, he hit .300 and swiped 78 bases before being traded to Montreal at the end of the year. With the Expos, LeFlore stole a career-high 98 bases in 1980, his second and last stolen base title. Free agency brought him to the White Sox the following year. Losing his starting position, LeFlore retired after the 1982 season with a career .288 batting average. In nine major league seasons, the fastest man in baseball stole an average of 50 bases a year. LeFlore later published a successful autobiography and his life story was made into a motion picture.

Similarly, Gates Brown serves 21 months for breaking and entering as a teenager before joining the Tigers.

Saul Lopez

Macon pitcher Saul Lopez, 19, of the South Atlantic League was arrested for murdering a 25-year-old female neighbor in June 1984. The Pirates farmhand was arrested during a game on the 22nd.

Julio Machado

Relief pitcher Julio Machado appeared in 101 major league games for the Mets and Brewers from 1989–91. On December 8, 1991, the 25-year-old was arrested for the murder of a young woman in his homeland, Venezuela. Machado sprayed bullets into another vehicle following a traffic accident with his car. A passenger in the other car died and he was sentenced to 12 years in prison.

J. C. McHaskell

Memphis Red Sox first baseman J. C. McHaskell's career ended when he was shot by teammate Robert Poindexter in a drunken argument in 1929. The wounds necessitated the amputation of both legs.

Denny McLain

Righthanded pitcher Denny McLain signed with the Chicago White Sox in 1962, receiving a $17,000 bonus. In his first professional game, he threw a no-hitter in the Appalachian League, striking out 16 batters. Another 16 whiffed in his next start. The White Sox were flooded with young pitchers in 1963 and rules dictated that they could only keep two bonus babies. They left him unprotected in favor of Dave DeBusschere and Bruce Howard. The Tigers snatched McLain up for the $8,000 waiver fee.

In 1965, McLain developed a curve and changeup and joined the rotation, winning 16 games with 192 Ks and a 2.61 ERA. The following year, he won 20 for the first time but his ERA ballooned to 3.92 as he led the league in runs, earned runs, and homers allowed. Pitching coach Johnny Sain, formerly of "Spahn and Sain and pray for rain," taught McLain a sidearm slider the next year, 1967, and, though his ERA rested at 3.79, he won 17 games and Detroit finished one game behind the Boston Red Sox for the pennant.

McLain put it all together in '68. In the "Year of the Pitcher," Bob Gibson and McLain dominated. McLain was both the American League Cy Young Award winner and the MVP, leading the league in starts, complete games, innings pitched, wins, and winning percentage. He also posted 280 strikeouts. His 31 wins were the most since Dizzy Dean 34 years earlier and made McLain the last 30-game winner of the century.

McLain's 1.96 ERA was only good for fourth place behind Luis Tiant and lefties Sam McDowell and Dave McNally. In the National League, Gibson, also winning the Cy Young and MVP awards, allowed opponents a mere 1.12 runs a game. He also led the league with 268 strikeouts, 13 shutouts, a .184 opponent batting average, and a scant .237 opponent on-base percentage. It's hard to imagine how he lost nine games.

Detroit was equally devastating in 1968. They scored the most runs, allowed the fewest, and had the highest fielding percentage in the league. They ran away with the last pure American League pennant, finishing 12 games ahead of Baltimore. In the World Series versus Gibson's Cardinals, McLain won one and lost two but, luckily, lefthanded pitcher Mickey Lolich stepped up for three victories.

McLain won another Cy Young award, though it was shared with Mike Cuellar of Baltimore, in 1969 with 24 wins and a 2.80 ERA. He had pitched 1,380 innings in the last five years. His arm would soon show the effects. McLain was also drunk with success. He soon ran into trouble—a lot of it. The pitcher would be gone within three years at age 28, posting a 17-34 record with a 4.78 ERA in his final 67 games.

His main problems were gambling, a lack of ethical boundaries, and close-knit friendships with undesirables who led him to bookmaking operations and organized crime. McLain quickly found himself more than $400,000 in debt and declared bankruptcy. The public became aware of his difficulties in a February 3, 1970, article by *Sports Illustrated*.

Among other allegations, *SI* discovered that a debt collector had stomped on his foot in 1967, dislocating his toes. The injury affected his play during the tight pennant race. Commissioner Bowie Kuhn assigned baseball's security director, former FBI agent Henry Fitzgibbon, to investigate and suspend McLain.

McLain returned in July, though, causing criticism directed at Kuhn for being too lenient. Easing his frustrations, the pitcher dumped buckets of ice water over the heads of two sportswriters on August 28. Irate Tiger management suspended him. Then, McLain was found to be carrying a gun and Kuhn suspended the pitcher again, this time for the rest of the season.

McLain was shuffled to Washington, then Oakland and Atlanta. He lost a league-worst 22 games for the Senators in 1971, fueling manager Ted Williams' disgust. He couldn't make the Braves lineup in spring training 1973 and never played in the majors again. Life went downhill from there.

After a slew of unsuccessful business deals, McLain was indicted on five charges of racketeering, extortion, and narcotics in 1984. He had allegedly scammed thousands from trusting individuals, including the elderly. A year later, he was convicted on four counts and sent to prison. It was overturned on appeal in '87 but he would serve another jail stint in the 1990s.

Dobie Moore

Dobie Moore possessed a rifle arm and outstanding range. He was a favorite of Casey Stengel, who claimed that he was the best shortstop that ever played the game. As the story goes, Stengel first noticed Moore and Bullet Joe Rogan playing ball in the military in 1919. He relayed the information to the Kansas City Monarchs of the Negro leagues. Moore anchored the team in the black World Series in 1924 and again in '25.

The righthander was also a powerful line drive hitter—an asset anyone would love to have in the middle infield. His brief career came to an end at age 31 because of injuries suffered in 1926. The married player was fighting with his madam girlfriend when she shot him in his leg as he jumped out of a brothel window. His leg was broken in six places. Moore never played another game.

Ed Morris

Ed Morris won 19 games as a rookie for the Red Sox in 1928. While celebrating at a party in his honor before leaving for spring training in February 1932, Morris became involved in a dispute with a fellow partier. The 32-year-old pitcher was stabbed twice and died three days later.

Hiroshi Ogawa

Hiroshi Ogawa won 21 games for the Lotte Marines from 1985–90. In December 2004, he was arrested for robbery and homicide. Owing money to a loan shark, Ogawa went to his boss' home to borrow money. There, he encountered the housekeeper, whom he knocked unconscious and then ransacked the house, taking cash. He then drove the housekeeper to the Arakawa River and drowned her. Her body was found two days later. Ogawa was sentenced to life in prison.

Bud O'Laughlin

A jealous husband shot and killed Kitty League player Bud O'Laughlin on January 19, 1915. The Owensboro player died on the street in Booneville, Indiana. He was 24 years old.

Steve Palermo

Well-respected 15-year American League umpire Steve Palermo was having dinner at a Dallas restaurant with former Miami Dolphins defensive lineman Terrence Mann in July 1991. Outside, two waitresses were being robbed. The men interceded and Palermo was shot in the back. He sustained permanent partial paralysis that ended his on-the-field career.

Jose Piloto

Memphis Red Sox pitcher Jose Piloto finished his third year in the Negro leagues in 1950. At season's end, he traveled to Mexico, where he was killed in a tussle.

Alabama Pitts

Washington created a stir in the baseball community in the 1930s when they signed paroled convict Alabama Pitts to a minor league contract. He was convicted of armed robbery at age 19 and served five and a half years at Sing Sing Prison for stealing

$72.50. The controversy attracted national attention, with even his warden championing his cause.

National Association president William Branham ruled Pitts ineligible to play for Albany in the International League. Always one to exert his power and grab the national limelight, Judge Landis overruled the minor league executive on June 17, 1935. Pitts signed with Albany in the International League, which was owned by Joe Cambria, future Latin America scout for Clark Griffith.

Concerns subsided after it was determined that he would never hit well enough to make the parent club. He moved on and played three games in the NFL as a halfback for the Philadelphia Eagles at the end of the season, making a ridiculous and wholly undeserved $1,500. However, the controversy did attract badly needed attention to a floundering NFL.

Pitts spurned a lesser offer to continue his football career and then attempted professional basketball and to renew his baseball career. It didn't pan out, so he went to work in a mill. The ex-con was stabbed to death in a North Carolina bar fight in June 1941. He was attempting to "cut in" during a dance. The knife wound severed a shoulder artery.

Gus Polidor
Infielder Gus Polidor played seven seasons in the majors from 1985–93. Two years later, the 33-year-old was gunned down in his driveway by drug dealers trying to steal his vehicle in his native Caracas, Venezuela. He had just returned from the States trying to catch on with the Expos as a replacement player.

Alex Pompez
Alejandro Pompez exemplified the one legitimate gripe that Judge Landis held against the Negro leagues. Owner of the Cuban Stars and New York Cubans from 1916–50 and member of Dutch Schultz's mob, Pompez was one in a long list of racketeers who infused ready cash into the leagues.

Chased by New York authorities in 1936, he landed in France and, later, Mexico. Pompez did not oversee his baseball interests for two years as he returned to the United States and turned state's evidence against Tammany leader James Hines. For such, Pompez was given a suspended sentence and probation for his gambling and racketeering activities by lead prosecutor Thomas Dewey.

Jim Rivera
Outfielder Jungle Jim Rivera didn't make the majors until he was almost 30 years old because he was held in an army prison for four years in the late 1940s for the attempted rape of his commanding officer's daughter.

Fred Saigh
Cardinals' owner Fred Saigh was sent to jail for tax evasion and forced to sell the franchise to beer king Gussie Busch of Anheuser-Busch in 1953. Saigh's accounting practices came to light after he sold pitcher Murry Dickson to the Pirates. The $125,000 never found its way into the club's coffers; rather it was fed into a private account.

Dan Shay

American Association Milwaukee manager Dick Shay shot and killed a black waiter in an Indianapolis hotel on May 3, 1917. Ridiculously, the argument concerned the amount of sugar in a sugar bowl. He was indicted but later acquitted, claiming self-defense because he was insulted.

Shay's major league playing career ended in 1907 after a brief attempt to come back from an amputated finger.

Dave Shotkoski

Replacement player Dave Shotkoski was gunned down during spring training on March 25, 1995, in an attempted robbery in West Palm Beach, Florida. The 30-year-old was trying to make the Braves pitching staff.

Pacer Smith

Former long-time minor leaguer from 1886–93, Pacer Smith was executed by hanging on November 29, 1895, in Decatur, Illinois, for murdering his 18-year-old sister-in-law and her 6-year-old daughter on September 28. Estranged from his wife and habitually drunk, Smith had often threatened to kill his family. He finally showed up and took four shots at his wife, two that missed and two that hit their mark.

Ridiculously, the newspaper reported that the rope for the hanging cost the sheriff $5; however, a local drug store would purchase it for $10 after the hanging to display it in their sales window.

George Steinbrenner

George Steinbrenner led a group of 15 limited partners that purchased the New York Yankees from CBS for $10 million in 1973. A year later, Commissioner Bowie Kuhn suspended him for two years after "The Boss" pled guilty to making illegal campaign contributions to United States President and baseball enthusiast Richard Nixon. Steinbrenner was reinstated 15 months later.

Steinbrenner was suspended again in 1990 when it came to light that he had paid small-time gambler Howard Spira $40,000 to "dig up dirt" on future Hall of Famer Dave Winfield. Steinbrenner was seeking to back out of an agreement he had with the ballplayer. With one of his last acts in office, Commissioner Fay Vincent reinstated the magnate in March 1993. New York newspapers hailed, "The Boss is back."

Dernell Stensen

At age 25, Dernell Stensen finally made the majors with the Cincinnati Reds in 2003. Honing his skills in the Arizona Fall League that November, the outfielder met a violent death after being beaten, dragged by his vehicle, and finally shot execution-style in an apparent carjacking.

Antonio Susini

Antonio Susini only played one year in the Negro leagues with the All Cubans in 1921 before he clubbed fellow ballplayer Julio LeBlanc to death with a bat. He was sentenced to more than 10 years in jail.

Danny Thomas

Religious devotee Danny Thomas refused to play ball between sundown Friday and sundown Saturday. The Brewers finally had no need for the part-time player and sent him to the minors in 1977. Thomas later killed himself in 1980 in an Alabama jail awaiting trial for the alleged rape of a 12-year-old girl.

Ray Treadaway

After appearing briefly in the majors with Washington in 1930, third baseman Ray Treadaway slipped to the minors. In July 1935, he was shot in the left leg during a bar fight. He died that October at age 27 from complications after an amputation.

Boss Tweed

Boss Tweed held power within of the best baseball franchise, Mutuals, in the richest baseball town, New York, during the amateur National Association from 1860 until his incarceration in 1871. Though they were not the first, Tweed's administration highlights a classic example of how amateurs were paid to play the game. Many of his players were listed on the payrolls of city administrations, such as the coroner's office and the street-cleaning department.

History books show that William Marcy Tweed sat at the helm of New York's Tammany Hall, a Democratic Party organization known for its strong influence over New York politics and ceaseless corruption. Tweed's looters are thought to have absconded with $40–$100 million of taxpayer's money. Future generations of New York baseball owners owed allegiance at one time or another to Tammany Hall. The relationship continued well into the 20th century.

Eddie Waitkus

Eddie Waitkus's story may have inspired the book and movie *The Natural*. The first baseman was shot in the chest and nearly died in June 1949 by a crazed 19-year-old female fan in a Chicago hotel. Four operations later, Waitkus recovered to help the Phillies in their drive for the pennant in 1950. The lefthander retired in '55 with a career-.285 batting average.

Likewise, fellow Cub Billy Jurges drew the ire of a showgirl in 1932. He was shot in the hand and chest but recovered to have a long career as a shortstop for Chicago and New York in the National League. Negro leaguer Dimps Miller was shot in his pitching arm by his wife in 1926 but recovered quickly.

Mother Watson

Pitcher Walter "Mother" Watson was murdered in a Middleport, Ohio, bar in November 1898 at age 33. In the minors at the time, Watson was a year removed from appearing in three games for Cincinnati in the American Association.

Sam White

Umpire Sam White was killed in 1899 in Alabama while working a game when he was hit in the head with a bat by a player.

Bill Wilson

Tough catcher Bill Wilson played parts of three seasons in the National League during the 1890s. Rumors allege he was a member of an organized crime family. Indeed, his resume shows two separate prison stints.

He was killed breaking up a robbery of a soda shop in St. Paul, Minnesota, on May 9, 1924. Some suggest that it was a setup designed as a "hit" on Wilson. He was stabbed 10 times in the neck and chest.

CHAPTER FOUR

Suicide

John Allen
Shortstop John Allen of the Portsmouth A's in the Class-D Ohio–Indiana League killed himself at age 29 in 1950.

Steve Ashe
New Haven pitcher Steve Ashe of the Connecticut State League killed himself at Grace Hospital on November 28, 1904. He had attempted suicide two days prior by slashing his throat. Ashe reopened the wound in the hospital.

Marty Bergen
Marty Bergen was the starting catcher for the Boston Beaneaters from 1896 to '99. He became depressed over the sudden death of his son in 1898. Then, a hip injury looked to end the backstop's career. His erratic behavior began to scare teammates, forcing team owner Arthur Soden to release Bergen near the end of the 1899 season.

On January 19, 1900, in Worcester, Massachusetts, the 28-year-old Bergen murdered his wife, 6-year-old daughter, and 3-year-old son with an axe and razor. He then killed himself.

Bergen's brother Bill also caught in the majors, for Cincinnati and Brooklyn from 1901–11. In the lineup for his catching skills and strong arm, Bill owns the lowest career batting average, .170, for a player with 1,000 + at-bats (and he had over 3,000). Of any player ever qualifying for a batting title, he owns the lowest mark, .139 in 1909.

Randolph Blanch
See Sportswriters.

Carl Britton
Minor league pitcher Carl Britton killed himself in Canton, Ohio, on October 11, 1916. He was 40 years old.

Charlie Brown
Minor leaguer Charlie Brown shot himself on March 14, 1910, in Albion, New York. He was 27 years old.

Hugh Casey

Brooklyn ace reliever Hugh Casey is best known for throwing the pitch that went by catcher Mickey Owen for a passed ball that would have ended Game 4 of the 1941 World Series. His career saves total of just 55 cannot be measured by today's standards. Three times he led the league in relief wins (twice in double digits) and twice in saves. The righthander won two games in the 1947 World Series.

Casey missed three seasons to World War II service. An interesting facet of his life is his friendship with Ernest Hemingway. With Kirby Higbe, the three would carouse to the wee hours of the morning, especially when spring training was conducted outside the country in Cuba. They would typically begin drinking after practice, go shooting, gambling, and barhopping. By the end of the night, the trio would end up at Hemingway's place. Then Casey and Hemingway would box each other for entertainment. The following passage is from Higbe's book *The High Hard One*:

> We would have a few drinks and bat the breeze and listen to Ernest tell about the experiences he had based his books on. Then you could see them itching to put the gloves on—and I don't mean big pillow gloves. Both of them could hit like a mule kicks. Old Ernest would belt Case one, and down he would go. Case would belt old Ernest, and down he would go. They brawled all over the room for five or ten minutes, laughing all the time. . . . The furniture would really take a beating.

On July 3, 1951, Casey killed himself with a shotgun in an Atlanta hotel while on the phone with his wife. He was allegedly despondent over the break-up of their marriage. Casey had also recently lost a paternity suit. He was 37 years old.

Cannonball Crane

Fireballer Ed Crane played in all four major leagues of the 19th century. Breaking in as a utility player with Boston in the Union Association in 1884, Crane hit 12 home runs to finish second in the league. Moving to the National League, he turned to pitching when he couldn't hit in the tougher league. Crane won 64 games from 1889–92 and led the American Association in ERA in '91.

As a member of Al Spalding's world tour in 1888–89, Crane began drinking heavily, probably out of boredom from traveling. He continued imbibing after his marriage to Nellie Dolan deteriorated.

Facing pressure from her parents and Crane's unpredictable behavior, Nellie sought the dissolution of her marriage. By this time, Crane was relegated to the minors. Released by his club at the end of the season and with no home to go to, Crane checked into a Rochester hotel on September 19, 1896. Hotel staff found his body the next day clutching a picture of his wife. The pitcher had consumed chloric acid, killing him at the age of 34.

Clay Dailey

Young, minor league pitcher Clay Dailey committed suicide on May 21, 1921, in Frankfort, Kentucky. He was apparently depressed after being released by the Louisville club during spring training.

Ned Egan

Ned Egan had a mild stroke in the fall of 1917, requiring his resignation as manager of Milwaukee in American Association. On May 6, 1918, he was found in a hotel room dead by a self-inflicted gun shot. He was upset by the recent death of his wife.

Benny Frey

The Reds demoted righthanded pitcher Benny Frey after he went 10-8 with a 4.25 ERA in 1936. He refused to report to Nashville, prompting management to add him to the voluntary retired list. The pitcher committed suicide in November 1937 at age 31 by inhaling exhaust fumes.

Willard Hershberger

Reds Bill Hershberger hit extremely well for a backup catcher, highlighted by his .316 batting average in 402 career at-bats. However, he frequently experienced insomnia, extended depression, headaches, and paranoia. Hershberger constantly brooded over losses and feared that teammates disliked him.

The 30-year-old became despondent after calling for a pitch that the Giants Harry Danning hit for a game-winning home run. He even told manager Bill McKechnie that he was going to kill himself like his father had done years before. His body was found on August 3, 1940, in a Boston hotel room slashed at the throat. Hershberger remains the only major leaguer to take his own life during the season.

Bob Langsdorf

Popular minor leaguer Bob Langsdorf committed suicide by imbibing carbolic acid on January 10, 1907, after a failed attempt to woo actress Elsie Cressy.

Danny Mahoney

In his only major league appearance, Danny Mahoney pinch ran for the Cincinnati Reds on May 15, 1911. That year, the 22-year-old attempted suicide by drinking carbolic acid.

Dan McGann

In mid-1902, first baseman Dan McGann jumped the Baltimore Orioles for the New York Giants with teammates John McGraw, Joe McGinnity, and Roger Bresnahan. McGraw was set to take over the National League franchise. In the 1905 World Series, the Christy Mathewson showcase, McGann knocked in four runs in Game 3.

A career .284 hitter, McGann slipped to the minors in 1909 after his average dropped. In December 1910, he was found dead by a gun shot to the chest in a Louisville hotel at age 38. The McGann family had a history of suicide and it was ruled as such, though questions remained concerning a missing diamond ring.

Edgar McNabb

Ed McNabb was a rookie pitcher for the National League Baltimore Orioles in 1893. In 14 starts, he accumulated an 8-9 record with a 4.12 ERA. He was released at the end of the season and signed with Grand Rapids. However, McNabb became involved with Louise Kellogg (a.k.a. Mrs. Louise Rockwell), wife of the president of the Pacific and Northwest League.

On February 28, 1894, after an argument in a Pittsburgh hotel, McNabb shot Kellogg twice in the neck. He then shot himself through the mouth. She survived but was paralyzed, eventually dying of complications from her injuries. McNabb was dead at age 28. At the time of his death, McNabb was also suffering from tuberculosis.

Back in 1889, McNabb won 20 games for last place Waco of the Texas League. The young pitcher could boast credit for 60% of his teammate's 33 victories.

Win Mercer

Win Mercer was an ace righthander for the Washington Senators in the 1890s, winning 49 games from 1896–97. The Detroit Tigers named him their player–manager for the 1903 season. However, he killed himself by inhaling poisonous gas (hooking a hose to a gas jet) in a San Francisco hotel on January 12, 1903, while on a barnstorming trip in California. The 28-year-old left a note detailing the evils of women and gambling.

Katsutoshi Miwata

Orix Blue Wave executive Katsutoshi Miwata committed suicide at age 53 in 1998. Miwata was allegedly linked to underhanded practices in the draft system. He originally convinced Orix executives to sign Ichiro Suzuki and was responsible for switching him from a pitcher to an outfielder.

The pressing problem was the signing of number one draft pick Nagisa Arakaki. Club executives demanded that Miwata get the job done; however, Arakaki wanted to sign with Sadaharu Oh's Daiei Hawks. Miwata became increasingly stressed over his failure to ink the prospect's signature to a contract. After begging his parents for the young man's signature and failing in November, Miwata jumped to his death from the 11th floor of an office building.

Donnie Moore

Righthander Donnie Moore pitched in 13 major league seasons for five teams. He finally made his breakthrough in 1985 for the California Angels. Over the two-year period of 1985–86, he won 12 games with 52 saves while posting a 2.36 ERA.

However, Moore was plagued by two pitches to Dave Henderson in Game 5 of the 1986 American League Championship Series that tied the game with a two-out homer in the 9th and, eventually, won the game in the 11th on a sacrifice fly. Boston went on to win the series and the pennant.

His life went downhill from there. The heavy drinker turned to the bottle even harder, limiting his games to only 14 in 1987. Moore was released by the Angels and then again by the Royals system. Moreover, his marriage failed and he was near bankruptcy.

On July 18, 1989, Moore lost it. He shot his estranged wife and then killed himself as his 10-year-old son was forced to watch. His wife survived. She later blamed his depression on the fans for booing the pitcher.

Johnny Mostil

Fleet-footed Johnny Mostil was one of the finer center fielders of the 1920s, certainly a jewel on the second division White Sox. In March 1927, he attempted suicide in his hotel room by slashing his arms, wrist, and neck 13 times with a razor. Having an affair with teammate Red Faber's wife, Mostil became distraught when Faber found out and threatened retaliation. The outfielder recovered to reappear in the lineup at the end of the season.

Bull Perrine

American League umpire Fred Perrine suffered sunstroke while working a game in Cleveland in 1911. It partially led to a nervous breakdown, requiring admittance to the Napa Asylum for the Insane. He committed suicide in 1913.

Robert Poindexter

Spitball pitcher Robert Poindexter played six seasons in the Negro leagues. The end of his career was marred by habitual drunkenness and violence. After shooting teammate J. C. McHaskell, Poindexter's career ended after imbibing bichloride of mercury in an apparent suicide attempt in 1929. He survived, but died the following year.

Jim Price

See Sportswriters.

Harry Pulliam

Quiet, nervous, and introverted, Harry Pulliam was elected president of the National League in 1903. He had previously been road secretary and part-owner of the Louisville Colonels–Pittsburgh Pirates. Ban Johnson and his ally Garry Herrmann usually pushed around the compromise candidate on the National Commission. Furthermore, he was ill-supported and often attacked by National League owners. His ruling against the Giants in the Merkle Boner game of 1908 proved to be the beginning of the end for Pulliam.

The acrimony caused him to suffer a nervous breakdown at an owners' meeting in February 1909. After a leave of absence, Pulliam resumed his duties in June. On July 28, he retired to his hotel room and killed himself with a revolver. He was 40. The Giants were the only team to skip the funeral. To illustrate his hard-nosed nature, manager John McGraw could muster no sympathy, only the offhanded comment, "I didn't think a bullet in the head could hurt him."

Sy Sanborn

See Sportswriters.

Tom Senior

32-year-old minor league umpire Thomas Senior shot himself to death in Chester, Pennsylvania, on February 6, 1911.

John Sheridan
See Sportswriters

Sportswriters
Johnstown, Pennsylvania, sports editor Randolph Blanch committed suicide by gun on November 29, 1911. He was 30 years old. Other sportswriters who killed themselves include Jim Price (gun in 1929), John Sheridan (hanging in 1930), and Sy Sanborn (gun in 1934).

Chick Stahl
Boston Beaneater Chick Stahl hit .354 in his rookie season in 1897 and batted .351 in '99. When the American League declared itself a major league, he jumped to the cross-town Pilgrims. In the 1903 World Series, the first baseman hit .303 with 3 triples, 3 RBIs, and 6 runs for the world champions. Toward the end of the 1906 season, Stahl replaced Hall of Famer Jimmy Collins as the team's manager but failed to lift the club out of last place.

Citing pressure, Stahl resigned his managerial post during spring training 1907. Two weeks later, he was found dead in a West Baden, Indiana, hotel after consuming carbolic acid. It seems that the ballplayer was involved with two women other than his wife. Other reports suggest drug usage led to his demise. Stahl died at age 34.

Ed Strickland
After killing his 18-year-old girlfriend, Ida Williamson, and her escort on January 2, 1909, at a dance in Chandler, Indiana, pitcher Ed Strickland, formally of the Carolina Association, shot himself in the head, dying at age 26. He had signed to play the upcoming season with Evansville in the Central League.

John Wakefield
In 1924, John Wakefield was one of many young men in the burgeoning Cardinals farm system. On December 11, he killed himself in Memphis after an argument with his girlfriend.

Don Wilson
Righthanded pitcher Don Wilson was a steady producer for some not-so-great Houston Astros teams from 1967–74, posting 104 victories with a 3.15 ERA. He is one of few to have multiple no-hit games. The first occurred on June 18, 1967, while striking out 15 Atlanta Braves at the Astrodome. The Reds fell to his second no-hitter on May 1, 1969, at Crosley Field. Wilson whiffed 13.

He was lifted in the ninth for a pinch-hitter by manager Preston Gomez after completing eight no-hit innings on September 4, 1974, though losing 2-1. On January 5, 1975, Wilson was found dead in his car in his garage of carbon monoxide poisoning. His 5-year-old son, who was sleeping in the house, also died.

CHAPTER FIVE

War

Cuban War of Independence

Three Cuban baseball Hall of Famers perished during the War of Independence against Spain. Outfielder Ricardo Cabaleiro, a captain in the Cuban Army, was killed in action in 1897. Pitcher/infielder Juan Pastoriza was killed in action in 1896. Catcher Emilio Sabourin, an early founder of Cuban baseball, died in prison in 1896 opposing Spain.

World War I

The impact of World War I on major league baseball was minimal compared to the conflict of the 1940s. The *work or fight rule* didn't even affect the game until 1918, just months prior to the armistice. 250 major leaguers ended up in the military. Others joined the reserves, found war-related work, or played ball in an industrial league. Few actually left the game for an extended period of time. Hall of Famers Christy Mathewson, Ty Cobb, Pete Alexander, George Sisler, and Branch Rickey were among those sent to Europe.

On July 19, 1918, Secretary of War Newton Baker decided that baseball was not an essential occupation. Baseball executives were thrown into a panic, but the season managed to stay open until Labor Day. The World Series was even played with the Boston Red Sox the victor for the fourth time that decade.

However, the war effort did close down the racetracks, reviving gambling in baseball. Attendance suffered as 1918's mark was the lowest since '02. More importantly, three major leaguers were killed in action. Because of travel restrictions, clubs held spring training within 500 miles of home. Also, a percentage of league profits were diverted to the Red Cross and marching drills became a pregame staple.

Members in Service

	American Leaguers	National Leaguers	Total
By 1917	48	28	76
By the end	144	103	247

Major League Attendance

	American League	*National League*	*Total*
1916	3,451,885	3,051,634	6,503,517
1917	2,858,858	2,361,136	5,219,994
1918	1,707,999	1,372,127	3,080,126
1919	3,654,236	2,878,203	6,532,439
1920	5,084,300	4,036,575	9,120,875

Military Personnel Deaths

Major Leaguers

Alex Burr	Larry Chappel
Harry Glenn	Eddie Grant
Newt Halliday	Ralph Sharman
Bun Troy	

Minor Leaguers

Harry Acton	John Cooper
Frank Healey	John Inglis

Negro Leaguers

Arthur Kimbro	Pearl Webster

Killed In Action and Combat Deaths

John Cooper	Eddie Grant
Robert Troy	

Former White Sox farmhand John Cooper was killed in action on September 2, 1918. He was 30 years old.

Eddie Grant graduated from Harvard in 1905 and later became the regular third baseman and leadoff hitter for the Phillies. He would top the league in games, at-bats (twice), putouts, and double plays. However, he could never break the .270-batting barrier. Philadelphia traded him and Grant soon lost his starting job. Ending up with the Giants as a utility infielder, Grant retired from the diamond in 1915 to practice law.

When war broke out, he was among the first to enlist, becoming a captain in the 77th Infantry Division. Grant, 35, was killed in the Argonne Forest, France, during the Battle of Meuse-Argonne by an exploding shell on October 5, 1918, one month prior to the war's ending. He was part of a rescue mission at the time to find the fabled "Lost Battalion." A monument was erected in his honor in center field at the Polo Grounds in New York. Today, the Edward L. Grant Highway runs by Yankee Stadium.

One-game major leaguer Robert "Bun" Troy was killed in action at Petit Mau-jouym, France, on October 7, 1918.

Noncombat Deaths

Alex Burr	Newt Halliday
Ralph Sharman	Pearl Webster

One-game major leaguer Alex Burr was killed when his plane went down above Cazaux, France, and landed in a lake on October 12, 1918.

Newt Halliday joined the navy the year after his one-game stint with the Pirates in 1916. While in service, he contracted tuberculosis and died in April 1918 at a base hospital.

Ralph Sharman appeared in 13 games in the outfield for the Philadelphia Athletics in 1917, then joined the Army. He drowned in the Alabama River near Camp Sheridan on May 24, 1918, at age 23.

Reports suggest that Negro league catcher Pearl Webster died in France shortly after the cease-fire in 1919.

Spanish Flu Deaths

Harry Acton	Larry Chappell
Harry Glenn	Frank Healey
John Inglis	Arthur Kimbro
Ralph Worrell	

The Spanish flu was first detected at an army barracks in Kansas in March 1918. It spread quickly, killing 675,000 Americans and between 20 and 40 million world-wide within months. This epidemic was unusual in that the bulk of its sufferers were neither young nor old.

Central Leaguer Harry Action died from the effects of Spanish flu in October 1918 at Camp Sheridan, Ohio.

Five-year reserve major league outfielder Larry Chappell joined the U.S. Army Medical Corp. after the 1917 season. He contracted pneumonia and influenza on assignment in San Francisco and died on November 8, 1918, at age 28.

Harry Glenn played six games at catcher for the St. Louis Cardinals in 1915. The Spanish flu ended his life in October 1918 at the U.S. Army Aviation School in St. Paul, Minnesota. He was 28 years old.

Western Association umpire Frank Healey passed away in October 1918 at Fort Riley, Kansas. The Army sergeant was 31 years old.

John Inglis played in the New York State League and the New York–New Jersey League. He died on October 7, 1918, at the Pelham Bay Park Naval Training Station in New York.

Negro league star third baseman Arthur Kimbro contracted the flu in the last days of his military service and died soon after his discharge in 1918.

Baltimore Orioles pitcher (of the International League) Ralph Worrell was of millions to die from the WWI-era Spanish flu epidemic. At the time, he was stationed at an Army truck training facility on the University of Virginia campus. Nineteen years old in 1918, the southpaw won 25 games for Baltimore. He enlisted at season's end and died that November, just five days before the war ended.

Grover Cleveland Alexander

Pete Alexander is the other man with 373 wins, though he thought Mathewson only had 372 at retirement. Researchers later discovered an additional tally. As a rookie in 1911, Alexander led the league with 28 wins, 31 complete games, 7 shutouts, and 367 innings pitched. He also finished second in strikeouts and fourth in ERA. 1915–17 were even finer years, as he won the pitching Triple Crown each year; that's three straight. The feat is even more impressive if you consider that his home field was the tiny Baker Bowl in Philadelphia, home to many dead ball era slugging feats. Some stats:

- 1915–17 wins: 31, 33, 30 = 94
- 1915–17 ERA: 1.22, 1.55, and 1.83
- 373-208 career record
- 2.56-career ERA
- 1920: 27-14, 1.91 ERA, 173 strikeouts = another pitching Triple Crown
- 90 shutouts
- ERA under 2.00 six times
- Led league in innings pitched seven times
- 20+ wins nine times
- 4 one-hitters in 1915

One of the most staggering statistics of his storied career is that as a rookie Alexander committed a balk but never would again. The Phillies were fearful that Alexander was going to be drafted into World War I so they sold him to the Cubs along with his designated catcher Bill Killefer after the 1917 season. The Cubs later traded Alexander to the St. Louis Cardinals where his exploits in the 1926 World Series at the age of 39 would become legendary. After retiring, the righthander pitched for the barnstorming House of David team until 1938, once a teammate of the great female athlete Babe Didrikson.

It turned out the Cubs were right because Alex spent much of 1918 in France in General Pershing's American Expeditionary Force. As a sergeant in an artillery division, he suffered shell shock. The resulting loss of hearing and increased seizures only fueled his existent epilepsy and alcoholism. Alexander battled all four until his death in 1950.

Forever linked with Alexander, Tony Lazzeri is another who suffered from epilepsy, as did Sherry Magee, Hal Lanier, Buddy Bell, and top Negro league hitter Jud Wilson.

Charlie Becker

Former Senators pitcher Charlie Becker was in the ambulance corps during WWI when he was gassed. The lingering effects led to his death in 1928 at age 39.

Ray Cahill
Suffering from asthma and the lingering effects of being gassed in France during WWI, minor league catcher Ray Cahill was forced to retire. He then scouted for the St. Louis Browns from 1924–41.

Oran Dodd
Oran Dodd played five games at second base for the Pirates in 1912. From there, he returned to the Texas League and later joined the cause during WWI. He was gassed and suffered lingering effects until his early death at age 39 in 1929.

Tony Mahoney
Like Christy Mathewson, Negro league southpaw Tony Mahoney was gassed during his military service in WWI. Never fully recovering, he died in an army hospital on September 25, 1924.

Christy Mathewson
Christy Mathewson was one of the all-time greats. His 373 wins are tied for third on the career list. Matty led the league at one time or another in every major pitching category including winning the pitching Triple Crown, wins, ERA, and strikeouts, in 1905 and 1908. Mathewson's out-pitch was the "fadeaway," known today as a screwball. The following statistics are a mere sample:

- 373-188 career record
- .655 winning percentage
- 2.13 career ERA
- 30+ wins, four times
- 94 victories from 1903–05
- 20+ wins 13 times, 12 in a row
- 79 shutouts
- ERA under 2.00 five times, four straight between 1908–11
- Walked less than one man per game in 1908
- Pitched 68 consecutive innings without issuing a walk in 1913

The highlight of Matty's career came in the 1905 World Series versus Connie Mack's Philadelphia Athletics. He pitched three shutouts while striking out 18 and walking only one.

However, his intangibles were worth a lot more than mere numbers to the Giants. Whenever Matty stepped on the mound, his teammates had a reasonable expectation of winning. From 1903–06, Matty and Joe McGinnity totaled 61, 68, 52, and 49 wins. Likewise, he combined with Rube Marquard in 1911–13 for 50, 49, and 48 victories—a one-two pitching punch any manager would crave.

As skipper of the Cincinnati Reds in 1918, Mathewson left his team to join the war effort. The Army captain was sent to France with Ty Cobb, among others, to become an instructor in the Chemical Warfare Service. During a training exercise, he suffered gas poisoning. His lungs were permanently damaged and Matty developed an alarming cough. Ty Cobb, who was present, said that Matty missed the signal and just didn't get his mask on fast enough.

Big Six was diagnosed with tuberculosis two years later. He spent much of the next few years in and out of Sarnac Lake Sanitarium while coaching the Giants and serving as president of the Boston Braves. Matty died in 1925 at age 47.

Red Ormsby
American League umpire, 1923–41, Red Ormsby was gassed during World War I and continued to show effects for years.

Marsh Williams
A's righthander Marsh Williams lost all six of his decisions in his only major league season, 1916. He was part of one of the worst teams of the 20th century, a collection of ballplayers Connie Mack patched together after dismantling his dynasty in the face of Federal League competition.

Williams was gassed by the Germans while in the Army during World War I. He suffered for years and died in 1935 at age 43. Another American League pitcher Ed Klepfer was similarly gassed but suffered no long-term effects.

World War I Injuries
Injuries sustained or illnesses contracted while in service during World War I ended or shortened the following baseball careers:

Swede Carlstrom	contracted rheumatism in Europe
Walt Kuhn	lost an eye
Pat Maloney	injured in France
Hughie Miller	wounded in action
Finners Quinlan	injured in France

World War II

War would have a much greater impact on major league baseball in the 1940s than in the 1910s. By January 1945, 5,400 of the 5,800 professional ballplayers in organized baseball in 1941 were in the service. More than 50 were killed.

Without a doubt, the quality of play on the field was diminished. League champions and statistical leaders are questioned to this day. Lou Boudreau in his book, *Lou Boudreau: Covering All the Bases*, states "It was still called 'major league' baseball, but I'd have to say the caliber of the game . . . was Triple-A, at best, maybe only Double-A." However, there were enough stars left to entertain the masses and new heroes would come.

To baseball historians, the most significant telltale factor of on-the-field play during the war is that St. Louis won the American League pennant in 1944. Vying against cross-town, defending world champion Cardinals to fill their seats, the Browns drew a meager 81,000 fans at the height of the Great Depression in 1935.

One of the true second-tier franchises in sports, the Browns were able to put it together for one year while the brightest major league stars were overseas. A mere six times they had finished higher than fourth and only once in consecutive years. Ridiculously, the Browns had only risen above the second division nine times since 1901. When the regulars returned in 1946, naturally, the Browns slipped to the bottom of the standings. They wouldn't compete again until 1960, long after moving to Baltimore.

On January 15, 1942, stressing the importance of baseball on the nation's morale, President Franklin Roosevelt urged the game to proceed as usual in a letter to Judge Landis. This was a huge relief to the baseball community, which had feared the loss of the entire 1942 season after Pearl Harbor was bombed on December 7.

Senators' owner Clark Griffith, unbeknownst to Landis, had been courting General Lewis B. Hershey, who was in charge of the Selective Service System. Through this friendship and his personal relationship with President Roosevelt, Griffith was able to gain a favorable position for baseball. Landis would have never stood for asking for special favors, especially from a liberal reformer like Roosevelt. The judge especially disliked night games, which Griffith was able to have President Roosevelt push for to accommodate day workers in the capital.

However, players were still subject to the draft, but those in winter war-related employment were permitted to leave in time for spring training. Travel restrictions still applied and night games were limited, except in Washington, DC. Spring training was held exclusively above the Mason-Dixon Line to restrict Southern travel, for some reason. Ultimately, the 1945 All-Star Game was cancelled. The majors also experimented with a balata ball in 1943.

Some important advances were spurred by the war. Teams, Washington especially, increased the signing of Latin American players because they weren't subject to the military draft. A proliferation of night games and radio broadcasts occurred. As a result of contract disagreements by some service returnees, the first semi-effective player and umpire unions developed after the war. In 1946, the American Baseball Guild, a players' union, was formed. It gained payments for spring training expenses, known as "Murphy Money" after union organizer Robert Murphy. The Guild also established the first pension plan.

The most significant headway was in the area of racial integration. Throughout the service, African-American men played with white men. It became apparent to many that if African-Americans were expected to fight beside white men than why should they be excluded in other areas? Of course, this did not happen overnight and, in fact, difficulties continued for decades. Another seemingly significant factor is the death of Judge Landis in November 1944, opening new possibilities.

Major League Attendance

	American League	*National League*	*Total*
1941	4,911,956	4,777,647	9,689,603
1942	4,200,216	4,353,353	8,553,569
1943	3,696,569	3,769,342	7,465,911
1944	4,798,158	3,974,588	8,772,746

1945	5,580,420	5,260,703	10,841,123
1946	9,621,182	8,902,107	18,523,288

Military Personnel Deaths

Major Leaguers

Elmer Gedeon   Harry O'Neill

Minor Leaguers

This list was compiled mainly from the Deadballera.com website:

Herman Bauer	Fred Beal
Keith Bissonette	Davis Blewster
Joe Boren	Lefty Brewer
Merrill Brown	Ordway Cisgen
Howie DeMartini	Harold Dobson
James Doyle	William Fash
Frank Faudem	Ray Flaherty
George Gamble	Robert Gary
Conrad Graff	Alan Grant
William Hansen	Billy Hebert
Nay Hernandez	Bob Hershey
Robert Holmes	Gordon Houston
Ernie Hrovatic	Harry Imhoff
Frank Janik	Art Keller
Lester Kirkkala	Stan Klores
Carlisle Koop	Walt Lake
Gene Lefler	Walt Loos
Andy Lummus	Henry Martinez
John McKee	Louis Miller
Marcus Milligan	Joe Moceri
John Muller	John Munro
George Myers	Walt Navie
William Niemeyer	Hank Nowak
John Ogden (front office)	Joe Palatas
Jack Patteson	Charlie Percod
Metro Persoskie	Harold Phillips
Joe Pinder	Robert Price
Ernie Raimondi	Mike Sambolich
Glenn Sanford	Bill Sarver
Robert Schmukal	Ed Schohl
Frank Schulz	Norman Smith
Marshall Sneed	Rod Sooter
Billy Southworth Jr.	Earl Springer
Gene Stack	Don Stewart

Al Stiewie
Fred Swift
Bob Trench
Wirt Twitchell
Art Vivian
Roman Wantuck
Dick Williams
Elmer Wright
Marion Young
George Zwilling

Sylvester Sturges
John Tayler
Jimmie Trimble
Lewis Varanese
Elmer Wachtler
James Whitfield
Lester Wirkalla
Joe Yeske
Peter Zarila

Negro Leaguers

Ralph Johnson

Killed In Action and Combat Deaths

Herman Bauer
Ordway Cisgen
William Fash
Elmer Gedeon
William Hansen
Manuel Hernandez
Ernie Hrovatic
Ardys Keller
Walter Loos
Henry Martinez
John Muller
Walter Navie
Henry Nowak
Harry O'Neill
Charles Percod
Joe Pinder
Ernie Raimondi
William Sarver
Ed Schohl
Marshall Sneed
Don Stewart
John Tayler
Wirt Twitchell
Arthur Vivian
Roman Wantuck
Elmer Wright

Forrest Brewer
Howard DeMartini
Frank Faudem
Conrad Graff
Billy Hebert
Robert Holmes
Harry Imhoff
Lester Kirkkala
Andy Lummus
John McKee
George Myers
William Niemeyer
John Ogden (front office)
Jack Patteson
Metro Persoskie
Robert Price
Michael Sambolich
Robert Schmukal
Franklin Schulz
Earl Springer
Sylvester Sturges
Jim Trimble
Lewis Varanese
Elmer Wachtler
James Whitfield
Marion Young

Herman Bauer was killed in action in 1943 in Europe. Bauer, a minor league catcher from 1938–41, was the brother of Hank Bauer.

Lefty Forrest Brewer, a minor league pitcher with Charlotte, was killed in action in 1944 at Normandy, France. He was a member of the 82nd Airborne.

Ordway Cisgen, a minor league pitcher with Utica, was killed in action in 1944.

Former Jacksonville minor leaguer Howard DeMartini was killed in action in 1944.

29-year-old Bill Fash was killed due to an explosion onboard the USS John Hancock, an aircraft carrier, in 1945.

23-year-old ex-minor leaguer Frank Faudem was killed in action in 1943. The private died at Leyte Gulf in the Philippines. The battle of Leyte Gulf in October 1944 is considered the largest naval battle in history. The Allied forces soundly defeated the outnumbered Japanese navy, inflicting a serious blow to their strategic capabilities. It was also the site of the first kamikaze bombings.

Bomber Captain Elmer Gedeon was shot down and killed over St. Pol, France, on April 20, 1944, just past his 27th birthday. He had appeared in five games for the Washington Senators in 1939.

Former minor leaguer Conrad Graff was killed in action in 1944.

Bill Hansen, formally with Milwaukee in the American Association, was killed in action in Belgium in 1945.

Oakland second baseman Billy Hebert was the first professional baseball player killed in action in World War II. He died on October 31, 1942, at Guadalcanal.

Manual Hernandez, formally with San Diego in the Pacific Coast League, was killed in action in Germany in 1945.

Bob Holmes was killed in action on Iwo Jima in 1945. The 22-year-old lieutenant was a former Yankee farmhand.

On January 14, 1944, former two-season minor leaguer Ernie Hrovatic was killed in action in Belgium. The Private First Class was 20 years old.

Former Baltimore Orioles catcher Harry Imhoff was killed in action on Okinawa in 1945. He was 19 years old.

Ardys Keller caught in the minors with Toledo. A member of the 82nd Airborne, he was killed in action in 1944.

Toledo minor leaguer Les Kirkkala was killed in action in France in 1945.

Lt. Walt Loos, a minor leaguer from 1939–41, was lost in action on an air transport flight in 1944. He was 27 years old.

Medal of Honor recipient Andy Lummas was killed in action on Iwo Jima on March 28, 1945. The Reds farmhand had played center field for Wichita Falls in the West Texas–New Mexico League in 1941.

Henry Martinez played in the minors for seven seasons. The 28-year-old was killed in action in the Central Pacific in 1945.

Lt. John McKee was killed in action in Belgium in 1945. The 34-year-old had played with Columbus and Atlanta.

Former minor leaguer Lt. John Muller was killed in action in September 1943. The Army Air Force pilot was serving in the Pacific theatre.

21-year-old former minor leaguer George Myers was killed in action in Belgium in 1945.

Walt Navie, formally with Shreveport in the minors, was killed in action in 1945.

Private Bill Niemeyer was killed in action in Germany in 1945. The 24-year-old was a former Cubs farmhand.

Former New Orleans and Houston pitcher Henry Nowak was killed in action in Belgium on January 1, 1945.

21-year-old John Ogden was killed in action in 1944. He had been a member of the front office of the Elmira club.

Harry O'Neill died at Iwo Jima on March 6, 1945. He had played one game in 1939 for Connie Mack.

Minor leaguer Jack Patteson, a Marine, was killed on Guadalcanal in 1942.

Charles Percod, a minor leaguer from 1937–43, was killed in action in France in 1944.

Metro Persoskie, a minor leaguer from 1939–42, died over England in 1944. The 23-year-old was returning from a bombing mission in Germany.

Minor league pitcher Joe Pinder, 1935–41, died on Omaha Beach on D-Day, June 6, 1944. He was posthumously awarded the Congressional Medal of Honor. His citation reads:

> For conspicuous gallantry and intrepidity above and beyond the call of duty on 6 June 1944, near Colleville-sur-Mer, France. On D-day, Technician 5th Grade Pinder landed on the coast 100 yards off shore under devastating enemy machinegun and artillery fire which caused severe casualties among the boatload. Carrying a vitally important radio, he struggled towards shore in waist-deep water. Only a few yards from his craft he was hit by enemy fire and was gravely wounded. Technician 5th Grade Pinder never stopped. He made shore and delivered the radio. Refusing to take cover afforded, or to accept medical attention for his wounds, Technician 5th Grade Pinder, though terribly weakened by loss of blood and in fierce pain, on 3 occasions went into the fire-swept surf to salvage communication equipment. He recovered many vital parts and equipment, including another workable radio. On the 3rd trip he was again hit, suffering machinegun bullet wounds in the legs. Still this valiant soldier would not stop for rest or medical attention. Remaining exposed to heavy enemy fire, growing steadily weaker, he aided in establishing the vital radio communication on the beach. While so engaged this dauntless soldier was hit for the third time and killed. The indomitable courage and personal bravery of Technician 5th Grade Pinder was a magnificent inspiration to the men with whom he served.

Bob Price was killed in action at sea in 1945. The 26-year-old had played catcher and first base in the minors.

Ernie Raimondi was killed in action in Italy in 1945. The 24-year-old had played seven minor league seasons.

22-year-old, former minor leaguer Mike Sambolich was killed in action on November 5, 1944.

Bill Sarver, formally a center fielder with Augusta in the minors, was killed in action in 1945.

Bob Schmukal signed a contract with the Boston Braves prior to joining the service. He was killed in action in France in October 1944.

Ed Schohl played in the minors from 1933–41. On November 1, 1943, the Private First Class died from wounds in Italy.

Franklin Schulz, a former minor leaguer with Flint, was killed in action on June 17, 1945.

Former Topeka minor leaguer Marshall Sneed was killed in action in 1943.

Sgt. Earl Springer was killed in action on January 25, 1945. The 26-year-old had been a member of the 1940 Baltimore Orioles of the International League.

Don Stewart played in the Pacific Coast League and also umpired in the Western International League. A Canadian, Stewart served with the Calgary Highlanders. He was killed in Glasgow, Scotland, during a bombing raid in 1941.

Sylvester Sturges played in the minors from 1929–41. The lieutenant was killed in action on D-Day. He was piloting a paratroop ship at the Normandy invasion on June 6, 1944.

John Tayler, a minor leaguer from 1938–41, was killed in action in August 1944. He was a Marine.

Jim Trimble, a former Senators prospect, was killed by a suicide bomber on Iwo Jima in 1945.

Marine Wirt Twitchell was killed in action on Saipan, an island chain north of Guam, in 1944. He had played in the minors from 1938–41. The Japanese had ruled the islands from 1914 until Allied forces secured it after three weeks of heavy fighting in July 1944.

Lewis Varanese, a minor leaguer from 1933–39 known as Lou Vann, was killed in action on May 18, 1943. The 31-year-old Marine was serving in the southwest Pacific.

Art Vivian, a Newark Bear, was killed in action in 1944.

Elmer Wachtler was killed in action in Belgium in 1945. The 26-year-old had been in the Cardinals chain.

Roman Wantuck, a minor leaguer in 1941, was killed in action in October 1944. He was serving in the Pacific.

Jim Whitfield was killed in action in September 1944. The 24-year-old staff sergeant was serving in the Southwest Pacific.

Former San Antonio minor league pitcher Elmer Wright was killed in action in 1944 at Omaha Beach.

Marion Young was killed in action on December 13, 1944, in the southwest Pacific theatre. The 22-year-old had played in the minors from 1941–42.

Noncombat Deaths

Fred Beal	Merrill Brown
Harry Dobson	Robert Gary
Alan Grant	Gordon Houston
Harold Phillips	Rod Sooter
Billy Southworth Jr.	Gene Stack
Peter Zarila	

On February 11, 1943, Fred Beal, a minor leaguer from 1941–42, died at Camp White in Oregon.

21-year-old Merrill Brown died in a plane crash in Jacksonville in 1943. He had played in the minors.

Harry Dobson was killed when his plane went down in England in 1943. The 28-year-old Army lieutenant had played in the minors from 1941–42.

Former minor leaguer Bob Gary died on February 5, 1944, at Briggs Field in Texas. He was an aviation cadet.

Alan Grant, a minor leaguer from 1939–42, died when his plane went down at Victoryville, California on May 23, 1943.

Lt. Gordon Houston, formerly a Texas League outfielder, was killed in February 1942 in a training flight accident near Tacoma, Washington. He was the first professional ballplayer to die in WWII. Houston led the East Texas League with a .384 batting average in 1938.

Lt. Harold Phillips died when his military plane went down in 1945. The former Piedmont League catcher was returning from a semi-pro baseball tournament in Texas.

Rod Sooter, previously with Seattle in the Pacific Coast League, died in a plane crash in 1946.

Major Billy Southworth Jr., a Distinguished Flying Cross medal earner who flew 25 bombing missions, was killed after his B-29 took off from Long Island (heading to Florida), experienced trouble and crashed during an emergency landing at LaGuardia Airport in New York on February 15, 1945. The plane crash-landed into Flushing Bay. His body wasn't recovered until six months later. Southworth was the first man from organized baseball to enlist, in December 1940. The 27-year-old had played in the minors with the Toronto Maple Leafs in the International League. His father was respected major league player and manager Billy Southworth.

White Sox prospect Gene Stack had a heart attack while pitching for his Army team in Michigan. He died on the mound in on June 26, 1942.

Corporal Pete Zarila, formerly with the Knoxville Smokies of the Southern Association, died in the same plane crash as Harold Phillips.

Negro Leaguers

At least 89 Negro leaguers joined the armed forces during WWII. Thankfully, none perished (some reports suggest that Ralph "Botts" Johnson was killed in action in 1945). Many Negro leaguers left the game for a job in a defense plant. Here, one could gain a measure of stability and control over their personal life, combined with equal or greater pay and certainly less travel than offered in baseball.

Administratively, Negro league executives faced many of the same challenges that their counterparts in organized baseball did.

Prisoners of War of Germany

Augie Donatelli (umpire)	Mickey Grasso
Dixie Howell	Phil Marchildon
Bert Shepard	

Umpire Augie Donatelli was a prisoner of war. The Army tail gunner with 18 missions under his belt was shot down over Berlin in 1944 and sent to German Stalag VI for 15 months. It was there that he first began umpiring. Donatelli worked in the National League from 1950–73, officiating in five World Series.

Backup catcher Mickey Grasso played seven seasons in the majors from 1946–55. He brought home a World Series ring with Cleveland in 1954. Before that, he was captured by the Germans in North Africa. The Army Technical Sgt. was encamped in Tunisia from 1943–45.

Righthanded pitcher Dixie Howell hit the show in 1940 with Cleveland but did not reappear in the bigs until 1949. He would be in and out of the minors for 18 years before he finally found a slot in the White Sox bullpen in 1955. Howell went the longest from his major league debut until his first victory, 15 years. He continued pitching, in and out of the majors, until dying of a heart attack during spring training in 1960 at age 40. Howell spent five months in a German POW camp. He was finally liberated on April 30, 1945.

Phil Marchildon won 27 games for the Athletics in 1941–42 before joining his native Royal Canadian Air Force. German anti-aircraft fire brought down his plane over Denmark in September 1944. He was captured and sent to a POW camp in Poland and remained there until it was liberated in May 1945. The tail gunner was force-marched from camp to camp during his imprisonment. Combined with malnourishment, he lost 40 pounds. Marchildon was the only member of the crew to survive. Connie Mack called him back and pitched the underweight and unsteady righthander in three late-season games in 1945. Marchildon's health remained shaky into 1946. He had trouble maintaining concentration and often appeared jittery and nervous from his ordeal, though the hurler calmed himself enough to lead the hapless team with 13 victories. He took it up a notch in 1947 with 19 wins and a 3.22 ERA.

Fighter pilot Bert Shepard was shot down over France in May 1944. His right leg was amputated below the knee. Captured by the Germans, Shepard was liberated from prison camp, Stalag IX-C, in October. He was fitted for an artificial limb and practiced his pitching technique. On August 4, 1945, mere weeks from the prison camp, he pitched for the Senators, allowing just one run in 5.1 innings. Shepard continued in the minors, even playing first base. In 1949, remarkably, he stole five bases.

World War II Injuries
Injuries/illnesses contracted while in service during World War II ended or shortened the following baseball careers:

Ernest Payne (Negro leagues)   stabbed with a bayonet

Didn't Return to the Game
After winning 197 major league games, 35-year-old Larry French joined the Navy in 1943, eventually retiring as a captain in '69. Stationed at a nearby shipyard, the Brooklyn Dodger unsuccessfully petitioned the Navy to allow him to pitch eight

games in 1943 to pick up his 200th victory. French was even willing to donate his salary to the Naval Relief Society.

Others who did not return after serving include:

Russell Awkard   Boze Berger
Bubby Burbage   Harry Danning
Jake Dunn   Buddy Hassett
Red Moore

Pushed Out

To compensate for the returnees, major league rosters expanded to 30 after the war. Still, every spring training camp was flooded with talent in 1946. The following players could not find work when they returned from the service. They threatened or actually pursued legal action to protect their re-employment rights under the G.I. Bill.

Bruce Campbell   Bob Harris
Tony Lupien   Pinky May
Al Niemiec   Steve Sundra

Also, to make way for others, some ballplayers were dismissed at the end of 1945. One, Tony Cuccinello, was released by the White Sox with only two days left in the season, ending a 15-year major league career. He was 37 years old and did not figure into the team's future. Cuccinello was battling Yankee George Stirnweiss for the batting title. Without the extra at bats, Cuccinello lost by 0.00009, the smallest difference in history.

Lou Brissie

Lou Brissie's patrol unit was shelled on December 7, 1944, in Italy. He was the only survivor, though Brissie suffered two broken feet, a smashed left ankle, a broken left leg, and injuries to his hands and shoulders. It took two years, 23 operations, and a leg brace for Brissie to continue his baseball career.

Pitching for Savannah in the South Atlantic League in 1947, he rebounded with a 23-5 record and a 1.91 ERA. Connie Mack brought him up at the end of the year to pitch one game. Brissie won 30 games over the next two seasons and even made the All-Star team in '49.

Creepy Crespi

Cardinals second baseman Frank Crespi led the league in putouts and double plays as a rookie in 1941. He also hit .279 with 85 runs. In 1943, he broke his leg playing army baseball and then re-broke it during a training exercise (his tank overturned). In the hospital recuperating, Crespi again broke the same leg in an ill-advised wheelchair race. Not surprisingly, it never healed sufficiently for Crespi to return to the majors.

Johnny Grodzicki

After pitching in five games in 1941 for the Cardinals, John Grodzicki was in the club's farm system when he was drafted into an army paratrooper unit in 1942. After being involved in heavy combat for three years, his unit dropped into Germany in March 1945. There, his four-man squad was hit by an enemy shell. Grodzicki lost part of his right leg but was lucky enough to be the only one to survive.

After months of intensive therapy, he learned to walk with a brace and stubbornly rejoined St. Louis as a batting practice pitcher in 1946. He got into three games that summer and 16 the next; however, he couldn't claim a victory. The righthander lasted in the minors until 1953.

Satoshi Hirayama

Satoshi Hirayama, a Nisei with Japanese-born parents, was born in Hawaii and moved with his family to first Utah and then Fresno following employment opportunities. The entire Hirayama family was confined to an internment camp in Poston, Arizona, during the war.

There, Satoshi played ball with and against other Nisei. After the war, the family returned to Fresno and Satoshi won an athletic scholarship to Fresno State. He later joined the Browns organization and was sent to Stockton in the California League. From 1955–64, he played third base and outfield for the Hiroshima Carp.

Gerald Juzek

Gerald Juzek, a Marine, was crippled at the Battle of Guadalcanal in January 1943. Not expected to even walk again, Juzek rehabbed and pitched an inspirational three innings for Los Angeles Angels on April 1, 1944. The rookie was soon released by the club and sent to Portsmouth. He had showed promise but his battered legs weren't up to Pacific Coast League competition.

Ken Noda

Many Japanese–Canadians played ball throughout Canada. One of the strongest and most popular teams was the Asahis. Often, they would recruit Japanese nationals to fill out their roster. One such man was their star pitcher in 1934, Ken Noda. Later, he would be killed in action in China during WWII.

Cecil Travis

Cecil Travis was a popular shortstop–third baseman for the Washington Senators. In 1941, he led the league in hits with 218 while slugging .520, belting 101 RBI, and scoring 106 times. He finished second in batting to Ted Williams with a .359 average. The lefthanded hitter was particularly adept at hitting to the opposite field. In a 12-year career, his batting average rose above .300 seven times.

After the war, Travis returned to the majors at age 32 but was never the same. His feet froze during the Battle of the Bulge, limiting his mobility. He also hadn't played regularly in four years. Travis batted a mere .252 and then .216 before retiring. His prewar production, though, was strong enough to sustain a .314 career average despite the lackluster 1946 and '47 seasons.

Japan in World War II

Baseball was first introduced to Japan in the 1870s. Big league teams began touring the Asian country in 1913. Many Negro league teams would follow during the 1920s and '30s. In 1920, the first professional team, the Nihon Undo Kyokai, was formed. Sixteen years later, the first pro league assembled with Eiji Sawamura starring for the Tokyo Giants.

Japan became involved in World War II in 1937. The seasons were curtailed but play continued until August 1944 when Allied air raids forced its closing. The pro leagues did not operate in 1945. After the war, occupation commander General Douglas MacArthur promoted the reformation of the league. It thrives today.

Military Personnel Deaths

Seizaburo Amakawa	Tsutomu Aoki
Kenichi Aoshiba	Masakimi Araki
Chujiro Endo	Isamu Fukushi
Goro Fushimi	Tadashi Goto
Ichiro Hara	Yasuo Hayashi
Eiji Hirabayashi	Shuichi Hirose
Hisayuki Ikeda	Yutaka Ishii
Shinichi Ishimaru	Jinkichi Ito
Kentaro Ito	Masaru Kageura
Daichi Kaino	Noboru Kato
Norihisa Kawamura	Noboru Kitahara
Kazuo Kito	Matsuichi Kunihisa
Nobuo Kura	Hajime Kuwashima
Kiyoshi Maeda	Masayoshi Maekawa
Iwao Masano	Riichi Mastumoto
Shigeji Mastushita	Satoshi Matsuda
Hachiro Miwa	Bikichi Miyaguchi
Kunigoro Mori	Minoru Morita
Shigeo Murakami	Chotaro Muramastu
Yokio Muramastu	Ichizo Murase
Takeo Nagai	Miyoshi Nakagawa
Masao Nakamoto	Masami Nakamura
Saburo Nakamura	Hisashi Nakao
Yonekichi Naya	Yukio Nishimura
Noboru Noguchi	Toshiyasu Ogawa
Toshio Ohara	Fukukichi Okada
Muneyoshi Okada	Hiroshi Onodera
Yoshizo Oribe	Kenichi Ota
Adelano Rivera	Masao Santa
Eiji Sawamura	Yoshifumi Shimamoto
Usaburo Shintomi	Kajuji Shiraki
Toyo Sugiyama	Takeo Tabe

Momosuke Takano
Genbe Tsuji
Shizuka Watanabe
Masaki Yoshihara

Kazutaka Terauchi
Tadashi Ueda
Susumu Yagi

Killed in Action and Combat Deaths (Place of Death)

Seizaburo Amakawa (Leyte)
Chujiro Endo
Goro Fushimi (Marianas)
Ichiro Hara
Eiji Hirabayashi
Hisayuki Ikeda
Shinichi Ishimaru
Kentaro Ito (Guam)
Daichi Kaino
Norihisa Kawamura
Matsuichi Kunihisa (Burma)
Hajime Kuwashima
Masayoshi Maekawa
Riichi Mastumoto
Satoshi Matsuda
Bikichi Miyaguchi
Minoru Morita
Yokio Durmast (Guam)
Takeo Nagai
Masao Nakamoto (At sea)
Saburo Nakamura (Nomonhan)
Yonekichi Naya (Bataan)
Noboru Noguchi (At sea)
Toshio Ohara
Muneyoshi Okada
Yoshizo Oribe
Adelano Rivera
Eiji Sawamura
Usaburo Shintomi (Burma)
Toyo Sugiyama (Philippines)
Momosuke Takano
Genbe Tsuji
Shizuka Watanabe
Masaki Yoshihara

Tsutomu Aoki
Isamu Fukushi (Luzon)
Tadashi Goto
Yasuo Hayashi
Shuichi Hirose
Yutaka Ishii
Jinkichi Ito
Masaru Kageura
Noboru Kato
Kazuo Kito (Marianas)
Nobuo Kura (Okinawa)
Kiyoshi Maeda (China)
Iwao Masano
Shigeji Mastushita
Hachiro Miwa (China)
Kunigoro Mori
Shigeo Murakami (Leyte)
Ichizo Murase
Miyoshi Nakagawa
Masami Nakamura
Hisashi Nakao
Yukio Nishimura
Toshiyasu Ogawa
Fukukichi Okada
Hiroshi Onodera
Kenichi Ota (Burma)
Masao Santa
Yoshifumi Shimamoto
Kajuji Shiraki
Takeo Tabe
Kazutaka Terauchi
Tadashi Ueda
Susumu Yagi

Adelano Rivera returned home to the Philippines after a brief stint with the Tokyo Giants in 1939. He was drafted into the Philippine Army and killed in action on September 10, 1945, at age 35.

Shinichi Ishimaru played for Nagoya from 1941–43. He was drafted into the

Japanese Imperial Army Air Corps and joined a kamikaze squadron. Ishimaru died in a kamikaze attack on May 11, 1945, at age 22.

Noncombat Deaths

Kenichi Aoshiba   Masakimi Araki
Noboru Kitahara   Chotaro Muramastu

Kenichi Aoshiba pitched for the Tokyo Giants from 1936 until he was drafted in the Fall of 1938. He died from disease in a Pyongyang, North Korea, military hospital on November 1, 1945, at age 33.

Masakimi Araki was drafted into the military in 1940 after amassing a 9-2 record and a 1.72 ERA for Hankyu the previous summer. He died from sickness while serving near the Soviet–Manchurian border during the war.

Noboru Kitahara died from tuberculosis in 1945 at age 28. He had been drafted in 1943. Kitahara played shortstop and second base for Nankai from 1941–42.

Chotaro Muramastu pitched and played the outfield from 1939–42. He was killed when his plane crashed during a training flight on June 20, 1944, at age 22.

Military Deaths of Hall of Famers

Masaru Kageura   Miyoshi Nakagawa
Yukio Nishimura   Eiji Sawamura
Takeo Tabe   Masaki Yoshihara

Japanese Baseball Hall of Famer Masaru Kageura played the outfield and pitched from 1936–39 and again in '43. He was drafted into the military during the 1940–42 seasons. He reenlisted in 1944. Kageura was killed in action at the battle for Philippines on May 20, 1945. He was 29 years old.

Japanese Hall of Famer Miyoshi Nakagawa pitched and played first base for the Eagles from 1937–41. He was one of the top-fielding first sackers. Drafted after the 1941 season, Nakagawa was killed in action in Luzon in the Philippines in 1944. The lefty was 22 years old.

Yukio Nishimura was drafted in 1944 and killed in action in the Philippines on April 3, 1945. The Hall of Famer was a top pitcher for the Tigers from 1937–39 and then joined the industrial leagues. The righthander was 24 years old.

In America, the award for best pitcher every year is named after Cy Young. In Japan, the award is named for Eiji Sawamura. He was the first Japanese pitcher to win 30 games, posting a 33-10 record in 1937. In 1934, the 17-year-old high school student became a national phenom when he fanned Hall of Famers Charlie Gehringer, Babe Ruth, Lou Gehrig, and Jimmie Foxx in succession during a postseason exhibition tour, though he lost the game 1-0 on a home run by Gehrig. In all, he struck out nine and allowed only five hits. Instantly, Sawamura became a national hero. In the other 17 contests, the Japanese were outscored 188-39. In 1937, Sawamura led the league in victories and proved to be the postseason hero. The following year, he won the pitching Triple Crown with 24 wins, 196 strikeouts, and a 0.81 ERA in only 30 games during the spring season. For his efforts, he was named MVP. In a total of 86 starts during his career, the righthander won 63 games for a .741 winning percentage. His ERA calculates to a sterling 1.74. In all, Sawamura notched three no-hitters during his 5-year career. In 1959, Sawamura became one of the initial class to enter the Japanese Baseball Hall of Fame.

Sawamura reenlisted in the Imperial Army shortly after Pearl Harbor. He was killed, at age 26, on a troop transport in the Taiwan Strait on December 2, 1944, during the battle for the Ryuku Islands when his ship was torpedoed by an American warship.

Takeo Tabe first made a name for himself at Meiji University. During the U.S. tour in 1935, he stole 109 bases in 105 games, presenting an exciting form of ball for his countrymen. For this, the shortstop was elected to the Hall of Fame in 1969 without appearing in the pro league. He was killed in action in June 1945 at age 39.

Giants catcher, 1938–41, Masaki Yoshihara died in Burma on October 10, 1944. Drafted in 1942, the Hall of Famer was 25 years old.

Prisoners of War

Yoshio Gomi   Tokuji Kawasaki
Kenjiro Marsuki   Shigeru Mizuhara
Kichiharu Tosauchi   Kazuo Yoshida

Yoshio Gami played infield in Nippon Professional Baseball from 1936–42. In the service, he was captured by the Russians in 1945 and sent to a POW camp in Siberia.

Tokuji Kawasaki pitched in the Japan League from 1940–42 and 1946–57, amassing 188 victories and a 2.53 ERA. In between, he served in the military and spent time in a POW camp in Burma.

Kenjiro Matsuki played for the Osaka Tigers from 1936 until he was drafted in 1941. He was wounded and captured by American forces at the Battle of Okinawa. He returned to the Tigers for the 1950–51 seasons. In all, Matsuki hit .263 in 1,700 at-bats.

Shigeru Mizuhara played for the Yomiuri Giants from 1936–42 then joined the service and was stationed in Manchuria, eventually becoming a prisoner of war in a Soviet detention camp in Siberia. The Giants helped negotiate his release, which finally occurred in July 1949. He soon became the club's manager and led them to eight pennants, 1951–53 and 1955–59. Similar to Casey Stengel, Mizuhara was fired in 1960 after failing to win a ninth. Unlike Stengel, he copped another pennant with the Toei Flyers in 1962 before finally retiring in 1971. Mizuhara was elected to the Hall of Fame in 1977.

Kichiharu Tosauchi was drafted in 1943, imprisoned in a Siberian POW camp in 1945 and finally returned to Japan in 1948. He pitched and played the infield for the Kokutetsu Swallows from 1950–51.

Kazuo Yoshida played left field for Nagoya from 1939–44. Drafted in 1944, he was stationed in Manchuria. He was soon captured by the Russians and sent to a Siberian POW camp, where he resided for five years. Yoshida played ball again for Shochiku from 1950–52.

World War II Injuries

Shinichi Kimura   Sadao Kondo

Shinichi Kimura played shortstop and second base for Nagoya from 1939 until he was drafted in October 1942. He lost his right hand in an artillery explosion in Rabaul, Papua New Guinea, during the war.

Sadao Kondo won 55 games from 1943–54. As a pedestrian, he was sideswiped by a U.S. Army jeep and thrown into a river. As a result, the pitcher lost the middle finger on his right hand, his pitching hand. Adjusting, Kondo developed an effective palm ball. He later became the first Nippon Professional Baseball manager to strictly separate starters from relievers. For such, he was elected to the Hall of Fame.

Korean War

Military Personnel Deaths

Major Leaguers

Bob Neighbors

Minor Leaguers

Erwin Adamcewiez   William Crago
Leonard Glica   John Hrasch
James Hudgens   Ray Jankowski
Walt Koehler   John Lazar
Edward Leneve   Jack Leonard
Marcel Poelker   George Reedon
Carol Sweiger   Fred Tschudin
Carl Tumlinson   Charlie Wilcox

Killed In Action and Combat Deaths

Erwin Adamcewiez   William Crago
Leonard Glica   James Hudgens
Walter Koehler   John Lazar
Edward Leneve   Jack Leonard
Bob Neighbors   Marcel Poelker
Carol Sweiger   Carl Tumlinson
Charles Wilcox

Former Cardinals farmhand Erwin Adamcewiez died from wounds in Korea on November 21, 1952. He was 23 years old.

Bill Crago was killed in action in Korea in 1951. The 21-year-old had played with Dublin in the Georgia State League.

Leonard Glica, a former minor leaguer, was killed in action on May 26, 1951. The Army private was 22 years old.

Before joining the Navy, James Hudgens played for San Jose in the Pacific Coast League. The 22-year-old was killed in action on April 21, 1952.

Private First Class Walt Koehler was killed in action on July 28, 1952. The 25-year-old had played for Greensboro in the minors.

Former Browns prospect John Lazar was killed in action on September 7, 1951.

Marine Private Ed Leneve was killed in action on December 2, 1950. He was a Cubs farmhand.

22-year-old former minor leaguer Jack Leonard was missing in action in Korea in 1952.

Shortstop Bob Neighbors had a brief stint with the St. Louis Browns in 1939 before entering the Air Force. The major died in North Korea in August 1952. Missing in action, his body was never recovered. Neighbors was the only major leaguer to lose his life during the Korean conflict.

Marcel Poelker, a former minor leaguer, was killed in action on September 25, 1951. The sergeant was 23 years old.

Lt. Carol Sweiger was killed in action on October 4, 1951. The former minor leaguer was 23 years old.

Private Carl Tumlinson, a former Dodger hand, was killed in action on April 7, 1952.

Army Private Charles Wilcox was killed in action on September 8, 1952. He had played on an Anderson, Indiana, team in the minors.

Noncombat Deaths

John Hrasch	Raymond Jankowski
George Reedon	Fred Tschudin

Before being drafted, John Hrasch was a shortstop for New Orleans. The 24-year-old died in an auto accident at Camp Pickett in Virginia on September 18, 1952.

Private Ray Jankowski died from injuries suffered at Fort Huachuca in Arizona in 1951. The 22-year-old was a former Cardinals prospect.

George Reedon, formerly with Terre Haute in the Three-I League, died in a plane crash in Panama City, Florida in December 1953. He was 23 years old.

Fred Tschudin caught and managed in the minors. The 29-year-old was killed during an Air Force training flight on March 14, 1952.

Bo Wallace

Drafted during the Korean War, Negro league catcher Bo Wallace lost part of his left hand when a grenade exploded in 1952. Unfortunately, he was unable to resume his baseball career.

Vietnam War

Military Personnel Deaths

Minor Leaguers

Udell Chambers	Charles Chase
Eddie Glinnen	

Killed in Action and Combat Deaths

Udell Chambers   Charles Chase
Eddie Glinnen

Braves farmhand Udell Chambers was killed in action in a rocket attack outside Danang, Vietnam, on June 1, 1968.

Outfielder Charles Chase was drafted in the first round, 18th overall, by the Minnesota Twins out of the College of San Mateo in 1966. In June 1968, he was killed in action.

Giants farmhand Ed Glinnen died from wounds suffered in combat in a Vietnam hospital in 1970. He was 21 years old.

CHAPTER SIX

At the Ballpark

Grover Cleveland Alexander
Pete Alexander was beaned in 1907 while with Galesburg of the Illinois-Missouri League. He was hit in the head with the ball by a shortstop while trying to break up a double play. Alex fell unconscious for 56 hours. Dizziness and double vision persisted all year. Underhandedly, his manager quickly dealt him to Indianapolis. His first warm-up pitch broke his new manager's rib. Then Indianapolis merely gave Alexander to the Syracuse franchise—a move they would soon regret. The injury may have contributed to the pitcher's life-long battle with epilepsy.

Jessie Batterton
Swede Carlson of Omaha in the Western League beaned Springfield's 19-year-old second baseman Jessie Batterton on July 2, 1933, fracturing his skull. Batterton died the next day following surgery. He never regained consciousness.

William Bedford
Cuban Giants second baseman William Bedford of the Negro leagues was hit by lightning and died at Inlet Park in Atlantic City in 1909.

Bill Bradley
Bill Bradley and Jimmy Collins were the best third basemen in baseball during the first decade of the 20th century. Bradley, with Cleveland, led the league 16 times in major fielding categories, including four times in fielding percentage.

Prior to a pitch that broke his arm in 1906, Bradley had a career .298 batting average. After the beaning and a bout with typhoid fever, he hit a mere .216 over his last six seasons. Bradley later managed in the Federal League and scouted for the Indians for decades.

Gus Brooks
Page Fence Giants center fielder Gus Brooks died on the field of a heart attack while chasing a fly ball in 1890. To increase their gate attraction, black teams often performed various skits and clowning acts. This practice led many in the stands to initially view Brooks' collapse as just another performance.

Ray Brubaker
51-year-old Terre Haute manager Ray Brubaker died in the dugout of heart failure on May 1, 1947. The Three-I League team was in Waterloo, Iowa, at the time. He had been in the minors since 1912 and spent 15 years with the Oakland Oaks of the Pacific Coast League, mainly as an infielder.

Thomas Burke
Left fielder Thomas Burke, of Lynn in the New England League, was hit in the head by a Joe Yeager, of Fall River, pitch in the sixth inning on August 9, 1906, fracturing his skull. The speedy Boston University star immediately collapsed and was caught by the umpire. Burke passed away two days later, never regaining consciousness. He was studying law during his off-seasons.

Career-Ending Beanings
The following is an incomplete list of additional careers that were shortened by a beaning:

Pat Deasley	Jesse Duryea
Glenn Gardner	Bill Hobbs
Masaru Koda (Japan)	Bobby LaMotte
Hank Leiber	Cass Michaels
Reggie Richter	Al Schellhase
Ralph Shinners	

White Sox third baseman Cass Michaels was hit in the head by a Marian Fricano fastball on August 27, 1954. He was carried off the field and listed in critical condition. Michaels was even given the last rites. He recovered but his career was over at age 27.

Ed Cermak
Cotton States League umpire Ed Cermak died after taking a foul tip to the throat on November 23, 1911. He was 29 years old.

Frank Chance
Hall of Famer and Chicago baseball legend Frank Chance was bothered by a succession of beanings because of his aggressiveness at the plate. The repeated blows to his head forced him out of the starting lineup after the 1908 season. His hearing was diminished and he suffered blinding headaches, which frequently kept the cleanup hitter off the field. Luckily, the "Peerless Leader" was able to maintain his field management duties with the Cubs that he had attained at age 27 in 1905.

Just before taking over the New York Yankees in 1913, Chance had surgery to alleviate blood clots affecting his headaches, though the injuries forced him to retire from the majors in 1914. From 1916–18, Chance was part-owner of the Pacific Coast League Los Angeles Angels. He returned to the show in 1923 to lead the hapless Boston Red Sox that owner Harry Frazee had dismantled. He quipped to a reporter in a preseason interview that they ". . . will unquestionably finish last." And they did. Chance was fired, hired by the White Sox but retired again due to ill health and asthma in 1924. He died that September just past his 47th birthday.

Ray Chapman

Cleveland's Ray Chapman was an excellent shortstop who led his league in putouts and range three times and once in games and assists. He played "inside baseball" well by getting on base, advancing runners, and scoring. To this end, he led the league in runs and walks in 1918 and three times in sacrifice hits. His 52 stolen bases in 1917 was a club record until eclipsed in 1980. Chapman is the only man to die by being hit with a baseball during a major league contest.

The righthander came to the plate against the Yankees Carl Mays on August 16, 1920, at the Polo Grounds. The Yankees shared the Polo Grounds with the Giants prior to the opening of Yankee Stadium in 1923. As usual, Chapman crouched tight to the plate. Mays with his submarine delivery threw the ball, it sailed not too far out of the strike zone, Chapman froze, and the ball hit him on the left temple. Mays fielded the ball and threw to first for a force-out, thinking it made contact with the bat. Then, he noticed Chapman on the ground. The Yankees physician was summoned and applied ice to the injury. Chapman rose and began walking to the clubhouse in center field but collapsed near second base.

Chapman was carted off the field. Never regaining consciousness, the middle infielder died in a New York hospital twelve hours later. Blame was immediately placed on the already-despised Mays and his tricky delivery. Accusations were eventually flung at the umpires, club owners, and American League president Ban Johnson. As a result, baseball altered its policy concerning the use of dirty balls. No longer would it be acceptable for a dirty, nicked, or scuffed ball to remain in play. All balls hit into the stands would remain as souvenirs, departing from custom at most parks. To illustrate, the National League used 22,000 balls in 1919 but the number rose to 54,000 five years later. As a side note, batting helmets were not commonplace in the majors until the 1950s.

Hitting .303 with 97 runs at the time, Chapman was replaced at shortstop by future Hall of Famer Joe Sewell. The Indians edged the White Sox for the pennant. The resulting rule changes accounted for the power surge and increased batting averages during the 1920s, as much as the free-swinging style of Babe Ruth and the outlawing of the spitter.

Mickey Cochrane

Mickey Cochrane is regarded as one of the top catchers in major league history. Not only did he bat .320 for his career but he also led the league in every major defensive category at least once. He led in putouts six times, games five times, and assists and double plays twice. Eight times in 13 seasons, the lefthanded batter hit over .319. Cochrane amassed 80+ RBIs five times while fanning only 217 times in 5,169 at bats.

Twice the backstop was named American League MVP and led his team five times to the pennant. "Black Mike" was a key member of the A's dynasty of 1929–31.

Connie Mack disassembled his team once again, sending Cochrane to Detroit in '34. That year, he became a player–manager at age of 31 and won the MVP award. Cochrane immediately led his team to two pennants and a world championship in 1935, the franchise's first postseason appearances in 25 years.

On May 25, 1937, Yankee righthander Bump Hadley beaned Cochrane on his first at-bat after a prior home run off the pitcher. His skull fractured in three places. Cochrane lay unconscious for 10 days. His playing career was over but he continued to act as field manager. Cochrane left baseball in 1938, claiming the fire was gone. Hall of Fame enshrinement took place in 1947. He was the first lefthanded-hitting catcher elected to Cooperstown. Only Bill Dickey and Yogi Berra have followed.

Earle Combs

Lefthanded batter Earle Combs was the center fielder and leadoff hitter for the power-house Yankees "Murderers' Row" teams. His .325 batting average, .397 on-base percentage, and bunting ability proved to be essential to the run producing of the Babe Ruth/Lou Gehrig tandem. In 11 full seasons, from 1924–35, Combs scored an amazing 1,186 times. In four World Series appearances, he batted .350 and scored 17 runs.

On July 24, 1934, Combs smashed into the concrete center field wall at Sportsman's Park in St. Louis, fracturing his skull, kneecap, and shoulder. It was several hours before he regained consciousness. The outfielder returned in 1935 as a player–coach but retired from the active roster after 89 games at the age of 36. The Hall of Fame inducted the Yankee in 1970.

Tony Conigliaro

Tony Conigliaro immediately became a fan favorite in his hometown Boston after 24 rookie home runs in 1964. The next year, he became the youngest man, at 20, to lead the league with 32, 23 of them at Fenway. Another 28 homers and 93 RBIs in 1966 put Tony C on his way to becoming the youngest to reach 100 dingers.

Batting .287 with 20 homers and 67 RBIs on August 18, 1967, Conigliaro came to the plate in the fourth inning versus the Angels Jack Hamilton. A fastball sailed, breaking his cheekbone and blinding him in the left eye. He would be in the hospital much of the rest of the season and miss 1968 completely. Boston signed free agent Ken Harrelson at the end of August 1967 to replace Tony C's bat and continue the drive for the pennant.

With one eye, he won Comeback Player of the Year in 1969, posting 20 home runs and 82 RBIs. The following year, he notched an impressive 36 HR and 116 RBIs. Rarely playing healthy, Conigliaro also suffered a broken wrist, hand, shoulder blade, and fingers during his career.

He was shuffled to California in 1971 and announced his retirement in July after 74 games due to vision impairment. An ill-advised comeback in '75 lasted only 21 games. Off the field, Conigliaro recorded music, even singing a duet with Dionne Warwick. Sadly, he suffered an incapacitating heart attack in 1982 that left him bedridden until his death in 1990 at age 45.

Richard Conway

The Twins Falls Cowboys (Idaho), of the Pioneer League, rookie catcher Richard Conway was playing first during pregame drills on June 29, 1951. While he was fielding a popup, another ball slammed into his chest above his heart. The blow proved to be fatal to the 19-year-old.

Bill Craig

Steubenville pitcher Bill Craig of the Ohio–Pennsylvania League landed awkwardly trying to break off a curve on August 15, 1912. He broke his leg, which caused an internal rupture. It proved fatal.

Mario Cuomo

The Pittsburgh Pirates gave Mario Cuomo a $2,000 bonus to sign in 1951. He was assigned to Class-D Brunswick (Georgia). Hitting over .350 in '52, the center fielder broke his wrist crashing into the outfield wall. Later that year, a beaning ended his career. Hospitalized for two weeks, Cuomo suffered a blood clot. Doctors warned of additional injuries and he quit the game after batting .244 with 26 RBIs in 81 games.

Cuomo entered law school and went on to become Governor of New York in 1983. As the Democratic nominee in 1988, he would challenge George Bush for the presidency. Cuomo also pushed for major league expansion into Buffalo.

Stormy Davis

20-year-old Ballinger outfielder James "Stormy" Davis, of the Longhorn League, was beaned in the skull on July 3, 1947. He died a week later from a brain hemorrhage. Davis had been pounding the ball, posting 17 home runs and 64 RBIs in only 48 games.

Jay Hanna Dean

As great a pitcher as he was in his brief career, Dizzy Dean is remembered today as much for his engaging personality and grammatical botches. In his first six seasons, the four-time All-Star won 133 games, struck out 1,090 batters, and dominated in 23 shutouts. On July 30, 1933, Dean fanned 17 Cubs. In '34, the St. Louis Cardinal won the MVP award, became the last 30-game victor in the National League and won two games in the World Series versus the Tigers. Again, he dominated in 1935 and '36, posting 52 more victories

The Indians Earl Averill smashed a line drive off Dean's left foot in the first inning of the 1937 All-Star Game, breaking the small toe. Dean continued to pitch three more innings before leaving the game. He tried to come back too early while wearing a splint and a larger shoe. The altered delivery ruined his pitching arm and brought on bursitis. Dean would win only 17 more contests. Van Lingle Mungo's career was also derailed during that midsummer classic.

General Manager Branch Rickey quickly dumped him off to the Cubs. Dean attempted to sue Cardinals management for rushing him back too early from the injury but Judge Landis talked him out of it.

Dean pitched in parts of five more seasons but had lost his overpowering fastball and dazzling curve. His reputation was enough to gain Hall of Fame recognition in 1953 despite only 150 career victories.

Johnny Dodge
Former National League infielder Johnny Dodge, then with Mobile in the Southern Association, was beaned by a Shotgun Rogers, of Nashville, fastball on June 18, 1916. The ball crept inside on Dodge who was apparently expecting a curve and fractured the 27-year-old's skull. He immediately collapsed and died the next day from the concussion. Seemingly unaffected, Rogers then tossed five straight shutouts.

Mike Dorgan
Outfielder Mike Dorgan of the New York Giants hit .326 in 1885. Two years later, he scaled the fence to a make game-saving catch. Landing, Dorgan injured his knee. His career was effectively over, though he later appeared in 33 games for the American Association. Dorgan had previously missed the entire '82 season after being black-listed for insubordination.

Cal Drummond
Cal Drummond umpired in the American League from 1960–69. He fell ill after a game between the Orioles and Angels on June 10, 1969. Working behind the plate, Drummond may have taken a foul ball to the mask that caused the injury. He eventually underwent surgery to remove a blood clot in his brain.

Following rehabilitation, Drummond was working himself into shape in the minors. He collapsed in an American Association dugout during a game in early May 1970 and never recovered. The arbiter died from a cerebral hemorrhage at age 52.

Skeeter Ebnet
Winnipeg, of the Northern League, shortstop Linus "Skeeter" Ebnet passed away on July 21, 1938, five days after being beaned in a game versus Grand Forks pitcher Dutch Clawson. The 23-year-old's skull was fractured.

Alfredo Edmead
Santo Domingo-native Alfredo Edmead was a rookie in 1974 in the Pirates organization, playing for Salem in the Carolina League. In a game on August 22 versus Rocky Mount, the right fielder collided with second baseman Pablo Cruz while fielding a popup. Edmead took a knee to the head. He died in the hospital after being briefly revived. The 18-year-old was hitting .313 and had that day stolen his 60th and 61st bases.

Chico Fernandez
Baltimore farmhand infielder–coach Chico Fernandez, of Rochester, was beaned above the left ear on August 3, 1969, by a Larry Bearnarth, of Tidewater, sidearm fastball. An operation inserted a metal plate in his skull. It was 11 days before he

awoke and another 18 months before he could speak. He had appeared in 24 games with the Orioles the previous summer.

Jose Figarola
Cuban catcher Jose Figarola died when hit in the chest by a Jose Mendez pitch during batting practice in late 1915 in Havana. He was in his 12th Negro league season.

Tom Finley
Philadelphia Stars third baseman Tom Finley died from a spike wound in the inaugural season of the renewed Negro National League in 1933.

Phil Forney
Western Association umpire Phil Forney was immediately paralyzed and died after being hit by a ball above the left eye in 1910.

Chick Galloway
Chick Galloway joined the Tigers in 1928 after nine seasons as Connie Mack's shortstop. A pitch by Josh Billings fractured his skull during batting practice after his 53rd game of the year and ended his career.

Charlie Harrington
Dallas, of the Texas League, pitcher Charlie Harrington was hit in the stomach by a batted ball on the mound on July 5, 1902. He made the play at first but then collapsed and soon died.

Louis Henke
Atlanta, of the Southern League, first baseman Louis Henke put a ball in play and broke for first in a game on August 14, 1885. At first, he crashed into the knee of Nashville first baseman Marr. Henke collapsed and was led to the players' tent by his manager to obtain medical attention. He died the next day from a ruptured liver.

Frank Herbert
Dayton, of the Central League, infielder Frank Herbert crashed into Alvoy Spangler while trying to get to first on July 7, 1904. He died two days later.

Gerald Highfill
Wenatchee, Washington, of the Class-A Northwest League, batboy Gerald Highfill was killed after being hit by a line drive during pregame drills. He was 13 years old.

Ralph Hodgin
On April 21, 1947, White Sox outfielder Ralph Hodgin suffered a concussion after being beaned by Tiger ace Hal Newhouser. The career .285 hitter lost his aggressiveness at the plate and retired the following season.

Harold Jensen

Lightning struck first baseman Harold Jensen, of Urbana, Ohio, in the Miami Valley League, in the first inning on August 7, 1949. He was killed instantly. Three other teammates were knocked unconscious but recovered.

Otis Johnson

Dothan player Otis Johnson died after being beaned by Headland's Lefty Clifton in a Class-D Alabama–Florida League game on June 2, 1951. The 24-year-old was tearing up the league with a .393 average and 10 home runs at the time. In his next start, Clifton no-hit a tentative Panama City club.

Hal Lanier

Giants' infielder and future manager Hal Lanier was beaned in 1965, sparking a long-time battle with epilepsy.

Julio LeBlanc

Cuban pitcher Julio LeBlanc joined the Negro leagues in 1919 when his team, the Cuban Stars, signed on with Rube Foster's Negro National League. Playing winter ball in Havana, LeBlanc was beaten to death with a bat by fellow ballplayer Antonio Susini in February 1922.

Gardner Lowe

Butte pitcher Gardner Lowe succumbed to an infection on February 16, 1914. It might have been caused by a beaning the previous summer. (Note: penicillin was not in general use until the end of World War II.)

George McBride

Washington Senator George McBride was the premier American League shortstop of his era. Actually, the Senators were officially known as the Nationals, often called the Nats, prior to 1957. McBride led the league six times in double plays, five times in fielding average, four times in games, three times in putouts, and once in assists and range. Although the famed double-play combination of Tinker to Evers to Chance only copped one double-play crown between them (in fact, they only turned 56 double plays total in the pennant years 1906–10), McBride captured every one from 1908–12 and again in '14. He was your typical good-field, no-hit shortstop. After 16 years in the big leagues, his career batting average resided at a mere .218 and never did rise above .235.

McBride retired as an active player after the 1920 season and took over the reigns of the club. During the 1921 campaign, he was hit in the face by a ball in batting practice. Paralysis resulted on one side of his face. He subsequently suffered a nervous breakdown and retired.

Don McMahon

Long-time relief pitcher Don McMahon appeared in 874 games from 1957–74. He compiled a 90-68 record with 153 saves and a 2.96 ERA. McMahon pitched with no record in three World Series, including five shutout innings in three games during the Braves victory over the Yankees in 1957.

Tossing batting practice with the Dodgers in 1987, the 57-year-old scout collapsed on the mound. He died on July 22.

John McSherry

Long-time (1971–96) National League umpire John McSherry died behind home plate following a heart attack on Opening Day 1996 in Cincinnati.

Ducky Medwick

St. Louis Cardinal Joe Medwick was one of the most feared righthanded batters of the 1930s. As a rookie in '33, he knocked in 98 runs. In 1936, he posted an incredible 64 doubles. All else fails to compare with his '37 season. That year, Medwick won the Triple Crown and the National League MVP award while also topping the league in games, at-bats, hits, doubles, total bases, runs, slugging average, and fielding average. The 10-time All-Star would lead the National League in RBIs from 1936–38 and total bases from 1935–37. Rogers Hornsby, 1920–22, is the only other man to lead his league three consecutive seasons in RBIs.

Medwick was a vital cog of the Gas House Gang of the 1930s that featured Hall of Famers 1B Jim Bottomley, 1B Johnny Mize, 1B Walter Alston, 2B Frankie Frisch, LF Chick Hafey, 2B Hornsby, SS Leo Durocher, RHP Dazzy Vance, RHP Dizzy Dean, RHP Burleigh Grimes, and RHP Jesse Haines.

Ducky was combative on and off the field. At various times, Medwick was known to fight teammates Tex Carlton, Rip Collins, and Ed Heusser. He also engaged in some famous run-ins with Dizzy Dean. And if he fought with teammates, imagine Medwick's competitive blowups with opponents. His surly temper and resulting flare-ups often led to spats with fans and reporters, as well. During the 7th game of the 1934 World Series, he slid in hard at third, starting a fight. Commissioner Landis removed him from the game for his own safety, as fans were about to riot.

From 1933–39, Medwick knocked in an incredible 861 runs. St. Louis fans were shocked when their star was pedaled to the Brooklyn Dodgers in the middle of the 1940 season. Six days later, on June 12, he was beaned by those very Cardinals.

Prior to the game, Medwick and Dodgers manager Leo Durocher argued with Cardinals pitcher and former teammate Bob Bowman at the hotel. As soon as Medwick stepped to the plate, Bowman put the ball in his left temple. Ducky was rendered unconscious and carried off the field. New York police had to escort Bowman from the field. Dodgers' president Larry MacPhail went through the roof. Eventually, a Ford Frick investigation proved fruitless.

Bowman blamed the incident on Dodgers coach Charlie Dressen who was stealing signs. Dressen would whistle every time he picked off the sign for a curve ball. Bowman decided to cross him up and threw a fastball instead, high and tight. Medwick dove into what he thought was a curve and took a shot to the head instead. Remember, players did not yet wear helmets.

Medwick's bat was never as potent again. Over the last nine years of his career, Medwick managed 510 RBIs, good production but no longer great. His home run power also sharply declined. Ducky retired in 1948 with a career batting average of .324 and was elected to the Hall of Fame 20 years later.

Cass Michaels
See Career-Ending Beanings

Clyde Nelson
Infielder Clyde Nelson played in the Negro leagues from 1939 until his death on July 25, 1949. The Indianapolis Clown collapsed on the field of an apparent heart attack as he was positioning under a fly ball.

Paul O'Dea
A promising young lefthanded hitter with solid minor league credentials, Paul O'Dea went blind in his right eye in a spring training accident in 1940. Though he missed the rest of the season, O'Dea returned to the minors in '41. The Indians brought up the outfielder in 1944 and he hit .318 in 76 games in his rookie season. O'Dea lost his roster spot when the regulars returned from the war in '46. He finished with a .272 batting average in 400 at-bats.

James Phelps
Outfielder James Phelps, with an independent Rayville club, made a game-saving catch in the eighth inning on July 22, 1909, in Monroe, Louisiana. Unfortunately, he backed into a bog doing so and was bitten by a water snake. His leg swelled but Phelps finished the game. He died the next day. It was not the first snake-bite death at that park.

Charles Pinkney
A pitch struck Dayton second baseman Charles Pinkney of the Central League in the head in September 1909. The blow proved fatal to the 22-year-old.

Doc Powers
Mike Powers was Eddie Plank's personal catcher for the Philadelphia Athletics. In the inaugural game at Shibe Park in April 1909, he crashed into the wall behind home plate while chasing a foul ball. Other stories suggest he just dove for a foul ball. Either way, the catcher thought he pulled a stomach muscle; however, two weeks and three operations later, Powers died of gangrene of the bowels. The following year, a benefit game raised $8,000 for his widow and children. This little-known incident should surely be recognized on par with the Ray Chapman case.

Powers was a rarity in early 20th-century baseball. He had graduated from Holy Cross and was enrolled at Notre Dame Medical School.

Phil Reccius
Phil Reccius died in February 1903, nine years after being beaned. The injury fractured his skull and pressed it against his brain, causing continued difficulties. He

never fully recovered. Reccius pitched and played the infield off and on for eight years in the American Association during the 1880s.

Pete Reiser

Pete Reiser's hard play produced separated shoulders, broken ankles, torn cartilage and muscles in his left leg and knee, a broken elbow, a fractured skull, and numerous concussions. Eleven times he was carried off the field. The warning track and padded outfield walls were developed to protect future Pete Reisers.

The Cardinals began scouting him at age 12. Just prior to the 1938 season, Reiser was one of 74 low minor leaguers that Judge Landis freed from their contract with the St. Louis Cardinals in his continuing feud with Branch Rickey and the farm system. Supposedly, Rickey had struck a covert deal with Larry MacPhail to hide Pistol Pete in the Dodger organization until things quieted down and he could be retrieved. Reiser's aggressive style garnered too much attention for MacPhail to honor the deal. His speed would be the standard by which the Dodgers judged all future talent. In full baseball uniform, Reiser sprint a 9.8-second 100-yard dash. In 1946, the speedster set the record with seven steals of home, later matched by Rod Carew.

Reiser's first full season in 1941 saw him lead the league in batting with a .343 average, doubles, triples, runs, total bases, HBP, and slugging average. The center fielder sparked the Dodgers to their first pennant since 1920. Batting .381 on July 2, 1942, Reiser ran full speed into the concrete wall in St. Louis chasing an Enos Slaughter shot. Though a fractured skull, concussion, and separated shoulder could not keep him from the All-Star Game four days later, dizziness plagued him the rest of his life. Reiser was offered the last rites after a similar accident in 1947 that caused temporary paralysis. Later that season, he returned and broke his ankle in the World Series.

At age 28, Reiser never played regularly again. He averaged only 86 games a year over his 10-year career.

Goody Rosen

Goody Rosen was given a second chance in the major leagues during World War II and produced. In 1945, the Brooklyn Dodger hit .325 with 126 runs and 75 RBIs. He also finished second in runs, hits, and total bases and third in batting average and triples. Nonetheless, the Dodgers traded him after the regulars returned to the lineup.

In his 100th game with the Giants in 1946, Rosen crashed into the outfield wall, sustaining a career-ending clavicle injury at age 34.

Jim Scoggins

Jim Scoggins had a cup of coffee in the bigs with the White Sox in 1913. Ten years later in the minors, he died in August 1923 from a brain injury, six weeks after being beaned. The lefthanded pitcher was 32 years old.

Herb Score

A liner up the middle in 1957 changed the entire complexion of southpaw Herb Score's pitching career. The subsequent layoff and arm trouble the following year destroyed his effectiveness.

Score was a phenom in high school. Fourteen of the 16 major league clubs hounded him. He chose Cleveland for a lesser bonus of $60,000 because of his close relationship with scout Cy Slapnicka. The lefthander spent three years in the minors conquering his control problems, even being named Minor League Player of the Year in 1953.

In '55, Score joined the American League and set the rookie record with a league-leading 245 strikeouts to go with a 16-10 record and 2.85 ERA. On May 1, Score fanned nine Red Sox in the first three innings, 16 in all that day. Obviously, he won the Rookie of the Year Award.

The following year, the Indian went 20-9 with a 2.53 ERA and a league-best five shutouts and 263 Ks. At age 23, Score started the All-Star Game for the American League. After two-plus years, Score's record stood at 38-20 with 547 strikeouts and a meager 2.63 ERA. He would win only 17 more times.

In a night game on May 7, 1957, the second batter, New York Yankee Gil McDougald, screamed one back to the box into Score's face, shattering his cheekbone. Unfortunately, the great pitching technique made him vulnerable in the follow-through. The hurler was unable to defend himself. Eight days in a dark hospital room motionless saved his eye. Returning the following spring, the southpaw lost all effectiveness. Five years later, the 29-year-old retired. Score became a long-time Indians announcer.

Pete Scott

Pete Scott was a solid hitter, batting .303 in 208 major league games. 1928 found him in a Pirates uniform trying to break into an outfield that already included both the Hall of Fame Waner brothers. Chasing a deep fly ball at Forbes Field, Scott crashed into the outfield wall. The resulting concussion ended his promising career after only three seasons.

Ron Simms

Gulf Coast League infielder Ron Simms was beaned in the face in his first professional game on June 20, 1988. Surgeons had to remove his left eye.

Mac Smith

Hagerstown catcher Mac Smith of the Piedmont League had been fighting malaria for some time. Rapping a single in the fifth inning of a game against Portsmouth on July 2, 1954, he collapsed on the base path and died.

Moose Solters

Heavy-hitting outfielder Moose Solters knocked in 355 RBIs from 1935–37 with three different American League teams. With Cleveland on July 7, 1935, he smacked three home runs against the Browns. One day during batting practice, he waved to someone in the stands and was beaned from behind. The freak accident caused him to gradually go blind.

Andy Strong
Standing in center field during the sixth inning of an Evangeline League game in Alexandria, Louisiana, on June 16, 1951, Crowley outfielder Andy Strong was hit by a bolt of lightning. The 23-year-old died instantly. At the time, the summer clouds did not appear threatening.

Bill Taylor
Minor leaguer pitcher Bill Taylor died in a Cincinnati hospital soon after being beaned on September 13, 1905.

Charles Tenhuy
Charles Tenhuy, with Dayton in the Central League, was beaned by pitcher Hagerman of Grand Rapids on September 24, 1909. The resulting fractured skull caused his demise.

George Thach
Northern League second baseman George Thach, of Superior, died in Winnipeg five days after a beaning on August 27, 1936. The opposing pitcher was Alex Uffelman. The 25-year-old never regained consciousness.

Dickie Thon
Houston shortstop Dickie Thon was looking forward to a bright career. He had increased his batting average his first four years, culminating in a breakthrough 1983 when he hit .286 with 20 homers, 79 RBIs, 81 runs, and 34 stolen bases. He had even made the All-Star team.

In early April the following year, a Mike Torrez fastball ended Thon's season after only five games. A bright career was derailed. Suffering headaches, blurred vision, and nausea, the Astro couldn't return to the game until mid-1985. Struggling, Thon was shipped to the Padres, then the Phillies, until he finally became a regular again in '89.

Charlie Tumelty
Minor leaguer Charlie Tumelty died after a collision at home plate in 1938. He was 25 years old.

Umpires
Umpires have always been the objects of wrath from fans and players alike. National League president John Heydler felt that conditions were never as bad as "when the (1890s) Orioles were flying high." However, incidents still abound. In 1906, a thrown bottle fractured Bill McLean's skull. Bill Evans was likewise injured the following year at Sportsman's Park in St. Louis.

Bobby Valentine
Bobby Valentine was a high school football star who chose baseball instead. He was the fifth player selected in the June 1968 free agent draft, by the Dodgers. In '70, he lit up the Pacific Coast League with a .340 average and 211 hits to win the PCL Player

of the Year Award. He led the league in batting, runs, doubles, triples, and total bases. In the playoffs, he was beaned, breaking his cheekbone. In 1971, he joined the parent club as a utility player.

The hard-nosed player broke his right leg in two places on May 17, 1973, after crashing into the outfield wall at Anaheim Stadium. His spikes caught in the wall while leaping for a Dick Green home run. Valentine also suffered a serious spinal fracture. The accident left his leg misshapen and hastened the end of his active career. Again, in June 1974, he separated his shoulder. Valentine hung around part-time until 1979 but he was no longer productive.

In 1985, he became the Texas Rangers field manager. In 1995, Valentine became the first man to manage in Japan, with the Chiba Lotte Marines, and in the majors. Leo Durocher had actually been hired by Yokohama in 1976 to lead the Whales but he fell ill with hepatitis and never left the States. Valentine later returned to Chiba and won the Japan Series in 2005.

Herb Whitney

Catcher Herb Whitley, with Burlington in the Iowa State League, was killed by a Fred Evans, of Waterloo, fastball on June 24, 1906. The resulting skull fracture led to his death three days later.

Bill Williams

A broken leg suffered in a play at home plate in 1987 helped hasten the end of National League umpire Bill Williams' 25-year career.

Don Zimmer

Don Zimmer's career in baseball extends 50+ years on the field as a player, coach, and manager. It almost ended in 1953. On July 7, in the American Association, Jim Kirk beaned him. Zim lay unconscious, near death for two weeks. It was another six before he could speak. Zimmer finally left the hospital 44 pounds lighter with four screws in his skull. Another fastball cracked his cheekbone in 1956 while with Brooklyn.

"Popeye" recovered to have a quality, 12-year major league career as a utility player. Zim also played in Japan for the Toei Flyers when his major league career ended in '65. After a stint as manager for four minor league teams, he rejoined the majors as a coach for Montreal. In 1972, Zim was named manager of the Padres, replacing Preston Gomez. Managing his fourth team in 1989, he finally won a division title with the Cubs, led by control specialist Greg Maddux.

In 1999, while Yankee skipper Joe Torre underwent cancer treatment, Zimmer guided the team for 36 games. And he was still in the dugout after the turn of the century as a bench coach for yet another Yankee dynasty.

CHAPTER SEVEN

Football Opportunities

The NFL was known as the American Professional Football Association from 1920–21. The AAFC merged with the NFL for the 1950 season with Baltimore, Cleveland, and San Francisco being absorbed. Other players were reshuffled with the Browns and Giants receiving the biggest push. The AFL was formally melded into a revamped NFL in 1970. No teams were dropped. The AFL would form the American Football Conference and the NFL would comprise the National Football Conference. Pittsburgh, Baltimore, and Cleveland volunteered to shift to the AFC to even the conferences at 13 teams apiece. The following is a list of professional football leagues:

NFL	National Football League	1902
NFL	National Football League	1920–present
AFL	American Football League	1926
AFL	American Football League	1936–37
AFL	American Football League	1940–41
AAFC	All-American Football Conference	1946–49
AFL	American Football League	1960–69

Ed Abbaticchio

The first major hotbed for professional football was in eastern Ohio and western Pennsylvania in the late 1890s. The four-way rivalry between Latrobe, Canton, Massillon, and Greensburg later spurred the development of the modern game. To illustrate, the Football Hall of Fame resides in Canton. Ed Abbaticchio played fullback for Latrobe from 1895–1900. He is also reputed to be the first to boot a spiral punt. Because baseball bred a much more hospitable lifestyle, Abby played 28 games at third base for the Philadelphia Phillies from 1897–98 and was later picked up by the Boston Braves in 1903.

Abby led the National League in putouts both as a second baseman (1903) and as a shortstop (1905). In 1907, he caught on with Pittsburgh, sharing the keystone with Honus Wagner. The following year, he played a controversial part (on top of the Merkle incident) in the tight National League pennant race, whereby the Giants and Cubs tied with the Pirates finishing a half game out. Abby poked an apparent grand slam to defeat the Cubs late in the season but it was called foul. Later, in court, a woman who was beaned with the shot (and consequently suing) swore she was in fair territory. A Pittsburgh victory would have led to a three-way tie.

Abby was one of the first big name Italians in the majors. In all, he batted .254 in 3,000 at bats through 1910.

Red Badgro

Outfielder Red Badgro played part-time for the St. Louis Browns in 1929–30, batting .257. He had previously starred at end for the University of Southern California and played in the NFL with the New York Yankees from 1927–28. After leaving baseball, Badgro returned to the NFL for the New York Giants and Brooklyn Dodgers from 1930–36. His career highlight came when his Giants won the NFL championship in 1934. That year he led the NFL in receiving. Badgro entered Canton, the Pro Football Hall of Fame, in 1981.

Sammy Baugh

Sammy Baugh played 53 games at shortstop in the American Association and International League in 1938, hitting an even .200. Signed by Rogers Hornsby, he was merely one of hundreds of Branch Rickey's farmhands. On the gridiron, "Slingin' Sammy" revolutionized the game.

Baugh was an All-American at Texas Christian University in 1935 and '36 before joining the Washington Redskins in the NFL in 1937. By the end of his career 16 years later, he held every passing mark in the game. In fact, Baugh was the catalyst in transforming professional football from a mainly running game, almost infantry like, to one in which the forward pass electrified the offense.

Not only was Baugh the first great passing quarterback, he is still viewed by many as the best punter the game has seen. In 1943 alone, he led the league in passing, punting and interceptions caught. It wasn't until the Redskins shifted to the T-formation in 1944 that Baugh's days as a defensive back ended.

As a rookie, Baugh led the Skins to the NFL championship and again in 1942. Baugh retired in 1952 and later coached in the American Football League. He was elected to both the College and Pro Football Hall of Fames.

Cedric Benson

Chicago Bears 2005 NFL draftee Cedric Benson appeared in nine games in the Dodgers organization in 2002.

Charlie Berry

Reserve catcher Charlie Berry played eleven seasons in the American League from 1925–38 and coached for the Athletics, 1936–40. He also played in the NFL for two seasons with the Pottsville Maroons from 1925–26. In 1925, Berry led the league in scoring, 74, with six touchdowns, 29 extra points, and three field goals.

After retirement, Berry umpired in the American League for 21 years, 1942–62, and refereed in the NFL for 24 seasons. He was the head linesman during the famous 1958 championship game.

Larry Bettencourt

Larry Bettencourt played in parts of three seasons with the St. Louis Browns from 1928–32. In 1933, he also played two games in the NFL as center for the Green Bay Packers. He was elected to the College Football Hall of Fame out of St. Mary's College in California. Bettencourt toiled in the minors through 1944. He won the Triple Crown in the Class-C Northern League in 1941.

Hugo Bezdek

Hugo Bezdek was a powerful fullback for Amos Alonzo Stagg's University of Chicago teams from 1902–05. The following season, he began coaching college football himself at the University of Oregon, then at the University of Arkansas and at Mare Island, ultimately winning the Rose Bowl in 1917 and '18.

Later, Bezdek, who never played baseball but did work as a scout on the West Coast and as Pittsburgh's business manager, was hired by Barney Dreyfuss to manage the Pirates from 1917–19. He moved the team into the first division from last place his final two years. He left the majors to coach baseball and football at Penn State through 1929. Bezdek also coached the expansion Cleveland Rams of the National Football League in 1937. He is the only man to manage in MLB and coach in the NFL.

Josh Booty

Josh Booty was drafted by the Florida Marlins in the first round in 1994 out of high school and played five seasons in their organization. The third baseman made the parent club from 1996–98, appearing in thirteen games. He then went to LSU and was drafted by the Seattle Seahawks in 2001. The backup quarterback was cut before the season and joined the Cleveland Browns, remaining on their roster through 2003; however, he never took a snap.

Tom Brady

High school catcher Tom Brady was drafted in the 18th round by the Montreal Expos in 1995. Shunning baseball, Brady went on to quarterback the New England Patriots to three Super Bowl championships.

Bubby Brister

The Detroit Tigers drafted Bubby Brister out of high school in 1981. After 39 games playing shortstop and outfield with Bristol in the Appalachian League, he left baseball to enroll at Tulane in 1982. The quarterback joined the Pittsburgh Steelers in 1986 at 24 years old. He played in the NFL through 2000.

Tom Brookshier

Seven-year Philadelphia Eagles defensive back Tom Brookshier pitched in 11 games with Roswell in the Longhorn League in 1954, amassing a 7-1 record. Later, he was a longtime television football analyst for CBS.

Tom Brown

Tom Brown was the first major leaguer to play in the Super Bowl. The defensive back helped the Packers take the first two. He had played in 61 games for the Washington Senators in 1963.

Isaac Byrd

Isaac Byrd was drafted by the St. Louis Cardinals in 1996 and played a year in their system. The wide receiver out of Kansas played in the NFL from 1997–2002 for Tennessee and Carolina.

Charlie Caldwell

Charlie Caldwell pitched in three games for the Yankees in 1925. Throwing batting practice one day, he beaned first baseman Wally Pipp. In turn, Lou Gehrig replaced Pipp in the lineup. Gehrig wouldn't miss another game until May 1939.

Caldwell went on to coach Princeton football, where he had been its star fullback from 1922–24, to two consecutive undefeated seasons in 1950–51. His final coaching record lies at 146-67-9, prompting election to the College Football Hall of Fame.

Joe Carr

Joe Carr organized and promoted semi-pro and minor league baseball in his native Ohio from 1901 until his death in 1939. From 1933 on, he was the promotional director of the minors, helping the National Association expand from 12 to 41 leagues during the Depression. Carr was also a founder and president of the American Basketball League in 1925.

In football, he formed the Columbus Panhandles in 1904 and made them one of the strongest gridiron clubs in the nation for years. In 1920, they became one of the charter members of the NFL. He assumed the presidency of the league the following year and remained there until his death. He was the first true giant administrator in NFL history, facing and standing firmly behind his decisions as William Hulbert, Ban Johnson and Rube Foster did for their fledgling organizations. Carr was elected to the Pro Football Hall of Fame in 1963.

Quincy Carter

Quincy Carter played right field in the Cubs organization from 1996–99. He was originally signed for $450,000. The University of Georgia quarterback quit baseball to seek a career in the NFL.

Hopalong Cassady

Ohio State halfback Hopalong Cassady won the Heisman Trophy and was named AP Athlete of the Year in 1955. He was approached by the New York Yankees but signed with the NFL instead. He spent eight seasons there, mostly with the Detroit Lions. Cassady later coached in the minors and scouted as well.

Chuck Corgan

Chuck Corgan joined the National Football League out of Arkansas University in 1924 and played until he became ill in 1927. Likewise, the middle infielder appeared in 33 games for the Brooklyn Dodgers in 1925 and '27. On June 13, 1928, Corgan succumbed to stomach cancer at age 25.

Fred Crolius

See Pennsylvania, 1902

Paddy Driscoll

Paddy Driscoll played 13 games in the infield for the Chicago Cubs in 1917. It ended his amateur career as a star halfback and kicker at Northwestern University. After WWI, he helped Great Lakes win the Rose Bowl in 1919.

The following year, Driscoll became a charter member of the NFL as quarterback and halfback for George Halas' Decatur Staleys and the Chicago Cardinals. He rejoined Halas in 1926 with the club now renamed the Chicago Bears and played through 1929. He led the league in field goals: 1922–23, 1925–26; touchdowns: 1923, '27; scoring: 1923, '26.

Driscoll coached the Cardinals in 1920 and '22 and took over the Bears in 1956, while Halas was temporarily retired for two seasons, and took the team to the NFL championship game. Driscoll was elected to the Pro Football Hall of Fame in 1965.

John Elway

NFL great John Elway was drafted by the Yankees in 1982. That summer, he played 42 games in the outfield for Oneonta in the New York–Pennsylvania League, batting .318. However, when school started, he left the game for good to finish his football career at Stanford University. Originally drafted first overall in the NFL by the Baltimore Colts in 1983, Elway threatened to quit the game and play baseball if he wasn't traded.

Billy Evans

Longtime American League umpire (1906–27), farm director (Red Sox 1936–40), and general manager (Indians 1927–36, Tigers 1947–51) Billy Evans joined the NFL Cleveland Rams as general manager in 1941. In 1942, Evans began a four-year stint as president of the Southern Association. He was elected to the Hall of Fame in 1973.

Beattie Feathers

Beattie Feathers played seven seasons as a halfback in the NFL from 1934–40 after becoming an All-American at the University of Tennessee. As a rookie with the Chicago Bears, he led the league with nine touchdowns and made All-Pro. Feathers also manned the outfield in the minors from 1936 to '43. In more than 2,200 at-bats, he hit .318.

In the backfield, Feathers would follow behind Bronko Nagurski, who would break open the line, allowing Feathers to plow for a league-leading 1004 yards in 1934.

Freddie Fitzsimmons

Brooklyn released 217-game winner Freddie Fitzsimmons in July 1943 when the opportunity arose for the pitcher to manage the Philadelphia Phillies. Phillies magnate William Cox later owned the Brooklyn Dodgers of the All-American Football Conference. For two seasons, Fitzsimmons also held the general manager position for the football franchise after Cox was expelled from the major leagues.

Charlie Follis

Charlie Follis, a catcher, played three seasons with the Cuban Giants early in the century before his death from pneumonia at age 31 in 1909.

He also joined the Shelby football club of the Ohio League where he played beside and later against Branch Rickey. On September 15, 1904, with Shelby, the 6', 200-lb. halfback became the first African-American to officially sign a professional football contract. He made history when he donned the pads eight days later.

Follis actually played for Shelby from 1902–06 but it isn't clear if he was a professional or not until he formally signed the agreement in 1904. Prior to that, though, he was employed at a local hardware store at the behest of the club, which allowed him plenty of free time to pursue his gridiron obligations.

Here an interesting chain began, which linked integration in both professional football and baseball. Follis, the first African-American professional football player, was a teammate of Rickey who hired the first acknowledged African-American professional baseball player in organized baseball in the 20th century, Jackie Robinson. Robinson, in turn, was an UCLA teammate of Kenny Washington who, along with Woody Strode, re-integrated the NFL in 1946.

Walter French

West Point All-American halfback Walter French joined the NFL in 1922 for a game with Rochester. In 1923, he debuted with Connie Mack's Athletics. With Philadelphia, French hit .303 over six seasons as a part-time outfielder and pinch hitter. He also played nine games for Pottsville in the NFL in 1925, scoring five times. After sports, he returned to the Air Force, retiring as a lieutenant colonel in 1959.

Ted Fritsch

Ted Fritch played fullback and linebacker for the Green Bay Packers from 1942–50. In all, he scored 35 touchdowns, leading the league in 1946. In 1944, he joined the Los Angeles Angels in the Pacific Coast League. The rookie baseball player was soon sent to Nashville in the Southern Association for more seasoning.

Mike Garrett

Running back Mike Garrett won the Heisman Trophy in 1965 with the University of Southern California. The following year, he became a huge feather in the AFL's cap when he signed with the Kansas City Chiefs for five years and $450,000. He led the Chiefs to the AFL championship in 1966 and a berth in the first Super Bowl and again with a victory in Super Bowl IV over the Vikings.

When his contract expired, Garrett left football to join the Pittsburgh Pirates organization. He quit after being traded to the Padres and joined the San Diego Chargers instead. He played there through 1973.

Wally Gilbert

Wally Gilbert worked in the major leagues from 1928–32, mostly as a third baseman for Brooklyn; in the NFL as a back for Duluth from 1923–26, and he also played hoops professionally. He batted .299 between 1929 and '30 with 125 RBI and 180 runs.

Dale Hackbart

Defensive back Dale Hackbart played for five NFL teams from 1960 until a broken neck ended his career in 1973. Prior to that, he played a season at first base and outfield in the Pirates organization for Grand Forks in Class C.

Pat Haggerty

Future NFL referee Pat Haggerty won two minor league batting titles: 1948 Class-D PONY League, .369; 1950 Class-AA Southern Association, .346.

Hinkey Haines

Hinkey Haines played 28 games in the outfield for the Yankees first world championship team in 1923 and two games in the World Series itself. A running back out of Penn State, Haines also led the league in touchdowns for the NFL champion New York Giants in 1927. In all, Haines worked in the NFL from 1925–31 with New York and Staten Island.

George Halas

George Halas, football star at the University of Illinois, played twelve games in right field for the New York Yankees in 1919. The following year, Babe Ruth would occupy that position. After leaving baseball due to an injury, Halas went on to organize and coach, with Dutch Sternaman, the Decatur Staleys professional football team in 1920. As a representative of the club, he was part of the original contingent that formed the American Professional Football Association, later renamed the National Football League. By 1922, Halas assumed ownership, moved the franchise to Chicago, and changed the moniker to Bears. He would retain ownership until his death in October 1983. Halas was the only man continuously associated with the NFL throughout its first 50 years.

In 1925, "Papa Bear" signed running back Red Grange and began barnstorming. Their trip throughout the country helped popularize the sport. The Bears became one of the premier teams in the NFL and, later, dominated the 1940s. In the 1940 championship game, they demolished the Washington Redskins, 73-0.

His Bears participated in the forerunner to the NFL championship game. Prior to 1933, all league champions were declared by vote. In 1932, the Bears tied the Portsmouth Spartans for the league's best record. A tiebreaker was held on December 18 in Chicago. With a blizzard outside, play was moved to an indoor, 80-yard, mud-soaked arena, Chicago Stadium. The Bears won the title 9-0 on a two-yard pass from Bronko Nagurski to Grange plus a safety.

Head coach Halas led the Chicago Bears to six championships in 1921, '33, 1940–41, '46, and '63. His 324 managerial wins would stand as a record until Don Shula surpassed it in 1993. In 1963, Halas became a charter member of the Pro Football Hall of Fame. He also coached in the American Basketball League.

Carroll Hardy

Carroll Hardy is known as the only man to pinch hit for Ted Williams. It happened in 1960 after Williams fouled a ball off his foot. Hardy was originally signed by the Cleveland Indians in 1955 out of the University of Colorado. That same year, he was also drafted in the third round by the San Francisco 49ers and played 10 games for the franchise at half back, scoring four times. After his playing days, Hardy became assistant general manager for the Denver Broncos.

Kay-Jay Harris

Kay-Jay Harris was drafted out of high school by the Texas Rangers in 1997. The outfielder gave up baseball after hitting a mere .186 in 3 + seasons at Class-A. He then played running back for West Virginia. In 2005, the 26-year-old was drafted by the Miami Dolphins.

Bob Harvey

Right fielder for the champion Newark Eagles of the Negro National League in 1946, Bob Harvey had starred on the gridiron at Bowie State College in the late 1930s for which he was selected to the College Football Hall of Fame.

Drew Henson

Michigan quarterback Drew Henson was drafted by the NFL Houston Texans in 2003 but opted for a 6-year, $17 million deal from the Yankees instead. A year later, the third baseman asked out of his contract after grasping New York's penchant for purchasing talent over developing it. Henson had just completed a year in Triple-A, batting .234 with 78 RBIs but interlaced with 28 errors and 122 strikeouts. He subsequently signed with the Dallas Cowboys.

Chad Hutchinson

Chad Hutchinson was originally drafted by the Atlanta Braves in 1995 but chose college instead; however, he did sign with the St. Louis Cardinals after being drafted again in 1998. The pitcher spent four seasons in the minors working his way up to Triple-A. In all, he posted a 17-25 record and a 5.63 ERA. In 2001, he appeared in three games for the parent club.

In 2002, Hutchinson left baseball to pursue a career in the NFL. The quarterback went on to take snaps with Dallas and Chicago.

Don Hutson

Don Hutson played the outfield in the minors for two seasons, 1936–37, batting .301 in 800 at-bats in three different leagues. At the University of Alabama, he led the team to a Rose Bowl victory in 1935 with six catches and a 4th-quarter touchdown.

Later that year, Hutson signed with both the Green Bay Packers and the Brooklyn Dodgers in the NFL. Amusingly, both contracts arrived at the commissioner's office on the same day. Joe Carr awarded Hutson to Green Bay because their package was postmarked seventeen minutes earlier.

Hutson became one of the game's most productive players as an end and kicker through 1945. Eight times he led the league in receptions and five times straight, 1940–44, in scoring. The Packers copped the NFL championship in 1936, '39, and '44. Hutson was elected to the Pro Football Hall of Fame in 1963.

Bo Jackson

Bo Jackson was one of the premier athletes of the 20th century. In 1985, he won the Heisman Trophy as a running back for the Auburn University, rushing for 1,786 yards and 17 touchdowns. He was named MVP in both the 1983 Sugar Bowl and 1984 Liberty Bowl.

The Tampa Bay Buccaneers made him the #1 pick in the NFL draft in 1986 but Jackson opted to sign a $7 million deal with the Kansas City Royals instead. Then Bo announced his intention to play both baseball and football and signed with Al Davis' Los Angeles Raiders.

With Kansas City, Bo hit 107 home runs from 1987–90 but batted only .252, striking out too often. In fact, he fanned one out of every three trips to the plate over his career. Jackson's best year was '89 when he notched 32 home runs and 105 RBIs in only 135 games. He did produce a respectable .272 batting average the following year.

Jackson is often remembered today for:

- Breaking bats over his head and thigh
- Crushing a home run to open the 1989 All-Star Game
- Scaling the outfield wall a la Fred Astaire to slow his momentum
- A bare-handed grab off a carom in left field and nailing the runner at the plate
- Freak football injury
- His pure athletic build
- "Bo Knows . . ." advertising campaign

As a testament to his skills, Jackson was the first man to appear in the All-Star and Pro Bowl Games. On a routine tackle during a 1991 playoff game against the Cincinnati Bengals, Jackson suffered a career-ending injury (avascular necrosis) that required hip replacement surgery in 1992. He was able to return to baseball in '93 with the White Sox, becoming the first professional athlete to compete with an artificial hip. Bo ultimately retired with the California Angels at the end of the 1994 season at the age of 31.

Vic Janowicz

Vic Janowicz was one of the last great single-wing tailbacks. In 1950, he won the Heisman Trophy with Ohio State University as a junior. Then he signed a bonus contract with the Pittsburgh Pirates.

In 1953, the catcher became the first Heisman winner to play in the major leagues. After 83 games and a .214 batting average, Janowicz left the Pirates in '54 to join the NFL Washington Redskins. His football career was over two years later after a near-fatal auto accident during training camp.

Noel Jenke

In 1969, University of Minnesota star Noel Jenke was drafted by the Boston Red Sox, Minnesota Vikings, and Chicago Black Hawks. He eventually made it to Triple-A in 1971 but left baseball for the NFL. The linebacker played for three teams from 1971–74.

Doug Johnson

Doug Johnson was drafted by the Tampa Bay Devil Rays in 1996 out of high school. He played with them in the minors from 1996–97 while starring at quarterback for the Florida Gators. In 2000, he was drafted by and signed with the Atlanta Falcons.

Ken Kavanaugh

Ken Kavanaugh was one of hundreds of prospects buried in Branch Rickey's farm system. At Louisiana State, he made headlines finishing seventh in the Heisman running in 1939. The following fall, the end joined the Chicago Bears and won back-to-back NFL championships as Sid Luckman's deep threat. After three-plus years in the Air Force, Kavanaugh rejoined the Bears in 1946 and won another championship. In 1947, he led the NFL in touchdowns. Kavanaugh played through 1950.

Red Kellett

Red Kellett played nine games in the infield for the Red Sox in 1934. Falling back into the minors, he emerged as a broadcaster and television executive in Philadelphia. In 1953, he was hired as general manager by the NFL Baltimore Colts soon after Carroll Rosenbloom assumed ownership. From there until his retirement in late 1966, Kellett built one of the powerhouses of the NFL.

Wilbur King

Dolly King played in the Negro leagues from 1944–47. An end out of Long Island University, he also played minor league football in the American Association in 1941 for Long Island.

Yale Lary

Yale Lary joined the Detroit Lions out of Texas A & M in 1952. His first love, though, was baseball, so he played in the minors from 1953–57. Realizing his future was in the National Football League, Lary rejoined the Lions in 1956 after military service and played through 1964. In all, he played 11 seasons at defensive back and punter for Detroit, winning championships in 1952, 1953, and 1957. Lary is often referred to as the finest punter of his era and ranks just a notch below Sammy Baugh on the all-time list.

Bobby Layne

Quarterback legend Bobby Layne pitched in the minors for his hometown Lubbock Hubbers of the Class-C West Texas–New Mexico League in 1948. The righthander had come out of the University of Texas undefeated in three seasons.

Also that year, he was drafted in the first round by the Chicago Bears, beginning a 15-year NFL career that ended with the Steelers in 1962. Along the way, he led Detroit to their last three championships in 1952, '53, and '57. One of the last men to play without a facemask, Layne is credited with developing the "2-minute offense" when he led the Lions to a come-from-behind 17-16 victory in the 1953 championship game.

At retirement, Layne held all the significant career marks for a quarterback: most passing attempts, completions, passing yards, and touchdowns passed. He was elected to the Hall of Fame in 1967.

Jim Levey

Jim Levey came up at the end of 1930 and became the Browns starting shortstop through 1933. He had a decent year at bat in 1932 but Levey made a ton of errors and his dismal .936 fielding percentage eventually sparked a trade to the Red Sox in December 1933. He never played for the Sox but instead joined his hometown Pittsburgh Steelers in 1934—even though he never played college ball. Playing in the NFL through 1936, Levey scored four times in 1935.

Joe Lillard

Negro league pitcher–outfielder Joe Lillard toiled on the diamond from 1932–37 with the Chicago American Giants, among others, and returned to fill a war-depleted roster in 1944.

Lillard also played tailback at Oregon State College in 1930 but was suspended after two games when it was discovered that he had played baseball for pay with the barnstorming Gilkerson Giants. During the off-season in 1932 and '33, Lillard also donned the uniform of the NFL Chicago Cardinals as a halfback, punt returner, and kicker. As roster sizes shrunk during the Great Depression, Lillard and Pittsburgh Pirates tackle Ray Kemp would be the last African-Americans in the NFL until after World War II. In all, the NFL had fielded only 13 black players from its inception in 1920. Lillard also played basketball for the Chicago-based Savoy Big Five, a forerunner of the Harlem Globetrotters.

After the NFL, he played minor league football for Westwood in the Pacific Coast Football League in 1934 and in the American Association for Clifton in 1938, Union City and Brooklyn in 1939, and New York in 1941.

Dean Look

Dean Look appeared in three games for the White Sox in 1961. The following year, the quarterback played in one game for the New York Titans. Look later became an NFL referee.

Doc Lotshaw

Doc Lotshaw was a fixture in Chicago for decades. After playing 13 years in the minors, he became the trainer for the Chicago Bears in 1920, when they were called the A.E. Staleys. Likewise, Lotshaw was the Cubs trainer for 30 years, starting in 1922, until his death in February 1953.

Bobby Marshall

Bobby Marshall played first base and managed in the Negro leagues from 1909–11. At 40 years old in 1920, the former University of Minnesota star joined Rhode Island in the NFL. The end reappeared in the league for three games with Duluth in 1925.

Pepper Martin

See Brooklyn Dodgers

Christy Mathewson

See Pennsylvania, 1902

Jim McKean

Jim McKean umpired in the American League for more than 25 years, starting in 1974. Previously, he starred in the Canadian Football League as a quarterback and kicker.

Dutch Meyer

Dutch Meyer signed with the Cleveland Indians out of college in 1922 and played one season in the minors before developing arm trouble. He returned to Texas Christian University and led their football program until 1963. There, he developed the country's foremost aerial attack with Sammy Baugh and Davey O'Brien from 1934–38.

Keith Molesworth

Playing in the minors during the 1930s (including two stints with the International League Baltimore Orioles), Keith Molesworth, at one time, formed a double-play combination with Red Kellett (1937 Syracuse Chiefs). The two would later work together in a different capacity.

From the late 1920s, Molesworth was playing semi-pro football with Portsmouth and Ironton; in 1931, he joined the Chicago Bears as a halfback and quarterback. Like most men of the era, he also played on the other side of the ball at defensive back. By the time Molesworth left the field in 1937, the Bears had won two NFL championships.

In 1953, Molesworth was hired as the first head coach of the new Baltimore Colts (revamped Dallas Texans). At the end of the season, he moved into the front office as personnel director to build the team's scouting department, remaining until his death in 1966.

Mewelde Moore

Mewelde Moore was drafted out of high school by the San Diego Padres in 2000. After playing three seasons, he left baseball to play football at Tulane. The running back joined the Minnesota Vikings in 2004.

Charlie Moran

Pennsylvania clubs may have established the first professional football league in 1902 but the true development of the pro game grew out of an Ohio rivalry between Massillon and Canton, which began in earnest the following year. Charlie Moran, formerly a standout at the University of Tennessee and Bethel College, took over the reigns of the Massillon Tigers as player–coach in 1905.

In 17 seasons as a college football coach, mostly with Texas A&M, Carlisle, Bucknell, Centre College (Kentucky), and Catawba College, Moran amassed an impressive .766 winning percentage, including a highly respected and still acclaimed shutout victory over the powerful Harvard team of 1921. In 1927, he led the Frankford Yellow Jackets in the NFL.

Moran also umpired in the National League for 23 years between 1917–39 after brief stints as both ends of the battery for the St. Louis Cardinals in 1903 and '08.

Vernand Morency

Vernand Morency was drafted by the Colorado Rockies in 1998 out of high school and played outfield in their organization for three seasons. He left to play football at Oklahoma State. In 2005, the 25-year-old running back was drafted by the Houston Texans.

Frank Morris

Frank Morris played minor league baseball in the Provincial League in Canada during the late 1940s. He went on to a hall of fame career in the Canadian Football League as a guard and defensive tackle.

Greasy Neale

Greasy Neale starred in baseball, football, and basketball at West Virginia's Wesleyan College. He joined the Cincinnati Reds in 1916 and would later star in the infamous 1919 World Series, hitting .357.

Football was his calling, though. While still playing baseball, Neale both played football professionally and coached at Washington and Jefferson, a small Pennsylvania college that attained substantial national recognition and a Rose Bowl berth under Neale's guidance. The long-time college coach joined the NFL Philadelphia Eagles in 1941. He won the NFL Championship in 1948 and '49 before being ushered out by new ownership in 1950. Neale was elected to both the College and Pro Football Hall of Fames.

Frank Nesser

Frank Nesser, 1920–26, and his six brothers played football in the formative years of the NFL. His pro career lasted five seasons with the Columbus Panhandlers as a back, guard, and tackle. During the off-season, Nesser played minor league baseball for six seasons in Ohio.

Ernie Nevers

Ernie Nevers played three seasons with the St. Louis Browns, 1926–28. His first major league hit came off fireballer Walter Johnson. Nevers is best known in baseball for giving up two home runs to Babe Ruth during the famed 1927 season. His 6-12 record and 4.64 ERA did not distinguish him on the ball field. However, the gridiron was another matter. He was recognized by Pop Warner as the finest football player he ever coached, much to the dismay of Jim Thorpe fans.

His reputation was made in a well-fought contest against Knute Rockne's Four Horseman of Notre Dame in the 1925 Rose Bowl, though his Stanford team lost 27-10. Missing most of the season with two broken ankles, Nevers taped up to compete in all sixty minutes of the game.

He also ran track at Stanford. After turning pro, Nevers became a storied full-back with the Duluth Eskimos and Chicago Cardinals in the NFL from 1926–31. On Thanksgiving Day 1929, Nevers executed perhaps the finest individual performance in NFL history. He scored all the points for the Cardinals in a 40-6 rout over the Chicago Bears. Nevers rushed for six touchdowns and kicked four extra points. To date, no one has surpassed his point total; it is the oldest surviving record in the NFL. That year, he led the league in touchdowns and scoring. Nevers was inducted into both the College and Pro Football Hall of Fames.

Because each sport dominated a season (baseball: summer, football: fall, basketball: winter), Nevers was able to play three major professional sports in 1926. Besides time with the Browns and Eskimos, he played hoops with the Chicago Bruins of the American Basketball League.

Homer Norton

Homer Norton played outfield in the minors from 1916–19 in Alabama, Florida, and North Carolina; then left baseball to coach football at Centenary College through 1933. In 1934, he took over the reins of Texas A & M and won the national title in 1939 with a Sugar Bowl victory over Tulane. He was later inducted into the College Football Hall of Fame.

Ace Parker

Ace Parker hit a home run in his first at-bat in the bigs for the Philadelphia Athletics in 1937. Playing baseball and football full-time, the infielder decided to concentrate on football in '39, though he did sneak away during the spring and summer to swing a bat in the minors through 1952. The quarterback became the NFL's MVP in 1940 with Brooklyn and was elected to the Hall of Fame in 1972.

Previously, Parker starred at quarterback for Duke University, where he also played baseball and basketball. From 1953–65, he was the school's baseball coach. Starting in 1966, Parker became a long-time NFL scout for the San Francisco 49ers and St. Louis Cardinals.

Pennsylvania, 1902

Professional football initially developed from a rivalry among Pittsburgh area clubs in the 1890s. One of the game's foremost coaches and promoters was Dave Berry, who formed the Latrobe, Pennsylvania, team in 1895. Suffering financial hardship personally, Berry encouraged the baseball Phillies owner John Rogers to form a professional football team in 1902. Of course, this was during the Philadelphia baseball war against the upstart American League, a battle that was especially acrimonious due to the loss of Napoleon Lajoie, Bill Bernard, Chick Fraser, and Elmer Flick to the cross-town Athletics.

A's owner Ben Shibe would not be outdone. He recruited his manager, Connie Mack, and University of Pennsylvania tackle Blondy Wallace to build a better team. A couple more clubs signed up and the first professional football league was established, called the National Football League. The league folded after only one season when the Athletics pulled out after losing $4,000 operating the club. However, it did make an impact. During the season, the aptly named Philadelphia Athletics won the first professional football night game, under a crude lighting system aligned along the sidelines. Christy Mathewson, a former halfback at Bucknell, played punter for the Pittsburgh All-Stars and it is unclear whether guard Rube Waddell saw action, though he did suit up for the A's. Fred Crolius, on loan from the Pirates, was a teammate with Mathewson.

Cy Rigler

See Umpires

Art Rooney

After a successful career as a gambler, racetrack operator, and boxing promoter, Art Rooney founded the Pittsburgh Steelers and inserted them into the NFL in 1933. Rooney guided the club through numerous losing seasons and financial battles during WWII, when the club merged with Philadelphia and Chicago to stave off bankruptcy. Finally, he hired Chuck Noll as head coach and the club won four Super Bowls during the 1970s.

During the 1920s, Rooney, the athlete, boxed as a middle and welterweight, played semi-pro football, and manned the outfield in the minors. After playing 10 games for Flint in the Michigan–Ontario League in 1922, he batted .369 over 106 games for Wheeling in the Middle Atlantic League in 1925, leading the league in games, hits, runs, and steals.

Kyle Rote

Kyle Rote was an All-American football player at Southern Methodist University. After joining Corpus Christi in the Gulf Coast League in April 1951, he was offered a bonus contract by the NFL New York Giants. Reporting to training camp, Rote's baseball career ended after 22 games. He went on to score 52 touchdowns in an 11-year career as a halfback and end.

Deion Sanders

Deion Sanders was drafted by the Kansas City Royals out of high school. He chose to go to Florida State University instead. There, he starred in baseball, football, and track and field. He qualified for the 1988 Olympic trials as a sprinter. At FSU, Sanders played in the College World Series. As one of the top defensive backs in the country, "Prime Time" was named All-American twice.

In 1988, Sanders was selected by the New York Yankees in the baseball amateur draft. The NFL Atlanta Falcons drafted him the following year. He played both sports for eight years, then retired from baseball after the 1997 season. In September 1989, Sanders became the first athlete to hit a home run and score a touchdown for major league sports teams in the same week.

In 1992, the cocky center fielder hit .304 with a league-leading 14 triples in only 97 games. In the World Series with Atlanta that year, Sanders posted a .533 batting average. In '97 with the Reds he stole 56 bases in his only 100-game season.

Sanders earned two Super Bowl rings in the 1990s, becoming the first man to play in both the Super Bowl and the World Series. In the NFL, he is recognized as one of the all-time great cornerbacks. The two-way player would often line up as a wide receiver and return kicks for special-teams units, as well. Sanders briefly returned to the diamond in 2001.

Jay Schroeder

Jay Schroeder joined the Blue Jays organization in 1979 as its number one draft pick, while continuing his education and quarterbacking at UCLA. In all, he played three seasons in the minor leagues. In 1984, Schroeder was drafted by and signed with the Washington Redskins, beginning an 11-year NFL career.

Akili Smith

Akili Smith signed with the Pirates out of high school in 1993. He spent two seasons in the minors before returning to college to play football. Smith was drafted by the Cincinnati Bengals as the third overall pick in 1999. The quarterback played for the team from 1999–2002. He later worked in NFL Europe.

Ken Strong

New York Yankees power-hitting prospect Ken Strong suffered a baseball career-ending wrist injury in 1931 while with the Toronto Maple Leafs. He originally broke the bone against the center field fence making a catch. It was misdiagnosed as a sprain. After the season, a doctor performed surgery on his right wrist but removed the wrong bone. Strong had lost the flexibility needed to play baseball.

The previous summer he went deep four consecutive times on June 8 in an Eastern League game and set the season mark with 41 round trips while also batting .373 and knocking in 130 runners.

The 200-pounder had starred at New York University, kicking, passing, and running during their successful 1926–28 campaigns. Strong returned to football and became a Hall of Fame halfback and kicker for the NFL Staten Island Stapletons and New York Giants. In 1931, he led the league in field goals and in 1933 topped all with 64 points scored. The following year, Strong led the Giants to their first NFL title with two touchdowns in a 30-13 romp of Bronko Nagurski's undefeated Chicago Bears on an ice-covered field.

In a salary dispute with the Giants, Strong jumped his contract and signed with the New York Yankees of the American Football League in 1936. The NFL banned him for three years for doing so. Strong returned to the Giants in 1939 but retired the following year as the all-time NFL scorer. He later returned to the gridiron as a kicker during World War II. Retiring for good in 1947, he amassed a total of 479 points.

Strong holds a place in both the College and Pro Football Hall of Fames. Returning to the diamond, Strong later served as president of the Colonial League.

Jim Thorpe

Jim Thorpe is generally regarded as the finest male athlete of the 20th century. He initially gained fame as a two-time All-American halfback at the Carlisle Indian School. The versatile competitor also excelled at archery, baseball, basketball, boxing, ice hockey, lacrosse, swimming, tennis, and track and field. At the 1912 Summer Olympics in Stockholm, Sweden, he won the pentathlon and decathlon, a feat no other iron man has duplicated. The accomplishment gained him instant recognition as the world's greatest all-around athlete.

Unfortunately, the Amateur Athletic Union stripped his medals and amateur status in 1913, after it was discovered that he had played Class-D baseball from 1909–10. Many college athletes of the era would compete under an assumed name, but Thorpe failed to do so. He played for Rocky Mount, North Carolina, of the Eastern Carolina League for $60 a month.

John McGraw stepped in and signed the Olympian to a three-year contract with the New York Giants in February 1913. McGraw's motives were mixed. Of course, he wanted Thorpe to help the team on the field but a stronger interest was Thorpe's drawing appeal. Retiring with a career .252 batting average over six seasons, Thorpe proved that you need more than raw athletic ability to hit a major league curveball.

Thorpe helped re-organize the Canton Bulldogs in 1915, beginning his professional football career. In the years prior to the development of the NFL, Thorpe enjoyed his most productive seasons on the gridiron. He could do everything well: run, pass, kick, catch, and tackle.

At the time, the professional game was battling an unsavory reputation because of gambling scandals, uncontrollable player conduct, and rowdy patrons. In fact, the first highly publicized pro football game-fixing scandal took place between two Ohio teams in 1906: Canton and Massillon. Thorpe is credited by many with reviving the pro game and almost single-handedly improving its financial future.

Thorpe later served as figurehead president of the American Professional Football Association, forerunner of the NFL, which was formed on September 17, 1920, at an automobile agency in Canton, Ohio. The fledgling league used his popularity to gain credibility. During the 1920s, Thorpe donned the uniform of eight different teams. In 1929, he retired from the game.

Utilizing his hero status, Thorpe appeared in motion pictures. Eventually, the offers dried up and he was left destitute. In 1963, he was elected to the Pro Football Hall of Fame. In 1982, the International Olympic Committee restored the medals to his memory.

Charlie Trippi

Charlie Trippi played a season with Atlanta in the Southern Association in 1947, hitting .334. Later that year, he signed an incredible four-year, $100,000 contract to play for Chicago in the National Football League. The rookie halfback led the Cardinals to the NFL Championship.

Earlier in his career, Trippi was MVP in Georgia's Rose Bowl victory over UCLA in 1943 and starred again in the 1946 Sugar Bowl defeat of North Carolina. Trippi, the first overall draft selection of 1945, played with Cardinals through 1955 and was elected to the Pro Football Hall of Fame in 1968.

Bobby Vandever

Speedster Bobby Vandever played infield with the Kansas City Monarchs in 1944. The halfback also played minor league football for Des Moines from 1936–40 and with San Francisco in 1944.

Rube Waddell

See Pennsylvania, 1902

Chris Weinke

Chris Weinke joined the Blue Jays organization in 1990, out of high school. Seven years later, he left baseball and returned to school as a quarterback for Florida State University. In 2000, Weinke won the Heisman Trophy at age 28, the oldest man to do so, and joined the Carolina Panthers of the NFL.

Ricky Williams

Outfielder Ricky Williams ended a four-year minor league career in the Phillies organization in 1998. That year, the Texas running back won the Heisman Trophy and, later, established himself in the NFL.

Mike Wilson

Catcher Mike Wilson appeared in five games for the Pittsburgh Pirates in 1921. He also donned football gear professionally prior to the existence of the National Football League. Later, Wilson became an assistant to NFL Commissioner Bert Bell and supervisor of officials until his retirement in 1962.

Major Leaguers in the Pro Football Hall of Fame

Red Badgro	Paddy Driscoll
George Halas	Cal Hubbard (umpire)
Greasy Neale	Ernie Nevers
Ace Parker	Jim Thorpe

Negro Leaguers Who Played in the NFL

Sol Butler	Joe Lillard
Bobby Marshall	

Major Leaguers Who Played in the NFL

Cliff Aberson	Red Badgro
Norm Bass	Gene Bedford
Charlie Berry	Howard Berry
Larry Bettencourt	Lyle Bigbee
Josh Booty	Tom Brown
Garland Buckeye	Bruce Caldwell
Ralph Capron	Jim Castiglia
Chuck Corgan	Shorty DesJardien
D.J. Dozier	Chuck Dressen
Paddy Driscoll	Ox Eckhardt
Steve Filipowicz	Paul Florence
Walter French	Wally Gilbert
Norm Glockson	Frank Grube
Bruno Haas	Hinky Haines
George Halas	Carroll Hardy
Drew Henson	Chad Hutchinson
Bo Jackson	Vic Janowicz
Rex Johnston	Brian Jordan
Matt Kinzer	Bert Kuczynski
Pete Layden	Jim Levey
Dean Look	Waddy MacPhee
Howie Maple	Walt Masters
Bill McWilliams	Johnny Mohardt
Ernie Nevers	Ossie Orwoll
Ace Parker	Jack Perrin
Al Pierotti	Pid Purdy
Dick Reichle	Deion Sanders
John Scalzi	John Singleton
Red Smith	Evar Swanson
Jim Thorpe	Andy Tomasic
Luke Urban	Joe Vance
Ernie Vick	Tom Whelan
Hoge Workman	Ab Wright
Tom Yewcic	Russ Young

NFLers Who Played in the Minor Leagues (without promotion to majors)

Sammy Baugh	Cedric Benson
Bubby Brister	Tom Brookshier

Terrell Buckley
Isaac Byrd
Bob Douglass
Beattie Feathers
Mike Garrett
Joe Guyon
Kay-Jay Harris
Don Hutson
Noel Jenke
Ken Kavanaugh
Bobby Layne
Keith Molesworth
Vernand Morency
Frank Nesser
Jay Schroeder
Ted Strong
Chris Weinke
Ricky Williams

Adrian Burk
Quincy Carter
John Elway
Ted Fritsch
Joe Girard
Dale Hackbart
Chuck Hunsinger
John Jackson
Doug Johnson
Yale Lary
John Lynch
Mewelde Moore
Tom Nash
Kyle Rote
Akili Smith
Charlie Trippi
Ray Weitecha

CHAPTER EIGHT

~

Basketball Opportunities

Danny Ainge
Danny Ainge batted only .220 in 211 major league games with the Blue Jays from 1979–81. At the same time, he played hoops for Brigham Young University, where he was named All-American and won the Wooden Award in 1981.

He left the ball field at age 22 to embark on a long career for Red Auerbach's Boston Celtics in the NBA. He joined Larry Bird, among others, to form perpetual contenders during the 1980s, winning the NBA championship in 1984 and '86. Ainge went on to play in the second most basketball playoff games, 193. Ainge later coached in the NBA as well. In 2003, he was named director of basketball operations for the Celtics.

Benny Borgmann
Benny Borgmann played middle infield in eight different minor leagues from 1928–42, compiling a lifetime .304 batting average. The speedster scored more than 1,000 runs and nearly stole 300 bases. He also managed numerous clubs through 1950; however, Borgmann would not report to his baseball club until after the basketball season. This probably derailed any major league opportunities. As a scout for the Oakland A's, he finally retired from baseball in 1974 at age 75.

Though only 5'8" tall, Borgmann, an original Celtic, was a standout hoopster during the game's barnstorming heyday. He led the American Basketball League in scoring four times from 1926–31 with Fort Wayne. He was elected to the Basketball Hall of Fame in 1961.

Sweetwater Clifton
Six-foot, eight-inch Nat Clifton donned the red, white, and blue of the Harlem Globetrotters from 1947–50 but left to join the NBA when it was deemed acceptable to include a black player. From 1946–47, he played for the New York Rens.

In 1950, he became the first African-American to sign with an NBA team, the New York Knicks after being sold by Abe Saperstein for $25,000. Earl Lloyd was the first to actually play and Chuck Cooper was the first African-American drafted. Clifton played in the NBA through 1958, averaging 10 points per game for a total of 5,444. From 1949–50, he manned first base in three different minor leagues.

Jocko Collins

Longtime baseball scout Jocko Collins worked in the NBA as a referee, scout, and supervisor of officials. In the majors, he scouted for more than 30 years, finally retiring at the age of 75.

Gene Conley

Gene Conley starred in baseball and basketball at Washington State University. He signed on with the National League Boston Braves and became Minor League Player of the Year in 1951 and '53. Sticking with Milwaukee in 1954, Conley finished third in the Rookie of the Year voting with a 14-9 record, 2.96 ERA, and two shutouts. He also pitched and was credited with the loss in the All-Star Game. The following year, Conley was the winning pitcher.

By 1957, the righthander was pushed to middle relief but did appear in the World Series victory over the Yankees. With the Phillies in '59, Conley regained a starting spot and was selected to his last All-Star Game. His arm gave out with the Red Sox in '63 after 91 major league victories.

Conley began playing in the NBA in the winter of 1952 with the Boston Celtics. After a five-year absence, the 6′8″ Conley returned to the Celtics in '58 to help them win three consecutive NBA titles with his fine defensive play and rebounding. He played in the NBA through 1964, ending one of the finest two-sport professional careers and helping in three more championship marches. Conley also played in the American Basketball League during the 1961–62 season.

Chuck Connors

Seton Hall University basketball center Chuck Connors played beside future NBA great Bob Davies. Connors then played in the NBA with the Boston Celtics in 1946–47. He also appeared in 67 major league games for the Brooklyn Dodgers in 1949 and Chicago Cubs in '51 as a first baseman. The Cubs demoted him to Los Angeles in the Pacific Coast League.

After the 1952 PCL season, a small part in a Katharine Hepburn/Spencer Tracy film helped convince Connors to pursue acting full-time. He landed starring roles in the television series The Rifleman and Branded, though Connors won his critical acclaim for his part in the mini-series Roots.

Chris Crawford

Chris Crawford pitched in the Houston organization while attending Marquette. In 1997, the forward joined the NBA as a member of the Atlanta Hawks.

Dave DeBusschere

Dave DeBusschere was a $75,000 White Sox bonus baby who only pitched 36 major league games, though one was a shutout. While playing baseball, he also gained fame as a dominating forward in the NBA.

The Detroit Pistons enticed him away from baseball by making him their player–coach at age 24, the youngest head coach in history. The 6′6″ athlete later won two world championships with the New York Knicks. After 12 seasons in the

NBA, he became commissioner of the American Basketball Association. DeBus-schere was elected to the Pro Basketball Hall of Fame in 1982.

Larry Doby
Larry Doby played a season, 1947–48, in the American Basketball League with Paterson, New Jersey, integrating the league. He later worked for the New Jersey Nets in the NBA.

Eddie Ehlers
Out of Purdue, Eddie Ehlers was drafted by the Boston Celtics and the Chicago Bears. He played in the National Basketball League from 1947–49 and accepted $10,000 from the New York Yankees. In 1947, Ehlers played in the Three-I League and International League. Ehlers was the first man selected in the first NBA draft in 1947.

Ed Fitzgerald
Ed Fitzgerald was one of seven brothers that barnstormed as the Traveling Fitzgerald Basketball Team.

Frank Forbes
Frank Forbes spent more than 20 years in the Negro leagues as an infielder, pitcher, umpire, business manager, and promoter. He also was a boxing judge and played basketball professionally with the Renaissance Five.

Harry Gallatin
NBA Hall of Fame coach and forward Harry Gallatin played two seasons in the Cubs organization beginning in 1948.

Johnny Gee
After pitching for the Pirates and Giants from 1939–46, Johnny Gee joined Syracuse of the National Basketball League in 1946.

Don Grate
Don Grate pitched in seven games for the Phillies from 1945–46, earning a single victory. Then, he joined the NBL in 1947 and enjoyed three seasons with Indianapolis and Sheboygan.

Vic Hanson
Vic Hanson is a member of the College Football Hall of Fame and the Pro Basketball Hall of Fame. The multi-talented athlete also played briefly in the Yankees organization during the 1920s. The Syracuse University standout was named to Grantland Rice's All-Time All-American (basketball) Team for the first half of the century.

Harlem Globetrotters
The Harlem Globetrotters were formed in 1927 or 1928 or 1929, depending on what version of history you believe. Abe Saperstein claimed he started the enterprise in 1927. Another version traces the roots of the franchise from the Chicago-based Giles

Post club to the Savoy Big Five to the Tommy Brookins' Globe Trotters to Saperstein's club. In short, Saperstein was recommended to the Giles Post basketball team
as a booking agent in 1927. The Giles Post soon became the Savoy Big Five. In a
financial dispute, much of the Savoy roster splintered off in 1928 and eventually
formed the Globe Trotters (a popular name at the time) headlining Tommy Brookins.
Brookins brought Sapertstein in to book contests. Without Brookins' knowledge,
Saperstein formed a second Globe Trotter club, thus booking both traveling teams.
By 1929, Brookins retired to a singing career and left Saperstein to merge the two
clubs, eventually settling on the moniker *Harlem* as a marketing ploy to spark interest
throughout the Midwest (though it would be decades before they actually played in
Harlem).

Quite a few major league and Negro league players have donned their red, white,
and blue, the most prominent being Goose Tatum. Tatum was a showman and a
comedian for the Cincinnati and Indianapolis Clowns barnstorming team of the
Negro leagues. From 1941–42, the first baseman toiled on the diamond goofing with
the crowd, umpires, and fellow players. On occasion, Tatum would even wear a dress
to entertain the audience.

Tatum and his teammates would do a shadow ball routine during pre-game
warm-ups. The players would perform acrobatic feats with an invisible ball in play.
The Globetrotters borrowed the idea, set it to *Sweet Georgia Brown*, and hired Tatum
to enhance their act. Along with Marques Haynes, Tatum made the team a national
sensation. Finally, in 2002, the Globetrotters, as a group, were inducted into the
National Basketball Hall of Fame.

The following baseball professionals played or worked for the basketball Globetrotters:

Bobby Anderson	assistant coach, Savoy Big Five
Rock Anderson	
Joe Bankhead	1947–48, guard
Zach Clayton	
Sweetwater Clifton	
Piper Davis	1934–44, also road manager
Bill Dumpson	
Greene Farmer	
Bill Foster	manager
Sammy Gee	
Bob Gibson	1957
Hallie Harding	Brookins' Globetrotters
Ferguson Jenkins	1967
Collins Jones	
Ezelle King	
Joe Lillard	Savoy Big Five
Ziggy Marcell	
George "Sonny" Smith	
Ford Smith	
Othello Strong	1949–52

Ted Strong	1937–48
Goose Tatum	1942–54
Fred Thomas	minor league baseball player
Bill Watson	1927–30
Winfield Welch	coach and business manager
Sam Wheeler	1946–59, guard, and Harlem Magicians
Johnny Wilson	1949–54
Parnell Woods	business manager, 24 years

Harlem Renaissance Five

The first black professional basketball team was formed by Bob Douglas and New York Lincoln Giants (Negro leagues) owner Jess McMahon five years before the Globetrotters. Later, the team was renamed the Renaissance Five. For a time, the club was also owned by New York Lincoln Giants magnate James Keenan.

Like all African-Americans, the Rens faced numerous indignities. They would often have to leave the city they just played in and travel hundreds of miles by bus to find a hotel that would accept them.

Games between the Rens and the Original Celtics were big gate attractions during the 1930s. The Rens finally folded after World War II with a sterling 2,588-529 record.

The entire franchise was later inducted into the Pro Basketball Hall of Fame. The NBA itself did not admit African-Americans until the Boston Celtics signed Charles Henry Cooper in 1950. The following baseball professionals played or worked for the Rens:

Zach Clayton	1939–46
Sweetwater Clifton	1946–47
George Crowe	1947–48
George Fiall	1924–29
Frank Forbes	1923–24
Johnny Holt	1931–38
Fats Jenkins	1923–39
James Keenan	business manager
Wilbur King	1942–48
Lennie Pearson	1944–46
Johnny Wilson	1942–44
Willie Wynn	1943–45
Bill Yancey	1929–37

Chuck Harmon

Negro leaguer Chuck Harmon played for the Saratoga Harlem Yankees of the American Basketball League during the 1951–52 season.

Billy Harrell

Negro leaguer Billy Harrell played for the Saratoga Harlem Yankees of the American Basketball League during the 1951–52 season.

Arnie Heft

Lefthander Arnie Heft pitched for the International League Orioles and in the Red Sox farm system before enlisting in the Navy in 1943. In the service, he began refereeing basketball games. After WWII, Heft found a career in the Basketball Association of America and, later, the NBA. A sportsman, Heft would become a part-owner of the Washington Bullets and Capitals and of race horses.

Fats Jenkins

Speedy center fielder Fats Jenkins played and managed in the Negro leagues from 1920–40, starring at leadoff for the New York Black Yankees and Harrisburg Giants. During the off-season, he played professional basketball for the Harlem Renaissance Five starting in 1924 and achieved legendary status during their peak seasons, 1932–36, in which they went on a 473-49 tear. Only 5'7", Jenkins captained the team from 1932–42 and is considered one of the best of his era.

Kevin Johnson

Phoenix Suns guard Kevin Johnson had a brief stint with Modesto in the California League in 1986.

Donald Johnston

Donald Johnston played eight seasons in the NBA with the Philadelphia Warriors beginning in 1951, ultimately scoring 10,000 points. He led the league three times in scoring and once in rebounds. Earlier, Johnston pitched two seasons in the Phillies farm system, starting in 1949.

Neil Johnston

Basketball Hall of Fame coach and player Neil Johnston's first love was the diamond. He pitched three seasons in the Phillies organization before a sore arm forced his priorities to shift to the court.

Michael Jordan

Hailed as the greatest basketball player of all time, five-time MVP Michael Jordan turned to minor league baseball with the Chicago White Sox organization between stints in the NBA.

No one can suddenly develop a knack in their 30s for hitting a little white ball whizzing at 90–100 mph in his direction, intermixed with knee-buckling curveballs and hand-cuffing changeups. It cannot be done. Baseball requires skills developed and honed from youth. Jordan never made it to the parent club.

Doggie Julian

Al Julian had a full career in college and professional athletics from the early 1920s until his death in 1967. Some highlights:

College baseball player	College basketball player
College football player	Minor league baseball player

| College basketball coach | College football coach |
| NFL backfield coach | NBA head coach |

Julian amassed 386 college basketball victories as a coach and was named to the Pro Basketball Hall of Fame one year after his death.

Wilbur King
Negro leaguer Wilbur King had three different stints with the basketball New York Rens: 1942–43, 1945–46, and 1947–48. During the 1946–47 season, he played for the Rochester Royals of the National Basketball League. King also played pro football for Long Island in 1941.

Johnny Kundla
Johnny Kundla spent a season in the minors for the Brooklyn Dodgers before starting in 1948 a basketball coaching career, which eventually led to five NBL and NBA championships with the Minneapolis Lakers.

William Lampkins
Negro leaguer William Lampkins played pro basketball for the Washington Bruins during the 1940–41 season.

Emil Liston
Basketball pioneer and Hall of Famer Emil Liston played five seasons of minor league ball.

Ziggy Marcell
Ziggy Marcell was the son of top Negro league third baseman Ghost Marcelle. Ziggy was a backup catcher and outfielder for much of his career in the league, 1939–48. He also played pro football in the Pacific Coast Football League for Los Angeles in 1944 and '46. Ziggy further played guard for the Harlem Globetrotters and in the Pacific Coast Basketball League.

Bill McCahan
Bill McCahan won 16 games for the Philadelphia A's from 1946–49. He also played in the NBL during the 1948–49 season with Syracuse.

Cotton Nash
Cotton Nash saw action in 13 major league games from 1967–70, mostly at first base. He also played in the NBA during the 1964–65 season and the American Basketball Association in 1967–68.

Andy Phillip
Andy Phillip played parts of three seasons in the minors from 1947–52. At the University of Illinois, he set the Big Ten basketball scoring record in 1943. After World War II, Phillip became one of the standout backcourt men during his 11-year career

in the NBA. As a member of the Boston Celtics in 1957, Phillip won the NBA Championship. Like Borgmann, he was elected to the Basketball Hall of Fame in 1961.

Cum Posey

Longtime Negro league outfielder and officer Cum Posey, 5'9", played and managed professional basketball as a guard for the Pittsburgh-based Monticello Delaney Rifles and Leondi Big Five from 1909–20. He had originally played at Penn State and Holy Ghost.

Del Rice

Seventeen-year major league catcher Del Rice played for the Richmond Royals of the National Basketball League during the 1945–46 season while still in the minors. The Royals eventually joined the NBA and are known as the Sacramento Kings today.

Red Rolfe

Third baseman on some powerful Yankee teams, Red Rolfe coached the Toronto Huskies in the first season, 1946–47, of the Basketball Association of America, the forerunner of the NBA. He started the season as the team's general manager but descended to the bench after his first three coaches failed to pan out. Later, Rolfe held the position of athletic director at Dartmouth from 1954 to '67.

John Russell

Honey Russell is another athlete and coach with a distinguished career. Among other accolades, he was elected to the Pro Basketball Hall of Fame in 1964. Some highlights:

College basketball player	Pro football player
Minor league baseball player	Pro basketball player
College basketball coach	ABL basketball head coach
BAA basketball head coach	Major league baseball scout
NFL football scout	Boxing and wrestling promoter

Russell toiled as a scout for 26 years with the Braves, Expos, and White Sox, signing Joe Torre, among others.

Rusty Saunders

Rusty Saunders played five games in the outfield for the Philadelphia A's at the end of the 1927 season after Connie Mack lost hope of catching the powerful Yankees. Thirteen years later, Saunders appeared on the court with Detroit of the NBL and again during the 1945–46 season with Indianapolis at age 39.

Howie Schultz

Howie Schultz joined the Brooklyn Dodgers in 1943 during World War II and quickly became a fan favorite. In his only full season, 1944, Schultz knocked in 83 runners.

After two games in 1947, he was sold to the Phillies in May for $50,000 to make room at first for Jackie Robinson.

During the off-season in 1946, the 6'6" Schultz had joined Anderson of the National Basketball League and later moved with the team into the NBA in 1949 and even coached the team. Capping his hoops career, Schultz was a member of two champion Minneapolis Lakers teams from 1951–53.

Bill Sharman

Bill Sharman was called up by the Brooklyn Dodgers in late 1951 but just rode the bench during the famed pennant race. On September 27, umpire Frank Dascoli cleared the entire Dodger dugout for excessive bench jockeying after a disputed call. Sharman may be the only major leaguer thrown out of a game without ever appearing in one. He was also on the bench for Bobby Thomson's shot during the playoffs. Sharman did, though, play parts of five seasons in the minors from 1950–55.

At Southern California, Sharman was a two-time All-American basketball player. He went on to play for four championship Boston Celtics teams in the NBA. Accurate, he is one of the all-time leading foul shooters at 88%, and led the league seven times in the category. The Celtics with Bob Cousy, Ed Macauley, and Sharman are considered one of the finest scoring clubs of all time.

Sharman is also the only coach to win championships in three leagues: ABL, ABA, and NBA. He was elected to the Pro Basketball Hall of Fame in 1975 after spending 30+ years in the league as a player, coach, and executive.

Goose Tatum

Goose Tatum was originally signed by Abe Saperstein to play baseball in 1941. He was such a clown that the team moved him from the outfield to first base to place his act closer to the crowd. Never a great baseball player, he left the game the following year and joined the Globetrotters. Tatum was the biggest draw in basketball until he left the club in a spat in 1955. He subsequently formed the Harlem Magicians and was joined by 'Trotter dribbling showman Marques Haynes. At the height of his career, Tatum was earning $25,000 a year, making him the highest-paid player in the sport.

Bill Tosheff

1952 NBA Rookie of the Year, Bill Tosheff also played baseball in the minors and in South America from 1952–57.

Bill Yancey

Long-time Negro league shortstop Bill Yancey was a guard for the powerful Renaissance Five basketball teams of the mid-1930s that was inducted into the Pro Basketball Hall of Fame in 1963. His professional baseball career began in 1923 with the Philadelphia Hilldales in the first year of the Eastern Colored League.

By the time his career was over in 1936, Yancey became known as one of the finest shortstops in Negro league history. His contributions were even more profound in Panama. There, he was hired by the national government to prepare and train the Panamanian baseball team for the upcoming 1936 Olympic Games. A baseball exhibition was scheduled for the summer games in Berlin. In fact, he created the two national teams, Atlantic and Pacific. Yancey would continue to visit the country for years, helping to promote the fledgling sport and feed ballplayers to the Negro leagues.

Yancey later found work as a major league scout, signing Bill Bruton and Al Downing among others, and even helped the Manleys in Newark find up-and-comers.

Pro Basketballers before World War II

Larry "Rock" Anderson (Negro lg.)	Ernie Andres
Joe Bankhead (Negro lg.)	Jim Begley
Scrappy Brown (Negro lg.)	Lou Boudreau
Zack Clayton (Negro lg.)	Sweetwater Clifton (Negro lg.)
Piper Davis (Negro lg.)	Snooks Dowd
Bill Dumpson (Negro lg.)	Greene Farmer (Negro lg.)
George Fiall (Negro lg.)	Frank Forbes (Negro lg.)
Sammy Gee (Negro lg.)	Wally Gilbert
Hallie Harding (Negro lg.)	Bucky Harris
Johnny Holt (Negro lg.)	Carl Husta
Fats Jenkins (Negro lg.)	Collins Jones (Negro lg.)
Ted Kearns	Al Kellett
Pip Koehler	William Lampkins (Negro lg.)
Bert Lewis	Joe Lillard (Negro lg.)
Ziggy Marcell (Negro lg.)	Gordon McNaughton
Ralph Miller	Ernie Nevers
Tony Ordenana (Cuba)	Lennie Pearson (Negro lg.)
Cum Posey (Negro lg.)	Harry Riconda
Dick Seay (Negro lg.)	George "Sunny" Smith (Negro lg.)
Ford Smith (Negro lg.)	Hank Soar (coach)
Ted Strong (Negro lg.)	Goose Tatum (Negro lg.)
Jim Thorpe	Bucky Walters
Bill Watson (Negro lg.)	Ed Wineapple
Bricktop Wright (Negro lg.)	Willie Wynn (Negro lg.)
Bill Yancey (Negro lg.)	

Pro Basketballers after World War II

Danny Ainge	Frankie Baumholtz
Hank Biasatti	John Candelaria
Frank Carswell	Gene Conley
Chuck Connors	George Crowe (Negro lg.)
Dave DeBusschere	Larry Doby
Johnny Gee	Bob Gibson
Don Grate	Dick Groat
Steve Hamilton	Chuck Harmon

Billy Harrell
Ezelle King (Negro lg.)
Bill McCahan
Irv Noren
Billy Reed
Del Rice
Jackie Robinson
Howie Schultz
Othello Strong (Negro lg.)
Sam Wheeler (Negro lg.)

Fergie Jenkins
Wilbur King (Negro lg.)
Cotton Nash
Lennie Pearson (Negro lg.)
Ron Reed
Dick Ricketts
Rusty Saunders
John Simmons
Kite Thomas
Johnny Wilson (Negro lg.)

NBAers to Play Minor League Baseball

Carl Braun
Harry Gallatin
Michael Jordan
Erick Strickland

Bob Davies
Jim Holstein
Pep Saul

CHAPTER NINE

Other Sports Opportunities

Athletics

Giant Baba

Shohei Baba dropped out of high school to join the Yomiuri Giants organization in 1955. The Eastern League pitcher went 12-1 in 1956 and was named the league's Pitcher of the Year. He made the parent club for three games in 1957, amassing an 0-1 record and 1.29 ERA. That was all he would see of the major leagues. In 1960, Baba signed with the Taiyo Whales but fell in the bathtub and severely cut his pitching hand, ending his baseball career.

That September, Giant Baba, listed anywhere from 6'6" to 6'11", took part in his first wrestling match. In 1963, the father of professional wrestling in Japan, Riki-dozan, was murdered. The industry didn't stabilize until Baba and Antonio Inoki formed competing organizations in the early 1970s. The rivalry implanted professional wrestling as one of the nation's leading forms of entertainment.

George Bone

George Bone played 12 games for Milwaukee during the American League's inaugural season. He was also a professional roller polo player, a sport popular at the turn of the century, pitting teams of five men on roller skates trying to score hockey-style.

Don Carter

Considered by many to be the greatest bowler of his time and by some as the best all-time, Don Carter first played in the minors for the Philadelphia A's in 1947. He was the first bowler to earn six figures.

Junior Johnson

Junior Johnson was reared to be a moonshine runner. His family transported the "Wilkes County Champagne" in and out of Charlotte, North Carolina, for years during and after Prohibition; it was a lucrative cash business. All you had to do was avoid the revenuers, who wanted to tax you, and local sheriffs, who wanted to impound your speedster and sell it. Johnson made good money but he also spent some hard days in an Ohio jail.

153

After watching a stock car race in the early 1950s, Johnson figured he had the qualifications to join the circuit. And he did. He soon became the biggest name in NASCAR, entering 313 races from 1953–66. In all, Johnson won 50 times, 13 in 1965 alone, and finished in the top ten 148 times, earning more than $300,000. After retiring, he became one of the most successful team owners.

Johnson, a lefthander, pitched in the minors in his home state during the late 1940s and early '50s before injuring his arm in a farm accident.

Johnny Kling

Johnny Kling was one of the game's outstanding catchers at the beginning of the 20th century. He led the National League six times in putouts and twice in assists, fielding average, and double plays. He was a key member of the championship Cubs teams of 1906–8 and '10. Unfortunately for the Cubs, he won the World Pocket Billiard Championship in the winter of 1909. Kling retired from baseball to pursue the lucrative business but returned after he failed to repeat. Many believe his absence prevented the Cubs from winning five consecutive pennants.

While away from the game, he played ball against banned players. The National Commission only accepted his return after levying a $700 fine.

Edmund Lamy

Speed Skating Hall of Famer Edmund Lamy played minor league baseball in Canada during the 1910s. He was at one time the world's pro speed skating champion.

Strangler Lewis

Ed Lewis began wrestling for cash in 1912. Prior to that, he played semi-pro baseball. In 1920, he claimed the wrestling world championship and kept it, on and off, through 1933. His era straddled the old-time serious nature of the sport and the new theatrical entertainment angle. By the end, he was nearly blind from trachoma after wrestling 6,000 matches on unsanitary mats.

Line Drive Nelson

Lynn Nelson was nicknamed "Line Drive" for all the ropes peppered off his pitching. In seven major league seasons in the 1930s, Nelson posted a 33-42 record with a bloated 5.25 ERA. His hitting was much better, though. In 367 career at bats, he managed a .281 average, not bad for a pitcher. Nelson was known as the Masked Marvel in professional wrestling.

Tadaomi Nishino

After playing second base for Yomiuri from 1960–63, Tadaomi Nishino became a bicycle racer.

Randy Poffo

18-year-old Randy Poffo signed with the Cardinals out of high school in 1971. The outfielder hit .286 in his first year in the rookie leagues. In 1973, he became one of the first designated hitters in the minors. Promoted to Single-A after 25 games, Poffo's poor fielding and declining batting average signaled the end of his baseball career in 1974.

Randy performed for over 25 years in professional wrestling, like his father Angelo Poffo, as Randy "Macho Man" Savage, at times holding belts as the world champion in the WWE and WCW. Even during his minor league days, Savage was performing while wearing a mask.

Herb Washington

Herb Washington appeared in 105 major league games as a pinch runner without ever batting, pitching, or fielding. He also owns a World Series ring. The Michigan State sprinter set world indoor track records in the 50- and 60-yard dashes.

Professional Bowlers

Cap Anson
Tom Candiotti
Jean Faut (AAGPBL)
Dolly Niemiec (AAGPBL)
Kip Selbach

John Burkett
Shirley Danz (AAGPBL)
Jean Havlish (AAGPBL)
Takayori Ryu (Japan)

Professional Wrestlers

Giant Baba (Japan)
Lynn Nelson

Ken Kaiser (umpire)
Hugh Nicol

Boxing

The Babe's First Catcher

Meyer K. O. Christner amassed a 57-45-4 record in the ring from 1927–40. The heavyweight fought one-time champions Jack Sharkey, Max Baer, and Primo Carnera (twice). Christner also played professional football and semi-pro baseball around his hometown, Akron, Ohio. The catcher spent time at St. Mary's Industrial School in Baltimore with Babe Ruth.

Harry Bauchman

Good-field, no-hit Chicago Giants (Negro league) second baseman Harry Bauchman went four rounds with top heavyweight Fireman Jim Flynn in 1912. Flynn is the only man ever to knock out Jack Dempsey during his professional career, doing so on February 13, 1917.

Biddy Bishop

Featherweight Biddy Bishop boxed once in 1895 and again in 1900 for a 1-1 record. He later umpired in the Texas League.

Johnny Broaca

Yale graduate Johnny Broaca was a starter for the great New York Yankees teams from 1934–37 and later relieved for the Indians in '39. He jumped the Yankees twice to fight in professional boxing matches, missing chances to pitch in the World Series. He failed to ever post a win in the ring.

Zach Clayton

Negro leaguer and Harlem Globetrotter Zach Clayton worked as a boxing referee from 1952–84. He was in the ring for the 1952 heavyweight championship pitting Jersey Joe Walcott against Ezzard Charles, becoming the first African-American to referee a heavyweight championship match.

Clayton also worked the following title fights: 1972 Joe Frazier versus Ron Stander and 1974 Rumble in the Jungle, Muhammad Ali versus George Foreman. Also, he oversaw two *Ring Magazine* Fights of the Year: 1965 Floyd Patterson versus George Chuvalo and the Ali/Forman bout. Clayton was there for Ali's final bout against Trevor Berbick in 1981.

Frank Forbes

Fellow Negro leaguer Frank Forbes was a boxing judge from 1944–67. He was at ringside for the following heavyweight title fights: 1946 Joe Louis versus Billy Conn, 1950 Ezzard Charles versus Joe Louis, 1954 Rocky Marciano versus Ezzard Charles, and 1967 Muhammad Ali versus Zora Folley. Ali was prevented from defending his title after the Folley fight. He finally retired in February 1970, so Joe Frazier and Jimmy Ellis could fight to unify the title.

Boob Jackson

Robert Jackson was a catcher for the Chicago Unions of the Negro leagues from 1897–1900. Previously, he boxed professionally and was billed as the middleweight champion of New Jersey back in 1888.

Jack Johnson

Heavyweight champion Jack Johnson found extra cash playing first base in the Negro leagues for the Philadelphia Giants during the 1903–04 seasons. The years coincide with his reign as Negro heavyweight champion. There, he forged a life-long friendship with teammate Rube Foster.

On December 26, 1908, Johnson knocked out Tommy Burns in the 14th round in Sydney, Australia, to become the first black heavyweight champion. He also gained the ire of white America, partially because he refused to be told how to live. The son of a former slave, Johnson saw no reason to accept the limitations America enforced on African-Americans. As a child in Galveston, Texas, he was not even permitted to use the same sidewalk as whites.

Eventually, the establishment could no longer accept his lifestyle and Johnson escaped the country to avoid prosecution under the Mann Act for transporting his young, white girlfriend across state lines. He fled by posing as a Negro league player en route to a game in Canada. The last years of his heavyweight reign were spent abroad.

Topeka Jack Johnson

Topeka Jack Johnson played and managed in the Negro Leagues for two Kansas City clubs from 1909–10. He was also a professional boxer with the same name as the heavyweight champ. Johnson fought some of the toughest black heavyweights of the era, including drawing with Sam Langford on December 21, 1911. On November 25, 1920, Topeka Jack lost to former heavyweight champion Jack Johnson at Leavenworth Federal Prison.

Honest John Kelly

Big, 6′, 185 lb., John Kelly was a tough kid from Paterson, New Jersey who spent three seasons as a catcher in the big leagues between 1882–84, bouncing from the National League to the American Association and the Union Association. Kelly spent the rest of the 1880s playing sporadically, managing, Louisville Eclipse of the American Association 1887–88, umpiring full-time, National League 1882, '88, '97, and American Association 1883–86, and filling in where needed. In 1892, he managed the Mobile club in the Southern Association.

In fact, Kelly was the premiere postseason umpire of the era. In 1884, he witnessed Hoss Radbourn and the Providence Grays of the National League dominate the American Association New York Mets in major league baseball's first official postseason series and the first unofficial World Series. Kelly also oversaw postseason competition in 1885 and '87.

Kelly refereed professional boxing matches including three heavyweight championship bouts. He was in the ring for champion Jim Corbett's only successful title defense against England's Charley Mitchell, an old Sullivan foe, in January 1894, a third-round knockout. He also oversaw another Corbett match versus Tom Sharkey in 1898 and title matches involving Kid Lavigne and Frank Erne. He quit refereeing the following year in a cloud of controversy centering on his gambling interests. Kelly operated gambling parlors throughout New York City.

Bill Maharg

Bill Maharg, a central figure in the Black Sox affair, accrued a 45-11-17 record in 73 bouts. The 5′4″ lightweight from Philadelphia fought professionally from 1900–07.

Jim McDonald

Jim McDonald umpired in the National League in 1895 and from 1897–99. Prior to that, he umpired and played minor league ball on the West Coast. He also refereed boxing matches, including a Kid Lavigne versus Mysterious Billy Smith bout in San Francisco on March 10, 1899, prior to departing for spring training.

Art Shires

Art Shires was a pain in the neck for baseball executives his entire four-year career. He was tough, loud, and walked around calling himself "Art the Great." The first baseman managed to hit .291 in 290 games from 1928–32 when he wasn't fighting. In late 1929, the 21-year-old from Texas was cash poor, so he started boxing professionally. He was currently serving a suspension from the White Sox for getting drunk and punching manager Lena Blackburne in the eye, something he did twice that year. (Blackburne would later, in 1937, discover the famous South Jersey mud that is still used today to rub the shine off new baseballs. It came about because American League umpire Harry Geisel pushed MLB to do something about the slickness of new balls.)

The brawler's first fight was against a competitor named Dan Daly who later confessed to tanking the match. Soon, Shires found that he could make more money promoting bouts with other sporting celebrities than by playing ball. Art the Great fought George Trafton, the rugged Chicago Bears center; Cleveland Indians Tony Faeth; and Boston Braves Al Spohrer. Cubs owner William Wrigley canceled a proposed bout with star Hack Wilson. In all, the heavyweight amassed a 5-2-0 record in seven matches.

Judge Landis began to fear that Shires' associations might lead to gambling, or probably had. He was already banned in 32 states for allegedly participating in the rigged bout with Daly. In early 1930, Landis gave him an ultimatum to choose either baseball or boxing. Shires left baseball but returned in '32. Shires also had a brief career as a pro wrestler.

John L. Sullivan

John L. Sullivan, the Boston Strong Boy, was the heavyweight boxing champion from 1882–92 and perhaps the most famous of all 19th-century athletes. He knocked out Paddy Ryan in the eighth round to become the last bare-knuckles world heavyweight champion. The last significant heavyweight bare-knuckles match saw Jake Kilrain go down after 75 rounds in 1889.

Sullivan was the first American sportsman to be paid to advertise products. It is estimated that he was the first to earn more than $1,000,000 in his career, primarily from personal appearances, advertising, and, especially, the vaudeville circuit, rather than gate receipts from actual boxing matches.

As a youngster in Boston, Sullivan developed a lifelong love for baseball and even played semi-pro games. Later in life, Sullivan would claim, though unsubstantiated, that the Cincinnati Red Stockings offered him $1,300 to join their club back in 1879 and '80.

Having already achieved fame in boxing, Sullivan played baseball with various clubs for half the gate receipts. He would attract huge followings at the Polo Grounds, Sportsman's Park, or wherever he played. With the St. Louis Browns in 1884, Sullivan pitched and batted first in an exhibition game but succeeded at neither. He was guaranteed 60% of the gate though, a total of $1,400. Sullivan would later organize traveling teams and play or umpire for them. Up until his death, Sullivan was a welcomed visitor in the Red Sox dugout.

Professional Boxers

Ed Barrow	Harry Bauchman (Negro lg.)
Johnny Broaca	Dolf Camilli
Robert Carpenter (trainer)	Dean Chance (manager)
Zach Clayton (Negro lg., referee)	Tony Faeth

Rick Ferrell
Jack Hannibal
Tim Hurst (promoter)
Jack Johnson (Negro lg.)
Wade Johnson (Negro lg.)
George Magerkurth (umpire)
Bill McLean (umpire)
Ernie Orsatti
Boss Schmidt
Art Shires
Bill Summers (umpire)

Frank Forbes (Negro lg., judge)
Don Hoak
Robert Jackson (Negro lg.)
Topeka Jack Johnson (Negro lg.)
Honest John Kelly (referee)
Bill Maharg
John Morrissey (owner)
Bill Pettus (Negro lg.)
Frank Selee (promoter)
Al Spohrer
Jack Watts

Golf

Horace Allen

Horace Allen played four games in the outfield for Wilbert Robinson's Brooklyn Dodgers in 1919. He also played football professionally. In 1926, he left baseball altogether to pursue a professional golf career.

Sammy Byrd

Sammy Byrd was known as "Babe Ruth's Caddy" partially because he served as the Bambino's late-inning, defensive replacement. He later claimed that his baseball career was derailed after running into the outfield wall in Cincinnati during the major's first night game in 1935. Byrd was probably the best golfer to play major league baseball.

On the PGA tour, Byrd won the 1942 Greensboro Open, 1943 Chicago Victory Open, 1944 New Orleans Open, 1944 *Philadelphia Inquirer* Open, 1945 Texas Open, and 1945 Mobile Open. However, his greatest moment may have come in losing to Byron Nelson in the finals of the 1945 PGA Championship, 4 and 3, at the Morraine Country Club in Dayton, Ohio, back when the major was still decided by match play.

Walter Hagen

PGA founding member Walter Hagen's first love was baseball. In 1914, the semi-pro shortstop was vacillating between pursuing a golf career and an opportunity to impress the Philadelphia Phillies. That August, he won the U.S. Open and, choosing golf, went on to win 10 more majors.

Ken Harrelson

Ken Harrelson signed with the Kansas City A's at age 18 and, eventually, became their starting first baseman. In 1965, he hit 23 home runs with 66 RBI but carried only a .238 batting average. Two years later, he was given free agency, a decade before Andy Messersmith and Dave McNally.

In August 1967, Harrelson blasted KC owner Charlie O. Finley as "a menace to baseball." Finley was so mad (he had already suspended pitcher Lew Krausse and fired manager Alvin Dark) that he released the player, forfeiting a $50,000 paycheck if he had placed him on waivers. The silly thing is that the "Hawk" was still a viable major league player. The bidding began. Harrelson eventually accepted a $73,000 offer to join the Boston Red Sox.

He helped the Sox down the stretch with 14 RBIs in 23 games. They won their first pennant since 1946; though, Harrelson managed only one hit in the World Series versus the Cardinals and their three-game winner Bob Gibson.

In 1968, Harrelson hit 35 homers, three consecutive in one game, with a league-leading 109 RBIs. He smacked another 30 dingers the following year, 27 after being shipped to Cleveland. Boston fans picketed Fenway after the popular player was traded. After two unproductive seasons, Harrelson left baseball to join the professional golf tour. He is credited with introducing the batting glove to baseball, probably a carryover from his love of golf.

In 1980, Harrelson finished 75th at the Pleasant Valley Jimmy Fund Classic and played in another tournament the following year but didn't make the cut. In 1994 and '96, he played a tournament each year on the Champions Tour, finishing 37th at the Ameritech Senior Open that first season.

Harrelson became a baseball broadcaster in 1982. In 1985, he became the White Sox executive vice-president of baseball operations. Sparking a lot of controversy, Harrelson was soon fired and went back into the booth.

Jumbo Ozaki
Masashi Ozaki pitched for the Nishitetsu Lions from 1965–66, posting an 0-1 record with a 4.83 ERA in 20 games. In 1967, he was switched to the outfield but made only two hits in 42 at bats with 24 strikeouts.

Ozaki took up professional golf at age 23. In all, he's won over 90 tournaments worldwide, becoming the most successful golfer in Japanese history.

Jerry Priddy
Second baseman Jerry Priddy hit .265 in nine major league seasons from 1941–1953. He led the league four times in putouts and three times in assists, double plays, and range. At the plate, Priddy's finest season was 1948 with the Browns when he hit .296 with 79 RBIs and 96 runs scored. His last play in the majors (as a third baseman) nipped Al Rosen at first in the final game of the 1953 season, in effect, costing Rosen the Triple Crown (losing the batting championship to Mickey Vernon.)

After retiring, Priddy joined the PGA tour, though his winnings amounted to little. During the 1973 U.S. Open at Pebble Beach, he was arrested and charged with extortion. Priddy was found guilty of demanding $250,000 from a cruise line, threatening the bombing of one of their ships. Two live bombs were found aboard the Norwegian ship *Island Princess*. He was sentenced to nine months in jail.

Rick Rhoden
Rick Rhoden, a one-time teammate of Don Sutton, was often accused of scuffing the ball on his way to 151 major league victories. He was also one of the top-hitting hurlers, posting three .300+ seasons. While with the Yankees in 1987, Rhoden became the only pitcher to start a game at designated hitter.

When he retired in 1989, Rhoden was a self-taught, two-handicap golfer. For years, he was the best golfer on the Celebrity Players Tour. After turning 50, Rhoden joined the Champions Tour in 2002, finishing as high as fifth in the 2003 Allianz Championship.

John Montgomery Ward

John Montgomery Ward was one of the most significant figures in 19th-century baseball. He is also the only player in major league history with 100 victories and 2,000 base hits.

The righthander won 22 games and led the league with a 1.51 ERA as a rookie in 1878 with Providence. Joined by Hall of Fame shortstop-manager George Wright and right fielder Orator Jim O'Rourke, the Grays won the National League pennant by five games the following year. Ward added a league-leading 47 wins, .712 winning percentage, and 239 strikeouts.

In 1880, he won 39 more times, eight of them shutouts. On June 17 that year, Ward pitched the National League's second perfect game in a 5-0 victory over Buffalo. There wouldn't be another until Jim Bunning's in 1964. The 2,400 innings over the last six seasons took their toll, forcing an end to Ward's pitching career in early 1884. Along the way, he compiled a 164-102 record and a 2.10 ERA. He is credited by some with inventing the pitcher's mound and the intentional base on balls.

Ward then became one of the National League's best shortstops for the New York Giants, leading the league 14 times in major fielding categories over the next six seasons. He also shined as a speedy, aggressive base runner, though stolen base totals for the era are virtually meaningless (the stats count additional bases taken on hits).

The Giants of the late 1880s featured Hall of Famers RHP Tim Keefe, RHP Mickey Welch, C Buck Ewing, 1B Roger Conner, OF O'Rourke, and Ward. They won pennants in both 1888 and '89. Ward particularly excelled in the World Series match-ups against St. Louis of the American Association by hitting .379 in 1888 and .417 the following autumn.

Off the field, Ward gained his law degree from Columbia University. On October 22, 1885, with eight New York Giant teammates, he formed and organized the Brotherhood of National League Players, baseball's first players union. Their main gripes were the reserve clause, and money, of course. Ward would recruit and establish Brotherhood chapters in every National League city.

While Ward was out of the country with Al Spalding's world tour in 1889, National League owners adopted a salary classification plan that froze players' salaries in five tiers between $1,500 and $2,500. It was called the Brush Classification Plan after Indianapolis owner John T. Brush. Also, the magnates tightened their control by blanketing the reserve clause over all players. Now, a standard contract was developed that bound each player to his team, was renewable at the *club's* option, and was transferable to another owner at the *club's* discretion.

The noose was tightened. Ballplayers were now fully bound to an owner that enjoyed exclusive rights to their contract, set territorial rights, a standardized pay scale, and an unquestioned authority to fine and blacklist.

Upon Ward's return, the owners refused to negotiate with him. In response, Ward called for the players to develop their own league at a meeting on July 14. The Players League of 1890 was the result. It lured the biggest stars of both the National League and the American Association and, consequently, outdrew the two established leagues. In fact, 80% of the National League's players jumped their contract.

The Players League had no reserve clause, salary classification, or blacklist. Nevertheless, it folded after one season because of lack of financial backing. The American Association followed a year later. The National League would be alone at the top of organized baseball for another decade.

After serving as player–manager for Brooklyn in the Players League, Ward was accepted as player–manager and part-owner of the Brooklyn Bridegrooms of the National League in 1891. The following year, he won part-ownership of the New York Giants in a bet and promptly took over as the club's player–manager.

In 1894, the Giants defeated the Baltimore Orioles in the postseason Temple Cup series. Ward retired after the victory partially because of his poor relationship with majority-owner Andrew Freedman. As a litigator, Ward would later punish Freedman in court on several occasions. The lefthanded batter finished with 2,104 hits, 1,408 runs, and 867 RBI. His record as field leader stood at 412-320 for a .563 winning percentage.

Ward devoted himself to his law practice but resurfaced as a leading candidate for the post of National League president in 1909. He was passed over, probably because of his reputation as a rebel. In 1911–12, he served as president and part-owner of the Boston Braves. Ward was lured to the upstart Federal League in 1914, serving as general manager for the Brooklyn Tip-Tops and unofficial league spokesman. In 1964, he was belatedly elected to Cooperstown.

Outside baseball, Ward pursued golf. In 1897, he became founder and president of one of the first American golf clubs, the Long Island Golf Association. Later that year, Ward won his first golf tournament at age 37. Golf at the time was an upper-class sport dominated by the Scottish and British. Ward, among others, sought to change this during the early decades of the century. Harry Vardon's tour of the States in 1900, sponsored by Al Spalding, introduced many to the sport itself and was the first event to spark the interest of the masses, not to mention igniting equipment sales for Spalding. By 1913, there were more than 1,000 golf courses nationwide with over 350,000 enthusiasts.

In 1903, Ward finished second at the Southern Open in Pinehurst, North Carolina. Eventually, he found his forte to be match play, as he won all of his head-to-head matches versus a traveling British team in 1904. In fact, Ward didn't lose a match in Lesley Cup play until his sixth year of competition in 1910. Ward's career highlight was beating four-time U.S. Amateur and U.S. Open champion, Jerry Travers. Only Bobby Jones won more amateur titles than Travers.

Ward died in 1925 at the age of 65 after developing pneumonia while hunting in Georgia. He had just recently competed in The Masters.

Robin Yount

At age 22 in 1978, future Hall of Famer Robin Yount temporarily retired from the typically hapless Milwaukee Brewers to pursue a career in professional golf or possibly motorcycle racing. More likely, he was nursing an injury sustained while riding a motorcycle. That spring, Paul Molitor was called up to replace Yount at shortstop.

Professional Golfers

Horace Allen
Johnny Bench
Jeanie Descombes (AAGPBL)
Sammy Hale
Vic Lombardi
Koichi Nishimura (Japan)
Albie Pearson
Jerry Priddy
Mike Schmidt
Ichiro Togawa (Japan)

Yasuhiro Aratake (Japan)
Sammy Byrd
Whitey Glazner
Ken Harrelson
Mark Mauldin
Jumbo Ozaki (Japan)
Charlie Perkins
Rick Rhoden
Isao Sugimachi (Japan)
Ralph Terry

Hockey

Toe Blake
Hockey Hall of Famer Toe Blake played minor league ball in the Canadian Provincial League. The left winger played professional hockey from 1929–51, including 14 seasons in the NHL, mostly with the Montreal Canadians. He was named MVP in 1939 after leading the league in scoring. On the ice, he won Stanley Cup championships in 1944 and '45. Blake later coached the Canadians to another eight Stanley Cup titles.

Bob Bourne
Future NHL star center Bob Bourne joined Clark Gillies on the Covington Astros of the Appalachian League in 1972.

Lionel Conacher
Similar to Jim Thorpe, Lionel Conacher is considered the top Canadian athlete of the first half of the 20th century. Not only did he play minor league baseball in his homeland but he led the Toronto Argonauts to the CFL Grey Cup title with two touchdowns in the championship game in 1921.

The Toronto-native played pro hockey from 1918–37, including the final twelve seasons in the NHL. The defenseman helped lead the Chicago Black Hawks to Stanley Cup championships in 1934 and '35.

Well-rounded, Conacher later served in the Ontario Legislature and in the House of Commons in Parliament. He is a member of the Canadian Sports, Canadian Football League, Canadian Lacrosse, and Hockey Hall of Fames.

Bob Dill
Bob Dill played ball in the minor league American Association and later managed in the Yankees, Giants, and Reds organizations. The defenseman was also a professional

hockey player from 1938–52, including two seasons in the NHL. Dill later coached in the American Hockey League and was elected to the United States Hockey Hall of Fame in 1979.

Norm Dussault

Norm Dussault played minor league baseball during the 1940s and '50s, mostly in his homeland of Canada. He also played professional hockey from 1945–55, including four seasons with the NHL Montreal Canadians.

Babe Dye

Babe Dye hit .311 over seven minor league season from 1920–26, spent mostly in the International League. There, he caught the eye of Connie Mack, who offered him $25,000 to leave his other interests and play baseball. A broken leg ended his baseball career in 1927.

Dye achieved his ultimate fame, though, in the National Hockey League, where he became one of the leading scorers of the 1920s. In 1922, he led the Toronto St. Pats to the Stanley Cup title with four goals in the final game of the championship. Dye led the league three times in scoring during a career that lasted from 1919 until 1931 when he finally retired after being hampered for four seasons by the leg injury. In 1970, he was elected to the Hockey Hall of Fame.

Chaucer Elliott

Chaucer Elliott was one of the first referees elected to the Hockey Hall of Fame. He worked games from 1903 until his death in March 1913 of cancer. Elliott, at various times, coached hockey, football, and baseball. Plus, he played professional baseball in Toronto in 1903 in the Eastern League.

Bill Galloway

Early Negro league, 1899–05, outfielder Bill Galloway also played for Woodstock in the Canadian League. While north of the border, he played hockey in the Central Ontario Hockey Association in 1899.

Clark Gillies

Canadian Clark Gillies played minor league baseball in the Appalachian League from 1970–72 prior to beginning his hockey career. He played professionally from 1971–88, mostly with the New York Islanders in the NHL. The left winger helped the franchise take four consecutive Stanley Cups from 1980–83. Gillies was elected to the Hockey Hall of Fame in 2002.

Leroy Goldsworthy

Righthanded pitcher Leroy Goldsworthy played minor league ball in Canada, capping with a 22-6-season with Winnipeg of the Northern League in 1933. Meanwhile, he starred as a professional hockey player from 1924–42, including ten seasons in the NHL. Goldsworthy was a right winger on the Stanley Cup champion Chicago Black Hawks in 1934.

Johnny Gottselig
Russian-born and Canadian-bred Johnny Gottselig played professional hockey for 23 years from 1922–45, mostly as a left winger for the Chicago Black Hawks in the NHL. He was a key member of the Stanley Cup champions of 1934 and '38 and coached the team from 1944–48.

During the off-season late in his career, Gottselig managed the Racine Belles and Peoria Red Wings of the All-American Girls Professional Baseball League. In 1943, he led the Belles to the championship. Gottselig also played minor league ball.

Wayne Gretzky
The Toronto Blue Jays offered hockey great Wayne Gretzky a contract after seeing him play semi-pro ball in the late 1970s.

Bruno Haas
Bruno Haas, who played briefly for the Philadelphia A's in 1915, was a backup goalie for St. Paul in the American Hockey Association in the early 1920s.

Doug Harvey
Doug Harvey played outfield for four seasons with Ottawa in the Border League from 1947–50, hitting .344. In 1949, he led the league in runs, RBIs, and average. An attempt by the Boston Braves failed to lure him from hockey. Harvey, a Canadian, stuck with his national sport.

An all-around athlete, Harvey was one of the top three defensemen in NHL history in a career that lasted from 1947 to '69. Harvey and his teammates hoisted the Stanley Cup in 1953 and from 1956–60. His achievements earned a spot in the Hockey Hall of Fame in 1973.

Andy Kyle
Joining the Cincinnati Reds as an outfielder for nine games in 1912, Canadian Andy Kyle became the first pro hockey player in major league baseball. He played with Toronto of the National Hockey Association, forerunner of the NHL.

Gilles Marotte
Canadian Gilles Marotte played minor league baseball in his homeland during the mid-1960s. Meanwhile, the defenseman was playing professional hockey from 1962–78, including 12 seasons in the NHL.

Maurice Richard
Maurice Richard was the leading all-time scorer in the National Hockey League until his mark was eclipsed by Gordie Howe. During his 18 seasons with the Montreal Canadians, 1942–60, the right winger was named MVP in 1946–47, served on 13 all-star teams, led the league in goals five times, and played on eight Stanley Cup champions.

Richard also played minor league baseball with Drummondville of the Provincial League in the late 1940s. He was elected to the Hockey Hall of Fame in 1961.

Jim Riley

Jim Riley is the only man to play in both the NHL and major league baseball. He played professional hockey for 10 seasons, mostly in the Pacific Coast Hockey Association. Riley spent the 1926–27 season with the Chicago Black Hawks and Detroit Cougars in the NHL.

Throughout his hockey career, he played baseball as well. He made it to the majors in 1921 with the Browns and again in 1923 with the Senators.

Fred Thurier

Canadian Fred Thurier played minor league ball in the Provincial League. He also played pro hockey from 1936–52, mostly in the American Hockey League. Thurier did lace them up for parts of three seasons in the NHL.

Lloyd Turner

Lloyd Turner was elected to the Hockey Hall of Fame in 1958 as an early contributor and builder of the sport. He was one of the first Canadians in the Western Canadian League, a baseball minor league.

Jimmy Williams

Jimmy Williams was a longtime minor league player, coach, and manager in the Dodger organization. He also coached for the Astros and Orioles at the major league level. In 1947, he turned down the NHL Toronto Maple Leafs' offer of a contract and played for Cleveland and Boston in the minor American Hockey League instead.

Pro Hockey Players to Play Minor League Baseball

Jack Caffery	Gary Collins
Michel Dion	

Professional Hockey Players

Bill Galloway (Negro Leagues)	Bruno Haas
Andy Kyle	Kirk McCaskill
Jim Riley	Bill Stewart (umpire)

Soccer

Frank Borghi

National Soccer Hall of Famer, 1976, Frank Borghi also played minor league baseball. He set his place in history as the goalkeeper who shut out England in the 1950 World Cup finals. He was a member of the U.S. National team from 1949–54.

Stan Chesney

Stan Chesney is a member of the National Soccer Hall of Fame, 1966, for his work as a goalie over 17 years with the New York Americans in the American Soccer

League. He was also signed out of high school by Branch Rickey and sent to Danville (Illinois) of the Three-I League in 1932.

Billy Gonsalves
Soccer player Billy Gonsalves turned professional in 1927. He didn't retire until 1952. Along the way, he was hailed as the dominant U.S. player of the 1930s and '40s. Gonsalves was one of the few who could actually make a living in the sport. It allowed him to reject a contract offer from the St. Louis Cardinals. He was elected to the National Soccer Hall of Fame in 1950.

Dick Spalding
Dick Spalding was a professional soccer player who played extensively through the minors and finally made the big leagues with the Phillies at age 33. The outfielder hit .296 for Philadelphia in 1927, his only full season in the majors.

He is best known as a fullback for the U.S. National team of 1916, the first to travel overseas to Scandinavia. He also played in the American Soccer League from 1921–25. Spalding was elected to the National Soccer Hall of Fame in 1950.

Soccer Players

Bill Abstein
Eddie Mulligan
John Reder
Dick Spalding
Harry Wendelstadt (umpire)

Bobby Avila
Harry Pearce
Charlie Reilly
Sam Thompson

CHAPTER TEN

Professional and Personal Opportunities

Homer Abele

Homer Abele played in the minors for Nashville in 1938. He was also a U.S. Representative from Ohio from 1963–65 and later a judge.

All-American Girls Professional Baseball League Women

Many young athletic women and girls were drawn to baseball simply because the All-American Girls Professional Baseball League was the rarity, a successful professional female sports organization. Some grew up with brothers and had a leg up pitching, tossing, and hitting a baseball. Others had to adapt their softball techniques to the new game.

Few players stayed in the league for an extended period of time. In fact, only Dottie Schroeder played in all 12 seasons. Like the rest of the country, they had to muddle through two wars and take care of their families, often as a result of the loss of a brother, husband, or boyfriend.

Here, the pressures were exponentially placed on women who were expected to maintain family and home. It simply was not acceptable for respectable women to roam the country and play ball, regardless of the strides women like Babe Didrikson made. Society's attitudes would not begin to change until the days of Billie Jean King.

The following is an incomplete list of reasons for many that left the game:

- To attend college
- To marry
- To enter the military
- To gain war-related employment
- Pregnancy and child rearing
- To establish a career
- To return home

Others left because they simply saw no future in the league. These were young, sports-minded people who had other interests, such as bowling, tennis, golf, softball, and other amateur athletics. A high percentage of the AAGPBL athletes were later inducted into local hall of fames; a few for their professional feats. Professional bowlers include Shirley Danz, Dolly Niemiec, Jean Faut, the league's top pitcher, and Jean Havlish. Lefty Descombes became a pro golfer. Dottie Ferguson won the North American speed-skating championship in 1939.

Johnny Berardino

Infielder Johnny Berardino left the majors in 1952 after 11 seasons to pursue an acting career. He landed a soap opera role and played Dr. Steve Hardy on *General Hospital* for the next 30 years. In total, Berardino appeared in 29 movies and made 78 television guest appearances from 1948–82.

Moe Berg

Moe Berg was possibly the smartest man to play professional baseball. Certainly, he was well-read. The third-string catcher had plenty of time to do so in the bullpen. Over 15 major league seasons, he averaged only 44 games a year.

Berg attended Princeton, Columbia Law School, and the Sorbonne. He is reputed to have spoken English, French, German, Greek, Hebrew, Italian, Japanese, Latin, Russian, Sanskrit, and Spanish.

After the 1934 season, Berg secretly filmed downtown Tokyo. The pictures were later used by the American military in devising bombing targets during World War II. Berg went on to spy for the OSS, forerunner of the CIA.

At CIA headquarters in Langley, Virginia, in the Exhibit Center sit two baseball cards of Moe Berg. Beside them it reads:

> . . . Following his 15-year career with five different major league teams, the Princeton-educated Berg served as a highly successful Office of Strategic Services (OSS) operative during World War II. Among his many missions on behalf of OSS, the former catcher was charged with learning all he could about Hitler's nuclear bomb project. . . .

One of his missions sent him to Switzerland to attend a lecture by German physicist Werner Heisenberg. If Berg determined that Germany was close to developing an atomic bomb, he was to kill Heisenberg on the spot. However, he correctly surmised that a German breakthrough was not imminent. Despite countless experiences and contacts, Berg died in poverty.

Dr. Bobby Brown

Dr. Bobby Brown was a third baseman for the great Yankees teams of the 1940s and '50s. He batted .439 in four World Series. New York helped pay for his medical training at Tulane, where Brown graduated in 1950. After a stint in the Army during the Korean War, Brown retired from baseball to pursue a medical internship. He later spent 25 years as a cardiologist in Texas. From 1984–94, Brown served as American League president.

Fred Brown

Outfielder Fred Brown went to bat for the Boston Braves 20 times from 1901–02. He attended law school during the off-season and left the game to pursue his new profession. In 1923, he became governor of New Hampshire and took a run at the presidency as a Democrat in 1924. Brown's career also included stints as a U.S. Senator, 1933–39, and Comptroller General of the United States.

Charlie Buffington

Charlie Buffington won 233 games over an 11-year major league career. His specialty was an overhand, hard-sinking curveball that he placed with amazing accuracy. In 1884, while pitching for the National League Boston Beaneaters, Buffington amassed 48 victories, 417 strikeouts, 63 complete games, and an ERA of 2.15. The previous year, he had led the team to the pennant. Buffington once fanned 17 Cleveland players in a game, eight of them in a row.

The American Association failed in 1891 and, in turn, the National League ordered across-the-board pay cuts. Buffington, one of the league's highest-paid players at $2,800, refused to accept Baltimore's offer and simply quit. At 30, he never played organized baseball again.

Morgan Bulkeley

The National League's first president Morgan Bulkeley was born into a prominent family. His father was the founder of Aetna Insurance Company. It is interesting to note some highlight's of Morgan's career:

- President of Hartford baseball club
- Bank founder in Hartford
- Successful merchant in both Hartford and Brooklyn
- Hartford major, 1880–89
- Republican Connecticut governor, 1889–93
- United States Senator, 1905–11
- President of Aetna, 1879–1922

Bulkeley, a National Association holdover, left the game after 1876 and sportswise focused on his horseracing enterprise. At his death in 1922, Aetna was the largest insurance company in the nation. Bulkeley was elected to the Hall of Fame as a pioneer of the National League. He technically was the first commissioner of the league but he won that title from the pick of a hat. William Hulbert was the actual driving force behind the league.

George W. Bush

Texas Rangers managing partner, 1989–94, George W. Bush divested from the club after being elected Governor of Texas. For his $605,000 investment, Bush sold out for a cool $10 million. Six years later, he became the 42nd President of the United States. In his first national address as President, he quoted one of Yogi Berra's malapropisms. His father, George Bush, 40th President of the United States, was a left-handed first baseman for Yale.

Bill Carrigan

Manager Bill Carrigan led the Boston Red Sox to world championships in 1915 and
'16. He retired at the height of success to become a banker. Red Sox officials coaxed
him out of retirement in 1927 but he left again after the stock market crash in 1929
to tend to his investments.

Fact is, Carrigan didn't adjust well to the lively ball era. Plus, the team was at a
low point in franchise history after repeatedly shipping its best talent to the Yankees.
To this day, New England cusses former team owner Harry Frazee for dismantling the
dynasty.

Fidel Castro

As a boy, Fidel Castro would attend Cuban winter league games. He would follow the
Negro league greats to the ballpark and was occasionally allowed to play catch during
pre-game warm-ups. The righthander later pitched for Belan College and the University of Havana. Supposedly, the radical student turned down a $5,000 bonus offer
from the New York Giants to pursue a law degree.

Castro soon became a revolutionary leader, organized a coup to overthrow the
government of corrupt dictator Fulgencio Batista, and became the head of Cuba's
government in February 1959. The flow of top Cuban talent to the major leagues
was severely curtailed after President Eisenhower broke diplomatic relations with the
country in January 1961.

Baseball has been a staple in Cuba since Frank Bancroft toured the country
with fellow major leaguers in 1879.

Joe Charboneau

Joe Charboneau will be remembered for two things in baseball: for being a one-year
wonder and for his outrageous antics. In 1980, he won the Rookie of the Year Award
with Cleveland by posting an impressive .289, 23, 87 season. Unable to contain himself, Charboneau was back in the minors the following year, developed a back problem, and was never heard from again.

Among his antics, "Super Joe:"

- Opened beer bottles with his eye socket
- Shaved his head, long before it was fashionable
- Removed a tattoo with a razor blade
- Ate cigarettes
- Engaged in fistfights in boxcars for $25

After giving Buffalo fans a one-finger salute in 1983, Charboneau was released by the
Indians.

Jim Cohen

After four years playing ball in the military and another seven with the Indianapolis
Clowns as a pitcher, business manager, and bus driver, Jim Cohen's salary was cut in

1952 to help the team compensate for the low revenues generated after Jackie Robinson and others joined the bigs.

Cohen decided to quit instead and take a job in a Washington, DC, post office, where he stayed for 35 years.

Bert Convy
Actor, director, and game show host Bert Convy played three seasons in the Phillies organization.

Harry Davis
Harry Davis was a 22-year major league veteran who led the league four times in home runs, three times in doubles, twice in RBIs, and once in triples and runs. While still an active player with the Athletics, he became a city councilman in Philadelphia.

Iron Davis
George Davis was a Harvard law student who played ball during the summer. The righthander threw a no-hitter for the Miracle Braves on September 9, 1914. He retired from the game after four years at age 27 to pursue a law practice in Buffalo. The list of manager/attorneys includes Monte Ward, Hughie Jennings, Branch Rickey, Miller Huggins, and Tony LaRussa.

Al Demaree
Righthander Al Demaree won 80 games with a 2.77 ERA for four National League teams from 1912–19. He helped the Giants win the pennant in 1913 and, likewise, the Phillies in '15. After leaving the game, Demaree became a sports cartoonist syndicated in over 200 newspapers.

Bob Dillinger
Third baseman Bob Dillinger led the American League in hits with 204 in 1948 and in stolen bases for three straight years, 1947–49, for the hapless St. Louis Browns. Posting a career .306 batting average over six seasons, Dillinger quit at age 33, claiming to have lost interest in the game.

Turkey Mike Donlin
Mike Donlin was an extremely popular and talented ballplayer. He topped a .300 batting average 10 times in a 12-year career, aggregately hitting .333. For the 1905 World Champion Giants, Donlin added 124 runs, 80 RBIs, and a .356 batting average. He also placed six hits in the World Series. In 1908, he swatted .334 with 106 RBIs.

The glove in his hand was another matter. For the Reds in 1903, Donlin committed 25 errors. The resulting .900 fielding average was the lowest for a major league outfielder in the 20th century.

Donlin probably would be mentioned with the all-time greats if he had focused on the diamond. Missing the 1907, '09, and '13 seasons, Donlin left baseball to tour the vaudeville circuit with his wife, actress Mabel Hite. After retiring from baseball, he acted and produced silent films in Hollywood. His movie career lasted nearly 20 years. In all, he appeared in 56 films from 1917–35.

Dwight D. Eisenhower
Dwight Eisenhower was a star halfback at West Point and also allegedly played center field for Junction City in the Class-D Central Kansas League under an assumed name in 1912. Later, he ascended to commander of the allied forces in Europe during World War II. In 1953, Ike became the 33rd President of the United States.

Mrs. Fields
Innovative Oakland A's owner Charlie Finley was the first to position young girls in foul territory to retrieve foul balls and entertain the crowd in the 1970s. One of the ball girls was Debbie Fields.

In 1977, the 20-year-old Fields opened her first cookie store. Today, the diversified Mrs. Fields Famous Brands, Inc. has more than 4,000 franchises, under differing dessert concepts, throughout the world in shopping malls and airports.

Fred Glade
Nebraska businessman Fred Glade was torn between playing baseball and running his mill enterprise, which made him a millionaire. He left the game in 1908 but made several aborted attempts to return.

Mike Griffin
Mike Griffin was an outfielder who had knocked in 477 runs for Brooklyn the previous eight years. He had also scored 100+ runs in 10 of his 12 major league seasons, leading the league in 1889 with 152. His batting average eclipsed .300 six times. Griffin also led the league six times in fielding percentage as probably the best center fielder of the 1890s.

The Brooklyn Superbas rewarded Griffin with a contract as player–manager for the team in 1899 for $3,500. Then Brooklyn merged with the Baltimore Orioles and team management decided they wanted future Hall of Famer Ned Hanlon as manager. The team offered Griffin $300 as a conciliation. Griffin refused and would not report. He was quickly peddled to Cleveland and then St. Louis.

Because they were not offering the same money, Griffin declined to play for either team. He sued Brooklyn for failing to honor his contract. Monte Ward, as council for Brooklyn, opposed Griffin. The player was eventually awarded $2,300 in 1903, though he never played in the majors again.

M.C. Hammer
Stanley Burrell, nicknamed Hammer for his resemblance to a young Henry Aaron, was a batboy–clubhouse kid–between inning entertainer for Charlie Finley in Oakland. After dismantling his roster and cutting jobs in the front office, Finley named the young Burrell his executive vice-president.

After a stint in the Navy, Burrell gained a stake from ballplayers Mike Davis and Dwayne Murphy and began his career as a singer and actor. In all, Hammer has sold over 30 million records.

Warren G. Harding
Prior to becoming the 29th President of the United States, Warren Harding twice owned part of his hometown Marion, Ohio, franchise of the Class-C Ohio–Pennsylvania League in 1907 and Class-D Ohio State League in 1911. Harding was proud of helping develop and promote Wilbur Cooper and Jake Daubert to the majors. All major leagues games were postponed when Harding died in office in 1923.

Harry Harper
Lefthanded pitcher Harry Harper won 57 games from 1913–23, mostly with Washington. Perennially, he was among the league leaders in walks, wild pitches, and hit batsmen. On August 25, 1921, the Yankees were being beat by Cleveland 15-1, so Harper plunked three consecutive batters in the eighth inning, precipitating a brawl. He also set an organized baseball record of 20 walks in a game that wasn't topped until 1951.

After leaving the game, the industrialist made millions in trucking and road construction back home in New Jersey. He even took a run at the U.S. Senate.

Emmet Heidrick
St. Louis outfielder Emmet Heidrick was born to wealth, a luxury afforded few ballplayers at the turn of the 20th century. By his seventh season in 1904, he had lost the confidence of his teammates, who felt that his numerous claims of leg injuries merely masked his lack of enthusiasm for the game.

After his father's death later in the season, Heidrick quit the game at age 28; though, he did reappear for 26 games in 1908.

Shozo Higuchi
Nankai Hawks first baseman and outfielder Shozo Higuchi hit .281 from 1962–71. He retired in 1971, when his father died, to take over the family's nut-and-bolt manufacturing company.

Jay Hook
Righthanded pitcher Jay Hook signed a bonus contract with the Cincinnati Reds. He left baseball in 1964 after eight major league seasons, a 29-62 record, and a 5.23 ERA to pursue a job with the Chrysler Corporation. He had recently attained his Master's Degree in Thermodynamics.

J. Edgar Hoover
On March 10, 1951, J. Edgar Hoover, FBI director from 1924–72, declined baseball's $65,000/year offer to become their third commissioner, replacing the outgoing Happy Chandler. Why he was under consideration is up to various interpretations, probably based on his law and order reputation. It would have been quite a different game in

the 1950s, not for the better. Hoover had previously been approached by the NFL to succeed Joe Carr, deceased, as commissioner in 1939.

Harry Hughes
Maryland Governor Harry Hughes, 1979–87, played in the Yankees farm system at Easton.

Jesse Jackson
Jesse Jackson was a 3-letter athlete in high school in baseball, basketball, and football. The San Francisco Giants offered the 18-year-old pitcher a $6,000 bonus to sign with the club in 1959. He turned it down when the Giants offered caucasian catcher Dickie Dietz a $95,000 bonus. Jackson was affronted when the club offered a white, local athlete more money.

Japanese Diet Members

Shigejiro Kanbayashi   Jun Misawa
Giichiro Shiraki

Edward Kelly
Ed Kelly played pro ball from 1912–16. He also served two stints as a U.S. Representative from Illinois from 1931–43 and '45–47.

John Kennedy
In 1941, there was talk of patriarch Joseph Kennedy purchasing the Brooklyn Dodgers and installing his frustrated (back injury) athlete son, John, at the helm of the baseball franchise. The deal fell through and JFK headed to the Navy instead.

Bill Klem
Hall of Fame umpire Bill Klem controlled National League games from 1905–40. Describing his last game, he noted on a close play that he was "almost certain" the player was tagged out. For the first time in his career, he only *thought* rather than *knew* the player was out. He retired that afternoon.

Ed Lafitte
Ed Lafitte jumped the Tigers after one game in 1912 to pursue a dental career at age 26. The righthander did return to pitch in the Federal League, notching the circuit's only no-hitter on September 19, 1914, for the Brooklyn Tip-Tops.

David Lander
David Lander, better known as Squiggy on the *Laverne and Shirley* television sitcom during the 1970s, began scouting in 1997 for the Angels before joining the Seattle Mariners in 2004.

Bill Lange
Outfielder Bill Lange, nicknamed Little Eva, was a big RBI man who batted .330 for his career. After being discovered by Frank Chance, Little Eva joined the Chicago

Colts and hit .389 after only three years in the league. In fact, after his first season Lange never hit below .319. His base-running style rivaled that of Ty Cobb's for its intensity.

Lange held out for a $500 raise at the beginning of spring training 1897. Chicago paid but he still wouldn't report. What he really wanted was to attend the heavyweight championship fight between his hometown hero, James J. Corbett, and Bob Fitzsimmons in March. Feigning injury, Lange refused to report until after the bout. That night, Fitzsimmons began a two-year title reign. Incidentally, that fight sparked the era of sports video coverage, making an estimated $750,000 for the Veriscope Company.

Lange quit baseball at the height of his career at age 29 to wed the daughter of a San Francisco real estate magnate. Her father had forbidden her to marry a lowly baseball player, an attitude that many in American society shared at the time. Lange was quoted as saying, "Plant flowers on my baseball grave out in center field, for I am in love and will never play there again."

Despite the offer of a substantial raise and even though the marriage ended in divorce, Lange never returned to play in the majors. Later, he became a scout and helped his nephew George "High Pockets" Kelly, a future Hall of Fame first baseman.

Alfred W. Lawson

London-born Al Lawson pitched in only three games in the National League back in 1890, losing all, but continued playing and managing in the minors until 1907. Lawson, a huckster, aggressively promoted minor league ball. He claimed to have sparked the formation of 16 associations and led world tours to Australia, Cuba, Great Britain, Hawaii, and New Zealand. He was also among the earliest to experiment with illuminating the sky so that ball could be played in the evening.

Other Lawson commercial endeavors include religious and economic publications and political and philosophical associations. He called his religion/philosophy Lawsonomy.

In 1906, Lawson became enchanted with the breakthroughs by Orville and Wilbur Wright and other aviators. Two years later, he began publishing the industry's first magazine, *Fly*. Eventually, the entrepreneur amassed enough capital to form Lawson Aircraft in Green Bay, Wisconsin, with the idea of producing affordable passenger planes to compete with the railroad industry. The company soon moved to Milwaukee and manufactured a series of commercial aircraft. Today, Lawson's contributions as an aviation pioneer go largely unnoticed.

Doc Leitner

Doc Leitner, a pitcher for the 1887 Indianapolis Hoosiers of the National League, used baseball to fund his participation in medical school. Upon graduation, he quit the game.

Animal Lesley

Relief pitcher Brad Lesley appeared in 54 major league games from 1982–85, mostly with Cincinnati. He then joined the Hankyu Braves and made a name for himself as a character in Japan. He left the Braves in 1987 to join the cast of a television comedy, shown now in the United States as *The Most Extreme Elimination Challenge*. Between 1992–2000, Lesley appeared in six American movies as well.

Ted Lewis

Ted Lewis won 93 games for the Boston Beaneaters from 1897–1901. He went 46-19 during the 1897–98 championship seasons. During the off-season, Lewis coached baseball and continued his education at Harvard. After the 1901 season, the 29-year-old retired from baseball to teach full-time at Columbia University. Eventually, Lewis became president of Dartmouth College. A pasttime of his was playing catch with Robert Frost while discussing poetry.

Lewis, a minister, was one of the first National Leaguers to jump contract for the American League's maiden season. His personal justification was the illegality and immorality of the reserve clause.

Douglas MacArthur

After forcing Happy Chandler from the commissioner's chair, in part because of his support of integration, major league executives sought the prestige of a military figure for the top job. General MacArthur refused citing his advanced age.

Later, Major General Emmett O'Donnell was elected but could not leave his post. They eventually settled on National League president Ford Frick.

Dave Malarcher

Dave Malarcher was a star player for New Orleans University as a high school student. He went on to become a long-time third baseman and manager in the Negro leagues from 1916–34. The speedy switch-hitter kept his average around .300 and gained a reputation as a productive clutch hitter.

Out of college in 1916, "Gentleman Dave" joined the Indianapolis ABCs for $50 a month. In 1918, Malarcher joined the Army and served as a member of the 309th Pioneer Infantry. In a bunker in France, he received a letter from Rube Foster asking him to join the Chicago American Giants after the war. The thought must have been a big morale boost.

After a stint with the Detroit Stars, he did indeed join Foster and became his chief understudy. In fact, Malarcher replaced Foster as the team's manager in 1926 and gained a reputation as the finest leader in the game.

Malarcher quit baseball in 1934 to enter the real estate business. Summing up his experiences on the road in the Negro leagues, he stated, "They were conditions, which I could not continue to bear."

Cy Malis

Righthanded pitcher Cy Malis appeared in one game for the Philadelphia Phillies in 1934. Then, he became an actor for MGM Studios, where he worked for 35 years. He appeared in more than 35 film and television roles from 1938–60.

Doc Medich

Doc Medich earned his medical degree from the University of Pittsburgh. One day during the summer of 1978, he jumped into the stands at Memorial Stadium in Baltimore and performed heart massage on a fallen fan, saving his life. After retiring from the game, Medich went into sports medicine.

Minor League Actors

The following minor leaguers had significant Hollywood or television careers as actors, directors, and/or producers:

Byron Browne	15 + film and TV roles	1997–
Wibur Higby	69 film roles	1914–34
Sean McCann (scout)	100 + film and TV roles	1974–
Stack Pierce	100 + film and TV roles	1971–98
Jeff Richards	30 + film roles	1948–86
Lew Temple	30 + film roles	1993–
Guinn "Big Boy" Williams	200 + film and TV roles	1919–61
Jim Van Wyck	30 + films	1979–

Richard Nixon

President Nixon was a life-long baseball fan. At one point or another, he was considered as for executive positions, such as general counsel for the Players Association, league president and commissioner. In 1985, Nixon served as an arbitrator in the impending strike negotiations.

Rosey O'Donnell

Rosey O'Donnell was elected commissioner on August 21, 1951. However, President Truman would not allow the major general to step down from his post as commander of bomber forces in Korea. National League president, Ford Frick, eventually began an undistinguished reign as commissioner.

Franklin W. Olin

Frank Olin played 49 games between 1884–85 in three different leagues, the American Association, the Union Association, and the National League. The paychecks helped fund his engineering education at Cornell University. He went on to form a company in Illinois that supplied blasting powder to coal fields throughout the Midwest. The firm grew into a small arms ammunition supplier called Olin Industries. Later, it merged with another chemical supplier to form the current Olin Corporation. At retirement, Olin was said to be worth $60 million, making him the richest of the early baseballers. Today, a young student can study at the Franklin W. Olin College of Engineering in Massachusetts.

Wes Parker

Wes Parker won six Gold Gloves at first base for the Dodgers from 1967–72. Save 1970, he didn't pound the ball like a prototypical first sacker. Parker retired in 1972 but reappeared in Japan with Nankai in 1974. From 1970–88, he acted in five movies and made seven guest television appearances.

Art Passarella

American League umpire, 1941–53 minus military service, Art Passarella had a reoccurring role on the television show *The Streets of San Francisco* that aired on ABC from 1972–77.

Arlie Pond

Arlie Pond won 16 games for the pennant-winning Baltimore Orioles in 1896. Pond was also a doctor. He left the team in 1898 to enlist in an Army medical unit during the Spanish–American War. The medical officer traveled to Cuba and the Philippines during the conflict and remained in the Philippines for two decades to fight disease. Later, as a colonel in World War I, Pond became Assistant Surgeon General of the U.S. Army. His post took him to Siberia, Russia, but once again he returned to the Philippines. He died there in 1930. As a world traveler, Pond acted as an unofficial ambassador for the game and spurred its development abroad.

Charley Pride

After integration, Charley Pride pitched in the Negro leagues during the 1950s for Memphis and Birmingham. He became much more famous as a country singer with more than 50 top-10 hits, the first coming in 1966. As such, he was the first big time African-American country star, leading to induction in the Country Music Hall of Fame in 2000.

Hub Pruett

Hub Pruett pitched for four teams in seven seasons, notching a mere 29 victories and amassing a 4.63 ERA. His claim to fame is striking out Babe Ruth 10 times in their first 13 meetings. Studying medicine in the off-season, Dr. Pruett left baseball in 1932 to set up a practice in St. Louis.

Ronald Reagan

Dutch Reagan did studio re-creations of Cubs games for WHO radio in the 1930s. He gained a national following after NBC purchased his station. While covering the Cubs during spring training in California, the aspiring actor was signed by Warner Brothers. The impending movie career ended his broadcasting days.

Reagan later entered politics and became Governor of California and, in 1981, the 39th President of the United States. On September 30, 1988, while in office, President Reagan called an inning and a half of play-by-play with Cubs announcers Harry Carey and Steve Stone.

Lee Richmond

Pitcher Lee Richmond left the game at age 26 in 1883 to practice medicine in his home state of Ohio. He had won 71 games the three previous seasons for Worcester in the National League. In 1880, he led the league with 74 starts. Richmond did reappear for a couple of games in the American Association in 1886.

Al Rosen

Power-hitting third baseman Al Rosen joined the Cleveland organization after serving in the Navy in World War II. By 1950, Ken Keltner was released, allowing Rosen to move into the starting lineup. He set the rookie record with 37 home runs and also knocked in 116 runs. The following year, Rosen produced another 102 RBIs. The Indian took the league lead with 105 in '52.

In 1953, Rosen was dominating. He led the league in total bases, runs, on-base percentage, and slugging average. Plus, no one bettered his 43 homers and 145 RBIs. However, Rosen lost the batting title and, consequently, the Triple Crown in his last at-bat to Mickey Vernon. The slick fielder led all American League third basemen in assists and double plays. Rosen was unanimously elected MVP.

In 1954, the Indians took the pennant by eight games over the Yankees with 111 victories, though they were swept by the Giants in the World Series. In the All-Star Game that year, Rosen hit two home runs and a single for 5 RBIs in front of his hometown fans. Though he broke his finger, Rosen still managed 24 home runs and 102 RBIs. From 1950–54, Rosen notched impressive .298, 156, 570 marks.

An off-season auto accident caused whiplash that impaired the superstar all of 1955. A combination of nagging injuries, contract disputes, fallen production, booing by fickle Cleveland fans, and a successful brokerage career led Rosen to call it quits after the 1956 season at the age of 32.

He later had a noted front-office career with the Yankees, Astros, and Giants, signing Dave Righetti, Dickie Thon, Ray Knight, Mike Scott, Kevin Mitchell, and Dave Dravecky, among others. In 1979, working for Bally's Hotel and Casino, Rosen hired Willie Mays, causing Commissioner Bowie Kuhn to ban the Hall of Famer.

Kurt Russell

Kurt Russell played parts of three seasons as a second baseman in the Northwest and Texas Leagues from 1971–73 in the Angels organization. He tore his rotator cuff in a collision at second base and returned to acting. Russell had started acting in films at age 10 in 1961. He went on to have a long career as a movie star and action hero performing in *Silkwood*, *Backdraft*, and *Tombstone*, among others.

Henry Schmidt

Texan Henry Schmidt joined the Brooklyn Superbas in 1903. He got the nod to start the opening day game versus the Giants at the Polo Grounds and beat the great Christy Mathewson. The righthander went on to record 21 more victories. After a tremendous rookie season, Schmidt refused to continue his baseball career, stating his dislike for life in the eastern United States. He is the only man to win 20 games in his sole major league season.

Two years later, he was booted out of the Pacific Coast League for suspicion of tainted play.

Tillie Shafer

Tillie Shafer came from money. Playing baseball for John McGraw, starting in 1909, was merely a distraction for him; in fact, it was an annoyance. He had no patience for the discipline the profession required. He would much rather travel and enjoy the benefits his parent's money could afford. It was an effort for McGraw to keep Shafer, who continually jumped the team, focused. He finally gave up in 1913.

Al Simmons

Hall of Famer Al Simmons was one of the most feared hitters of his day and a personal favorite of Connie Mack. "Bucketfoot Al" was so called because the righthanded batter's left foot pointed down the third base line and he stepped that way when swinging. Mack refused to tinker with the natural hitter's stance.

The rookie hit .308 with 102 RBIs in 1924. Simmons would knock in 100 + runs his first 11 seasons, 12 total in 20 major league campaigns. He killed the ball his sophomore year, hitting .384 with 253 hits, 43 doubles, 24 home runs, 122 runs, and 129 RBIs. Ty Cobb joined the team in 1927 and proved to be a good influence on Simmons, who constantly sought his advice on hitting. For a time, the A's outfield boasted Simmons, Tris Speaker, and Cobb, though the latter two were well past their prime.

Simmons was a part of the Philadelphia dynasty from 1927–32 that produced three second-place finishes, three pennants, and two world championships with fellow Hall of Famers MGR Connie Mack, OF Cobb, C Mickey Cochrane, 2B Eddie Collins, OF Zach Wheat, LHP Lefty Grove, 1B Jimmie Foxx, OF Speaker, and RHP Waite Hoyt. The Foxx/Simmons duo rivals that of the Yankees Ruth/Gehrig, Braves Aaron/Mathews and Japan's Sadaharu Oh/Shigeo Nagashima for power and production.

During the three-year pennant stretch 1929–31, Simmons hit .378 with 92 home runs and 453 RBIs. He copped one RBI crown and two batting titles. Incredibly, 14 of his 36 home runs in 1930 occurred in the eighth or ninth inning. In four World Series, he batted a cool .329 with 6 homers, 15 runs, and 17 RBIs. Simmons finished his career with 307 home runs, 1,827 RBIs, and a .334 batting average.

By 1939, he was 37 years old and had lost his starting job. Simmons stayed until he was 44 trying to notch his 3,000th hit. Meanwhile, he lamented about the times he begged off playing because of a hangover or left one-sided contests early to catch a shower and hit the town. He also lost a lot of time from injuries and sickness. Distressed, Simmons claimed that he lost a little of his aggressiveness after gaining success so quickly in the majors. Ultimately, Simmons fell 73 hits short. He advised an up-and-coming Stan Musial to "never relax on any time at bat; never miss a game you can play."

Likewise, Senators outfielder Sam Rice retired 13 hits shy of 3,000 in 1934. He had no internal drive, though, to reach 3,000. In fact, he claimed he didn't even know how many hits he had. Plus, at that point in history, 3,000 wasn't the magical number it is today.

Albert Goodwill Spalding

Al Spalding was one of the pioneers of the National League. Joining the Chicago White Stockings in 1876, he pitched the league's first shutout on April 25. Spalding had already led the National Association the previous four years in victories. His Boston team won the pennant each of those years. In the National League's first year, Spalding also led in victories with a 47-12 record and eight shutouts. Arm strain relegated him to playing first base the following year.

Spalding was the first professional to win 200 games. In the National Association, he put together a 207-56 record in five years that included 20 straight victories to begin the 1875 season. He bettered his win total every year, going 20-10, 37-8, 41-15, 52-18, and 57-5 from 1871–75. Spalding's career winning percentage was an outstanding .787. The versatile athlete also batted .320 in 1,400 at-bats.

Spalding quit playing baseball at age 28 to devote himself to the sporting goods company that still bears his name. The business eventually made him a multi-millionaire. His friendship with National League president William Hulbert ensured him of supplying the official league balls. In 1882, Spalding assumed the presidency of the Chicago National League club upon Hulbert's death.

At the end of the 1888 season, Spalding led the first international tour promoting baseball, traveling to Ireland, England, France, Italy, Hawaii, New Zealand, Australia, Ceylon, and Egypt. Surely, part of his plan was to increase the customer base for his company. In fact, he opened a branch of operations in England.

Spalding later published *America's National Game*, one of the first extensive chronicles of early baseball history. Much of its content highlights his personal contributions to the development of the game, real or imagined.

State Legislature Members

Victor Aldridge	Indiana	majors
Chuck Campbell	Illinois	minors
George Hurley	Washington	minors
Larry Jackson	Idaho	majors
Bobby Pafford	Georgia	minors (umpire)
Herman Wademeyer	Hawaii	minors

Billy Sunday

Billy Sunday was discovered by Cap Anson at a firemen's skill tournament in Iowa. Anson judged him to be the fastest man he ever saw and assigned him to the major leagues without any lower classification experience. Not surprisingly, he struck out his first 13 times at bat. Over eight seasons, Sunday proved little more than a spray hitter but at times he did shine on the base paths, as Anson suspected.

Undistinguished as a ballplayer, Sunday quit the game at age 28 to take a job with the YMCA in Chicago. His pay cut exceeded $2,500 a year, but he deemed the religious calling more powerful. The epiphany came to him while drinking on a street corner with King Kelly, Ned Williamson, and Silver Splint and listening to a gospel service in 1887. Sunday became one of the nation's leading evangelists as an ordained

Presbyterian minister. His flamboyant sermons led the prohibitionist movement and decried science and liberalism.

Ron Taylor
Righthanded pitcher Ron Taylor, a reliever with the champion 1969 Mets, retired at age 34 in 1972 to pursue a medical career. He later became the Blue Jays team physician.

Joe Tepsic
Bonus baby Joe Tepsic played in only 15 games for the Brooklyn Dodgers. He quit in 1947, refusing a demotion to the minors. His case along with numerous others highlighted the economic inefficiency of the bonus program and later bore the amateur free agent draft.

Conway Twitty
Upon graduation of high school, singer Conway Twitty was offered a contract by the Philadelphia Phillies but he was drafted into the military instead.

Fred Vinson
Fred Vinson was offered the commissioner's job after Judge Landis' death in 1944. However, Vinson was in FDR's cabinet at the time and felt he couldn't leave his post during the war. He later became Chief Justice of the United States.

Blue Washington
Blue Washington pitched for Rube Foster's Chicago American Giants in the mid-1910s. In all, he appeared in 58 films from 1919–57. He also worked with Buster Keaton in silent movies. Similarly, St. Louis Cardinals outfielder Ernie Orsatti worked as a stunt double for Keaton for several years. Blue's son Kenny integrated the National Football League in 1946.

Herman Wedemeyer
From 1948–49, Herman Wedemeyer played in the All-American Football Conference as a tailback for the Los Angeles Dons and Baltimore Colts. He then played baseball for the PCL San Francisco Seals' farm club in Salt Lake City in 1950.

Wedemeyer went on to serve in the Hawaiian state congress from 1971–74. He also found a role on the television show *Hawaii Five-O* in which he played Duke Lakela from 1972–80.

Dave Wills
Dave Wills was a first baseman for the Louisville Colonels in 1899. After hitting only .223 in 24 games, he fell back on his previous training as a medical student and joined the Marines. Wills served more than 20 years before retiring as a major.

Al Worthington
Seven-year major league veteran Al Worthington was picked up by the Chicago White Sox in mid-1960. He quit the team after realizing that they stole signs through

the scoreboard. Worthington commented, "Baseball is a wonderful game. When it's not played on the up and up, it's time to quit."

The righthander would pitch another seven years in the big leagues but didn't return until 1963. In July '53, Worthington pitched shutouts in his first two major league starts. Converted to a reliever, he led the league in saves with Minnesota in 1968, totaling 110 in his career.

CHAPTER ELEVEN

~

Illness and Dependency

Willie Adams

Righthanded pitcher Willie Adams was in the majors from 1912–14 and again 1918–19. He was still in the minors in 1922, when he suffered a career-ending heart attack at age 31.

Jabo Andrews

Jabo Andrews played in the Negro leagues from 1930–43. He retired as manager the Philadelphia Stars, suffering from tuberculosis.

Albert Belle

Outfielder Albert Belle was one of the top hitters in baseball during the 1990s, perhaps of all time. However, he will forever be remembered as a malcontent who left the game with few fans.

Belle's most productive year was 1995 with the Indians when he clobbered 50 home runs, the 12th man to do so. He also batted .317 with a .401 on-base percentage and led the league in runs scored, doubles, homers, RBIs, and slugging.

Through twelve seasons in 2000, Belle amassed 381 dingers, 1,239 RBIs, a .295 batting average, and a .564 slugging average. He never fell below 100 RBIs after his first full season in '91. Production any team would love to bat at cleanup. Belle's 1,199 RBIs in his last 10 seasons are eclipsed only by Babe Ruth, Lou Gehrig, Jimmie Foxx, Al Simmons, and Mel Ott for a 10-year period.

An arthritic hip forced his retirement in spring training 2001 at age 34. Belle had three years remaining on a 5-year, $65 million contract with Baltimore. The money was guaranteed. In order to capitalize on an insurance policy that would pay 70% of the remaining salary, the Orioles declared their right fielder "totally disabled and unable to perform." The hip injury was diagnosed as degenerative with no possibility for improvement.

While Belle's numbers compare favorably with 2001 Hall of Fame inductee Kirby Puckett, it is doubtful the bad actor will garner the support that the affable Puckett fostered.

Frank Bird

Frank Bird collapsed on the field during an exhibition game in 1893. The resulting paralysis ended his career at age 24. The rookie catcher had spent the previous summer with St. Louis in the National League.

Don Black

Tired of pitcher Don Black's heavy drinking, the A's suspended and shipped him to Cleveland in 1945. On July 10, 1947, the righthander pitched a no-hitter against his old team in front of 48,000 at Municipal Stadium. The masses had shown up to witness Larry Doby's first appearance in the bigs, but he didn't even play.

The next season, on September 13, Black collapsed at home plate, suffering a brain hemorrhage. Though the pitcher recovered, his major league career was over. In six major league seasons, Black compiled a 34–55 record with a 4.35 ERA. Black did not live to see his 43rd birthday.

Vida Blue

Most baseball scouts ignored Vida Blue because he had signed a letter of intent to play football for the University of Houston. Undeterred, Oakland's Charlie Finley offered him a $25,000 bonus and Blue accepted. In and out of the minors in 1969–70, he threw a no-hitter versus Minnesota on September 21, 1970.

In 1971, Blue had one of the finest pitching seasons since World War II. Going 24-8 with 301 Ks, eight shutouts, and a 1.82 ERA, the lefthander won the Cy Young and MVP Awards. The following year, he held out for more money. Baseball enthusiast and U.S. President Richard Nixon even made a comment in support of the superstar. Blue eventually signed for a $35,000 raise to $50,000.

Oakland proceeded to win three consecutive world titles. The southpaw won 20 again in 1973 and '75. Then Finley set about to dismantle his team and attempted to sell Blue for $1.5 million-plus in deals to the Yankees and Reds in late 1977. Continuing his feud with the A's owner, Commissioner Bowie Kuhn vetoed both deals as detrimental to baseball. Twenty years later, Bud Selig had no problem allowing Wayne Huizenga to dismantle the World Champion Marlins.

Blue was later sold to the Giants for a lesser sum. In 1978, Vida had a fine season for San Francisco, winning 18 and starting the All-Star Game. He became the first man to start the Midsummer Classic for both leagues.

In August 1983, it was revealed that the federal government was investigating several Royals players for the use, distribution, and sale of cocaine. Blue, Willie Mays Aikens, Jerry Martin, and Willie Wilson were sentenced to a year in prison with nine months suspended. Suspended by Commissioner Bowie Kuhn, Blue sat out all of 1984, as well.

After leaving the Giants in 1986, Blue attempted to re-sign with Oakland; however, he failed a urine test. The player meekly retired instead of facing further controversy. Aikens and Martin were already gone. The pitcher left behind a 209-win career with an impressive 3.26 ERA.

Asa Brainard

Asa Brainard was the star pitcher of the great Cincinnati Red Stocking team of 1869, baseball's first openly declared professional team. The Reds went 65-0 that year as they traveled throughout the country. He threw hard, varied speeds, and usually hit his mark, meaning he was a control specialist. Also, Brainard had no qualms about working inside.

Brainard was at the forefront of the alleged game-fixing scandal that tainted the Red Stockings run in 1869. Supposedly, he was offered $500 to throw a game to the Troy Haymakers. His errant pitching yielded 13 runs in the first two innings. In the end, Troy walked off the field with the score tied at 17, thus, preserving the wagers of its owner John Morrissey and his friends, estimated at $60,000.

Off the field, Brainard fit in well in an era of heavy drinking. Often begging off work, he suffered from many self-claimed injuries and illnesses. Eventually, Brainard lost his edge, in part because of alcoholism. This affliction would shorten and derail many a bright baseball career in the decades to follow.

Dick Brown
Dick Brown caught for four teams over nine major league seasons. In 1965 with Baltimore, he was diagnosed with a brain tumor. Brown died in 1970 at age 35.

Pete Browning
Pete Browning was the original "Louisville Slugger," the man the bat was named to honor. In 1884, while playing for his hometown team, the Louisville Eclipse of the American Association, he broke his favorite bat. John Hillerich, a woodworker's son, was at the game and brought Browning back to his father's shop. The two designed and built a new bat to the ballplayer's specifications out of white ash. Thus, the family entered the bat making business that still bears its name. Or so the story goes.

Browning was one of the best hitters of the 19th century, winning four batting championships. The righthander was the premier hitter of the American Association. His .341 lifetime batting average ranks among the all-time greats. Browning scored 100 + runs three times and knocked in 118 runners in 1887.

Yet, his career was marred by chronic drunkenness and horrible defensive play. Browning bragged, "I can't hit the ball until I hit the bottle." He was also illiterate, partially because he skipped school in his embarrassment over a hearing problem. In fact, as a child he went completely deaf for a time and incurred some permanent hearing loss. He suffered from mastoiditis, an infection of the bone behind the ear. From his position in the field, he could not hear the calls of teammates or the crack of the bat.

Browning's suffering led, in part, to heavy drinking, the effects of which, combined with the worsening of the mastoiditis, led to his retirement in 1894. He died at the age of 44 in 1905.

Mike Chartak
Outfielder Mike Chartak spent four seasons in the American League from 1940–44, making it to the series with the Browns in '44. Then his career was cut short by tuberculosis complications.

Russ Christopher
Righthander Russ Christopher led the league in saves in 1948, helping the Indians claim the pennant. In all, he notched 54 wins in the majors from 1942–48. He was

forced to retire because of rheumatic heart disease, which led to his early death at age 37 in December 1954.

Rich Coggins

In his rookie season in 1973, Rich Coggins produced 54 runs, 17 stolen bases, and a .319 batting average. The Baltimore Orioles were looking forward to a long, productive career. Unfortunately, a thyroid condition forced his retirement in the spring of 1975.

Larry Corcoran

Larry Corcoran was one of the best pitchers of the 1880s. He won 170 games from 1880–84, 43 as a rookie in '80. At one time or another, he led the league in wins, ERA, strikeouts, and winning percentage. Helping himself in the field, Corcoran twice led the league in putouts. The righthander is one of only a handful of men who threw three no-hitters.

Corcoran was one of the first pitchers to use signals with his battery mate, King Kelly. He would move his tobacco wad from one side of his mouth to the other to indicate a curveball or fastball. Overworked, 2,281 innings in five years, and suffering from Bright's disease, Corcoran ended his career at age 27. He died five years later.

Bright's disease, named after 19th century English physician Richard Bright, is an inflammatory kidney disease prevalent in males. At times, it is also referred to as acute nephritis.

Buddy Daley

Buddy Daley, a natural righthander, contracted polio as a child. It caused his right arm to wither and become shorter than his left. Nevertheless, he pitched lefthanded in the American League for 10 seasons, amassing 60 victories including the finale of the 1961 World Series for the Yankees.

Bill Delancey

Bill Delancey hit .316 with 13 homers and 40 RBIs while platooning at catcher for the World Champion Cardinals in 1934. Branch Rickey had high hopes for the rookie. However, he was diagnosed with tuberculosis in 1935 and left the game. A return in '40 proved to be unsuccessful. Delancey died six years later on his 35th birthday.

Ed Doheny

Lefthander Ed Doheny helped the Pittsburgh Pirates win pennants in 1902 and '03 with a 32-12 record, a solid .727 winning percentage. He also went 6-2 for the pennant-driving '01 team after being traded for in June. The totals account for half the wins of his nine-year career.

In 1902, Doheny with fellow pitchers Jack Chesbro, Deacon Phillippe, Jesse Tannehill, and Sam Leever helped the Pirates finish 27.5 games ahead of their closest rival in the National League. This accomplishment, along with consecutive pennants in 1901–'02–'03, makes Pittsburgh the first dynasty of the 20th century and one of its most underrated.

In late July 1903, Doheny disappeared. He had been acting paranoid, especially when drinking. He believed that detectives were following him and departed for home to avoid them. He returned to the club two weeks later.

Just prior to the inaugural modern World Series in 1903 versus Boston, Doheny attacked several men with a poker. The delirious and paranoid Doheny believed they were the detectives sent to spy on him. His brother picked him up on September 22 and escorted him home. In October, Doheny was committed to an Andover, Massachusetts, mental facility. There, he assaulted a medical aide with a cast iron stove leg. At age 29, Doheny never again played in the majors.

Dave Dravecky

Fans of the current generation will forever remember the images of the snapping of Joe Theismann's leg and the breaking of Dave Dravecky's arm and his subsequent flailing around on the pitcher's mound in pain.

Dravecky went 14-10 for the Padres in 1983 and appeared in the All-Star Game. In '84, the lefthander won nine with eight saves and a 3.58 ERA in 156 innings for the National League Champions and pitched 10 2/3 shutout frames in the postseason. A trade brought him to San Francisco in 1987.

Arthroscopic surgery revealed a cancerous tumor in his pitching arm. It was removed in October 1988, along with half the deltoid muscle. Dravecky rehabilitated and made an improbable return the following season. In his first game back with the Giants, the southpaw picked up the win, capping an amazing comeback.

In the sixth inning of his next start, the weakened bone gave out (it had been frozen during the operation to help kill the cancer), and Dravecky fell to the ground, bringing a sickening feeling to all. The Giants won the pennant that year. During the celebration, someone fell on his arm and re-broke it. An examination discovered that the cancer had returned. Dravecky's left arm was later amputated.

Ed Dundon

Ed Dundon pitched two years, 1883–84, in the American Association for the Columbus Buckeyes. The righthander had lost his hearing because of a childhood illness. He was the first deaf-mute to play in the majors. Some say hand signals for balls and strikes were developed to keep him informed. While in the Army in 1880, Dundon was assaulted with a knife and nearly killed when another soldier took his lack of verbal reply as an insult.

Ryne Duren

Ryne Duren was an intimidating reliever with a 95-mph fastball and a touch of wildness. He was also a chronic alcoholic who went downhill after joining the heavy-drinking Yankees, a group that, he estimates, included 13 alcoholics.

As a rookie in 1958 with New York, the righthander led the league with 20 saves, won 6 games, posted a 2.02 ERA, and joined the All-Star team. In the World

Series, Duren won a game, lost a game, and picked up a save, posting a 1.93 ERA over nine innings pitched.

On June 9, 1961, Duren fanned a major league record seven consecutive batters. A month later, he appeared in his third All-Star game. Duren would be gone four years later. His drunken antics eventually led him to a bridge in August '65 where Gil Hodges stopped him from killing himself. Subsequently, Duren burned his house down and passed out at the wheel.

Several failed rehabilitation stints and suicide attempts later, Duren finally cleaned up in 1968. He became a hospital director and alcohol educator.

Jim Eisenreich

Jim Eisenreich hit .290 over 15 major league seasons. But first, he had to overcome Tourette's syndrome which forced him out of the game in 1984 after only 48 games. The lefthander returned in '87 with the help of medication to become an extremely popular and productive player, five times hitting over .300.

Dock Ellis

Righthanded pitcher Dock Ellis was constantly at odds with Pirates management, fans, and sportswriters. At times, though, he looked brilliant on the mound. In 1970, Ellis threw a no-hitter against San Diego even though he claimed to have been under the influence of LSD.

In 1971, he started the All-Star Game and went 19-9 with a 3.06 ERA for the world champions.

Ellis was known as perhaps the most hated ballplayer in Pirates history, often making outrageous statements and showing ambivalence to the resulting furor. He won just enough for the team to keep him around for eight seasons. In December 1975, Pittsburgh management finally shipped the disgruntled pitcher to the Yankees.

Ellis flourished in Billy Martin's hectic clubhouse, winning 17 games with a 3.19 ERA and copping the Comeback Player of the Year Award. Then, he was quickly pedaled to the A's, Rangers, Mets, and Pirates before finally seeking help for his drug and alcohol problems. Eventually, he sobered up, became a drug counselor, and ran a rehabilitation center.

Nick Esasky

First-round draft pick Nick Esasky was brought up by the Reds in 1983 to replace Johnny Bench at third base. After six unfulfilled seasons in Cincinnati, Esasky was traded to Boston, where he posted a .277, 30, 108 season in 1989 in righthanded-hitter friendly Fenway Park. The free agent then signed a big deal with Atlanta.

His career was over the following season at age 30 due to dizziness caused by an ear infection, vertigo. Likewise, Ken Dayley's career also ended because of vertigo.

Charles "Victory" Faust

Thirty-year-old farm boy Charles Faust ran into a fortuneteller one day in 1911 who told him that he was destined to pitch for the New York Giants and win the pennant.

He feverishly approached John McGraw with the news. McGraw, probably amusing himself, offered the man a tryout the following day.

Throwing with a silly windup, Faust set out to impress the manager. His lack of skill was obvious but McGraw let him continue to the amusement of his players. Faust even took batting practice and the players, joining in on the joke, let Faust hit and run around the bases.

Amused, McGraw let Faust sit on the bench during that day's game. The Giants began a winning streak. The good luck charm was allowed to travel with the team, warm up prior to each contest, and sit on the bench in full uniform. Soon, the press caught on and began printing the exploits of Charles "Victory" Faust. A vaudeville promoter lured Faust away from the team, offering him $200 a day. Without their good luck charm, the Giants began losing.

Faust jumped his theatre contract and rejoined the Giants. By now, the entire league was in on the joke. Opposing teams would allow Faust to come to bat after the third out of an inning to take his licks to the delight of the crowd. McGraw even inserted Faust as a relief pitcher in two games at the end of the season. He gave up one run on two hits in two full innings. At bat, he was hit by a pitch, allowed to steal second and third by the laughing Dodgers and even scored. The Giants, indeed, won the pennant.

Faust reappeared during spring training 1912. But McGraw, still upset over the World Series loss the previous year, prohibited Faust from wearing a uniform. Nevertheless, he was allowed to sit on the bench in street clothes. All the while, Faust was trying get back in uniform to help the team. He even appealed to the National Commission for reinstatement, to no avail. Finally, he gave up and left the club.

In December 1914, Faust was committed to a mental hospital in Washington State. He died there six months later of tuberculosis and the hapless Giants finished at the bottom of the standings the following season.

Rube Foster

Negro league pitcher and pioneer Rube Foster possessed a nasty screwball that he flung from a submarine delivery. In 1903, he struck out 18 batters in a single game. Around that time, no box score has been found to solidify the date, Foster defeated Philadelphia Athletic and future Hall of Famer Rube Waddell in a barnstorming contest. Hence, he gained the nickname "Rube." It is further rumored that Foster taught the screwball to Christy Mathewson at John McGraw's behest.

Foster is considered one of the premier Negro league pitchers at the turn of the century along with Dan McClellan, Harry Buckner, and Walter Ball.

While playing for the Chicago Leland Giants in 1907, Foster began negotiating gate receipt payments to help boost each player's income. It would be a life-long mission. In 1911, he formed the Chicago American Giants with John Schorling, Charles Comiskey's son-in-law. Foster would gain fame as a manager of "inside baseball." He taught and promoted base running skills, the hit and run, and sacrificing. Foster loved the double steal, squeeze play, and the hit and run bunt, the latter being a well-placed bunt drawing the third baseman away from the bag so a speedy runner could advance from first to third. It never caught on in the majors. Opposing teams feared giving up a walk to his aggressive Giants.

After World War I, Foster, like most in the industry, was experiencing a financial pinch. He found himself continually at the mercy of white booking agents. Financially, black teams received a greater payday when vying against white independent clubs. In fact, teams that could not find white opponents or who played in areas where integrated play was prohibited by law were at a serious disadvantage. Stronger barnstorming Negro league teams would often raid a weaker club's roster.

Foster was also beginning to feel greater race relation difficulties. Moreover, he was involved in bidding wars with more lucrative eastern teams for talent. His relationship was especially strained with the East's most powerful booking agent, Nat C. Strong. Foster was particularly bitter over the loss of John Henry Lloyd, the "black Honus Wagner."

Foster felt that he needed to form a strong league to set a full schedule for his team and to avoid self-defeating bidding wars for players. He also understood the profit-making potential of pennant races and rivalries.

Consequently, Foster, along with a consortium of Western team owners, formed the Negro National League in 1920 at a YMCA in Kansas City, home of the current day Negro Leagues Baseball Museum. He became president and secretary of the league. Though he took no salary, Foster claimed 5% of all gate receipts. The teams included: Chicago American Giants, Chicago Giants, Detroit Stars, St. Louis Stars, Indianapolis ABCs, Kansas City Monarchs, Dayton Marcos, and the Cuban Stars.

The first major course of business was to keep the league afloat. To this end, he continually loaned money to players and other team owners. Foster also balanced competition by moving talent around to lesser teams, even at the expense of his own Giants.

Eastern teams finally organized in 1923 and formed the Eastern Colored League. Bidding wars erupted for player loyalties. Matters cooled down long enough to initiate the first real black World Series in '24.

However, in 1926 it became apparent that Foster was losing touch with reality. His actions and words became bizarre and erratic. He suffered from delusions and became a danger to himself and others. Once, Foster locked himself in the bathroom, requiring his players to climb in to get him out. In another incident, he almost gassed himself to death by accident. He also hit a female pedestrian with his automobile and attacked a friend with an ice pick.

One day in 1926 in his apartment with his wife, Foster began tearing the place apart. It took several police officers to subdue him. This incident led him to be committed to a state mental hospital in Kankakee, Illinois. He died there in December 1930. Hall of Fame voters overlooked his contributions until 1981.

Lou Gehrig

Everyone knows the story of Lou Gehrig. His power and run production, though, are often overlooked. No one was a better RBI man; do not forget the only way to win a ballgame is to score more runs than the other team. Moreover, a major reason Babe Ruth had so many good pitches to hit was that the feared Gehrig stood in the on-deck circle. Thirteen times, he knocked in 100 + runs. Gehrig led the league five times in RBI and on-base percentage, four times in total bases and runs, three times in home runs and walks, twice in slugging and doubles, and once in hits, triples, and batting average. The only year Gehrig led in batting average he also won the Triple Crown, 1934. Gehrig copped the MVP award in 1927 and again in 1936.

Gehrig particularly excelled at World Series play. In eight of them, he hit .361 with 10 home runs and 35 RBIs. In the 1928 series alone, he batted .545 with 4 home runs and 9 RBIs in the four-game sweep over St. Louis. In another sweep, in 1932, Gehrig swatted 3 home runs and 8 RBIs while hitting .529.

The winter of 1938–39 saw Gehrig lose his strength, stamina, and agility. It became apparent to his teammates during spring training. The mysterious illness forced him from the lineup on May 2, after 2,130 consecutive games. Later, he was diagnosed with Amyotrophic Lateral Sclerosis, a muscle atrophying disease. The Iron Horse died two years later at age 37.

Jake Goodman

After two brief stints in the majors in 1878 and '82, Jake Goodman was in the minors when he was beaned in 1884. Reports suggest that the blow to the head caused him to become mentally unbalanced and brought on palsy. He died from complications of such on March 6, 1890, at age 36.

Jackie Hayes

Second baseman Jackie Hayes formed half of the famed White Sox double-play combination with Luke Appling. During spring training on March 28, 1940, a cinder flew into Hayes' eye. He later noticed cloudiness in his eye, stemming from an infection. He was blind in that eye by August, ending his 14-year career. Three years later, he lost sight in the other eye.

Charlie Hodnett

Pitcher Charlie Hodnett's career ended after spending a year with the St. Louis Maroons of the Union Association in 1884. The 23-year-old was suffering from an ulcerated foot. He finished with a career 14-4 record.

Ken Holcombe

Bursitis caused righthanded pitcher Ken Holcombe's career to fluctuate between the majors and minors in the decade following World War II. It eventually ended his promise altogether.

Charlie Hollocher

Shortstop Charlie Hollocher began his career with a bang. In his rookie season in 1918, the Cub led the league in games, at-bats, hits, and total bases. He also finished second in on-base percentage, third in stolen bases, and fourth with a .316 batting average. Other career highlights include a 3-for-3 performance in Game 5 of that year's World Series, two league-leader awards in fielding percentage and a .340 batting average in 1922, the highest by a shortstop since Honus Wagner in 1908.

Hollocher's career was cut short by recurring abdominal pains. On July 26, 1923, he left the following note for manager Bill Killefer:

> . . . feeling pretty rotten so made up my mind to go home and take a rest and forget about baseball for the rest of the year. No hard feelings, just didn't feel like playing anymore.

No medical doctor could determine the root of his injury. All x-rays were negative. Unfortunately, his problems were probably psychological.

Hollocher returned to the team the following year but soon left again to regain his health. Returning home to Missouri, the 28-year-old never appeared in the majors again. Tormented, he killed himself by a gunshot to the throat in 1940 after complaining of severe abdominal pain.

Tony Horton

Indians first baseman Tony Horton had his best year in 1969: .278, 27, 93. His career ended the following season after suffering an emotional strain and being subsequently hospitalized.

On May 24, 1970, Horton belted three homers but was distressed that his team lost when he failed to connect for a fourth. In June, he crawled back to the dugout after striking out. After the final out of another game, Horton went to field his position at first. Concerned, manager Alvin Dark physically led the player back to the dugout by hand. Cleveland found the player counseling but he never returned to the diamond.

Steve Howe

When one points to the inadequacies of baseball's drug policy and to the stiff penalty imposed on Pete Rose, the Steve Howe case is inevitably cited.

At times, Steve Howe looked brilliant. In 1980, the Dodger was named Rookie of the Year after compiling 7 wins, 17 saves and a 2.66 ERA. In 1983, '91 and '94 the southpaw's ERA fell well below 2.00, though it was never consistent from year to year.

Along the way, Howe accrued seven suspensions for continued cocaine usage. Los Angeles couldn't handle him, so they suspended and shipped him off. Playing for the Sacramento Bees of the Pacific Coast League in 1986, the pitcher was blacklisted. The Texas Rangers got permission from Commissioner Peter Ueberroth to sign Howe to a minor league contract and quickly promoted him to the majors without formal approval. The $250,000 fine meant little to the franchise because they were able to keep the lefthander.

On June 8, 1992, Commissioner Fay Vincent suspended Howe for the seventh time for one year following an off-season arrest for the sale and possession of drugs. The players union filed a grievance and an arbitrator reinstated Howe.

LaMarr Hoyt

Chicago White Sox pitcher LaMarr Hoyt had a huge second half in 1983 winning 15 games to bring his record to 24-10 with a 3.66 ERA. He led the league in wins and opponent on-base percentage. It was good enough to cop the Cy Young Award. The righthander also won Game 1 of the American League Championship Series. Three years later, he would be out of baseball at age 31.

The bottom fell out in 1984, though Hoyt recovered to post a good 1985 with a 16-8 record. The Padre also started and won the All-Star Game.

1986 was not his year. On February 10, he was arrested at the Mexican border for possession of marijuana, Valium, and a knife. Eight days later, the San Diego police stopped his car and found a switchblade and more marijuana. Hoyt entered an alcohol rehab center but was arrested again at the Mexican border in October with 500 sleeping pills and marijuana. In December, Hoyt was convicted and sentenced to 45 days in jail.

Upon release, Commissioner Peter Ueberroth suspended Hoyt for one year and San Diego cut him. The players union filed a grievance because Hoyt still had three years and $3.2 million left on his contract. An arbitrator ruled in favor of Hoyt and even reduced his suspension to 60 days.

The Padres still didn't want the pitcher, so the White Sox invited him to camp but shoulder problems signaled the end of his baseball career. Hoyt was arrested again in December 1987 for possession with intent to distribute cocaine. He began serving a year in federal prison that February.

Hughie Jennings

Hughie Jennings' historic and often overlooked career spanned 35 years from his tenure as the team captain and probably best player in the National League for the championship Baltimore Orioles of the 1890s to field manager of three Detroit Tiger pennant winners fueled by the incomparable Ty Cobb to third base coach/part-time manager for the New York Giants dynasty of the 1920s.

In 1893, Jennings was traded to the Orioles. They would go on to win pennants in 1894–96 and the Temple Cup in '97. The Temple Cup series was played during the 1890s to foster postseason competition. Because there was only one major league at the time, the top two teams in the National League met to determine the winner. The Orioles of the era boasted Hall of Famers: MGR Ned Hanlon, 1B Dan Brouthers, SS Jennings, 3B John McGraw, LF Joe Kelley, RF Wee Willie Keeler, C Wilbert Robinson, and RHP Joe McGinnity. The only two regulars from the 1894 team that are not in the Hall of Fame are center fielder Walter Brodie and second baseman Heinie Reitz, the first major leaguer to die in an automobile accident.

Between 1894–98, Jennings led the league every year in being hit by pitches, while finishing in the top five in major batting categories 12 times. The shortstop also led the league three times in fielding average and twice in putouts, double plays, and range. In 1896 he hit .401. For the five-year period, Jennings accumulated 521 RBIs, 686 runs, 248 stolen bases, and a .361 batting average. *Total Baseball* ranks his "total player rating" as tops in the league three times and second once during this period. In 1896, he was hit by pitches 49 times, a record that stood until 1971. It's hard to imagine a more productive shortstop.

In 1899, he was traded straight up for Honus Wagner. However, Jennings personally called the Louisville owner to tell him that his arm was dead. The deal fell through and Jennings was remitted to Brooklyn to play first base. During the off-season, he studied law at St. Bonaventure University and Cornell. He also coached Cornell's baseball team. While there, he dove into an unlit, empty pool and fractured his skull. Later, Jennings was admitted to the Pennsylvania bar.

By 1902, Jennings' playing career was over primarily due to a weak arm and the effects of skull fractures incurred by a beaning and the diving accident. In 1907, after four years of managing Baltimore in the Eastern League, he became the field manager of the Detroit Tigers, who had finished sixth the previous year.

Jennings proceeded to guide the team to three consecutive pennants. His success with the Tigers was in spite of a dislike for star Ty Cobb. Jennings learned the best way to get production out of the fiery center fielder was to leave him alone. In 1911, Jennings again fractured his skull when his vehicle went off the side of a mountain. After the 1920 season and 1,131 victories, Jennings turned the managerial reins over to Cobb.

John McGraw quickly convinced Jennings to become his third base coach instead of pursuing a law career. An ill and often absent McGraw would have Jennings sub for him in 1924 and '25. The strain became too much for Jennings and he suffered a nervous breakdown. While recovering at a sanitarium in Asheville, North Carolina, Jennings found that he also suffering from tuberculosis. Jennings died in 1928 but his memory found a home in the halls of Cooperstown in '45.

Alex Johnson

Alex Johnson hit .288 over a 13-year career that included only six 120+-game seasons. He broke into the majors with Philadelphia in 1961, hitting .303 in 109 at bats. The outfielder soon established himself as a threat at the plate after joining Cincinnati as a regular in '68. The following year, he produced a .315, 17, 88 season.

On November 25, 1969, Johnson was traded to California, causing him to declare, "I'd rather play in hell than for the Angels." His attitude didn't get much better, though he soon won the batting title with a .3289 mark to edge Carl Yastrzemski's .3286.

The bad actor was surly and self-centered which caused tension among his teammates. Then, Johnson's behavior became erratic, including:

- Becoming a clubhouse troublemaker
- Continuing battles with teammate Chico Ruiz, including gun play at one point
- Growing more and more lackadaisical on the field
- Alarmingly declining stats
- Dumping coffee grounds on a reporter's typewriter
- Continual run-ins with sportswriters

It all tried manager Lefty Phillips' patience. In 1971, Johnson was benched four times, fined 29 times, and improperly placed on the restricted list without pay for "failure to give his best efforts . . ." Both American League president Joe Cronin and Commissioner Bowie Kuhn backed the Angels in this regard.

Players Association executive director Marvin Miller filed a grievance, claiming that Johnson was suffering from emotional stress. Others just thought he was a malcontent. For his part, Johnson recounted numerous racial incidents both in the minors and majors and other pressures doled out by the press and team management. Clearly, to Miller at least, he needed help, not continued banishment.

An arbitrator ruled in Johnson's favor, restoring his pay but enforcing the countless fines. The events established mental disorders as grounds for benefit compensation in baseball, like most other industries. It is important to note that other similar cases surely existed (in fact, the Rube Waddell case screamed it), but the difference now was that the players had an effective voice, Marvin Miller. Times were changing; no longer would the word of select management and their paid czar, the commissioner, be law. The players could now take their case to an impartial arbitrator.

Duane Josephson

Catcher Duane Josephson led the league in assists and double plays with the White Sox in 1968. Four years later, he was forced to retire because of a heart condition.

Dummy Kihm

George Kihm played first base in the minors from 1895–1911. As his nickname suggests, Kihm was a deaf-mute. In 7,600 at bats, he hit a solid .293 and amassed 2,245 safeties, mostly in the International League and American Association.

Sandy Koufax

Sandy Koufax was one of the most dominating, if not the dominate, lefthanded pitchers in major league history. He rates with Rube Waddell, Lefty Grove, Bill Foster, Steve Carlton, Carl Hubbell, Whitey Ford, and Warren Spahn as the game's best ever. Many managers would tell you that if they had one game to win, they would choose Koufax to do it. Simply stated, no one ever dominated as Koufax did in the early to mid-1960s.

He was the unanimous Cy Young Award winner three times—1963, 1965, and 1966—in an era when only one represented both leagues. Koufax won the pitching Triple Crown each of those years: 1963 (25-5, 306, 1.88), 1965 (26-8, 382, 2.04), 1966 (27-9, 317, 1.73). In 1963, he also was chosen as the MVP. The southpaw tossed four no-hitters and 40 shutouts. In 1965, he set the major league strikeout record with 382. All of this occurred before he retired at age 30 because of a chronically swollen, arthritic pitching elbow. Despite those problems, Koufax won the ERA crown each of his last five seasons.

Koufax signed with the Brooklyn Dodgers in December 1954 for a $14,000 bonus that required him to be assigned to the parent club. The 19-year-old was ill prepared. He would be hounded by continual wildness; though, on August 31, 1959, he struck out a record-tying 18 Giants.

His breakthrough came in 1961 with 18 wins after catcher Norm Sherry asked him to stop throwing so hard and compact his motion, thus improving his control. Koufax would later cite a number of other factors that aided his turnaround. That year, he was selected to the first of eight All-Star Games.

From 1961–66, Koufax posted 130 wins, 1,713 Ks, a 2.19 ERA, 35 shutouts, and a 4:1 strikeout-to-walk ratio. The man was nearly unhittable. He led the league seven times in opponent batting average; five times in ERA; four times in strikeouts and opponent on-base percentage; three times in wins and shutouts; and twice in complete games, innings pitched, and winning percentage.

On June 30, 1962, he pitched his first no-hitter. Dominant from the start, Koufax fanned three batters on nine pitches to start the game, the first time in the National League since 1924. In 1963, he pitched an incredible 11 shutouts.

To start 1966, Koufax and teammate righthanded pitcher Don Drysdale caused a stir holding out in tandem for more money. It was an attempt to strengthen their salary demands by threatening the Dodgers with the loss of both of their aces, a tactic first utilized by Ty Cobb and Sam Crawford in 1912. It worked. They each gained six-figure salaries. The idea was potentially dangerous to Major League Baseball if others had followed the example.

That year, Koufax posted a National League record 27 wins for a southpaw. But Koufax was done at the pinnacle of his career after losing to Jim Palmer in Game 2 of the Fall Classic. For years, Dodgers team physician Dr. Robert Kerlan had been monitoring the arm's condition. Rather than risking permanent crippling, Koufax called it quits. Minor arthroscopic surgery, common today, might have eased his circulatory problems.

He retired with a 165-87 record, 2,396 strikeouts, and a 2.76 ERA. In four World Series, Koufax compiled a 4-3 record with a stellar 0.95 ERA and 61 Ks. In 1972, he became the youngest man to enter the Hall of Fame.

Hideki Kuriyama

Hideki Kuriyama played for Yakult in Nippon Professional Baseball from 1984–90, hitting .279 in 1,200 at bats. He was forced to retire because of Meniere's disease.

Joe Kustus

Joe Kustus played 53 games in the outfield for the Brooklyn Dodgers in 1909. He was forced to retire from the game due to tuberculosis, which later claimed his life in 1916 at age 33.

Harvey McClellan

Chicago White Sox utility infielder Harvey McClellan hit .221 in 344 major league games. Two painful gallstone operations in 1924 forced his retirement. He died within a year of liver cancer at age 30.

Jim Nealon

Pirates rookie first baseman Jim Nealon led the National League in RBIs in 1906 with 83. The following year he contracted tuberculosis, necessitating the end of his baseball dreams. He died three years later of typhoid pneumonia at age 25.

Don Newcombe

Don Newcombe was a big, 6'4" 220-lb., hard-throwing righthander. The Dodger was the first great African-American pitcher in the bigs. He is also the only man to win the Rookie of the Year, Cy Young, and MVP Awards.

In 1944, he joined the Newark Eagles of the Negro National League. Playing an exhibition game in Ebbets Field in October 1945, Newk impressed Brooklyn Dodgers scout Clyde Sukeforth. Branch Rickey signed him the next day. The following year, he paired with Roy Campanella in Class B. Promoted to the show in 1949, Newcombe went 17-8 with a 3.17 ERA to win the Rookie of the Year Award. He was one of six African-Americans to win the award in the National League in the seven years since of its inception (and since integration): Jackie Robinson in '47, Newk, Sam Jethroe in '50, Willie Mays in '51, Joe Black in '52, and Junior Gilliam in '53.

In 1951, Newcombe won 20 for the first time, but his 1950 and '51 seasons will forever be remembered for their final days. Dick Sisler homered off Newcombe in the season's finale to win the pennant for the Phillies in '50. In the rubber game of the 1951 National League playoffs, he took a 4-2 lead into the ninth but left after putting two men aboard. Reliever Ralph Branca surrendered a 3-run homer to the Giants Bobby Thomson. The "Shot Heard 'Round the World" won the pennant.

Newcombe was one of the best hitting pitchers of all time. In 878 at bats, he produced a .271 average with 15 homers and 108 RBIs. Seven of the home runs came in 1955 to set a National League record.

Out of the majors in 1952–53, serving in the military during the Korean War, the four-time All-Star shined again in '55 and '56. For the 1955 World Champion Brooklyn Dodgers, Newcombe went 20-5 with a 3.20 ERA, even though he was suspended by manager Walter Alston for refusing to pitch batting practice. The following year, Newcombe tossed a masterful 27-7 season, leading the league in wins, winning percentage, opponent batting average, opponent on-base percentage, and fielding putouts. He won both the Cy Young and MVP Awards.

Unfortunately, his dominance did not carry over into the postseason. In five World Series starts, he put up an unimpressive 0-4 record and 8.59 ERA. After an off season in 1957, he was shipped to Cincinnati, then Cleveland. At age 31, Newcombe's major league career was over, partially due to alcoholism. Newk's drinking didn't sit well with the Japanese Chunichi Dragons in '62, either.

Several serious alcohol-related lapses led him to hit rock bottom. Fortunately, Newk quit drinking and regained control of his life. Later, he counseled young major leaguers.

Mike Norris

Billy Martin came to Oakland and squeezed the most out of Mike Norris. Some say he used him up, as well as the rest of the staff. In 1980, Norris doubled his innings to 284 and produced a 22-9, 180, 2.53 season. In the strike year of 1981, Norris was 12-9, helping the A's win the American League West title. Two years later, arm difficulties and drug usage curtailed his major league career. Norris toiled in the California League before returning to the majors briefly in 1990.

Johnny Oates

Johnny Oates was diagnosed with a malignant brain tumor in 2001, ending a 30 + year career as a catcher, coach, and manager.

Dave Orr

Dave Orr was a big, powerful first baseman who amassed 627 RBIs in eight major league seasons. Weighing over 250 pounds and standing just 5'11" tall, Orr was the first player to top 300 total bases in a season in 1886. He also hit .368 that year and led the league in 1884 with a .354 mark. His career .342 batting average ranks among the 19th century's best. Orr is one of few players of the era with a career slugging average over .500.

In the Players League in 1890, Orr was batting .373 with 124 RBIs after 107 games when he suffered a paralyzing stoke during an exhibition game in Renova, Pennsylvania. His career was over at age 31.

Ben Petrick

After appearing in 46 games in 2003, catcher–outfielder Ben Petrick was hoping to find a permanent slot on the Tigers roster. Instead, he retired in May 2004 at age 27 at the onset of Parkinson's disease.

Bill Pettus

Catcher–first baseman Bill Pettus was one of the top hitters of the dead-ball era in the Negro leagues. He began playing the game in 1904 and remained in uniform until contracting tuberculosis in 1923. He died the following August at age 40.

Horace Phillips

Horace Phillips, a former National League manager and the head of a Philadelphia team, and Opie Caylor, representing Cincinnati interests, got together one night in September 1881 to lament the fact that neither city fielded a team in the National League. Within months, the American Association was born.

Phillips would later manage Columbus and Pittsburgh in the American Association. He followed the Pirates into the National League in 1887 and managed them until a nervous breakdown eventually forced his commitment to an institution in 1889. He died there but researchers are unsure of the date.

Jimmy Piersall

Jimmy Piersall's bout with mental illness awoke the nation's consciousness in the 1950s. His story was eventually made into an overdone movie, *Fear Strikes Out*, starring *Psycho*'s Anthony Perkins. Piersall was the product of a domineering father who pushed him hard into baseball and a mother who would later be institutionalized. As he sadly comments about his father, "he set down my rules, and I tried hard not to disobey, for I lived in fear of his wrath."

Signing a $4,000 bonus contract with Boston, Piersall joined the Red Sox in spring training 1952, where they tried to convert the outfielder to shortstop, as player–manager Lou Boudreau was trying to ease himself out of the lineup. Then, the rookie started exhibiting a rash of strange behavior, including fistfights with a teammate and the hard-nosed Yankee Billy Martin. Noticing the breakdown, the Red Sox pushed him into counseling. The treatment included electroshock therapy.

Recovered, Piersall took over right field in 1953 to start a long career. Casey

Stengel referred to him as the "best defensive right fielder I have ever seen." By '55, he was switched to center field, playing the shallowest in the game. Piersall followed with two Gold Gloves, topping the league in fielding percentage three times, putouts and range twice, and double plays once. The slick glove man posted a .990 career fielding percentage.

Offensively, his best year was 1956 with a .293 average, 176 hits, and 87 RBIs. Piersall still had lapses in the field including once hiding behind the monuments in center field at Yankee Stadium. His most heralded stunt came with the Mets in 1963. Hitting his 100th home run, he ran around the bases backwards and slid into home plate at the Polo Grounds. Manager Stengel was not entertained, quipping, "There's only room for one clown on this team," and shipped the outfielder to the Los Angeles Angels.

Piersall eventually made his way into broadcasting with the White Sox and Rangers. Always controversial and sharp-tongued, he was fired by the White Sox but later hosted a popular radio show in Chicago.

Togie Pittinger

Togie Pittinger packed a lot into a brief major league career that didn't even get started until he was 29 years old. From 1900–07, he won 115 games for Boston and Philadelphia in the National League, including 27 in 1902 and 23 in 1905. The right-hander was a staff workhorse, averaging over 300 innings from 1901–05. However, diabetes forced him to retire from the game in 1907 and took his life two years later at age 36.

Kirby Puckett

Kirby Puckett was extremely popular in Minnesota among the sportswriters and with the baseball public in general. He was the star on the improbable Twins teams that surprised both the Cardinals and the Braves by taking 7-game World Series victories in 1987 and '91, respectively.

His career ended after 2,304 hits because of glaucoma damage in his right eye at age 34 in 1995. Puckett's last at-bat was a beaning by Dennis Martinez that broke the Twins' jaw. Puckett's .318 career batting average ranks among the leaders after World War II. Cooperstown invited the Twin in 2001. He passed away in March 2006.

Bill Reynolds

Bill Reynolds caught nine games for the Yankees in 1913–14. Later managing in minors, he was forced to retire with a malignant tumor in his jaw. He died at age 40 in June 1924.

J. R. Richard

Big J. R. Richard, 6'8" 222 lbs., threw smoke at upwards of 100 mph. Even his slider was clocked in the 90s. The righthander was on the verge of greatness when a debilitating stroke ended his career at age 30.

Richard's arm strength and blazing fastball drew a lot of attention from major league scouts. Houston offered a $100,000 bonus and he accepted. In his first major league start, Richard struck out 15 Giants on September 15, 1971.

1976 was his breakthrough season: 20-15, 214, 2.75. From then until the stroke in 1980, the pitcher posted 84 wins with 1,163 strikeouts and a 2.79 ERA in only four and half seasons. In 1978, Richard led the league in Ks with 303 and opponent batting average. The following year, he posted another 313 strikeouts and led the league with a 2.71 ERA.

In 1980, Richard was nearly unhittable with a 10-4 record and 1.90 ERA after seventeen starts. Then, he began to feel fatigued and complained of a "dead arm." Some accused him of malingering. Finally, Richard was placed on the DL and diagnosed with a blood clot in his neck but was told to continue playing anyway because the doctors did not feel he was in danger. While playing catch during pre-game warm-ups immediately after being diagnosed, Richard suffered a stroke and nearly died on July 30.

A blood clot had formed in an artery leading to his right arm. It moved to his brain, causing the stroke. Richard was paralyzed on his left side but was able, through therapy, to regain full use of his arm and leg; however, the facial muscles were still affected.

In the spring he tried to come back to no avail. In 1994, Richard was found homeless living under a bridge. Later, he became a minister. Likewise, Tigers left-hander John Hiller also suffered a stroke; however, he was able to come back mid-career and compete on the diamond for another nine summers.

John Ryn

John Ryn is generally considered the first deaf ballplayer. The catcher–first baseman worked throughout the minor leagues from at least 1883–95, perhaps as early as 1879. Much of his career was spent in and around Ohio, appearing at various times in the Ohio State Association, Ohio State League, and Tri-State League. At one point, Ryn worked the battery with another deaf player, Ed Dundon.

Bill Sarni

Bill Sarni entered the Pacific Coast League at age 15. Joining the National League Cardinals in 1954, he hit .300 with 70 RBIs in his rookie season and led all catchers in double plays and fielding average. Again in '56, Sarni led in double plays plus assists, while ending the season with the New York Giants.

During spring training the following year, he suffered a career-ending heart attack at age 29.

Rod Scurry

Rod Scurry was the Pirates #1 draft pick in 1974. He finally made the majors in 1980. Four years later, the lefthanded reliever was in drug rehab, eventually wearing out his welcome in the majors in 1988. Never quelling his demons, Scurry ended up in intensive care after scuffling with police in October 1992. He died there on November 5 at age 36.

Frank Selee

Frank Selee and Ned Hanlon are the two most acclaimed managers of the late 1800s. Both were enshrined in Cooperstown 100 years later. In 16 seasons, Selee won five pennants and 1,284 games. His .598 winning percentage is among the career leaders. Selee is primarily responsible for building the Boston Beaneaters and Chicago Cubs dynasties of the era. Unfortunately, Selee contracted tuberculosis and retired during the 1905 season. He died four years later at age 49. He is one of the first successful major league managers that never played in the bigs.

Mike Shannon

Mike Shannon was a valuable contributor and hometown favorite for the great Cardinals teams of the 1960s. So-so regular season stats belie his offensive spurt in the World Series. In Game 1 of the 1964 Fall Classic, Shannon homered off Whitey Ford. Additional home runs followed in '67 and '68, after he had moved to third base. In three World Series, he hit three home runs with eight RBIs and 12 runs scored.

A rare kidney disorder, nephritis, forced his retirement in 1970 at age 31. He then started a long broadcasting career for St. Louis as Jack Buck's partner.

George Sisler

George Sisler was one of the top first baseman in major league history and certainly the best of the St. Louis Browns. He is unheralded today primarily because of the talent-lacking teams he played for, his lack of postseason exposure, and his unassuming personality; though the great Ty Cobb referred to him as "the finest first baseman of them all."

Akron of the Ohio–Pennsylvania League sold 17-year-old Sisler to Pittsburgh in 1912, but his contract was later voided by the National Commission when it was discovered that he was under age. By then, he was attending and playing baseball at the University of Michigan for coach Branch Rickey. A "gentleman's agreement" apparently earmarked Sisler back to Pittsburgh. Rickey ignored the implications and signed Sisler for the Browns in 1915.

Sisler initially came up as a lefthanded pitcher and even gained two complete game victories over Walter Johnson. Like Babe Ruth, his bat was too good to keep out of the everyday lineup. The Browns placed him at first. Seven times, he led the league in assists and three times in double plays. He was just as potent on the base paths with 375 career stolen bases, virtually unheard of for a first baseman.

In St. Louis, the Browns ran a poor second to the Cardinals. However, they could boast a player that was nearly as good as Rogers Hornsby. In 1920, Sisler performed at a level few have matched. Playing every inning of every game, he went hitless in only 23 contests. Sisler broke Ty Cobb's string of batting titles with a .407 mark and set the all-time standard with 257 hits. He also finished first or second with 399 total bases, 49 doubles, 18 triples, a .632 slugging average, and 19 home runs. Remarkably, Ruth led the league with 35 more homers. Sisler finished the year batting .442 in August and .448 in September. Think of what that would have meant to a contending team.

The MVP award followed in 1922. He led the league with a .420 batting average, 246 hits, 134 runs, 51 stolen bases, and 18 triples. The first baseman added 105 RBIs, 348 total bases, 42 doubles, a .464 on-base percentage, and a .594 slugging average. Along the way, he compiled a 41-game hitting streak, then a league record. Impressively, Sisler fanned only 14 times in 586 at-bats. From 1920–22, Sisler batted an amazing .3997. The lefthander's career totals show six 200 + hit seasons.

The following year, he developed double vision stemming from a bout with the flu and sinusitis. It caused him to sit out the entire season. Sisler claimed that he was never the same hitter. He returned in 1924 as player–manager. By '28, he was being shuffled to Washington and then to the Boston Braves. In 1931, at the age of 38, Sisler played his first game in the minors. By then, he had amassed 2,812 major league hits and a .340 career average.

In 1943, he re-joined Branch Rickey in Brooklyn and again followed him to Pittsburgh for a long career as a scout and coach. George's son Dick hit the pennant-winning home run for the Philadelphia Phillies "Whiz Kids" in 1950.

Louis Sockalexis

Drinking also led to the premature ending of Louis Sockalexis' career. Sockalexis was a Penobscot Indian who was nicknamed Chief, like every other Native American ballplayer of the era. He was a phenomenal all-around athlete with blazing quickness and an exceptional arm. Sockalexis starred at Holy Cross before transferring with his coach to Notre Dame. He gained fame at both schools for hitting tremendous home runs and displaying his arm strength in exhibition feats. A monstrous home run against the New York Giants Amos Rusie, the fastest pitcher in the majors, in an exhibition game at the Polo Grounds brought the most acclaim.

Monte Ward recommended Sockalexis to Cleveland Spiders manager Patsy Tebeau. Cleveland signed him for 1897 but not before the outfielder was expelled by Notre Dame for public drunkenness.

Sockalexis was an immediate major league success, accumulating 10 outfield assists in his first six preseason games. He was an even bigger box office smash as the season began. The Indian chants began, as did the hounding by the press and fans. People even started calling the team the "Indians."

Sockalexis started to pound the bottle. In the midst of a July 4th celebration, he jumped out of a second-story window. The off-time from the resulting foot injury led to more opportunities to drink. He was suspended by the team even though he was hitting .413 at the time. His drinking was out of control by the end of the year. Sockalexis finished with a .338 batting average, but the team could only handle him for 28 more games over the next two seasons. A promising career was over by the age of 27. After a couple years knocking around in the minors, Sockalexis spent much of the rest of his life panhandling and living for the next bottle.

His legend was so popular that after his death in 1913 and Napoleon Lajoie's departure in 1914 (the team had been called the Naps in Lajoie's honor), the American League's Cleveland entry nicknamed itself the Indians after Sockalexis . . . or so that story goes.

Dummy Stephenson

Deaf-mute outfielder Reuben Stephenson appeared in eight games for the National League Philadelphia Phillies in 1892.

Darryl Strawberry

Darryl Strawberry arrived in New York and immediately won the National League Rookie of the Year Award in 1983. He followed with eight more years of serious power production, including helping the Mets win the world championship in 1986. The lefthander averaged less than 50 games a season after 1991 because of injuries, drug rehabilitation stints, suspensions, and cancer surgery.

In 1994, the player started the season in drug rehabilitation and ended it under indictment for tax evasion. The following year, Strawberry was suspended for drugs. In 1998, he was diagnosed with colon cancer. During recovery from surgery, he was arrested on drug and solicitation charges. In December '99, Strawberry failed a drug test and was suspended by baseball for one year. It was later discovered that the cancer had returned. The year 2000 brought another drug scandal and more soap opera drama the following year.

Tadayoshi Tamakoshi

Tadayoshi Tamakoshi retired with the Hankyu Braves in 1950, suffering from a respiratory ailment. The outfielder had hit .265 in 1,800 at bats from 1940–50. The disease ultimately took his life in January 1957 at age 36.

Specs Toporcer

Never playing ball in school or in the minors, Specs Toporcer became the first bespectacled infielder in the majors. Mainly a utility man with the Cardinals from 1921–28, Toporcer won back-to-back MVP crowns with Rochester in the International League from 1929–30.

While managing Buffalo in the International League in 1951, Toporcer finally lost his sight and was forced to retire.

Hal Trosky

Hal Trosky was one of the most powerful hitters of perhaps the most powerful decade, the 1930s. But the slick fielding first baseman never made the All-Star team because he had to contend with the popularity and production of Hall of Famers Lou Gehrig, Double X, and Hank Greenberg.

Trosky broke into the majors with Cleveland in 1934 to produce one of the finest rookie seasons on the books. The numbers are staggering for a fledgling: .330 batting average, 374 total bases, 89 extra base hits, 142 RBIs, 35 homers, 117 runs scored, and a .598 slugging average. He also led all first sackers in games, putouts, assists, errors, and double plays.

Numerous men entered the majors in the 1930s to produce big first seasons: Wally Berger, Cy Blanton, Dizzy Dean, Paul Dean, Paul Derringer, Joe DiMaggio, Lou

Fette, Cliff Melton, Johnny Mize, Trosky, Jim Turner, Joe Vosmik, George Watkins, Monte Weaver, Ted Williams, and Rudy York. Look 'em up.

Trosky punched through again in '36 with a .343 average, 42 home runs, and a league-leading 162 RBIs and 405 total bases. In the seven years from 1934–40, he produced 204 dingers and 852 ribbies while maintaining a .314 average. In his career, Trosky only fanned 440 times in 5,161 at-bats, impressive for a power hitter. In 1936, he connected in 28 straight games.

A potential Hall of Fame career was derailed in 1941 because of migraine headaches. Trosky missed all of 1942, '43, and '45. In a 10-year career, two of those parttime, he compiled 228 homers, 1,012 RBIs, and a .302 batting average.

Rube Waddell

Rube Waddell was one of the most effective lefthanded pitchers in major league history. However, four different teams, who were only too happy to be rid of his disruptions, happily released him.

Waddell possessed a fastball that has been compared to Walter Johnson's and a sharp-breaking, overhand curve. He routinely struck out batters in an era when most choked up and merely slapped at the ball. His strikeout-per-game ratio was the best in baseball prior to World War II. Moreover, his strikeout total nearly triples his total walks, signifying great control. From 1902–07, he led the American League every year in Ks. Waddell's 349 in '04 wouldn't be eclipsed in the majors until Sandy Koufax's 382 in 1965 and in the American League until Nolan Ryan's 383 in 1973.

Rube was originally signed by Louisville of the National League in 1897. He soon transferred with owner Barney Dreyfuss to the Pirates. Within a week, Waddell jumped the team to escape disciplinarian manager Fred Clarke. After returning, he was shipped to Connie Mack in the Western League, back to Pittsburgh, and then on to the Cubs. Chicago manager Tom Loftus suspended Waddell for the final month of the 1901 season.

What irked his managers and teammates the most was his penchant for skipping out on the team whenever it suited him to drink, wrestle alligators, join minstrel shows, hang around firehouses, chase fires, tend bar, or go fishing and hunting. No one could control his wanderlust. In fact, Waddell was probably mentally ill. Baseball history is littered with colorful stories about men with eccentric lifestyles or habits. Today, we would probably help that individual seek treatment.

Finally, Waddell ended up with Mack again in the American League in 1902. Apparently, Mack discovered a method to limit his carousing. He paid the pitcher in installments, $5 and $10 at a time. Once, he distributed his star's salary in $1 bills to try to make it last longer and to try to keep him under control.

Waddell shined in Philadelphia, going 24-7 his first season. On July 2, he became the first recorded major league pitcher to strike out the side on nine pitches. From 1902–05, he won at least 20 games a season, notching 97 in all. The southpaw also fanned 1,148 batters and accrued a measly 1.88 ERA. Hall of Famers Waddell, Eddie Plank, and Chief Bender formed the best rotation in the American League.

In 1905, he won the pitching Triple Crown by leading the league with 26 wins, 287 strikeouts, and a 1.48 ERA. In a 20-inning classic that year, he out-dueled Cy

Young. Waddell was sorely missed in the postseason after sustaining an injury to his left arm in a row with teammate Andy Coakley. Unsubstantiated rumors abound that gamblers had paid him off to skip the series.

Two years later, his teammates had enough and forced his sale to the St. Louis Browns. In his first game against his old teammates, Waddell struck out 16 on July 29, 1908, to set the American League record. By 1910, the Browns released him to the minors.

While in Kentucky in 1912, Waddell helped build a levee to fend off a flooded river. To do so, he stood for hours in freezing water. Rube became sick and never fully recovered. The following year, he collapsed while playing in the Northern League and ended up in a Texas tuberculosis sanitarium. He died there on April 1, 1914. In 1946, his 193-143 won-loss record, 2,316 strikeouts, 50 shutouts, and 2.16 ERA brought the pitcher to Cooperstown.

Art Weaver

Catcher Art Weaver played parts of four seasons in the majors during the first decade of the 20th century, amassing a scant .183 batting average. He had to leave the game suffering from asthma complications. Weaver eventually died from it in 1917 at age 37.

Ed Wilkinson

Ed Wilkinson appeared in 10 games for the New York Yankees in 1911. Soon after, he developed pulmonary tuberculosis ending his career. He died in April 1918 at the age of 27.

Willie Wilson

Kansas City wide-ranging center fielder Willie Wilson was fast, to say the least. He stole 668 bases (83% success rate), legged out five inside-the-park homers in 1979, and tripled more times than anyone but Roberto Clemente after WWII. Also, his 21 triples in 1985 were the most during the second half of the century.

The leadoff batter had 230 hits in 1980 and won the batting title in 1982 with a .332 mark. Versus St. Louis, Wilson hit .367 in the Royals World Series victory in 1985. In '83, his image became tarnished after becoming one of four KC players to admit to possession of cocaine and enduring a short prison sentence.

CHAPTER TWELVE

~

Injuries and Accidents

Charlie Abby
Charlie Abby played the outfield from 1893–97 with Washington in the National League. As a rookie in 1894, he knocked in 101 base runners. At age 30 in '97, Abby was run over in Washington, DC, ending his career with the loss of an arm.

Dale Alexander
First baseman Dale Alexander made a big splash when he reached the Tigers in 1929. His first two big league seasons produced 45 home runs, 272 RBIs, and a .335 average. Though his power diminished, Alexander was effective enough to lead the circuit in batting average in 1932 with a .367 mark, the first player to do so with two different teams.

   The following year the Red Sox team trainer, Doc Woods, treated his injured leg with a heat lamp. It stayed on too long while Woods was watching a Red Sox rally and the burns produced gangrene. Relegated to part-time status, Alexander was back in the minors in 1934. He would stay there until retiring eight years later.

Hugh Alexander
After two minor league seasons and appearing in seven games for the Indians at the end of the 1937 season, Hugh Alexander lost his left hand in an oil-drilling accident during the off-season. He became a full-time scout for the club the following year at age 20. Over the next 60 years, Alexander hit the back roads for the Indians, Dodgers, Phillies, and Cubs, signing Dale Mitchell, Allie Reynolds, Bill Russell, Don Sutton, Davey Lopes, Steve Garvey, and Frank Howard, among others.

Phil Ball
Phil Ball played minor league ball until stabbed in a fight that incapacitated his left hand. He went on to make a fortune in the cold-storage business. Backing the Federal League, Ball purchased the St. Louis franchise. When the league collapsed, he took over the American League Browns in 1916. In this capacity, Ball continued a running feud with Judge Landis until the magnate's death in 1932.

Charlie Bennett
Catcher Charlie Bennett played 15 major league seasons, mostly for the Detroit Wolverines and Boston Beaneaters of the National League. Perhaps the finest catcher of

his era, Bennett popularized the use of the chest protector. Some recognize him as the first to wear one; a model that was designed by his wife. Bennett also hit over .300 on three occasions.

On January 9, 1894, during a hunting trip in Kansas with his buddy and future Hall of Famer John Clarkson, Bennett attempted to re-board a moving train, slipped, and was run over. He lost both legs, one at the ankle and the other at the knee. To help defray medical costs, Detroit fans organized a benefit. Confined to a wheelchair, Bennett ran a newsstand in Detroit for the next thirty years. Later, the city named their American League ball field Bennett Park in his honor.

Les Cain

Detroit lefthander Les Cain put up impressive numbers in his rookie season: 12 wins, 156 Ks, and a 3.84 ERA. He was out of baseball two years later at age 24 because of nagging injuries and control problems. The pitcher filed a worker's compensation claim against the Tigers in 1973 alleging that manager Billy Martin pressed him to pitch with a sore arm and, thus, ruining his career. Cain was awarded $111 a week for life judgment against the club, but both sides agreed on a lump sum payment.

Roy Campanella

Roy Campanella joined the Brooklyn Dodgers in 1948 at age 26 after seven years in professional ball with the Baltimore Elite Giants of the Negro National League, two in Jorge Pasquel's Mexican League and two-plus in the minors. During a barnstorming trip after the 1945 season, Dodgers manager Charlie Dressen and general manager Branch Rickey lured the catcher away from the Negro leagues. Campanella went, even though his salary dropped by 63%.

He had a perfect body for a backstop: short, squat, and strong as an ox. Kept in the minors too long, Campanella won two MVP awards there. He joined Brooklyn's starting lineup in mid-1948. The righthander became the best catcher in the National League during the 1950s, leading the league in putouts five times, double plays and fielding average twice, and once in assists. The eight-time All-Star won the MVP in 1951 (.325, 33, 108), 1953 (.312, 41, 142), and 1955 (.318, 32, 107). The Dodgers followed his lead with pennants in 1949, 1952–53, and 1955–56.

Driving home from his Harlem liquor store on January 28, 1958, Campanella's car slid on the ice, rammed a telephone pole, and flipped over, pinning him behind the steering wheel. He suffered injuries to his fifth cervical vertebra and spinal cord, permanently paralyzing his arms and legs. The ballplayer was confined to a wheelchair until his death in 1993.

Roy Campanella Night in May 1959 drew the largest crowd in major league history, 93,000 +, even though he never actually played in Los Angeles. The Hall of Fame called a belated 10 years later.

John Castino

Minnesota Twins third baseman John Castino won the Rookie of the Year Award in 1979 with a .285 average, 52 RBIs, and 31 double plays. In 1980, he hit .302 and led the league with 340 assists. The next season, he led the league in triples, putouts, and fielding percentage. Soon, Castino became hobbled by back pain. A fused disc ended his major league aspirations after only eight games in 1984 at age 29.

Pug Cavet
Lefthander Pug Cavet pitched parts of three seasons for the Detroit Tigers from 1911–15 and another 20 in the minors. With the Tigers in 1914, he won seven games and posted a 2.44 ERA in 31 games. In all Cavet, won 301 professional games. The pitcher had only one eye.

Nate Colbert
Righthanded power-hitter Nate Colbert was a three-time All-Star for the San Diego Padres in the early 1970s. From 1969–73, the first baseman produced 149 home runs, 427 RBIs, and led the league in assists twice and putouts and double plays once.

On August 1, 1972, in a doubleheader, Colbert knocked in a record-breaking 13 runs on five homers on his way to career highs with 38 dingers and 111 RBIs. Back problems forced him to retire in 1976 at the age of 30.

Johnny Cooney
From 1921–30, Boston Braves part-time starter Johnny Cooney won 34 games with a 3.72 ERA. His arm went dead after 29 starts in 1925. After an operation, Cooney's left pitching arm was three inches shorter than his right. Ineffectiveness forced him out of the majors in 1930.

Six years later, at age 35, Cooney returned to the bigs as Casey Stengel's starting center fielder in Brooklyn. The former pitcher hit .282 and then .293 in 1937. He followed Stengel to Boston and posted a .318 average in 1940 and a .319 in 1941. Cooney was still playing at age 43 during World War II.

Con Daily
Catcher Con Daily appeared in three different major leagues from 1884–96. His career ended when he fractured his spine attempting to save a drowning child at Coney Island.

One Arm Daily
Hugh Daily lost his left hand while playing with an English flintlock musket as a child in a Baltimore theater. It didn't stop him from having limited success in the big leagues, though his inhospitable temperament and surly attitude did prevent him from attaining many friendships within the game.

In 1883, Daily won 23 games for the Cleveland Blues of the National League including a 1-0 no-hitter over the Philadelphia Quakers on September 23. Jim Abbott would later duplicate this feat.

The following year, he jumped to the Union Association and pitched for three different teams. In one game, he struck out 19 batters; 483 for the season. Not all that impressive though, if you consider the quality of play in the league, that seven balls equaled a walk and that the pitching distance stood at a mere 45 feet from home plate. Still, Daily overcame tremendous odds just to be there.

In 1885, he paid $500 for the right to be reinstated to the National League after jumping to the Union Association. Daily went on to pitch in only 33 more games over the next three years, losing 26 of them. His career ended with a 73-87 record and a 2.92 ERA.

Louis Drucke
Signed out of Texas Christian University, Louis Drucke took the mound between 1909–12 for John McGraw's Giants. His career ended at age 24 when he injured his arm in a subway accident.

Hank Erickson
Hank Erickson caught briefly for the Reds in 1935. His career ended after an automobile accident.

Ed Hawk
Ed Hawk appeared in five games for the Browns in 1911, losing four. Then a fall from a fourth-story hotel window ended his career with a broken leg and extensive internal injuries.

Percy Jones
Percy Jones was the Cubs swingman during the 1920s, starting or relieving as needed. In 1928, it caused quite a stir when he inherited a half million dollars. In April 1930, he was traded to the Pirates for Burleigh Grimes but only appeared in nine games before being sent to the minors. In 1931, with Columbus of the American Association the lefthander fell from a window and broke his neck, relegating Jones to a wheelchair until his death in 1979.

Chuck Koney
Red Sox prospect Chuck Koney returned home during the 1948 season to experience the birth of his child. Tinkering around the house, the young second baseman lost his leg when the gas furnace exploded. He subsequently became a scout for the organization.

Tony Kubek
Shortstop Tony Kubek joined the powerhouse Yankees in 1957, hit .297, and won the Rookie of the Year Award. To keep Kubek's lefthanded bat in the lineup, manager Casey Stengel would often use the athlete outside his natural position. Kubek went on to be selected to the All-Star Game in 1958–59 and '61.

Kubek the player is best remembered for a bad-hop, double-play grounder that bounced off his throat during Game 7 of the 1960 World Series. In six World Series, he hit .240 with 10 RBIs and 16 runs scored.

Slumping, Kubek visited the Mayo Clinic in 1965 and was diagnosed with three fused vertebrae in his neck, first injured in a touch football game while in the Army Reserves. Doctors advised him that a collision could potentially paralyze the infielder.

He retired at age 29 and became a long-time broadcaster for NBC, the Yankees, and the Brewers.

Ghost Marcelle

Ghost Marcelle was the best third baseman of his era from 1918–30, high praise, considering he was only average at best with the bat. He ranks among the top three third baseman in Negro league history with Hall of Famers Judy Johnson and Ray Dandridge.

The Creole was also known for his violent temper and fighting ability. Marcelle was with Dave Brown the night the latter killed a man in a drug-related argument. While playing winter ball in Cuba in early 1930, Marcelle fought with teammate Frank Warfield over a craps game. Warfield bit off part of his nose, forcing Marcelle to wear a patch over his injury for the rest of his life. Ghost only played four more games in the Negro leagues. The humiliation became too much for the handsome, dapper dresser and he quit the sport altogether in 1934.

Sis Moore

Prior to her first season in the All-American Girls Professional Baseball League in 1951, Sis Moore lost part of her hand working in an automobile plant. She still tried to make the team when spring training started but was held back until late in the season. She tried again the following season with minimal success.

Bert Niehoff

Paddles Niehoff led the National League with 42 doubles in 1916, while also besting all second baseman in twin killings. Those were the highpoints of a six-year career that saw him hit .240 in 583 games. A broken leg in 1918 ended his career.

Dolly Niemiec

Infielder Dolly Niemiec was forced to retire from the All-American Girls Professional Baseball League after an automobile accident prior to her fourth season in 1952. In 1958, she joined the professional bowling tour in its inaugural season.

John Paciorek

Eighteen-year-old Houston Colt .45's right fielder John Paciorek sparkled in his major league debut at the end of the 1963 season on September 29. He went 3 for 3 with two walks, three RBIs, and scored four times. Unfortunately, a back injury prevented the ballplayer from appearing in the majors again. Paciorek holds the record for most hits by a player with a 1.000 batting average. His brothers Tom and Jim also appeared on a major league diamond.

Mike Pazik

Lefthander Mike Pazik appeared in 13 games for the Minnesota Twins from 1975–77. In '77, he suffered numerous fractures to his legs in an auto accident, ending his career.

Old Hoss Radbourn

Charley Radbourn was a hard drinker with a personality to match. His 309 victories rank among the all-time leaders. Radbourn's 1884 season with the NL Providence Grays is particularly noteworthy. Providence's other pitcher Charlie Sweeney jumped the team at midseason. Radbourn offered to pitch the rest of the season if management forgave the suspension he was serving, gave him a bonus, and released him at the end of the year. Providence had no choice but to capitulate.

Radbourn pitched nearly every remaining game. In the process, he amassed many impressive statistics while leading the league in games, starts, complete games, wins, innings pitched, and strikeouts. His 59 victories that year are an all-time high. At one point, he won 18 straight. Staggering by today's standards, Radbourn pitched 678 innings. Equally impressive are his ERA of 1.38 and 441 Ks. He also pitched 11 shutouts. The toll on his arm required a friend to help him dress everyday. Keep in mind, though, that he was pitching underhand from 50 feet.

Providence won the pennant. At season's end, the National League and American Association staged a series to determine the championship of baseball. Some recognize this as the first World Series. Radbourn won all three games: 6-0, 3-1, 12-2. Instead of forcing the release, he accepted a $2,000 raise for 1885.

Radbourn originally entered the majors as a right fielder. Developing arm trouble, he quit the game in 1880 to become a butcher. In '81 repeated telegrams from the Providence Grays seeking his services as a right fielder and part-time pitcher went unanswered. Finally, a friend of his replied with an acceptance of the offer in Radbourn's name and, then, pushed him on a train to join the team. He reluctantly embarked on his pitching career.

On July 25, 1883, he pitched a no-hitter against Cleveland. Radbourn is also credited with seven one-hitters. Resilient, he pitched an amazing 489 complete games. Radbourn retired at age 36 in 1891, partially because of paresis and syphilis. He returned home to Bloomington, Illinois, and opened a pool hall. A hunting accident on April 13, 1894 blew away part of his face, including an eye. He also suffered some speech loss and partial paralysis. Old Hoss became a recluse, hiding in the back room of his saloon. In 1897, the retired pitcher drank himself to death at age 43.

Jack Ridley

Center fielder Jack Ridley joined the Nashville Elite Giants of the Negro leagues in 1927 and was still with them in 1934 when his career ended in an auto accident. His arm, which was hanging out the window, was torn off when his car swiped a trunk.

Minnie Rojas

Cuban righthanded pitcher Minnie Rojas was Fireman of the Year for the California Angels in his sophomore season of 1967 with 27 saves, 12 wins, and a 2.52 ERA. The following year, arm troubles forced him out of the majors. In 1970, a tragic car accident took the lives of his wife and two young daughters and left the pitcher paralyzed from the neck down.

Yoshitaka Sato

Brazilian Yoshitaka Sato played outfield for Hankyu in Nippon Professional Baseball from 1980–82. His career ended trying to break up a bar fight in March 1982. Glass shards damaged his right eye and the ballplayer returned home.

Tony Saunders

Tampa Bay Devil Rays pitcher Tony Saunders fell to the ground on May 16, 1999, after delivering a pitch versus the Rangers. He broke the humerus bone in his left, pitching arm, an uncommon injury in young players. The 25-year-old attempted a comeback the following summer but it ended in disaster as he re-broke the same bone, but in a different spot.

Saunders was the first player chosen by the Devil Rays from Florida in the 1998 expansion draft. In 61 starts, Saunders had a 13-24 record with a 4.56 ERA. After only 2 + seasons, his major league career seems over.

Skeeter Scalzi

Shortstop Skeeter Scalzi went 6 for 18 in his only major league games with the Giants in 1939. Managing in the minors until 1960, he was forced to retire after an auto accident, which left him permanently hobbled. Eventually, he would be confined to a wheelchair.

Lou Schettler

Lou Schettler hurled in 27 games for the Phillies in 1910. Six years later in the minors, his career ended with a broken leg sustained during a train wreck.

Jim Shaw

Grunting Jim Shaw four times won 15 + games for the hapless Washington Senators. Ten times, he led the league in some good and some not-so-good pitching categories. Nevertheless, his record shows a solid 3.07 ERA over nine major league seasons. A hip injury ended his career in 1921 at the age of 28. Shaw's nickname came from his guttural sounds while pitching, a la Monica Seles.

Syl Simon

Syl Simon was 29 years old and a six-year minor league veteran when he had his left hand mangled in a factory accident while working after the 1926 season. All that remained was his thumb and part of his palm and little finger. Simon, a righthanded third baseman, adapted a special glove for fielding and a mechanical grip for batting. He managed to play in 1927 and continued through 1932.

Dick Sipek

Deaf outfielder Dick Sipek appeared in 82 games for the Cincinnati Reds in 1945. He had fallen down a staircase at age five and virtually lost all hearing.

Casey Stengel

Casey Stengel was one of the true characters of major league lore. He created a language and wisdom that can only be explained as "Stengelese" and won him the title of the "Ol' Perfessor." No true fan can recall the legend without a chuckle. On the serious side, many consider Casey to have been one of the premier teachers of the diamond.

Stengel began his major league career for the Brooklyn Dodgers in 1912 with a four-hit game. As the club's starting right fielder in 1914, he posted a career-high .316 batting average. That year, he began his managerial education with one of the old-school masters, Wilbert Robinson. Stengel would further develop under the tutelage of John McGraw.

After being traded to the Pirates in 1918, Stengel returned to Ebbets Field facing heavy taunting. He found a sparrow, put it under his hat and waited for his next turn at bat. Approaching the batter's box, Casey turned to the crowd and doffed his cap. The laughter could be heard long after the bird flew away.

In 1921, he joined the New York Giants. McGraw platooned the lefthanded batter and Casey hated it. Nevertheless, it provided Stengel the opportunity to study the game with one of the finest field strategists of all time. In turn, the Yankees would later hate Stengel for platooning them.

Stengel's highlight as a player came in the 1923 World Series, as the Yankees won their first world championship in six games. In Game 1, Casey hit an inside-the-park homer in the 9th inning, the first postseason home run at the new Yankee Stadium. Likewise, he hit a 7th inning, game-winning four-bagger in Game 3.

Casey left the majors in 1925 to become player–manager–president for Worcester of the Eastern League. Prior to 1949, Casey Stengel had managed in the major leagues for nine years: 1934–36 Brooklyn Dodgers and 1938–43 Boston Braves. His teams were horrible, not once rising out of the second division. Casey's record stood at 160 games below .500. In 1943, he missed the first 47 games of the season with a broken leg after being hit by a taxicab. A local writer penned, "The man who did the most for baseball in Boston was the motorist who ran down Stengel and kept him away from the Braves." Casey was fired at the end of the season. At age 53, he returned to the minors to manage.

Yankees general manager George Weiss hired Stengel to assume the helm of the Bronx Bombers in 1949. Fans were shocked. Casey had long been known as a clown in New York. The irascible Joe DiMaggio was equally stunned.

What followed was the greatest run any manager has ever had in major league history. The Yankees won the world championship in 1949–53, '56, and '58, and the American League flag in 1949–53, 1955–58, and 1960. His 10 pennants are tied with his mentor, John McGraw, for the most in major league history. Al Lopez was the only other American League manager to win a pennant in the 1950s: 1954 Indians and 1959 White Sox. In 12 full seasons with the Yankees, Stengel won 1,149 games, an average of 96 a year. As Casey often said, you have to have the horses to win.

The Yankees lost the 1960 World Series in the bottom of the ninth of Game 7 on a home run by second baseman Bill Mazeroski. Yankee owners Del Webb and Dan Topping promptly fired Stengel and Weiss. The Yankees held a press conference to announce the "retiring" of the beloved manager. Casey set the record straight, "They paid me off in full and told me my services are not desired any longer by this club." The aged leader later quipped, "I'll never make the mistake of being 70 again." Another reason for his dismissal may be his surly attitude toward many of his players; consequently, he developed more than a few strained relationships. Stengel also made some highly questionable moves during his final Fall Classic, like refusing to open Game 1 with dominant southpaw Whitey Ford.

He joined George Weiss with the hapless expansion New York Mets in '62, perhaps the worst team of the 20th century. No one seemed to care as Stengel entertained the masses with his many incoherent soliloquies. The most-quotable man in baseball always had a throng of reporters at his side.

On July 24, 1965, the 75-year-old fell and broke his hip, ending a 50+-year professional career with 1,905 managerial wins, despite leading some truly awful Dodgers, Braves, and Mets clubs. Stengel entered Cooperstown the following summer.

Monty Stratton

After posting two 15-win seasons, White Sox pitcher Monty Stratton was just getting started in 1938 when a hunting accident ended his career at age 26. While seeking rabbits in Texas in November, he accidentally shot himself in the leg, severing the femoral artery. His right leg was amputated. An attempted comeback in 1946 fell short of the majors. Stratton is known today for the popular Hollywood movie about his life starring Jimmy Stewart.

Similarly, Cardinals shortstop Charlie Gelbert shot himself in the leg in early 1933 but was able to return to the majors two years later. His injury sparked the trade for Leo Durocher, which firmed up the Gas House Gang.

Marion Watson

All-American Girls Professional Baseball League pitcher Marion Watson broke her leg in a motorcycle accident prior to her sophomore season in 1948. She was in a cast for two years. Unfortunately, her rookie season was limited to only eight games after she broke her other leg sliding into home.

Norma Whitney

A detached retina ended Norma Whitney's All-American Girls Professional Baseball League career in just her second season in 1950.

Jimmy Wood

National Association second baseman–manager Jimmy Wood cut his left leg in 1873. The resulting infection spread to his right leg, leading to a botched surgery that eventually required amputation of that appendage. However, Wood found employment as manager of the White Stockings.

CHAPTER THIRTEEN

Death: Illness and Dependency

Harry Agganis

Former Boston University All-American quarterback Harry Agganis became the Red Sox starting first baseman in 1954 after signing for a $35,000 bonus. That year, he led the league in assists. Agganis died the following June of complications from leukemia. He was 26 years old.

Agganis was also drafted out of college by the NFL Cleveland Browns in 1952, though he never joined the club. The following year, his rights were shipped to the new Baltimore Colts as part of a huge 15-man trade. Likewise, Baltimore had no luck persuading Agganis to join the gridiron before he fell ill.

Lou Angemeier

Swamp fever took the life of 25-year-old Lou Angemeier on September 23, 1911. The Southwestern League Huntsville player was traveling through Kentucky at the time.

Bill Bailey

Bill Bailey pitched in the majors and minors for 20 years, beginning in 1906, then fell ill after the 1925 season and died the following November because of a ruptured vessel in his stomach, which some claim was a lingering effect of a baseball injury. The lefthander won 242 games in the minors and another 34 in the majors.

Bald Billy Barnie

Billy Barnie managed four major league teams in a 16-year career, spent mostly with Baltimore in the American Association. Though he never finished higher than third, Barnie made a name for himself as a strong backer of the association in its struggles with the National League.

While managing Hartford in the Eastern League in 1900, Barnie contracted and died of asthmatic bronchitis at midseason. He was 47 years old.

Bernardo Baro

Cuban baseball Hall of Famer Bernardo Baro passed away in June 1930 at age 37 after a mental breakdown the previous year. The speedy outfielder had toiled in the Negro leagues since 1913.

Francisco Barrios

Hard-throwing Chicago White Sox righthander Francisco Barrios won 38 and lost 38 with a 4.15 ERA in seven major league seasons. In 1981, he was arrested on narcotics charges. A year later, Barrios was found dead of an overdose at age 28.

Joe Bauldree

Righthanded pitcher Joe Bauldree died of heart disease in 2002. The 25-year-old was a farmhand in the Braves organization.

Steve Bechler

Orioles pitching prospect Steve Bechler died of heatstroke, temperature rising to 108 degrees, during spring training 2003. The 23-year-old had recently consumed a weight-loss drug that contained ephedrine, a controversial stimulant, that might have compounded his dehydration and organ system failures. Ephedrine had previously been banned by the National Football League, the NCAA and the International Olympic Committee.

Mark Belanger

Slick-fielding shortstop Mark Belanger replaced Hall of Famer Luis Aparicio in the Baltimore lineup in 1968. With Brooks Robinson, he formed one of the most efficient-fielding third base–shortstop combos in baseball history. "The Blade" won eight of the duos 24 Gold Gloves. When Bobby Grich joined the fold, no one could better the 4-5-6 combination the Orioles fielded. It was a pitcher's delight. Belanger led the league three times in assists, range, and fielding average, and once in double plays.

At the plate, Belanger had few highlights. It is a tribute to his skills with the glove that he stayed in the starting lineup for 13 years, 1968–80, as basically an offensive liability, though Nolan Ryan rated him as one of his toughest outs. Rod Guidry also had trouble with the slight righthander.

Belanger's finest year at the plate was 1969 under the tutelage of Charlie Lau when the righthander posted career highs with a .287 batting average, 50 RBIs, and 76 runs scored.

He played up the middle for six division winners, four pennant winners and a world championship team. After retirement, Belanger became a long-time special assistant to Don Fehr, chief of the Major League Players Association. He remained in that post until his death of lung cancer in October 1998 at age 54.

John Bender

Hall of Famer Chief Bender's brother John died of heart failure on September 25, 1911, in Edmonton. The attack came during a home game for the pitcher's Western Canada League club. Back in 1908, Bender stabbed his manager Win Clark while playing for Columbus. The subsequent suspension kept him away from the game for two years.

Cy Bentley

Cy Bentley died at the age of 22 in February 1873 of consumption. The previous summer, he had pitched for Middleton, Connecticut, in the National Association.

John Bergh

John Bergh had two stints in the National League, 1876 and 1880, but did not stick. Still playing ball, the catcher contracted consumption and passed away at age 25 in April 1883.

Babe Bigelow

Slugger Babe Bigelow pounded out a career .349 batting average and 848 RBIs over 12 minor league seasons, from 1920–32, spent mostly in the Southern Association and the Florida State League. In 1929, the outfielder appeared in 100 games for the Boston Red Sox, hitting .284. Following the '32 season, Bigelow became ill and died the following August at age 34. He had just led the league in games played.

Henry Blackman

Baltimore Black Sox third baseman Henry Blackman of the Eastern Colored League passed away on August 8, 1924, at age 36 from liver disease.

Though he didn't enter the league until after his 30th birthday, Blackman is recognized as one of the finer defensive third baseman of the 1920s, along with Judy Johnson and Ghost Marcelle.

Cy Blanton

Cy Blanton won 68 games over nine seasons in the National League from 1934–42. A sore arm relegated him to the minors where he was pitching for the Hollywood Stars of the Pacific Coast League in 1945. The club suspended him in March for habitual drunkenness. Years of alcohol abuse took his life in September at age 37.

Ned Bligh

Catcher Ned Bligh played four years in the American Association from 1886–90. Shortly afterward, he contracted typhoid fever and died at age 27 in April 1892.

Willie Bobo

Eight-year Negro league veteran first baseman Willie Bobo succumbed after consuming too much wood alcohol—moonshine—during a night trip with teammates to Tijuana in February 1931.

Walt Bond

After playing for the Kansas City Monarchs, Walt Bond joined the Cleveland Indians in 1960. In 1964 with the Houston Colt .45's, the first baseman–outfielder clubbed 20 homers and 85 RBIs while in remission from leukemia. In 1967, Bond was forced to leave his club after only 10 games. He died that September at age 29.

Tiny Bonham
Righthanded pitcher Ernie Bonham appeared in three World Series for the Yankees in the 1940s. In 1942, he went 21-5 while leading the league in winning percentage, complete games, opponent on-base percentage, and shutouts. Previously, he had copped the ERA crown in 1940 by posting a 1.90 mark.

Bonham was with Pittsburgh in 1949 when he died following complications after appendix surgery in September at age 36.

Frank Bonner
Blood poisoning killed 41-year-old Kansas City (American Association) second baseman Frank Bonner on New Year's Eve 1906. His wife had recently committed suicide.

Nick Bremigan
Nick Bremigan umpired in the American League from 1974 until his death on March 28, 1989, of a heart attack at age 43, shortly after working a preseason game.

Andy Briswalter
Pacific Coast League pitcher Andy Briswalter died of tuberculosis on May 12, 1912. The Los Angeles Angel was only 22 years old.

Babe Brown
New Orleans pitcher Babe Brown of the Southern Association died of spinal meningitis on September 4, 1904.

Buster Brown
Righthanded pitcher Buster Brown won 51 games in the National League from 1905–13; however, he lost 103. The following February, he died from complications related to an inflamed lymph gland under his left arm. Some reports suggest it developed from overtraining. Brown was 31 years old.

Willard Brown
Catcher–first baseman Willard Brown played seven years in the majors, National League and Players League, from 1887–94. He led the National League in fielding average the only two years he qualified, 1891 and '93. Brown died at age 31 in December 1897, after completing another season in the minors.

Randy Burden
Angels minor league pitcher Randy Burden died in his sleep in December 2002. He was 23 years old.

Tom Cahill
Tom Cahill studied medicine during his off-seasons while playing professional ball. During 1891, he appeared on the Louisville roster in the American Association. At age 26 on Christmas Day 1894, he died while suffering from consumption.

Bobby Cargo

Atlanta Crackers, of the Southern Association, infielder Bobby Cargo succumbed to typhoid pneumonia at the onset of a new season on April 27, 1904. The 35-year-old had played two games with Pittsburgh in the National League in 1892.

Bob Caruthers

Bob Caruthers won 191 games from 1885–90, helping the St. Louis Browns win the American Association title three times and Brooklyn twice (AA and NL). In all, the righthander was 217-98 for a .689 winning percentage that ranks among the highest in the sport. In 1885 and '89, Caruthers won 40 games. In 1886, he won the final game of the World Series over Chicago of the National League, giving the AA its lone world championship.

Caruthers often played in the outfield when not pitching, amassing a career .282 batting average in 2,500 at-bats over 10 seasons, 1884–93. In 1886 and '87, his slugging average topped an impressive .500. It is hard to top his 1887 season for batting production by a full-time pitcher.

Brooklyn's nickname was changed in 1889 to the Bridegrooms when Caruthers and three teammates were married prior to the season. Caruthers was one of the men who penned his signature to a letter in 1887 to club owner Chris Von der Ahe stating their refusal to play against black men. When the pitching distance was expanded to 60'6" in 1893, Caruthers left the mound and quickly slid to the minors.

Playing in the minors through 1898, Caruthers eventually turned to umpiring. In 1902 and '03, he did so for Ban Johnson in the American League. While umpiring in the Three-I League in 1911, he fell ill at midseason and passed away in August at age 48.

Joe Cassidy

Good-field, no-hit Washington Senators shortstop Joe Cassidy, out of Villanova University, was one of the first men to play at the major league level without any minor league experience. He led the league with 19 triples as a rookie in 1904 and in '05 with 520 assists. Cassidy died in the spring of 1906 of malaria at age 23.

Walt Cazen

International Leaguer Walt Cazen died of tuberculosis on May 7, 1946. The Syracuse player was 33 years old.

Henry Chadwick

Henry Chadwick was a baseball pioneer often called the "Father of Baseball." With his induction in 1938, Chadwick is the only sportswriter enshrined in the main hall of Cooperstown. As a rule interpreter in the old NABBP, he was instrumental in eliminating tie games as an official result, among other of the game's nuances. For years, he served as chairman of the rules committee of the National Association. Here he helped guide the fledgling sport through its numerous and complicated rule changes.

In the late 1860s, Chadwick was the editor of the first weekly devoted to baseball, the *Baseball Players Chronicle*. He also compiled the first baseball reference books, record books, and instructional guides. As chief baseball writer and editor, he contributed to the *Brooklyn Eagle* newspaper for 45 years. Chadwick became the nation's foremost authority on the sport.

Perhaps his greatest contributions lie in the development of a scoring system and his zero-tolerance for gambling and drunkenness. Numerous articles exposed gambling and game-fixing fraud to the public. He played a big part in the National League's banning of pool-selling at its parks in 1876. It was the most popular form of gambling at the time. In 1859, Chadwick produced the first known box score. Likewise, in 1858, he supplied the game's first rule book and scorecard. His work is largely responsible for the core of baseball statistics that we treasure today.

In later years, the English-born writer served as editor of the *Spalding Guide*. Insisting on attending the Brooklyn Dodgers' home opener in 1908 despite a lingering cold, Chadwick braved the wet, cold weather. He contracted pneumonia and died on April 20 at age 83. Sadly, he missed perhaps the most exciting pennant races in baseball history that year.

George Cole
Waterloo manager George Cole of the Iowa State League passed away after an appendicitis operation during the spring of 1905.

King Cole
As a rookie for the National League champion Chicago Cubs in 1910, righthander King Cole won 20 games with a league-leading .833 winning percentage. In all, he posted 56 victories between 1909–15. On January 6, 1916, he died of cancer at age 29. Cole was Ring Lardner's inspiration for his *Alibi Ike* series.

Bill Collins
Catcher Bill Collins appeared in only four major league games over three seasons, 1889–91. While playing in the minors, he contracted typhoid fever and died in June 1893 at age 30.

Dan Collins
Dan Collins appeared in seven games in the outfield for Louisville during the National League's first season. He died in September 1883 at age 29 while still active in the minors.

Hub Collins
Hub Collins was the starting second baseman for two pennant-winning Brooklyn Bridegroom teams. First, Brooklyn won the flag in the American Association in 1889. The very next year, the entire team joined the National League and won its crown. Collins, a fast and aggressive runner, scored over 100 runs in four different seasons. He was among a host of men that stole countless bases before they were calculated or included as official statistics.

During his seventh season in 1892, Collins began feeling cold symptoms on

May 14 and removed himself in favor of a pinch hitter. He was dead seven days later of typhoid fever at age 28. Monte Ward organized an all-star exhibition game that raised $3,000 for Collins' widow.

Bill Collver

Bill Collver appeared in one game in the National League with Boston at age 18 in 1885. Three years later, eyeing a new season in the minors, the outfielder died following spinal surgery.

Louis Comiskey

Louis Comiskey, son of White Sox founder Charles Comiskey, took over club operations in 1931 upon his father's death. The sickly, younger Comiskey had maintained a hospital suite at St. Luke's in Chicago since contracting scarlet fever in 1912. In '39, Comiskey had lights installed at the stadium, but died just prior to the team's first night game.

Red Connally

Red Connally played two games in the outfield for St. Louis in the National League in 1886. Ten years later, as an umpire in the minor leagues, he died from pneumonia at age 39.

Andy Cooper

Kansas City Monarchs manager Andy Cooper passed away after a stroke on June 3, 1941, at the age of 45. His Monarchs had won three of the previous four Negro American League titles. Cooper had been pitching in the Negro leagues since 1920.

Clint Courtney

International League manager Clint Courtney suffered a heart attack in his hotel room on June 15, 1975, and passed away at age 48.

Courtney was known as a hard-nosed catcher with five American League franchises. After a close play in a 1953 game, he took on Billy Martin, Phil Rizzuto, and Allie Reynolds at second base.

Forrest Crawford

Cardinals shortstop Forrest Crawford passed away from blood poisoning related to an injury to his side on March 29, 1908. He was 26 years old.

Amos Cross

In 1887, Amos Cross, his brother Lave, and Paul Cook shared the catching duties for Louisville in the American Association. Amos fell ill and died the following July of consumption at age 27. The severely bowlegged Lave went on to play another 20 years in the bigs.

Kiki Cuyler

Speedy outfielder Kiki Cuyler, pronounced "Cuy Cuy" Cuyler, stole 328 bases while leading the National League four times. He finished with 1,300 runs, 1,050 RBIs, and a .321 batting average.

In 1925, the right fielder propelled Pittsburgh to the pennant and world championship, leading the league with 153 games, 26 triples, 144 runs, and 13 HBPs. He complemented the huge year with second place finishes with 41 stolen bases, 369 total bases, 43 doubles, 228 runs produced, and a .598 slugging average. Cuyler placed third in hits with 220 and fourth with a .357 batting average and a .423 on-base percentage. Kiki also slugged 18 home runs and 102 RBIs.

In fact, all three Pirate outfielders hit above .325 that year. Cuyler was the hero of the 1925 World Series, producing six RBIs, including a game-winning home run in Game 2 against Stan Coveleski. In the seventh game, Cuyler made a great catch to keep the score close and hit a two-run double off the great Walter Johnson in the 8th inning to break the 7-7 tie. Pittsburgh held on to win, 9-7.

A feud with manager Donie Bush kept him from appearing in the rout by the Yankees over the Pirates in the 1927 World Series. Pirates owner Barney Dreyfuss, supporting his manager, traded Cuyler to the Cubs. He flourished in Wrigley Field, appearing in two more World Series in 1929 and '32. In 1932, he broke his foot and reinjured it in '33, eliminating his base-stealing threat.

As a coach with the Boston Red Sox, Cuyler died suddenly of heart failure on February 11, 1950, at the age of 51. The Veterans Committee elected him to Cooperstown in 1968.

Ed Daily

Louisville righthander Ed Daily's health started to decline early into the 1891 season, knocking him out of Louisville's lineup. He died in October from tuberculosis. Daily had won 66 games since 1885, including 26 as a rookie.

Jake Daubert

Jake Daubert was the best all-around first baseman of the 1910s. Rated below Hal Chase as a fielder, he nonetheless led the league three times in fielding average and double plays and once in assists and putouts. The steady lefthander hit .300+ ten times. Daubert produced 2,300 base hits, 400 sacrifice hits, 1,100 runs, 700 RBIs, 250 stolen bases, and a .303 batting average, mostly from the #2 spot in the lineup. He copped batting crowns in 1913 and '14.

In 1913 with Brooklyn, Daubert won the Chalmers' MVP award. Later, when the 1918 season was cut short for World War I, he sued to recover most of his lost salary. Owner Charles Ebbets felt betrayed and shipped him to Cincinnati. Daubert assumed the team's captaincy and led them to the World Series, his second in four years. At the age of 38 in 1922, Daubert had his finest season, batting .336 with 114 runs, 205 hits, and a league-leading 22 triples.

Toward the end of the 1924 season, the Red fell ill. The 40-year-old died on October 9 from complications after an appendectomy.

Herman Dehlman

Herman Dehlman succumbed to peritonitis in March 1885 at age 35, looking forward to another season in the minors. The first baseman had played for St. Louis during the National League's first two campaigns.

Steve Dignan
Outfielder Steve Dignan played for both Boston and Worcester in 1880. The following July, the 22-year-old died.

Pickles Dillhoefer
Part-time National League catcher, 1917–21, William Dillhoefer succumbed to typhoid fever on February 22, 1922. The 27-year-old had just married. He was the first of two Cardinals to pass away that year.

Cozy Dolan
The original Cozy Dolan fell to the minors after pitching briefly for the Boston Beaneaters in 1895–96. He reemerged in the National League in 1900, playing the outfield for five teams until 1906. He died in Louisville during spring training the following year from typhoid fever. Concerned for the club's health, the Braves cut spring training short. Dolan was 34 years old.

Tim Donahue
Catcher Tim Donahue played in three major leagues from 1891–1902, mostly for the Cubs. He fell ill after three games for the Nationals in 1902 and passed away from kidney and stomach ailments on June 12 at age 32.

Randy Donisthorpe
Reds farmhand Randy Donisthorpe, a lefthanded pitcher, died at age 23 after a seizure in his sleep during spring training in Plant City, Florida, on March 21, 1996.

Jimmy Doyle
Jimmy Doyle replaced longtime Chicago Cubs third baseman Harry Steinfeldt in 1911, hitting .282 and leading the league in double plays and errors. Over the winter, Doyle had his appendix removed. He died of blood poisoning on February 1, 1912, at age 30.

Valentin Dreke
Cuban Baseball Hall of Famer Valentin Dreke died on September 25, 1929, at age 31 from tuberculosis. The outfielder had played in the United States with the Cuban Stars from 1918–28.

Chuck Dressen
Manager Chuck Dressen won 1,008 games in 16 seasons with five different major league clubs from 1934–66, including two pennants with the Brooklyn Dodgers in 1952–53. A younger Dressen played third base in the majors for eight seasons, mostly with Cincinnati. Growing up in football-crazy Illinois, he later played for two NFL teams from 1920–23 at quarterback.

As the Detroit Tigers manager in May 1966, the 67-year-old became ill and left the team after 26 games to check into a hospital. He died three months later of a heart attack.

Charlie Duffee

Charlie Duffee left the majors four games into his fifth season, 1893, suffering from the effects of consumption. He died the following December at age 28. The outfielder had twice led the league in assists and double plays.

Jack Dunn

Jack Dunn, one of the most successful minor league owners and managers, died of a heart attack while riding a horse during a dog show in Towson, Maryland, on October 22, 1928. The International League magnate, 54, originally bought the Baltimore Orioles from Ned Hanlon in 1909 for $70,000. After Dunn's death, Hall of Famer George Weiss took over baseball operations for the club until New York general manager Ed Barrow tapped him to build the Yankees farm system in 1931. Dunn had managed in the International League for 24 years, winning more than 2,100 games and nine pennants.

Clyde Emsley

Western League Wichita pitcher Clyde Emsley succumbed to spinal meningitis on April 20, 1911, at the young age of 22.

Jack Farrell

After spending two seasons in the Federal League with the Chicago Whales, second baseman Jack Farrell could not crack a major league roster. He died in the minors from pneumonia in 1918 at age 29.

Charlie Ferguson

From 1884–87, Charlie Ferguson won 99 games, struck out 728 batters and compiled a 2.67 ERA for the expansion NL Philadelphia Quakers. He also hit .288 in 963 at-bats. In 1887, he won 22 games, batted .337, and knocked in 85 runners. The speedster also filled in at center field when he wasn't pitching.

Ferguson also coached Princeton baseball during the off-season. In early 1888, he contracted typhoid fever and died soon after turning 25 years old.

Pembroke Finlayson

Pitcher Pembroke Finlayson appeared in a game each year, 1908–09, for the Brooklyn Dodgers without a record. He died on March 16, 1912, from peritonitis of the heart at age 23. Some reports suggest it was caused by a pitching injury.

Mickey Finn

Phillies hard-nosed second baseman Neal Finn died following a stomach operation for duodenal ulcers on July 7, 1933. He was 29 years old.

Jim Fogarty

Jim Fogarty had outstanding range as a center fielder, leading his league multiple times in putouts, assists, double plays, range, and fielding percentage. His 42 assists in 1889 in particular stand out. Fogarty was also fast on the base paths, scoring 100+

runs on two occasions. In 1887, he became the second major leaguer to steal 100 bases. Fogarty impressed Al Spalding enough to slot him as the center fielder for the world tour after the '88 season.

Playing his entire career in Philadelphia, Fogarty became the Quakers team captain in 1889. He then jumped with numerous teammates to the Players League the following season and became a field manager. After the Players League dissolved, Fogarty was reassigned with Ed Delahanty to the Quakers. However, he contracted tuberculosis before the season began and died on May 20, 1891, at age 27.

Dave Foutz

Dave Foutz teamed with Bob Caruthers to win 198 games (99 each) for Charles Comiskey's American Association champion St. Louis Browns from 1885–87. Then, owner Chris Von der Ahe sold the duo to Brooklyn that winter for $13,500 but still managed to win the pennant in '88 by squeezing 90 wins from Silver King and Nat Hudson. Caruthers and Foutz, on the other hand, would lead the Bridegrooms to a championship in 1889 and again when the team joined the National League the following year. In the latter two seasons, Foultz mainly played first base, contributing 211 RBIs. In fact, he drove in 418 runners from 1887–90.

On the mound in 1886, Foutz led the league with 41 victories and a 2.11 ERA, while also tossing 11 shutouts. In all, the big, 6'2", righthander is second, behind Whitey Ford, in all-time winning percentage with a .689 mark, 146-66.

At the end of his career, Foutz managed Brooklyn from 1893–96. Falling ill from asthma complications, he retired at the end of the 1896 season and died in March the following year at age 40.

Masao Fujii

Masao Fujii pitched for Daiei in Nippon Professional Baseball from 1995–99. In January 2000, he was hospitalized with lung cancer. Fujii died that October at age 31.

Ned Garvin

Ned Garvin lost many more games than he won over seven major league seasons from 1896–1904. The mean-tempered and often violent pitcher fell ill after playing in the Northwest League in 1907. He died from tuberculosis at age 34 in June 1908.

Ben Geraghty

Ben Geraghty played infield in 70 games in the majors from 1936–44. In the minors, he began managing in 1947. With Jacksonville in the International League, Geraghty died at midseason in 1963. He was 48 years old.

A. Bartlett Giamatti

Lifelong Red Sox fan A. Bartlett Giamatti was named National League president in December 1986, requiring him to resign as president of Yale University. He was a scholar who first came to baseball management's awareness by publishing an op-ed piece in *The New York Times* during the 1981 players' strike lambasting the players.

His reputation today has survived despite the numerous controversies that surrounded his reign, first, in the National League, then, as commissioner. First, he alleg-edly fired umpire Dave Pallone without a hearing after his sexual preference became known. Giamatti was also allegedly part of the establishment that kept female umpire Pam Postema from cracking the major leagues.

Peter Ueberroth resigned as commissioner and touted Giamatti as his replace-ment, even though he had little to no experience in the economic factors that plagued the game. On April 1, 1989, Giamatti assumed the full duties of the post in the midst of the Pete Rose gambling controversy after being unanimously elected by the owners. Giamatti and Rose already had a combative past when the National League president fined Rose $10,000 and suspended him for 30 days after an on-the-field incident involving umpire Pallone the previous year.

In truth, Giamatti had been involved in the Rose affair from the beginning. It then dominated his 154-day term as commissioner. The case was almost botched after Giamatti was faced with charges of bias against Rose, who wrote an ill-advised letter lauding a known gambler and bumbled his testimony.

Finally, an agreement was reached wherein Rose accepted a permanent ban from the game. One week later, on September 1, Giamatti died of a massive heart attack at his home in Martha's Vineyard. He was overweight, chain-smoked, and rarely monitored his diet. His love of the game was unfulfilled during his rule, as con-troversy distracted from its potential. Giamatti was succeeded by his deputy and good friend, Fay Vincent.

Josh Gibson

Josh Gibson may have been the best all-around player in Negro league history, maybe in all of baseball, black or white. He was a feared line-drive hitter who drilled more than 800 home runs in his career, 75 in 1931 alone. Gibson was also a skilled catcher with a powerful arm in a career that spanned 17 seasons, from 1930–46.

Traveling across town in 1930, the 18-year-old was recruited to play in the sec-ond game of a doubleheader after the Homestead Grays catcher Buck Ewing was injured in Pittsburgh. The opponent that day was a white semi-pro club from Dor-mont. The upstart never relinquished the job.

From that moment, the legends of his hitting prowess grew. They are told and retold to this day. He is the only man to hit a fair ball out of Yankee Stadium. As Roy Campanella said, ". . . there were . . . a hundred legends about him. Once you saw him play, you knew they were all true. I couldn't carry his bat or glove. The stories about his 500-foot home runs are all true, because I saw them. And he was one of those sluggers that seldom struck out. You couldn't fool him; he was too quick with the bat. And he could do it behind the plate, including throw."

In 1932, Gibson jumped to the barnstorming Pittsburgh Crawfords. Here, he joined with showman Satchel Paige as the biggest draw in baseball. By 1940, Gibson was drinking heavily and became difficult to manage. In January 1943, he sought medical advice for severe headaches. He was diagnosed with a brain tumor but refused an operation.

Part of his problems stemmed from a failed marriage. After it failed, he took up with a girlfriend who shared his penchant for booze and upped the ante with the introduction of heroin.

Gibson continued to play and even captured batting titles in 1945 and '46; but his drinking was becoming out of control, as was his weight and general physical condition. He missed the 1945 East–West Classic because of a suspension for breaking training rules (a.k.a. drinking). In January 1947, he died in his sleep just months before Jackie Robinson would take the field in a major league game. He was 35 years old. Gibson was elected to Cooperstown in 1972.

Jim Gilliam
Longtime Brooklyn–Los Angeles Dodger fan favorite Junior Gilliam died of a brain hemorrhage just prior to the start of the 1978 World Series. He had been with the organization as a player and coach since leaving the Negro leagues in 1950.

John Gilroy
John Gilroy pitched in nine games for Washington in the National League from 1895–96. The hurler died the following summer from complications after appendix surgery. He was 27 years old.

Herb Gorman
San Diego outfielder Herbert Gorman suffered a heart attack during a Pacific Coast League game against Hollywood on April 5, 1953. The 28-year-old died before reaching the hospital. Gorman had appeared in one game for the Cardinals the previous spring.

George Grosart
Just as the season started in 1902, outfielder George Grosart succumbed to typhoid fever on April 18. The 23-year-old had played seven games for the Boston Braves the previous summer.

Marc Hall
Bright's disease took the life of Tigers pitcher Marc Hall on February 24, 1915. He was 27 years old.

Jimmy Hallinan
Ireland-born Jimmy Hallinan played for four National League teams from 1876–78 after spending two years in the National Association. On October 28, 1879, the 30-year-old died of inflammation of the bowels

Pete Harrison
England-born Pete Harrison joined the men in blue in the National League in 1916. He remained until tuberculosis forced his departure in 1920. Harrison died the following May.

Clyde Hatter
Lefthanded pitcher Clyde Hatter appeared for the Detroit Tigers in 1935 and '37. He died that October 16 of a heart attack at age 28.

Henry Heitmuller
The second Los Angeles player to die during the 1912 season, Henry Heitmuller succumbed to typhoid fever on October 8. The outfielder was 29 years old. He had recently played two seasons with the Philadelphia Athletics, 1909–10.

Gil Hodges
Slick-fielding, power-hitting first baseman Gil Hodges helped the Brooklyn–Los Angeles Dodgers win seven pennants and two world titles during an 18-year career that spanned 1943, '47–63. During World War II, the Marine took part in battles at Okinawa, Japan.

Returning to the Dodgers, Hodges' career as a catcher was aborted when Roy Campanella joined the club. He immediately shined at first base, leading the league four times in games, double plays, and fielding average and three times in putouts and assists. The righthander won the first three Gold Gloves for his position, 1957–59.

Hodges hit 30 + homers six times and seven times knocked in more than 100 runners, 1949–55. On August 31, 1950, he smashed four home runs for nine RBIs versus the Phillies, becoming the sixth man to do so. At the end of his active career, Hodges totaled 370 dingers, 1,274 RBIs, and a .273 batting average.

In 1963, he took over the helm of the expansion Washington Senators. In '68, the popular Hodges returned to New York as the manager of the hapless Mets. The following year, he guided the now "Miracle" Mets to the world championship, jumping from ninth to first place in the National League standings.

Just prior to the strike-delayed 1972 season, Hodges died after a heart attack on April 2, following a round of golf. It occurred a day after the first general strike in sports history. Hodges was two days shy of his 48th birthday.

Bill Hogg
Righthander Bill Hogg amassed 37 victories for the Highlanders from 1905–08. He was optioned to Louisville in the American Association in February 1909. He then fell ill and died of Bright's disease in December at age 29.

Eddie Holtz
Eddie Holtz played middle infielder in the Negro leagues from 1919 until his death in St. Louis on July 15, 1924.

Dick Howser
All-American Florida State University shortstop Dick Howser signed with the Kansas City A's for a reported $21,000 bonus. The athlete produced an exciting rookie season with a .280 average, 37 stolen bases, and 108 runs scored in 1961. He even appeared in the All-Star Game. His average plummeted from there and he was

shipped first to the Indians and then the Yankees. Leaving the active roster in 1968, Howser became a coach for New York for ten years.

In 1980, he assumed the helm of the Yankees. Winning 103 games, Howser was unceremoniously dumped by George Steinbrenner after refusing to fire his coach, Mike Ferraro, for waving Willie Randolph home to a waiting tag in Game 2 of the American League Championship Series against the Royals.

In '81, he took over the Royals, replacing Jim Frey. They won it all in 1985. The next summer, he began experiencing headaches and a stiff neck. Two days after managing the All-Star team in '86, Howser entered the hospital and was diagnosed with a brain tumor. He died on June 17, 1987, after several operations.

Highpockets Hudspeth
Tall, 6'6", first baseman Highpockets Hudspeth played in the Negro leagues for 14 years. The lefthanded batter died from tuberculosis shortly after joining the Brooklyn Royal Giants in 1933. He was replaced at first by an up-and-coming Buck Leonard.

Miller Huggins
Diminutive manager Miller Huggins took over the Yankees in 1918, built a dynasty, and guided the team until his death. He had to "spank" childlike superstar Babe Ruth several times along the way. Pennants in 1921–23 and 1926–28, three world championships, and more than 1,400 victories would later place Huggins into the Hall of Fame.

As a player, Huggins was a solid defensive second baseman for the Reds and Cardinals whose offensive value to his team transcended his career .265 batting average. The leadoff hitter sparked many a rally by leading the league four times in walks, once in on-base percentage, and six times stealing more than 30 bases. Huggins was a rare switch-hitter at the turn of the century. He came to the Reds slated as the man to replace the popular, barehanded second baseman and future Hall of Famer Bid McPhee.

Cardinals' owner Helene Britton dismissed the condescending and crass field manager Roger Bresnahan and replaced him with player–manager Huggins in 1913. He guided the Cardinals to third place in '14, the team's highest finish since 1876.

At the 1917 World Series, with his co-owner Colonel Huston overseas during World War I, Colonel Ruppert signed Huggins to manage the Yankees. Huston had been touting Wilbert Robinson to fill the job. It caused a rift between the two magnates that eventually led Huston to sell out in 1922.

Huggins immediately began making inquiries to obtain Ruth. The deal was finally struck on January 3, 1920, with Red Sox owner Harry Frazee. Boston received $125,000 and a loan on Fenway Park for $300,000. Frazee, a showman, needed cash to finance his Broadway plays and pay off former Red Sox owner Joe Lannin. In fact, in his seven years as owner, Frazee completely decimated the team. Dismantling the club's nucleus, Frazee peddled stars and Hall of Famers alike. By the time he left in 1923, Frazee was the most vilified man in Boston, no small feat.

Ruth soon became the toast of baseball. However, in 1925 the Babe's ego, continual breaking of training rules, and lack of respect for authority were disruptive to the team. Huggins fined the overweight ballplayer $5,000, fired him as team captain, and suspended him indefinitely. It was the largest fine in major league history to date. Ownership supported their manager and Ruth caved. He apologized to Huggins and the team and paid the fine. Ruth would somewhat toe the line thereafter.

Huggins was wiry and hyper, a chronic insomniac and worrier. In short, he looked perpetually worn out. Feeling ill in September 1929, Huggins told his coaches he'd be back the next day after seeing a doctor. Huggins had been ignoring soreness under his eye for some time. He never returned. The 50-year-old died a week later of influenza and erysipelas, an aggressive skin disease. The first monument in center field at Yankee Stadium was erected in his honor. Likewise, his memory would be installed at Cooperstown in 1964.

William Hulbert

Hall of Fame executive William Hulbert was the driving force behind the development of the National League. He slowly gained control over the fundamental issues facing the owners at the time: gambling, game-fixing, scheduling, ticket pricing, concessions revenue, reserve lists, blacklists, umpire staffing, revolving, Sunday ballgames, and numerous lesser concerns. He was the first of a long list of Chicago executives to exert their influence over the game. Among the others, Albert Spalding, Rube Foster, and Kenesaw Mountain Landis stand out.

Hulbert is credited with stabilizing the new league in its formative years. Just prior to the opening of the 1882 season, Hulbert died at his home of heart failure at age 50, turning over his White Stockings to Al Spalding. The American Association was about to present perhaps the biggest challenge to the league's survival.

Fred Hutchinson

Fred Hutchinson won Minor League Player of the Year honors by going 25-7 with a 2.48 ERA for the Seattle Rainiers in the independent Pacific Coast League in 1938. He was then sold to the Detroit Tigers for $35,000 and four players. After three lackluster seasons split between the minors and Detroit, Hutch joined the Coast Guard for three years, 1942–45, during the war.

Returning to the Tigers rotation in 1946, the righthander won 87 games over the next six seasons. In '52, Hutchinson succeeded Red Rolfe as the Tigers pitcher–manager. After 2 1/2 seasons in the second division, Hutch was let go. In 1956, he took over the Cardinals helm. The following year, St. Louis finished second to the World Champion Milwaukee Braves.

He then joined Cincinnati and the surprising Reds won the pennant in 1961, spurred by MVP Frank Robinson, RHP Joey Jay, and LHP Jim O'Toole. Years of smoking finally caught up to Hutch in 1963 when he was diagnosed with lung cancer. He died in November 1964, shortly after retiring as manager, with an 830-827 record. The Reds retired his uniform #1.

Mineo Itazawa

In December 1980, Seibu rookie infielder Mineo Itazawa passed away from heart failure. The 19-year-old had yet to play for the parent club.

Lou Jackson

Grambling star Lou Jackson cracked the show with the Cubs in 1958. He was back in the International League in the following season. In 1963 with Toronto, the outfielder hit .315 with 31 homers and 89 RBIs. That won him a promotion to the Orioles in 1964 but he only lasted four games before returning to the IL.

Jackson signed with the Sankei Atoms of the Japan League in 1966. In 1967, he hit .296 with 28 home runs, earning a spot on the All-Star team. During an exhibition game in 1968, Jackson collapsed at home plate but returned shortly to finish the season. In three seasons in Japan, he batted .257 with 68 homers in 1,200 at bats. Jackson died in Tokyo from pancreatitis in May 1969 at age 33.

Slim Jones

Negro league strikeout pitcher Slim Jones started both the 1934 and 1935 East–West games. In the former year, he went 22-3 for the Philadelphia Stars at age 21. The 6'6" beanpole southpaw was reputed to be faster than Satchel Paige and Lefty Grove.

From the beginning of his career, Jones started drinking heavily. One day in December 1938, he pawned his winter coat to purchase whiskey. Soon thereafter, Jones contracted pneumonia and died while living on a Baltimore street.

Addie Joss

Addie Joss is probably the least known of the great Hall of Fame pitchers of the 20th century. His 1.88 ERA is second all-time and no one in baseball history allowed fewer base runners per game, 8.73. In fact, Joss only walked an average of 1.43 batters per game. Five times, his ERA fell below 2.00, including every year from 1906–09. Ninety percent of his starts were complete games, 45 of them shutouts. Helping in the field, the Cleveland righthander led the league in double plays twice and once in assists.

On October 2, 1908, during the final week of the season in the heat of a pennant battle between Cleveland, Detroit, and Chicago (all within 1.5 games), Joss pitched a perfect game. The clutch performance came against Big Ed Walsh of the White Sox in a year in which he won 40 games. Joss notched another no-hitter on April 20, 1910, against Chicago.

In April 1911, Joss passed out on the bench during a preseason game. He died one week later of tubercular meningitis at age 31. The Hall of Fame waived its ten-year rule to include Joss in 1978. The move to include him in Cooperstown began soon after the momentous publication of *The Baseball Encyclopedia* in 1969. Historians and fans could now compare the greats (and not-so-greats). Joss' stats shined.

Kazuo Kageyama

Kazuo Kageyama played infield for the Nankai Hawks from 1950–59, hitting .264. On September 28, 1951, he amassed 17 total bases in a game including tripling three times. He died shortly after being named the Hawks manager in November 1965. Kageyama was 38 years old.

Harry Kane

Lefthander Harry Kane started nine games in the majors from 1902–06. In 1932, he was umpiring in the Pacific Coast League. He was found dead of a heart attack after calling a game on September 15.

King Kelly

Catcher–outfielder Mike Kelly was one of baseball's first superstars. He was a dapper dresser whose aggressiveness on the base paths earned him a huge following, especially among female fans. He could often be found strolling down the street, twirling a cane, dressed to the nines with an ascot and patent leather shoes. Occasionally, his entourage would include a monkey and a Japanese valet. Kelly was one of the first American sports figures to be heavily sought after for his autograph. Furthermore, his autobiography was the first to be published by a sport's hero.

The future Hall of Famer amassed a .308 batting average over 16 major league seasons. He led his circuit three times in doubles and runs and twice in batting average and on-base percentage. In 1886, Kelly batted .388, leading the Chicago White Stockings to the pennant. The city was stunned when their hero was sold to Boston the following year for $10,000, an outrageous sum for the era. In all, he played on eight pennant winners, five with Chicago.

Kelly became celebrated for his daring base running. To the delight of the fans, he was one of the first to experiment with various sliding techniques. The fans screamed "Slide, Kelly, slide" as soon as he reached first base to egg him on. In typical myth-creating fashion, a popular song featured his exploits. Occasionally, Kelly was known to run directly from first to third or second to home if the umpire was otherwise occupied.

Kelly is also said to have invented the hit-and-run play. One day, a foul ball was hit near him in the dugout. Capitalizing on the rules of the day, he yelled, "Kelly now catching . . . ," and caught the popup for an out. He is also said to be the first catcher to back up first base. The sly backstop even found a way to trip runners with his mask.

Dismissing greater financial rewards to stay in the National League, Kelly signed on as player–manager for the Boston entry in the new Players League. In 1890, he copped the league's only pennant.

Heavy drinking, gambling, and a fashion plate lifestyle began to catch up with Kelly, causing his physical skills to deteriorate. He appeared for four teams over the next three seasons, retiring in 1893. To maintain his income, Kelly appeared at vaudeville theaters reciting Ernest Thayer's *Casey at the Bat*. On the way to a performance in Boston in November 1894, he contracted pneumonia, compounded by alcoholism, and subsequently died. He was 36 years old.

George Kempf

Rookie Jimmie Louden had a good year for Ottawa in the Canadian League in 1912. Come spring training the following year, the club got word that their 21-year-old ballplayer was dead from undetermined, conflicting causes. They also came to understand that he was really a college student named George Kempf.

Darryl Kile

Cardinal pitcher Darryl Kile was found dead in his hotel room on June 22, 2002. An autopsy revealed severe clogging of the arteries and advanced heart disease.

The 33-year-old righthander won 133 games in a 12-year major league career. The highlights with Houston include a no-hitter versus the Mets in 1993 and a 19-7 season in 1997 that accompanied a 2.57 ERA. With St. Louis, Kyle broke the magical 20-win barrier in 2000.

Masao Kitai

Masao Kitai accumulated a 2.01 ERA in 31 games for Hankyu from 1936–37. He died suddenly on his 24th birthday in August 1937.

Lou Kolls

Lou Kolls umpired in the American League from 1933–40, after which he was assigned to the American Association. However, he died in February 1941, in an auto accident at age 48.

Red Kress

Red Kress coached the expansion New York Mets in 1962. He died of a heart attack that November.

Yuji Kubodera

Yuji Kubodera played infield, outfield, and designated hitter for the Nankai Hawks from 1977–84. He died suddenly on January 4, 1985, at age 26.

Toshio Kurosawa

Toshio Kurosawa of the Yomiuri Giants died from an intestinal ailment in June 1947 at the age of 33. The left fielder had hit .259 in 1,800 at-bats from 1936–47.

Ty LaForest

Ty LaForest played 52 games for the Red Sox at third base at the end of the war in 1945. Soon after, he caught pneumonia, which led to heart problems. The 28-year-old passed away on May 5, 1947.

Charlie Lau

Charlie Lau did not hit well enough to establish himself as a regular in the major leagues, though the backup catcher did hang around for 11 seasons with five teams. After injuring his right elbow and being unable to perform any catching duties, he came off the bench solely as a pinch-hitter

In 1969, Lau joined the Baltimore Orioles, embarking on a long, well-respected and controversial career as a hitting coach by championing a new branch of philosophy based on spray hitting. He helped weak-hitting shortstop Mark Belanger bat a by-far career high .287 with 50 RBIs for the American League champions. Lau is also directly credited with enhancing the careers of Harold Baines, George Brett, Reggie

Jackson, Hal McRae, and Willie Wilson during stints with the A's, Royals, Yankees, and White Sox.

In 1983, Lau volunteered to relinquish his spot on Chicago's bench so that scout Loren Babe could qualify for his 10-year pension. Babe was dying of cancer. Unfortunately, both Babe and Lau died in early 1984, Lau of colon cancer.

Lau's lasting contribution to the game rests in his use of video to dissect and either correct or exploit the mechanics of both pitchers and hitters, depending on which uniform they wore. He is credited with indirectly influencing the hitting style of many of today's athletes.

Frank Leary
Righthander Frank Leary broke into the show in April 1907, pitching in two games for the Reds. He died that October at age 26 after failing to be revived following appendix surgery.

Tom Lee
Tom Lee contracted malaria after posting six wins and playing the infield in the National League and Union Association in 1884. It manifested into tuberculosis and he died at age 21 in March 1886.

Jack Lelivelt
Jack Lelivelt played in the American League from 1909–14. The outfielder hit .301 in 382 games. He began managing in the minors in 1920. His teams finished first in the Pacific Coast League seven times. His last three years in Seattle, 1938–40, Lelivelt's boys won 313 games. The manager died over the winter on January 20, 1941, at age 55.

Joe Leonard
Senators' utility infielder Joe Leonard became ill in 1920 while on the road with the team in Boston. He was sent back to Washington for medical attention but died of a ruptured appendix after surgery on May 1. He was 25 years old.

Tom Lessord
Columbus, of the American Association, pitcher Tom Lessord died of quinsy on August 26, 1911. The Cincinnati Reds had already bought his contract for the 1912 season.

Howard Lindimore
Infielder Howard Lindimore spent 18 seasons in the minors from 1916–33, except for time spent in military service during World War I and a season on the suspended list in 1928. In 7,800 at-bats, the lefthander hit .306 in a career spent mostly in the Eastern League and the Pacific Coast League. The 39-year-old ballplayer died on November 16, 1933.

Bill Lindsay
The Kansas Cyclone, Bill Lindsay, passed away during the 1914 season while playing for Rube Foster's Chicago American Giants. The pitcher succumbed to tuberculosis on September 1 at the age of 24.

Steve Macko
Infielder Steve Macko appeared in 25 games for the Cubs in 1979–80. Soon after, he fell ill from cancer and died on October 17, 1981, at age 27.

Sherry Magee
Sherry Magee was one of the great players of the dead-ball era, leading the league at least once in virtually every major hitting category, including RBIs, four times. 1910 was his best year, when the Phillie led the National League in runs, RBIs, total bases, batting average, on-base percentage, and slugging average. He was also a fine defensive left fielder. Once, the hard-nosed ballplayer received a five-day suspension for knocking out umpire Bill Finneran after a called third strike.

After being passed up for manager in 1914, Magee demanded a trade. He ended up with the Braves one year after they won the World Series and the same year the Phillies went to the Fall Classic. Magee retired in 1919 with 441 stolen bases, 2,169 hits, and 1,176 RBIs. Subsequently, he took up umpiring and made it to the National League in 1928. In the spring of '29, he contracted pneumonia and died at age 44.

Rick Mahler
New York Mets Single-A pitching coach Rick Mahler died of heart failure at the start of spring training in 2005 at age 51. The righthander had pitched in the majors for 13 seasons, 1979–91, mostly with Atlanta.

Bob McClure
Righthander Bob McClure, 28, contracted pneumonia in early 1931 and died on September 6 in Baltimore. He had recently pitched for the Brooklyn Royal Giants in 1930.

Jim McGlothlin
Righthander Jim McGlothlin pitched in the majors from 1965–73, mostly with California and Cincinnati. In all he won 67 contests, was an All-Star in 1967 and started two World Series games for the Reds in 1970 and '72.

He fell ill soon after leaving the majors and died from leukemia just before Christmas 1975 at age 32.

Bill McGowan
Bill McGowan umpired in the American League from 1925 until his death in December 1954 from a heart attack at age 58.

Austin McHenry
St. Louis Cardinals left fielder Austin McHenry had a breakout year in 1921. He finished third in the league with 102 RBIs, 305 total bases, and a .350 batting average.

His totals were good enough to finish second in slugging average, fourth in home runs, and fifth in doubles. General Manager Branch Rickey, among others, looked forward to a promising career.

In early 1922, the outfielder began having trouble tracking fly balls. A brain tumor was detected. In November, McHenry died following an operation to remove the tumor. He was only 27 years old.

Ed McKeever

Like most owners, Charlie Ebbets ran into challenges trying to finance his new ball-park, Ebbets Field, in 1912. To offset costs, he courted Brooklyn contractors Ed and Steve McKeever. In exchange for their backing of $100,000, the brothers received half-ownership of the Dodgers, though Ebbets retained the club presidency.

Ebbets passed away from heart failure shortly after the season began in 1925 after 42 years with the franchise. Ed was named club president. The funeral was held on a cold, rainy April day and was extended while the burial hole was enlarged to fit the oversized casket. McKeever was already under the weather and the delay aggravated his misery. He awoke the next morning with pneumonia and died within a week. Field manager Wilbert Robinson took over the executive duties.

Alex McKinnon

In the middle of his fourth National League season in 1887, Alex McKinnon was batting .340 in 200 at-bats with Pittsburgh. The first baseman fell ill after the July 4th game and died 20 days later of typhoid fever at age 30. His career average rests at .296.

Sam McMackin

Lefthanded pitcher Sam McMackin made his major league debut on September 4, 1902. Over the winter, he caught pneumonia and died in February at age 30.

Jack McMahon

Catcher–first baseman Jack McMahon fell ill after his second season with the New York Giants in 1883. He died the following December from complications related to bladder stones at age 25.

Jack McQuaid

Jack McQuaid umpired in the American Association from 1886–88 until moving to the National League from 1889–94. He died from stomach trouble in April 1895.

Roy Meeker

Southpaw Roy Meeker won eight major league games from 1923–26. In the Reds camp in 1929, he suffered a heart attack and died during spring training. Meeker was 28 years old.

Clyde Milan

Clyde Milan was one of the best center fielders in Washington history. His speed allowed him to play shallower than the great Tris Speaker. In his career, Milan snatched 495 bases, topping at 88 in 1912.

Signed back in 1907 with Walter Johnson by Cliff Blankenship, Milan roomed with the fastballer for 15 years. Promoted to field manager in 1922, the lefthanded batter was let go because of his easy-going nature, a similar challenge that Walter Johnson would have to overcome as manager.

Milan retired as a player, finishing with 2,100 hits, 1,000 runs scored, a .388 on-base percentage, and a .285 batting average. He embarked on a long career as a minor league manager and coach for the Senators. While hitting fungoes in the Florida heat in spring training 1953, the 65-year-old suffered a fatal heart attack.

Charlie Miller
Catcher Charlie Miller passed away in April 1874. He was set to play in the National Association.

Dots Miller
Rookie second baseman Dots Miller led the league in games, assists, and fielding percentage in 1909. His glove helped the Pirates win the pennant. Surely not many balls leaked up the middle through Miller and Honus Wagner.

In all, Miller amassed 1,500 hits and a .263 batting average over 12 years in the National League. Soon after leaving the Phillies in 1921, he fell ill from tuberculosis. The 36-year-old died on September 5, 1923.

Reddy Miller
Backstop Reddy Miller died just as the National League began in May 1876. He had just finished his second season in the National Association.

Greg Million
Rockies farmhand Greg Million died at age 22 after an asthma attack in 1997.

Bill Monroe
One of the Negro leagues first big stars, popular Bill Monroe once hit a called–home run off Hall of Famer Joe McGinnity, winning a $500 bet from the hurler. The second baseman died suddenly just prior to his 20th season in 1915.

Estaban Montalvo
Cuban Stars power-hitting outfielder Estaban Montalvo died of tuberculosis in 1930, after six years in the Negro National League.

Pat Moran
Pat Moran was the best National League catcher of his era. His weak hitting, though, eventually led him to a dual role of catcher and pitching coach for the Phillies. In 1915, he became manager and, with Pete Alexander, led the team to the pennant in his first season. Philadelphia had finished sixth the previous year.

Managing Cincinnati in 1919, Moran again led a team to the pennant in his first season. They won the tainted World Series over the White Sox. In nine years as a major league manager, Moran finished either first or second six times. In spring training 1924, Moran died of Bright's disease. Tragically, Cincinnati would also lose their team captain that year as well.

John Morrissey
John Morrissey played third base in the National League with Buffalo and Detroit from 1881–82. Then, he began umpiring in the minors. In April 1884, the 27-year-old died of consumption.

Danny Murtaugh
Danny Murtaugh had an undistinguished nine-year playing career, except for his first season in Pittsburgh. In 1948, he hit .290 with 71 RBIs and 56 runs scored. In the field, he led all second baseman in games, putouts, assists, double plays, and range.

In '57, he began his first of four stints as the Pirates manager, intermixed with terms as a scout for the team. Four National League East titles and two world championships followed.

Rising from seventh place, the Bucs challenged the Milwaukee Braves for the pennant in 1958, ultimately falling eight games short in second place. They won it all in 1960 with the help of an astounding 23 victories coming in their final at-bat. Despite being outscored 2:1 in the World Series, the Pirates defeated the dominant Yankees with another game-ending homer by Bill Mazeroski in the finale.

A recurring heart condition was the reason for his first retirement at the end of the 1964 season. He also managed the team for the second half of '67 after Harry Walker was fired. In 1970, he rejoined the Pirates dugout to win the division title but lost to the upstart Big Red Machine in the playoffs. Again, Murtaugh led the Bucs to the World Series in '71, this time defeating another favored team, the Baltimore Orioles, in seven. He retired once more.

Returning, two more division titles in '74 and '75 followed. At the end of 1976, Murtaugh retired with a 1,115-980 record, an impressive .540 winning percentage. He died that December of a stroke at age 59.

Frank Nash
Southern League Columbus pitcher Frank Nash died of typhoid fever on August 16, 1885.

Simon Nicholls
Shortstop Simon Nicholls hit .302 as a rookie for Connie Mack in 1907. His hot bat proved to be a fluke, costing him his starting job two years later. He died after surgery for typhoid fever and peritonitis in March 1911 as a member of the Eastern League Baltimore Orioles at the age of 28.

Minoru Nishikura
Minoru Nishikura hit .192 in 230 at-bats for two clubs from 1952–55. He died in December 1955 at age 26.

Darby O'Brien

John O'Brien began his major league career as a pitcher in 1888. It ended four years later with 59 wins, 22 of them for the Cleveland Spiders in '89. After finishing the 1891 season with the AA Boston Reds, O'Brien became ill and died on March 11, 1892, of pneumonia at age 24.

Darby O'Brien

William O'Brien began his major league career as an outfielder in 1887. It ended five years later with a .282 average, after serving his best years with the champion Brooklyn teams of 1889–90. After finishing the 1892 season, O'Brien became ill and died on June 15, 1893, of consumption at age 29.

Tom O'Brien

Tom O'Brien's career was just getting started when he hit .290 with 61 RBIs for the pennant-winning Pirates. Somehow thinking that ingesting large amounts of seawater would help alleviate seasickness on a postseason barnstorming trip to Cuba in February 1901, O'Brien weakened his immune system and the functioning of his internal organs. He was rushed back to the States and sought treatment in an Arizona spa but it was too late; he died from pneumonia. Luckily, Kid Gleason, who also imbibed the water, recovered.

Big Mike O'Connor

Mike O'Connor was the only man to play in each of the Texas League's first 13 seasons. In 1905, he was player–manager for Austin and Waco; the following year, he died in a state hospital.

O'Connor was a player–manager in one of the most famous games in minor league history. His Corsicana Oilers defeated Texarkana 51-3 on June 15, 1902. In his cause, O'Connor homered three times while slapping seven of his team's 53 hits. Rookie catcher Nig Clarke belted eight consecutive homers over a short porch in right field. In all, Clarke drove in 20 runs.

Silk O'Loughlin

Silk O'Loughlin was brought in by Ban Johnson during the American League's infancy in 1902 to help stabilize a shaky umpiring crew. He stayed until his death of influenza after the 1918 season at 46 years old.

O'Loughlin was one of the earliest umps to use hand gestures to signify his calls. This was a great help to spectators who found games very difficult to follow. Often, fans and the press did not know who was at bat or in the field. Rarely did one know the count or even the score. Only the most attentive knew the details that we take for granted today. Scoreboards were rare, players could not be identified easily and lineup changes were often missed. Eventually, umpires were designated to announce the starting lineups via megaphone and players were issued numbers.

Bob Osgood

Nineteen-year-old catcher Bob Osgood died of heart failure during pre-game drills in the Ohio–Indiana League on May 11, 1948.

Claire Patterson

Twenty-five-year-old Claire Patterson died of tuberculosis on March 28, 1913. The outfielder was in the minors after a brief stint with the Reds in 1909.

Herb Pennock

Herb Pennock pitched 22 major league seasons without an overpowering fastball but still won 241 games, anyway. He was brought up by Connie Mack in 1912 but was soon shuffled to the Red Sox after a tiff with his manager, plus Mack figured American League batters would clobber a lefthander without heat. Pennock developed into a control artist on the mound. He was the consummate professional that was always in control, no matter the situation, even though he didn't possess the ability to strike out the side. Pennock used an array of screwballs, curves, and change-ups that he propelled from a variety of overhand and sidearm deliveries.

Mack had spied the pitcher at age 16 and coveted the teen's potential. He had Chief Bender teach the youngster the screwball. Pennock joined the A's two years later with no minor league experience behind him, as part of the 1910–14 dynasty that boasted fellow Hall of Famers MGR Mack, 2B Eddie Collins, 3B Home Run Baker, LHP Eddie Plank, RHP Bender, and RHP Stan Coveleski.

Pennock missed the 1916 World Series when he was sent to the minors and, likewise, in 1918 because of Navy obligations. After returning home, Pennock found his control and spun eight 16 + -win seasons. During the off-seasons, the pitcher became wealthy raising and breeding foxes.

On January 30, 1923, he became one of the great players, specifically pitchers, of the era hand-delivered from Red Sox owner Harry Frazee to the Yankees. Pennock immediately won 19 games plus two more in the World Series versus the Giants. Again, he won two games in the 1926 World Series loss to the Cardinals. In Game 3 of the 1927 Fall Classic, Pennock retired the first 22 batters before Pie Traynor of the Pirates singled. In a total of five postseason appearances, the lefthander was a perfect 5-0 with 3 saves and a 1.95 ERA.

In 1928, he developed a sore arm that led to the ballooning of his ERA throughout the rest of his career. Ridiculous for an arm injury, Pennock tried a "bee sting therapy" to fix his ailing arm. The mass of bees did nothing but agitate the existing injury.

After nine years as farm director for the Red Sox, Pennock became Philadelphia's general manger and vice-president in 1943. On January 30, 1948, at a National League directors meeting in New York, he suffered a cerebral hemorrhage and died. Pennock was elected to the Hall of Fame a month later. Much of the Phillies success in 1950 can be tied to his talent searches.

John Peters

John Peters started playing professional ball when he was 15 years old. He even appeared in parts of four seasons in the majors from 1915–22. The catcher died of a heart attack gearing up for a new season in the American Association on February 21, 1932. He was 38 years old.

Cy Pfirman

Cy Pfirman umpired professional baseball for 26 years, including a 15-year stint in the National League, 1922–36. He died in May 1937 at age 46 after a long battle with kidney disease.

Tom Power

Eight years removed from the Baltimore Orioles of the American Association and currently playing in the minors, first baseman Tom Power died of consumption in February 1898 at 29 years old.

George Prentiss

George Prentiss toed the rubber for the Red Sox during the first two seasons of the American League. He died at the end of the second season on September 8, 1902, of typhoid fever. The righthander was 26 years old.

John Puhl

Third baseman John Puhl appeared in three games for the New York Giants from 1898–99. The 24-year-old died the following August from tuberculosis.

Bill Quarles

After two short stints in the majors, pitcher Bill Quarles died after surgery in March 1897 at age 28 while still playing in the minors.

Ed Quick

Rocky Ford, Colorado, pitcher Ed Quick was found dead in his hotel room on June 19, 1913. He had appeared in one game for New York in their inaugural season of the American League.

Jerry Readon

Jerry Readon died of tuberculosis in February 1891 at age 24 while pitching in the minors. Five years prior, he toiled in both the National League and American Association while only 18 years old.

Nick Reeder

Third baseman Nick Reeder had a cup of coffee with Louisville in the last season of the American Association. Still active in the game, he died of brain fever at age 27 in September 1894.

Cananea Reyes

Cananea Reyes managed in the Mexican League for 23 years starting in 1968. In 1991, with the Mexico City Reds his team finished first; however, Reyes did not travel with the club on road trips. He died that November at age 54.

Art Rico

Catcher Art Rico joined the Boston Braves just past his 20th birthday in 1916. He died at age 22 in January 1919 from peritonitis after appendix surgery.

Cy Rigler

Longtime National League umpire, 1906–35, Cy Rigler died of a brain tumor that December at age 53.

Herman Rios

Cuban third baseman Herman Rios played 10 seasons in the Negro leagues for the western Cuban Stars. He died in midseason 1924 in Havana at the age of 28.

Jim Ritz

Third baseman Jim Ritz went hitless in his only major league game on July 20, 1894, with Pittsburgh. Still pursuing a pro baseball career, he fell ill two years later and died that November of typhoid fever at age 22.

Jim Rogers

Kidney problems claimed the life of infielder Jim Rogers in January 1900 at age 27. In the minors at the time, Rogers had played two seasons, 1896–97, for Washington and Louisville in the National League.

Ronaldo Romero

Heart disease caused Gastonia Rangers player Ronaldo Romero of the South Atlantic League to collapse in the dugout during a game on May 14, 1990. He later died. Romero had previously removed himself from the game after feeling chest pains.

Pythias Russ

Speedy catcher Pythias Russ died in August 1930 from tuberculosis shortly after his fifth Negro league season.

Kikuo Sato

Tokyo Senators outfielder Kikuo Sato died suddenly after 18 games in July 1936 during the spring season. He was 18 years old.

Germany Schaefer

Germany Schaefer's legend still grows today as one of the pure clowns of the game. Many books are full of stories of his zaniness. He later joined Nick Altrock, baseball's first full-time coach, as a comedy duo who enlivened the hapless Washington Senators as base coaches.

Schaefer is also known today as the man who stole first base. He set about to draw a throw from the catcher by stealing second, so the man on third could advance. When the catcher didn't react, he took off for first base on the next pitch. The crowd, as well as, the catcher was dumbfounded; however, no rule at the time prohibited his actions. On the next pitch, Schaefer took off for second again. This time, the catcher attempted to throw him out. Schaefer arrived safely as did the runner at home. The ploy was a success; the loophole in the rules was soon closed.

After World War I broke out, *Germany* requested that his nickname be changed to *Dutch*. After retiring as a player, he landed a job with John McGraw as a scout. While on a scouting trip in Canada in 1919, he died of a massive heart attack.

Joe Schultz

Joe Schultz hit .285 over 11 part-time seasons in the National League from 1912–25. He later coached, managed in the minors, and scouted. In 1939, he was named director of the Pirates farm system. On a scouting trip in South Carolina during the spring of 1941, Schultz fell ill of ptomaine poisoning and passed away on April 13 at age 47.

Lefty Seamon

Twenty-two-year-old pitcher Lefty Seamon died on October 14, 1948, after having a tumor removed from his chest. He had just produced a 21-4 record for Ottawa in the Border League.

Jimmy Sebring

Jimmy Sebring played outfield for four teams during his five-year major league career. With Pittsburgh in the 1903 World Series, he batted .367 with a home run and five RBIs. After a three-year absence, he returned to the majors in 1909. Sebring died that winter of Bright's disease at age 27.

Paul Sentelle

Umpire Paul Sentelle joined the National League in 1922. He worked there until his appendix ruptured, leading to his death the following April 27 at age 45.

John Sheridan

John Sheridan umpired three seasons in the National League and a year in the Players League before joining the American League in its inaugural season, 1901. He worked for Ban Johnson until his death from a heart attack in November 1914 at age 52. He had suffered sunstroke during a game that August, which may have complicated his heart condition.

Urban Shocker

One of Miller Huggins' first acts as Yankees manager was to trade away Urban Shocker. He lived to regret it, as Shocker proved effective against his old team. With the Browns from 1920–23 the spitballer amassed 91 wins and a 3.18 ERA. The Yankees gave up three players to get him back in December 1924.

The righthander won 49 games for the pinstripes over the next three seasons, including 37 in the pennant-winning 1926–27 seasons. After pitching in one game in '28, Shocker retired and returned home to run a radio shop in Denver. Heart disease and pneumonia hastened his death in September at age 38. His 187-117 record, .615 winning percentage, and 3.17 ERA rank him among the elite spitballers.

Harry Simpson

Harry Simpson was a semi-pro ballplayer from New Jersey employed by Al Spalding to work as a secretary for his world tour in 1888. Simpson would travel ahead of the contingent and drum up enthusiasm for their arrival. At the end of the tour, Simpson stayed in Australia to promote the fledgling sport.

In this capacity, he became the nation's first baseball development officer, which meant its first significant instructor and league organizer. He also helped put together the first clubs and promoted inter-colony play, thus extending interest for the game outside Sydney and Melbourne. Simpson was training the Australians to become competitive enough to warrant a tour of the United States. Unfortunately, he caught typhoid fever and died in September 1891 at the age of 27. The baseball spirit tapered off on the island over the next five years but eventually the Australians became the first foreign baseball players to tour America in 1897.

Will Smalley
Will Smalley was just getting started in his career when he died of stomach cancer at age 20, soon after the 1891 season ended. Before becoming ill, he led all National League third basemen in 1890 in putouts, assists, errors, double plays, and range. However, his .213 batting average necessitated a move to the American Association the following season.

Chino Smith
Lefthander Chino Smith was considered by Satchel Paige to be one of the three best hitters in Negro league history, along with Jud Wilson and Josh Gibson. The right fielder combined a high batting average with power and few strikeouts in a career that began in 1924. He died at age 29 in Cuba (winter league ball), most likely of yellow fever in 1931. Smith is one of the big "what ifs" of Negro league history.

Ed Somerville
During the National League's inaugural season in 1876, second baseman Ed Somerville of Louisville led the league in assists, errors, and range, but batted only .187. He died the following September in Toronto at age 24. He also appeared in 47 games for the National Association in 1875.

Allen Sothoron
Spitballer Allen Sothoron managed in the minors for 10 years after his pitching career ended. In 1939, he had to take leave from his duties after falling ill from years of alcohol abuse. He died that June.

Alan Storke
Utilityman Alan Storke played in the majors, mostly with Pittsburgh, from 1906–09. Just prior to spring training, March 18, the following year he died from complications after lung surgery. Storke was 25 years old.

Chub Sullivan
Chub Sullivan played first base in the National League from 1877–80. Shortly thereafter, he fell ill from consumption and died on September 12, 1881, at age 25. With Cincinnati in 1878, Sullivan led the league in fielding average.

Joe Sullivan
After finishing his fourth year in the National League in 1896 shortstop–outfielder Joe Sullivan fell ill to tuberculosis and died the following November at age 27.

Sy Sutcliffe
Sy Sutcliffe did everything but pitch as a part-time player for six major league franchises from 1884–92. The 30-year-old died of Bright's disease the following February.

Brewery Jack Taylor
Big Jack Taylor, 6'1", 190 lbs., hurled for three National League clubs during the 1890s, mainly Philadelphia. From 1894–96, the righthander won 63 games. In '96, he won 20 games despite being backed up by a lefthanded shortstop, Billy Hulen. In 1898, with the futile St. Louis Browns that lost 111 games, Taylor pitched in 50 of those games and lost 29. He led the league with 47 starts, 42 complete games, 397 innings pitched, and 465 hits allowed.

Shortly after finishing his ninth season, Taylor succumbed to a kidney disorder, Bright's disease, on February 7, 1900. He was 26 years old.

Candy Jim Taylor
Candy Jim Taylor played, managed, and administrated in the Negro leagues for more than 40 years from 1904–48. He was with the leagues virtually from beginning to end. Managing for the Baltimore Elite Giants in 1948, Taylor passed away during spring training at the age of 64.

Live Oak Taylor
Longtime pro outfielder Ed Taylor died in February 1888 from a lung ailment at age 33. He had appeared in the National League with Hartford in 1877 and the American Association in 1884 with Pittsburgh.

Danny Thompson
Twins shortstop Danny Thompson led all major leaguers at his position with a .276 average in 1972, his first year as a regular. Before the next season, he was diagnosed with leukemia. Bravely, Thompson played in another four campaigns, finally succumbing to the disease in December 1976.

Phil Tomney
Shortstop Phil Tomney played for the Louisville Colonels of the American Association from 1888–90. The final season, he upped his average to .277 and led the league in fielding percentage. Still, he was let go and continued his career in the minors. He died just before spring in 1892 at age 28 from a lung infection.

Brian Traxler
The Dodgers drafted Brian Traxler in 1988. The first baseman appeared briefly (nine games) for the parent club in 1990. Later, Traxler hit .263 with 15 homers and 62

RBIs for the Daiei Hawks in 1994. Working as a batting instructor for a Dodgers rookie club, he died from liver disease in November 2004 at age 37.

Tsunemi Tsuda
Hiroshima Toyo Carp closer Tsunemi Tsuda died of a brain tumor in July 1993 at age 32. He had been the Pacific League Rookie of the Year in 1982 with an 11-6 record. Tsuda had been forced to retire in November 1991.

Dutch Ulrich
Pitcher Dutch Ulrich died of pneumonia and pleurisy on February 12, 1929. The 29-year-old was in the minors after winning 19 games for the Phillies from 1925–27.

Jim Umbricht
Righthanded reliever Jim Umbricht had his breakthrough year in 1962 with the expansion Houston Colt .45's. Over the next two seasons, he went 8-3 with a 2.33 ERA. Umbricht died of cancer just prior to opening day 1964 at age 33.

Tony Venzon
Tony Venzon umpired in the National League from 1957 until his death in 1971 following heart surgery at age 56.

Ed Walsh
Ed Walsh, not the Hall of Famer, pitched for the Chicago White Sox during some of their bleakest seasons from 1928–32. Relegated to the minors, he died of rheumatic fever in October 1937 at age 32.

Dick Wantz
Righthanded pitcher Dick Wantz made his only major league appearance on April 13, 1965, facing six batters over an inning's work during the Angels home opener. A month later, he died at age 25, after an operation to remove a brain tumor.

Frank Warfield
Negro league second baseman Frank Warfield was a highly skilled base runner, team leader, and manager from 1916–32. The double-play combination he formed with John Henry Lloyd was one of the best in Negro league history. Warfield was among the first players to jump the Negro National League in 1923 in favor of the upstart Eastern Colored League. Working as player–manager for the Washington Pilots in July 1932, he died of a heart attack in a Pittsburgh hotel room after a game against the Crawfords.

Pop Watkins
Long-time catcher–manager Pop Watkins died in February 1923, just prior to his 24th season in the Negro leagues. At the time, he was set to manage a team bearing his name.

Shorty Wetzel

George Wetzel started two games for the American Association Baltimore Orioles in 1885 but lost both. He died from Bright's disease, looking forward to a new season in the minors in February 1899 at age 30.

Lee Weyer

Long-time National League umpire Lee Weyer died on July 4, 1988, after working a Cubs–Giants game at age 51. He had fought a long battle with Guilan-Barre syndrome and diabetes. The previous year, National League catchers had ranked Weyer as the best ball and strike caller.

John Weyhing

Lefthander John Weyhing pitched in the American Association during the 1888 and '89 campaigns. He succumbed to tuberculosis the following summer while in the minors, just short of his 21st birthday. He was the younger brother of longtime pitcher Gus Weyhing.

Jim Whitney

Jim Whitney won 187 games from 1881–88 in the National League. As a rookie with the Boston Red Caps, Whitney led the league in games, starts, complete games, innings pitched, hits allowed, walks, wild pitches, balks, wins, and losses. He became the first pitcher to lead the league in both wins and losses.

Fortunately, he quickly overcame his wildness and became one of the best control pitchers of his era. For the pennant-winning Beaneaters in 1883, Whitney won 37 games and compiled a league-best 345 Ks.

Whitney was also a powerful hitter who batted cleanup and played center field when he wasn't on the mound. In 1882, he became the only player ever to lead his team in victories, home runs, batting average, and slugging.

After 3,400 innings pitched in eight years, he lost his effectiveness and ended up in the American Association. Whitney developed tuberculosis and died in May 1891 at age 33.

Alan Wiggins

The California Angels selected Alan Wiggins in the first round of the January 1977 amateur free agent draft. He was later released, re-drafted by San Diego and signed for a $25,000 bonus. As a rookie in '82, he received his first drug suspension after an arrest for cocaine possession.

Wiggins was suspended again the following season. In 1984, the second baseman helped lead the Padres to the pennant with 70 stolen bases, 106 runs scored, and a league-leading 391 putouts. On May 17, the speedster tied a league record with five stolen bases in a game. In the postseason, Wiggins batted .316 in the National League Championship Series and .364 in the World Series versus Tiger pitching.

He was rewarded with a four-year, $2.5 million contract; however, in 1985, Wiggins entered rehab and was traded to the Baltimore Orioles. Two years later, he was out of the game completely due to his recurring drug problems.

On January 6, 1991, at age 32, Wiggins became the first known major leaguer to die from complications after contracting the AIDS virus. Admitted homosexual Glenn Burke, a major league outfielder from 1976–79, later died of AIDS in May 1995 after living on the streets in San Leandro, California. The first known pro athlete to succumb to the disease was former Washington Redskins tight end Jerry Smith in 1986.

Charlie Williams

Twenty-three-year-old Negro league infielder Charlie Williams died of ptomaine poisoning in July 1931.

Gus Williams

Gus Williams started two games for Brooklyn in the American Association in 1890, recording a loss. He died that October at age 20.

Ross Youngs

Ross Youngs was one of John McGraw's favorite players. His picture along with Christy Mathewson's hung above the manager's desk. The right fielder possessed a strong arm, leading the league three times in assists and double plays. His speed is evident by his 10 steals of home. Seven times in eight full seasons, the lefthander hit over .300.

Youngs' solid play in the outfield and career .322 batting average helped the Giants snare four consecutive National League championships from 1921–24. He hit .375 and .348 in the 1922 and '23 World Series, respectively.

In June 1926, Youngs was hospitalized by a mysterious ailment. He returned to the team and managed a .306 average but remained under a nurse's care. Bedridden all of 1927, the 30-year-old passed away in October of Bright's disease. The Veterans Committee elected him to the Hall of Fame 45 years later.

Toshihiko Yugushi

Pitcher Toshihiko Yugushi died suddenly at age 20 in March 1973. The first-round draft pick had yet to crack Yomiuri's roster.

CHAPTER FOURTEEN

Death: Injuries and Accidents

Oscar Acosta

An automobile accident in the Dominican Republic took the life of two members of the Yankees organization in April 2006. Oscar Acosta, a former coach with the Cubs and Rangers, was dually employed as manager of the Rookie League Gulf Coast Yankees and the organization's International Coordinator of Instruction. Humberto Trejo was the field coordinator for the Dominican Summer League Yankees.

John Ake

John Ake briefly saw action with the Baltimore Orioles in the American Association in 1884. Three years later, on May 11, as a member of Duluth, Minnesota, of the Northwestern League, Ake and teammates Bill Barnes, a former Union Association outfielder, and Billy Earle, a future major league catcher, were leisurely paddling a boat on the Mississippi River. A passing steamboat created enough turbulence to capsize the three ballplayers. Ake could not swim and he drowned at age 25. The other two swam safely to shore. His body was never found.

Vehicle Accidents, Minor Leaguers, Fatal

1929	Bill Albert	
	Clyde Nance	
	Denny Williams	
1950	Bill Corvallis	
	Rolland Dunn	
	Jimmy Groh	
	Jack Gutierrez	
	Cliff Janni	
	Richard Mix	
	Tony Smeraglia	
1951	Mickey Mahon	boat accident
	Jim Welch	umpire
1952	Sam Brewer	
	Bill Rakes	
	Al Sahlberg	
1953	Gilbert Shrink	

	Ray Cucchiarini	
	John Reese	
1954	Don Swanson	
1955	Richard Avery	
1956	Henry Holcombe	umpire
	Wilfredo Salas	
1957	Joel Parkey	
	Grover Seitz	manager
1958	Ron Anastasio	
	Keith Friend	
	James Grieves	executive
1961	Walter Cosgriff	executive
	Lionel Rogers	
1962	Bobby Case	
	Roberto Vea	bus accident
1964	Sammy Fountain	bus accident
	Jerome Hummitzsch	
	Larry Shoemaker	
	Richard Tams	
1967	Rick Davis	
1968	Mike McCready	
1969	Bill Seinsoth	
1976	Richard Ferrell	
	Tony Lathem	
1984	Steve Reish	
	Ramon Lora	
1985	Bob Souza	
1988	Greg Ferguson	
1996	Mike Diebold	
2001	Jody Gajewski	
	Miguel Del Toro	in Mexico
2003	Josh Brinkley	coach
	Stephen Gates	executive, hit and run

Automobile Accidents, Scouts, Fatal

1952	Mike Martin	Senators
1962	John Scalzi	Mets
1966	Julio DeArcos	Indians
1973	Frank Calo	
1979	Jack Butterfield	Yankees VP
1981	George Thompson	A's
1995	George Omachi	Astros

Leon Balser

South Atlantic League Greenville pitcher Leon Balser was fatally crushed between two railroad cars on January 11, 1947. He had been working during the off-season for the Nickel Plate Railroad in Cleveland. Balser had won 16 games the previous summer.

Nelson Barrera
Nelson Barrera was in his 26th Mexican League season, 1977–2002, when he was electrocuted and died while working at home on July 14, 2002. The 44-year old had recently become the league's all-time home run (455) and RBI champion (1,928). Barrera was elected to the Mexican Baseball Hall of Fame in 2003.

Gerik Baxter
Minor league pitcher Gerik Baxter and Oakland farmhand Mark Hilde were driving when a tire blew, causing them to swerve off the road near Indio, California, on July 29, 2001. Both were killed.

Bob Berg
See Spokane of the Western International League

Tony Boeckel
Boston Braves third baseman Tony Boeckel led the league three times in errors, twice in games and putouts, and once in double plays. He also swatted a career .282 with better-than-average power. He was killed on February 16, 1924, when his car collided with a truck in California. Boeckel was 29 years old. Passenger and future Yankee great Bob Meusel escaped unhurt.

Josh Brinkley
In 2003, former Expos farmhand Josh Brinkley played and coached for the Bangor Lumberjacks, an independent club in the Northwest League. That October, the 30-year-old was run over and killed while jogging on the side of the road in Wallace, North Carolina.

Buster Brown
See Cleveland Buckeyes of the Negro American League

John Carden
After serving in World War II, righthanded pitcher John Carden appeared in a game for the Giants in 1946 and then fell to the minors. He accidentally electrocuted himself while hooking up phone wires at home in Texas on February 8, 1949. Carden was 27 years old.

Tiny Chaplin
Pacific Coast League pitcher Jim Chaplin died during spring training in 1939 at age 33, after riding in a car that slammed into a stalled vehicle outside National City, California. The righthander had spent four seasons from 1928–36 in the National League, amassing 15 victories.

Nestor Chavez
In two games for the San Francisco Giants in September 1967, Nestor Chavez claimed one victory and an ERA of zero but failed to make the team the following year and was returned to the minors. Just prior to spring training 1969, the 21-year-old was killed when his plane went down above his native Venezuela.

Robert Chindamo
Infielder Robert Chindamo of the Medford Giants, a San Francisco farm club in the Class-A Northwest League, drowned in Snake River near Lewiston, Idaho, on July 26, 1967. The 21-year-old was riding a log raft with two teammates.

Earl Clark
Earl Clark was the Boston Braves fourth outfielder from 1927–33, amassing a career .291 average. After another year in the majors with the Browns in 1934, he fell to the minors. Clark retired at the end of 1937 to join the FBI. He was killed in Washington, D.C., in a streetcar accident on January 1938 at 30 years old.

Roberto Clemente Walker
Puerto Ricon–born Roberto Clemente is one of the storied players of the game's history, as much for his on-the-field exploits and warm personality as for his untimely death.

Clemente was originally signed by the Brooklyn Dodgers for a $10,000 bonus and assigned to Triple-A. The rules of the time stated that a bonus baby must be assigned to the parent club or be at risk of being drafted by another team for a $4,000 fee. Scout Clyde Sukeforth and general manager Branch Rickey had just left the Dodgers for Pittsburgh when they claimed the right fielder. He went on to become the most honored and respected Pirate in history.

Clemente had a gun for an arm in right field, continually nailing runners trying to reach second, third, or home. He won a Gold Glove in 12 straight years, 1961–72, tying Willie Mays for the most by an outfielder. Five times he led the league in outfield assists and twice in double plays. Stories and images of his skill in right field abound in the minds of those who saw him play and on video for those who didn't.

Clemente was also lethal with the bat. Thirteen times he hit over .300, eight of those years over .320, for a career .317 average. The 12-time All-Star won four batting crowns: 1961, '64–65, and '67. In 1960, Clemente found his power stroke, posting a .314, 16, 94 season. Eventually, he tagged 240 dingers and compiled 1,305 RBIs. In 1966, the Pirate won the MVP Award with a .317 average, 29 home runs, 119 RBIs, 105 runs scored, and 202 hits.

Clemente was just as potent in the postseason, batting .310 with three RBIs during the 1960 World Series defeat of the Yankees. October 1971 will forever be remembered for Clemente's heroics, offensively and defensively. In the National League Championship Series versus San Francisco, he notched a .333 average and four RBIs. The right fielder was on fire in the Fall Classic against Baltimore, killing the Orioles with both bat and glove. Clemente posted a .414 batting average with a more impressive .759 slugging average to lead the Pirates to victory in seven games.

Clemente's final hit in his 18th season was number 3,000. The double came off New York Mets Jon Matlack on September 30, 1972. It would be his last.

In December, a devastating earthquake shook Nicaragua, killing 6,000 people and injuring another 20,000. Clemente joined in the effort to aid the victims, toiling 16 hours a day. On New Year's Eve, he boarded a cargo plane loaded with supplies to ensure that the goods would be dispersed properly. He feared that Nicaraguan dictator Somoza and his military officials would abscond with the booty. The plane crashed into the ocean shortly after taking off from Puerto Rico. No survivors were ever found. Clemente was dead at age 38.

The Hall of Fame waived the five-year waiting period and immediately placed him on the ballot. In the summer of '73, he became the first Latino to enter Cooperstown. Clemente would have been proud to accept the plague the same year as his boyhood idol, Monte Irvin.

Cleveland Buckeyes of the Negro American League
After replacing a tire on September 7, 1942, outside Geneva, Ohio, six Cleveland Buckeye players hopped in the car. As they were returning to the highway, a truck smacked them from behind. Buster Brown, driver, and Smoky Owens were killed instantly.

Brown had been a catcher in the Negro leagues since 1937. Pitcher Owens arrived two years later. The others, returning home after a series with the Black Yankees, were Alonzo Boone, Eugene Bremmer, Herman Watts, and team owner, Wilbur Hayes. Bremmer sustained a fractured skull.

Cleveland Indians Pitching Staff, 1993
Cleveland pitchers Steve Olin, Tim Crews, and Bobby Ojeda were on a fishing boat in Florida during spring training in March 1993. They failed to see a pier and rammed it. Olin and Crews died and Ojeda was seriously injured. Olin, 27, had just gained the Indians closer role after posting 8 wins, 27 saves and a 2.34 ERA in 1992. 31-year-old Crews was just brought over from Los Angeles to strengthen the bullpen.

Thirteen-year veteran Ojeda also came over from the Dodgers with 113 wins under his belt. The lefthander would only appear in nine more games. The highlight of his career came in 1986 as he posted career-bests with an 18-5 record, 148 strikeouts, and a 2.57 ERA for the World Champion Mets. In the postseason, he won a game in each the National League Championship Series versus Houston's Nolan Ryan and in the World Series, Game 3 against Boston's Oil Can Boyd.

In November, rookie southpaw Cliff Young was killed after his vehicle hit a tree and flipped over. Also, righty Jerry DiPoto was hampered by thyroid cancer; though, he resumed a full schedule by 1995.

Bill Coffey
Bill Coffey drowned in 1951 at age 21. He was a ballplayer in the Class-C Wisconsin State League.

Brian Cole
22-year-old Mets prospect Brian Cole was killed in an automobile accident during spring training in 2001. The outfielder was rated as one of the top minor league prospects by *Baseball America*.

Mel Cole
See Spokane of the Western International League

Jim Creighton
Jim Creighton, star pitcher for the barnstorming Brooklyn Excelsiors in the early 1860s, was one of the game's first professionals. The Excelsiors were popular throughout the East Coast. They were the first team to go on an extensive traveling tour and pit their skills against local nines. With Creighton as its main attraction both pitching and hitting, Brooklyn drew big crowds and destroyed all competition in Maryland, Delaware, Pennsylvania, New York, and into Canada. Interestingly, the first truly national tour by a sports team or individual, or by a politician or entertainer for that matter, would not take place until boxing champion John L. Sullivan's endeavor in 1883–84, which was made feasible by a massive branching of the railway system during the 1870s.

Creighton, at age 19, became the nation's first baseball hero. With the pitcher's box only 45 feet away, he was one of the first men to put a little heat on the ball. He also varied his speeds and caused a little spin as he snapped his wrist. The term "cannon arm" was first used to describe his talents. Creighton's underhand fastball amazed the crowds and brought a new facet to the game. Of course, his pitching style created quite a stir. However, he was so successful that others began to emulate. Competitors even tried to lure him away from the Excelsiors.

This was during the genesis of sports reporting in newspapers. The hype of a sensational pitching talent that traveled into your community to play your local nine sparked a great deal of interest. Fans became territorial in response to another club coming to their community and defeating all comers. Naturally, they wanted to see firsthand the skills sensationalized in print. Communities also wanted a superior civic team to compete for bragging rights. No longer would a fan's interest be satisfied by merely local competition.

Creighton would also play the field to keep his potent bat in the lineup. On July 22, 1860, as a left fielder, he began what might have been the sport's first triple play. At the height of his stardom in October 1862, Creighton came to bat for the last time versus the Unions of Morrisania, New York. He swung hard, hitting a home run and sustaining some sort of internal injury, perhaps a ruptured bladder. The star passed out on the field and died a few days later at age 21. As with much of the early history of baseball, alternate stories indicate that Creighton died as a result of a cricket injury incurred earlier in the month.

Tim Crews
See Cleveland Indians Pitching Staff, 1993

Red Crowder
Red Crowder of the Birmingham Barons of the Double-A Southern Association drowned at age 23 in 1953.

Woodrow Crowson

Greensboro pitcher Woodrow Crowson died after his team bus collided with another vehicle on August 14, 1947. The only one injured, he was 28 years old. Crowson had had a cup of coffee in the American League with Philadelphia in 1945.

Jay Dahl

Lefthander Jay Dahl took the mound for the Houston Colt .45's for one game at age 17 in 1963. While gaining seasoning in the minors, he was killed in an automobile accident on June 20, 1965. Dahl never saw his 20th birthday.

Eggie Dallard

Thirteen-year Negro league veteran first baseman Eggie Dallard and his two-year-old son were killed in an automobile accident in December 1933. First appearing with the Hilldale Daisies in 1921, Dallard was 34 years old at the time of his death.

Mike Darr

San Diego Padres outfielder Mike Darr was killed when the car he was driving veered off the road in February 2002 near the team's spring training facility in Phoenix, Arizona.

Ed Delahanty

Big Ed Delahanty was one of the finest hitters in baseball history. One of five brothers to reach the majors, Delahanty was elected to the Baseball Hall of Fame with a career .346 batting average, 2,596 hits, and 1,464 RBIs in 16 seasons. Like any Hall of Famer, the left fielder and first baseman's statistics are staggering. Seven times he knocked in more than 100 runners. Delahanty led the league five times in doubles, three times in RBIs, twice in batting average, home runs, and total bases, and once in triples. Three times he hit above the .400 mark.

Delahanty was the premier power hitter of the 1890s, averaging an impressive 186 hits, 8 home runs, 107 RBIs, and a .354 batting average during the decade. The eight home runs are more extraordinary than they may appear. His career .505 slugging average is impressive by any era's standard.

On July 13, 1896, Delahanty became the second man to hit four home runs in a game, all inside the park, but it wasn't enough for his Phillies to defeat the Chicago Colts that day. Philadelphia's outfield of the era boasted Cooperstown-bound Delahanty, Billy Hamilton, and Sam Thompson, one of the finest ever assembled. In 1894, they each hit over .400. In fact, the entire team batted a collective .349, still a record. His legendary career is overshadowed only by the events surrounding his death.

In June 1903, with his Washington Nationals team on a Western trip, Delahanty didn't show up for a game in Cleveland, probably because of drunkenness. Manager Tom Lofton suspended the outfielder but allowed him to travel with the team. On July 2, Delahanty became uncontrollable on the train—even threatening passengers with a razor. The conductor escorted the drunken slugger off the train at Niagara Falls, Ontario, Canada, as the train was about to cross an international bridge.

The train pulled away and the drunken Delahanty pushed passed a guard and followed it. The draw was open on the bridge. Delahanty's body was discovered a week later 20 miles down the falls. The 35-year-old had apparently fallen off the bridge and been swept away.

Miguel Del Toro

Miguel Del Toro pitched in 23 games for the San Francisco Giants from 1999–2000. The following summer, the righthander appeared with Seibu in Nippon Professional Baseball. He died that October back home in Ciudad Obregon, Sonora, Mexico, in an automobile accident at age 29.

Joe DeSa

Hawaiian Joe DeSa appeared briefly at first base for the 1980 Cardinals and 1985 White Sox. He was killed in a head-on automobile accident in Puerto Rico on December 20, 1986, after a winter league game. DeSa, 27 years old, was looking forward to his third major league stint, with Kansas City.

Charles Dexter

New Orleans, of the Southern Association, first baseman Charles Dexter made headlines in April 1909 when he was involved in a brawl with Grover Land of the Cleveland Indians during a preseason exhibition contest. Dexter was hunting near his parents' home in Ohio that November 4th when he slipped down a hill. The 25-year old accidentally discharged a gun into his chest as he fell.

Bo Diaz

Hard-nosed, 13-year major league catcher Bo Diaz retired after the 1989 season and returned home to Caracas, Venezuela. A year later, he was killed by lightning while affixing a satellite dish to his roof.

Lou DiMuro

American League umpire Lou DiMuro was killed in a car accident in June 1982. He had just finished working a game between the White Sox and Rangers in Arlington, Texas. DiMuro had been working major league games since 1963. His son, Mike, would later umpire in the majors.

Wild Bill Donovan

Bill Donovan produced 186 wins, 1,552 strikeouts, and a 2.69 ERA in 18 major league seasons. Twice he won 25 games, in 1901 and '07. Eight times the righthander won 17 + games. In leading Detroit to the pennant three straight years from 1907–09, Donovan garnered 51 wins and a 2.17 ERA, though he only won one World Series game.

Donovan's arm gave out after the 1911 campaign. Stints as a manager in the minors and with the Yankees and Phillies followed. He was managing New Haven in the Class-A Eastern League when he died on December 9, 1923, en route to baseball's winter meetings. Donovan was sleeping in the lower berth during a train wreck. In the nearby berth was future Hall of Famer and Yankee dynasty builder George Weiss, who escaped without serious injury.

Pete Dowling
Lefthander Pete Dowling pitched in the National League from 1897–99 and reemerged with the American League in 1901. Four years later and still playing ball, Dowling was decapitated by a train in Hot Lake, Oregon, on June 30, 1905. His age is unknown.

Duluth of the Northern League
Three Duluth players and their business manager were killed in a bus accident near St. Paul, Minnesota, on July 24, 1948. 17 others were injured. The bus hit head-on with a dry ice truck, both vehicles catching fire. The truck driver was also killed. The team belonged to the Cardinals' chain. The following men passed away:

James Greelich (truck driver)	Gerald Peterson (outfielder)
Don Schuchman (pitcher)	George Treadwill (business manager)
Gilbert Trible (outfielder)	

Paul Edmondson
Righthander Paul Edmondson finally hit the bigs in June 1969 with the White Sox. The following February, he lost control of his vehicle on a slick road, slid into oncoming traffic, and crashed head-on with another vehicle, causing an explosion. Edmondson's passenger was also killed. The pitcher was 27 years old.

Emporia of the Virginia League
Emporia, Virginia, a Senators farm club, teammates Ralph Fraser (20) and Bert Roseberry (20) were killed in an auto accident during spring training on April 16, 1950. Fraser was the son of major league star Chick Fraser.

Robert Fontana
Robert Fontana pitched and played outfield for Bologna, Italy, in the Italian major league. After a game versus San Marino in May 2006, Fontana was killed in a motorbike accident.

Ralph Fraser
See Emporia of the Virginia League

Howard Freigau
Infielder Howard Freigau appeared in the National League from 1922–28. With the Knoxville Smokies of the Southern Association in 1932, he drowned after smacking his head on the bottom of a pool in Chattanooga. He was 29 years old.

Danny Frisella
Righthander Danny Frisella pitched for five major league clubs during a 10-year career. In 53 games with the Mets in 1971, the reliever won 8, saved 12, and posted

a 1.99 ERA. He was killed in a dune buggy accident on New Year's Day 1977 in Phoenix, Arizona.

Adolfo Garcia
See Monterrey of the Mexican League

Tom Gastall
Another Boston University quarterback, Tom Gastall signed a $40,000 bonus contract with the Baltimore Orioles in 1955. Going straight to the majors, the backup catcher hit only .181 in 52 games. In September '56, he drowned while piloting a plane that went down in the Chesapeake Bay. Just at the beginning of his career, Gastall was 24 years old.

Marv Goodwin
Seven-year veteran and grandfathered spitballer Marv Goodwin was the first major leaguer to die in an airplane. In October 1925, he was on board a military plane when it went down near Houston. Goodwin was on a training exercise with the Texas National Guard at the time. He died three days later at age 34.

Just prior to his death, Goodwin was sold from the Cardinals to the Reds. The sanctimonious St. Louis general manager Branch Rickey still demanded payment. Judge Landis thought otherwise.

James Greelich
See Duluth of the Northern League

Carl Hackford
Charleston, of the American Association, minor leaguer Carl Hackford was electrocuted and died in 1954. He was 24 years old.

Chris Hartje
See Spokane of the Western International League

Bruce Heinbechner
Bruce Heinbechner was trying to crack the Angels pitching rotation when he was killed in a car accident during spring training 1974.

Mark Hilde
Minor league pitcher Gerik Baxter and Oakland farmhand Mark Hilde were driving when a tire blew, causing them to swerve off the road near Indio, California, on July 29, 2001. Both were killed.

Herman Hill
Herman Hill played in the outfield for the division-winning Minnesota Twins from 1969–70. He drowned on December 14 at age 25.

Ken Hubbs

Cubs' second baseman Ken Hubbs won the Rookie of the Year Award in 1962. At one point, he fielded 148 consecutive chances without an error. Shortly after attaining his flying license (two weeks), the 22-year-old took flight during a snowstorm. The plane went down five miles later into Provo Lake (Utah). He died on February 15, 1964.

Jose Huelga

Cuban pitching phenom Jose Huelga was killed in an automobile accident on July 4, 1974, at the age of 27. The righthander was in his seventh Cuban League season. He owns the lowest career ERA mark for a Cuban pitcher, 1.50.

Huelga first made his reputation with a victory over Burt Hooten in the 1970 Amateur World Series.

Emil Huhn

Augusta manager Emil Huhn was killed in the same highway accident that took the life of Frank Reiger on September 5, 1925. Huhn had played first base and catcher in the majors from 1915–17. His only full-time action came with the Newark Peppers of the Federal League as a rookie.

Art Irwin

Eastern League Hartford skipper Art Irwin, a former major league shortstop and manager, went overboard into the Atlantic Ocean from a steamer en route to Boston from New York on July 16, 1921. No clear explanation has ever been given regarding the accident. Some say he committed suicide. Yet, others suggest that he was murdered or faked his own death. Further clouding the mystery was the discovery that he was hiding a second wife and that $5,000 had recently been withdrawn from his account. The body was never recovered.

Previously, Irwin had led four National League teams and took the Boston Reds to the American Association pennant in 1891. On the side, he also promoted other events, such as prize fights, roller hockey contests, and bicycle marathons, all of which made him wealthy. Some suggest he fashioned the first infielder's glove.

Robert James

See Spokane of the Western International League

David Johnson

Cardinals farmhand David Johnson was killed in a deer hunting accident in Missouri on December 6, 1952. The 21-year-old outfielder was moving his way up through the organization.

Otis Johnson

Otis Johnson played 71 games in the infield for Yankees manager Hal Chase in 1911. After another season in the minors in 1915, he accidentally shot himself during a fox hunt and died on November 9. He had just celebrated his 32nd birthday.

Takeshi Kato
Takeshi Kato pitched in 35 games for Chunichi from 1963–64. The 20-year old was killed in an automobile accident in January 1965.

Leona Kearns
Former Washington Senators catcher Eddie Ainsmith organized a group of Bloomer Girl players to tour Japan following the 1925 season. Ainsmith, born in Russia, and his wife convinced a dozen teenage girls to travel to the Orient under their care with the hopes of a $500 paycheck.

The tour immediately floundered, financial backers withdrew, and all were stranded in Japan. The group bickered and Ainsmith convinced three of the girls to go to Korea with him to hopefully renew interest in their mission. One of the three was 6′ lefthander Leona Kearns, who was one of the star pitchers.

The others stayed behind and found a generous banker who financed their return to the United States. In Korea, Ainsmith found no such funding. He wired the States and received enough cash for him and his wife to return home. They ditched the three young girls they were chaperoning, leaving them in a foreign land without any means of support. Furthermore, Ainsmith never contacted the girls' families to let them know of the predicament.

Kearns' parents, on their own, found out about their daughter's plight and wired cash to the three. Finally, in late January, they were bound for home. On deck, a large wave swept Kearns off the ship. The 17-year-old's body was never found.

Frank King
Minor leaguer Frank King of the Class-C Ohio–Pennsylvania League was killed by a train in 1906.

Bon Kinnaman
See Spokane of the Western International League

John Kyler
Western Association outfielder John Kyler fell down the steps at a 1938 New Year's Eve party. The 23-year-old broke his neck and died.

Bob Larkin
See Ottawa of the Border League

Dale Lenn
International League Orioles catcher Dale Lenn drowned when his boat capsized in the Clark Fork River in Montana on February 17, 1948.

Walt Lerian
Phillies catcher Walt Lerian had just gained the starting position in 1929 when he was killed in the off-season. He was walking on the sidewalk when a vehicle jumped the curb and crushed him against a wall in Baltimore.

Lucky Lohrke
See Spokane of the Western International League

George Lyden
See Spokane of the Western International League

Billy Martin
Billy Martin came to the New York Yankees in 1950 at the urging of Casey Stengel, who had managed him at Oakland in the Pacific Coast League. The second baseman brought the fire Stengel wished to instill in his team. In fact, Martin brought enough fire for the whole league. "The Ol' Perfessor" took the player under his wing and a father–son relationship developed.

Always a battler, Martin continually mixed his personality with alcohol to spark a riotous effect that continually embarrassed and, in the end, shortened both his life and baseball dreams.

"Billy the Kid" was named 1953 World Series MVP with a .500 average, 12 hits, 2 homers, and 8 RBIs. However, the second baseman will forever be remembered for darting in and scooping a fly underhanded near the pitcher's mound to kill a Dodger rally in Game 7 of the '52 series. The Yankee made the All-Star team in 1956.

Martin later took the fall for a nightclub melee in May 1957 and was shipped to Kansas City. Heartbroken to leave the Yankees and feeling double-crossed by mentor Stengel, Martin played for seven clubs over his last five seasons. In 1960, while with the Cincinnati Reds, he broke Cubs rookie Jim Brewer's cheekbone after the pitcher threw inside. Chicago sued Martin for $1 million, but charges were later dropped. Brewer did win $10,000 in a civil suit, though.

In 1969, Martin took over the helm of the Minnesota Twins, beginning a long cycle that defined his baseball career. He would be welcomed in, quickly find success, disrupt the clubhouse, possibly engage in a fistfight or two, and then be ushered out under embarrassment, all to be repeated over and over again, as a running sideshow to the baseball season.

In 1969, Martin won the American League West title, beat up pitcher Dave Boswell, rebuffed owner Calvin Griffith, and was fired. Hired by Detroit in 1971, Martin moved the team into second place, then took the American League East title the next summer. He was fired again at the end of '73 and took over the Rangers.

Texas jumped from sixth to finish an incredible second in 1974; along the way Martin punched the team's 64-year-old traveling secretary. That year, he won his first of four Manager of the Year Awards, only to be fired at midseason 1975 and take over his beloved Yankees. Martin and Steinbrenner only fueled the foolishness in each other. No less than five times was Billy hired and fired as Yankee skipper, creating a circus-like atmosphere in the clubhouse, later dubbed "the Bronx Zoo."

Martin won the pennant in 1976 and the world championship the following year. The battles continued as Martin clashed with Steinbrenner, Thurman Munson, and Reggie Jackson, including a highly publicized *Game of the Week* incident, where Martin pulled Jackson out of right field and had to be restrained in the dugout from going after the superstar. A drunken Martin lambasted Jackson and Steinbrenner to the press, saying that "one was a born liar and the other was convicted," referring to the fact that Steinbrenner was convicted of making illegal campaign contributions to President Richard Nixon. Martin was forced to resign in July 1978. Bob Lemon managed the team the rest of the way to the world title.

Martin was hired again as the Yankee manager in July 1979, only to lose his job three months later after a drunken fight in which he punched a marshmallow salesman. Then he took the show on the road in 1980 to Oakland for another difficult owner, Charlie Finley. "Billy Ball" revived a dying franchise that had drawn only 307,000 fans in '79; one contest saw a mere 653 attendees. The A's jumped from last to second in the AL West and won the division in the first half of the strike-split 1981 season. Again, Martin was fired at the end of '82.

Rehired by the Yankees in 1983, he would lose his job by the end of the year. The same goes for '85 and '88, after another nightclub incident. On Christmas Day 1989, Martin was driving home from a bar when he crashed within sight of his neighborhood and died. At the time, he was rumored to be gathering a coaching staff to take another run in the Bronx.

The overall value of Billy Martin, the manager, is difficult to decipher. At times, he could be the best in the business. If you had to win one year, all else be damned, one would probably love to see Martin at the helm. Unfortunately, in this respect, the game goes on year after year. Martin's lasting legacy to a franchise was usually negative, though a perusal of the record book shows an impressive .553 winning percentage and numerous top-two finishes.

Fred Martinez
See Spokane of the Western International League

James McAndrews
New York–Pennsylvania League, Class-A, umpire James McAndrews died in a train crash in 1933.

Doc McJames
Righthander Doc McJames won 46 games between 1898–99 for Baltimore and Brooklyn in the National League. Late in '99, he contracted malaria and missed all of 1900 as he also tried to start his medical career. A comeback in 1901 failed after 13 games. The pitcher died in September of that year at age 28 from complications after a carriage accident.

Bill McMillan
Bill McMillan of the Sioux City Soos in the Class-A Western League was killed in a hunting accident in 1953. He was 22 years old.

Greetchie Meredith
Birmingham Black Barons shortstop Greetchie Meredith died in a mining accident while working during the off-season during the Depression in January 1932.

Vic Michalec

Vic Michalec of the Tallahassee Rebels in the Class-B Florida International League drowned at age 26 in 1954.

Mike Miley

Angels shortstop prospect Mike Miley died in an automobile accident on January 6, 1977. He was only 23 years old. Miley lost control of his vehicle, which careened off road posts and flipped over, killing him instantly. He had been California's first round pick in 1974.

Monterrey of the Mexican League

Twelve Monterrey players were injured when the team bus crashed en route to Mexico City on July 15, 1952. Vincente Torrez and Adolfo Garcia did not survive.

Al Montgomery

Catcher Al Montgomery debuted with the Boston Braves in 1941. On his way from spring training to open the '42 season in the minors, he was killed in an auto accident in Virginia on April 26, 1942. The three-vehicle accident left six dead. Montgomery was 21 years old.

Bob Moose

Bob Moose played his entire 10-year career for the Pittsburgh Pirates, beginning in 1967. As a rookie in '68, the hard-thrower posted a 2.73 ERA. The following year, Moose had his breakthrough season with a 14-3 record, a 2.91 ERA, and a league-leading .824 winning percentage. He also tossed a no-hitter on September 20 against the soon-to-be World Champion New York Mets.

His postseason record is unflattering, though. In seven games, Moose failed to produce a victory. Embarrassingly, his wild pitch in the final game of the National League Championship Series allowed George Foster to score and gave Cincinnati the pennant in '72. It was also Roberto Clemente's final game.

Injuries began to plague the righthander. The most serious was a blood clot in his pitching shoulder that required surgery. In 1976, Moose was converted to a reliever. On October 9, his 29th birthday, Moose died after losing control of his vehicle in Martins Ferry, Ohio, returning from a postseason golf tournament. Two months later, the Pirates would also lose their skipper.

Porter Moss

Memphis Red Sox righthander Porter Moss played 11 years in the Negro leagues, pitching in three separate East–West games. While watching a dice game in July 1944, Moss was accidentally shot when a quarrel broke out.

He might have survived but the first doctor he saw refused to treat a black man. Moss had to be transported to an adjoining town.

Thurman Munson

Chosen in the first round of the June 1968 amateur baseball draft, Thurman Munson left Kent State University, where he was playing under a football scholarship, for a

$75,000 offer from the New York Yankees. Two years later, he took over the team's catching duties and posted a .302 average to win the Rookie of the Year Award.

His breakthrough came in 1973 with a .301, 20, 74 season and the first of three straight Gold Gloves. Munson was a tough backstop with a fireplug body and a powerful arm. Early in his career, he led the league three times in games, assists, and errors, twice in double plays and once in fielding average.

In 1975, Munson was named the first Yankee team captain since Lou Gehrig. He also hit .318 and knocked in 102 runners. In 1976, Munson's MVP .302, 17, 105 season helped lead the Yankees to the pennant. In the American League Championship Series versus Kansas City, he hit .435. His .529 average in the World Series meant little as the Yankees were swept by Cincinnati.

With the addition of Reggie Jackson and Munson's .308, 18, 100-season, the Yankees won it all in 1977. Munson also became only the second catcher to hit .300 with 100 + RBIs in three consecutive years. Another world title flag hung above Yankee Stadium in 1978.

On August 2, 1979, Munson was killed, at age 32, when the plane he was piloting fell 1,000 feet short of an airstrip in Canton, Ohio. He was flying home to visit his family. Jackson had just turned down Munson's offer to accompany him.

Leigh Neuage
The L.A. Dodgers plucked pitcher Leigh Neuage from Australia in 2001. The right-hander pitched in their system until 2003, rising to Single-A. Back home, the 20-year old fell 15 stories to his death at a Sydney hotel in August 2003.

Bobby Ojeda
See Cleveland Indians Pitching Staff, 1993

Steve Olin
See Cleveland Indians Pitching Staff, 1993

Ottawa of the Border League
Five members of the Ottawa club of the Border League were injured in an auto accident on July 31, 1950, pitcher Bob Larkin fatally. Their vehicle collided with an Army truck.

Smoky Owens
See Cleveland Buckeyes of the Negro American League

Robert Patterson
See Spokane of the Western International League

Charlie Peete
Outfielder Charlie Peete's professional career began with the Indianapolis Clowns in 1950. From there, he moved on to the minor leagues and eventually joined the St.

Louis Cardinals in 1956. Traveling to play winter ball in Venezuela, the 27-year-old died when his plane went down on November 27.

Delos Peterman
Pirates farmhand Delos Peterman was killed at age 26 in an industrial accident in 1920.

Gerald Peterson
See Duluth of the Northern League

Vic Picetti
See Spokane of the Western International League

McCoy Pitts
Appalachian League Johnson City player McCoy Pitts was accidentally shot in the head on November 30, 1911. He was being handed the gun by his brother when it went off. The 20-year-old died instantly.

Frank Reiger
Thirty-year old Frank Reiger hit .339 in the minors over five seasons prior to dying in a highway accident on September 5, 1925. He was traveling with his Augusta, Sally League, teammates after a game in Charlotte. Manager Emil Huhn was also killed.

Elio Ribet
Eighteen-year-old Elio Ribet of the Palatka Redlegs in the Class-D Florida State League drowned in 1960.

George Risk
See Spokane of the Western International League

Sherry Robertson
Sherry Robertson signed with the Washington Senators out of college and joined the team in 1940, playing there through 1952. One thing he had going for him was his pedigree. He was team owner Clark Griffith's nephew and brother to Calvin Griffith, future owner. Calvin's name was Robertson until Clark adopted him after his father's death.

After leaving the field, Robertson joined the front office and became farm director in 1956, staying with the club after its move to Minnesota. At the end of the 1970 season, October 23, he was killed in an auto accident while on a hunting trip with Twins officers and players. Robertson lost control of his vehicle, swerved off the road and smacked a tree, sustaining massive head trauma.

Ken Robinson
Looking forward to another spring in pro ball, Ken Robinson died in an auto accident on February 28, 1999, in Tucson. The 29-year-old had pitched in the majors with Toronto and Kansas City from 1995–97.

Bert Roseberry
See Emporia of the Virginia League

Chico Ruiz
Cuban Chico Ruiz is well-known today for allegedly pulling a gun on the irritable Alex Johnson in the Angels clubhouse in 1971. After eight years in the majors, the utility player was killed on February 9, 1972, after his car hit a sign post near Escondido, California. Ruiz was 33 years old.

Ken Ryback
Skin diving in Saginaw Bay (Michigan), 20-year-old Phillies farmhand Ken Ryback drowned on July 6, 1959.

Gus Sandberg
Former major leaguer and current Pacific Coast League catcher Gus Sandberg died a horrible death in February 1930. While draining a gas tank, he lit a match and incinerated himself.

Don Schuchman
See Duluth of the Northern League

Major Trammell Scott
Outgoing Southern Association president Trammell Scott accidentally shot and killed himself while starting out on a turkey hunt alone on December 20, 1942. Earlier in the month, league owners had dismissed him from his duties. The Atlanta businessman and judge was late arriving to a league meeting and, by the time, he arrived Billy Evans was named president. Scott assumed his regular chair before he was informed of the decision.

Mike Sharperson
Former major league all-star infielder Mike Sharperson died in an automobile accident on May 26, 1996. The 34-year-old was playing for Triple-A Las Vegas of the Pacific Coast League at the time. The crash ejected Sharperson through the sunroof as the car flipped over.

Jim Slowrey
A car accident took the life of Wisconsin Rapids player Jim Slowrey on September 2, 1947. The shortstop was only 22 years old.

Asa Small
Pitcher Asa Small of the Columbus Jets in the Triple-A International League died in a house fire in 1968. He was 26 years old.

Mike Smalling
While canoeing in the Conestoga River, Lancaster first baseman Mike Smalling drowned on August 9, 1911. The Tri-State League infielder was 22 years old.

Ray Spencer
En route to Fort Wayne, the train carrying the Dayton ball club of the Central league collided with another train at one a.m. on August 24, 1917. Twelve players were injured; right fielder Ray Spencer suffered a fatal blow to the back of the head.

Spokane of the Western International League
Nine members of the minor league Spokane team plus the driver were killed when their bus rode off the side of a Cascade Mountain in Washington State on June 24, 1946. Careening over an embankment, the bus fell 500 feet and caught on fire. Witnesses were aghast to hear the screams and to see the charred bodies. The bus veered to miss an incoming vehicle that was driving on the wrong side of the road. Six others were injured. The team was en route to Bremerton. The following did not survive:

Bob Berg (bus driver)	Mel Cole (manager)
Chris Hartje (catcher)	Robert James (outfielder)
Bon Kinnaman (pitcher)	George Lyden (pitcher)
Fred Martinez (infielder)	Robert Patterson (outfielder)
Vic Picetti (first baseman)	George Risk (infielder)

Lucky Lohrke gained his nickname because he found out that he was traded to San Diego during the bus trip. He hopped off at a road stop and hitchhiked back to his apartment. Similarly, Lohrke was bumped from a military plane during World War II for a superior officer. That plane crashed without any survivors.

Dick Stello
Dick Stello umpired in the National League from 1969 until his death in an auto accident in 1987.

Charlie Sullivan
In the minors after three years with the Tigers, 1928–31, pitcher Charlie Sullivan was killed by a train when he drove into a railroad crossing in North Carolina on May 28, 1935. He was 32 years old.

Al Thake
Brooklyn Atlantics outfielder Al Thake fell from a fishing boat and drowned on September 1, 1872 off Fort Hamilton in New York. He was 22 years old.

Bill Thomas
25-year-old Buffalo pitcher Bill Thomas of the Class-A Eastern League boarded a ship headed for New York City in May 1906. He was never heard from again. The mystery remains unresolved. Thomas had been lured East after successful seasons in the Pacific Coast League.

Vincente Torrez
See Monterrey of the Mexican League

George Treadwell
See Duluth of the Northern League

Humberto Trejo
See Oscar Acosta

Gilbert Trible
See Duluth of the Northern League

Mark Weems
Orioles farmhand Mark Weems drowned in the Caribbean Sea near Caracas, Venezuela on December 30, 1973. He was 22 years old. The reliever had led the league with a 2.61 ERA in 1971 with Dallas–Fort Worth.

Ben Young
Ben Young was a respected umpire in the American Association. The association was the first to strictly employ professional umpires. Young was an intellectual who worked to improve the job conditions of all umpires. He was instrumental in setting a code of ethics and pioneering a training program for arbiters. Young pushed the American Association to issue uniform attire for umpires and to experiment with a duel umpiring system. As a result, the American Association's quality of umpiring was greater than the National League's for a time.

In early 1887, Young was working on a ten-point plan for improving the status of the men in blue. Unfortunately, he was killed in a railway accident en route to a game.

Cliff Young
See Cleveland Indians Pitching Staff, 1993

Bibliography

Abrams, Roger I. *Legal Bases: Baseball and the Law*. Philadelphia: Temple University Press, 1998.

Acocella, Nicholas and Donald Dewey. *The Book of Baseball Lineups*. New York: Citadel Press, 1996.

Alexander, Charles C. *Ty Cobb*. New York: Oxford University Press, 1984.

———. *John McGraw*. New York: Viking Penguin, 1988.

———. *Our Game: An American Baseball History*. New York: Henry Holt, 1991.

Allen, Lee. *The Hot Stove League*. New York: A. S. Barnes, 1955.

Alvarez, Mark. *The Old Ball Game: Baseball's Beginnings*. Alexandria, VA: Redefinition, 1990.

Appel, Marty. *Slide Kelly Slide: The Wild Life and Times of Mike "King" Kelly*. Lanham, MD and London: Scarecrow Press, 1999.

Appel, Martin and Burt Goldblatt. *Baseball's Best: The Hall of Fame Gallery*. New York: McGraw-Hill, 1980.

Ardell, Jean Hastings. *Breaking into Baseball: Women and the National Pastime*. Carbondale: Southern Illinois University Press, 2005.

Associated Press. "Deaf Outfielder Hears Sound of Stardom." *Baltimore Sun*: June 4, 1993.

———. "A Legend is Lost on Death of Caray." *Baltimore Sun*: February 19, 1998.

———. "Saunders Breaks Arm Throwing Pitch." *Baltimore Sun*: May 27, 1999.

Baily, Bob. "Hunting for the First Louisville Slugger," *The Baseball Research Journal 30*. Cleveland, OH: SABR, 2001.

Barber, Phil and John Fawaz. *NFL's Greatest: Pro Football's Best Players, Teams and Games*. New York: Dorling Kindersley Publishing, 2000.

Bauer, Carlos. *The All-Time Japanese Baseball Register: The Complete Statistical Record of All the Great Japanese and American Players*. San Diego: Baseball Press Books, 2000.

Bjarkman, Peter C. *The Biographical History of Basketball*. Lincolnwood, IL: Masters Press, 2000.

———. *Diamonds Around the Globe: The Encyclopedia of International Baseball*. Westport, CT: Greenwood Press, 2005.

Bloomfield, Gary. *Duty, Honor, Victory: America's Athletes in World War II*. Guilford, CT: The Lyons Press, 2003.

Boxerman, Burton A. and Benita W. Boxerman. *Ebbets to Veeck to Busch: Eight Owners Who Shaped Baseball*. Jefferson, NC: McFarland, 2003.

Bronson, Eric. *Baseball and Philosophy: Thinking Outside the Batter's Box*. Chicago and La Salle, IL: Open Court, 2004.

Browning, Reed. *Cy Young: A Baseball Life*. Amherst: University of Massachusetts Press, 2000.

Boudreau, Lou and Russell Schneider. *Lou Boudreau: Covering All the Bases*. Champaign, IL: Sagamore Publishing, 1993.

Bowman, John and Joel Zoss. *Diamonds in the Rough: The Untold History of Baseball.* Chicago: Contemporary Books, 1996.

Brooks, Tim and Earle Marsh. *The Complete Directory to Prime Time Network and Cable TV Shows: 1946–Present.* New York: Ballantine Books, 1999.

Caren, Eric C. *Baseball Extra.* Edison, NJ: Castle Books, 2000.

Carroll, Bob, Michael Gershman, David Neft and John Thorn. *Total Football: The Official Encyclopedia of the National Football League.* New York: HarperCollins, 1997.

———. *Total Football II: The Official Encyclopedia of the National Football League.* New York: HarperCollins, 1999.

Casway, Jerrold. *Ed Delahanty in the Emerald Age of Baseball.* Notre Dame: University of Notre Dame Press, 2004.

Cayleff, Susan E. *Babe: The Life and Legend of Babe Didrikson Zaharias.* Urbana and Chicago: University of Illinois Press, 1995.

Charlton, Jim. *The National Pastime: A Review of Baseball History, No. 23.* Cleveland, OH: Society for American Baseball Research, 2003.

Clark, Dick and Larry Lester. *The Negro Leagues Book.* Cleveland, OH: Society for American Baseball Research, 1994.

Clark, Joe. *A History of Australian Baseball: Time and Game.* Lincoln, NE: University of Nebraska Press, 2003.

Cobb, Ty and Al Stump. *My Life in Baseball: The True Record.* Lincoln and London: University of Nebraska Press, 1993.

Connor, Floyd. *Baseball's Most Wanted.* Washington, DC: Brassey's, 2000.

Cottrell, Robert Charles. *The Best Pitcher in Baseball: The Life of Rube Foster, Negro League Giant.* New York: New York University Press, 2001.

Cox, James A. *The Lively Ball: Baseball in the Roaring Twenties.* Alexandria, VA: Redefinition, 1989.

Creamer, Robert W. *Baseball in '41.* Ashland, OR: Blackstone Audiobooks, 1997.

Crystal, David. *The Cambridge Biographical Encyclopedia.* New York: Cambridge University Press, 1994.

Daly, Dan and Bob O'Donnell. *The Pro Football Chronicle.* New York: Collier Books, 1990.

Dawidoff, Nicholas. *The Catcher Was a Spy: The Mysterious Life of Moe Berg.* New York: Vintage Books, 1994.

Dent, Jim. *Monster of the Midway: Bronko Nagurski, the 1943 Chicago Bears, and the Greatest Comeback Ever.* New York: Thomas Dunne Books, 2003.

Devaleria, Dennis and Jeanne Burke Devaleria. *Honus Wagner: A Biography.* New York: Henry Holt, 1995.

Dewey, Donald and Nicholas Acocella. *The New Biographical History of Baseball.* Chicago: Triumph Books, 2002.

———. *The Black Prince of Baseball: Hal Chase and the Mythology of Baseball.* Wilmington, DE: Sports Media Publishing, 2004.

———. *Total Ballclubs: The Ultimate Book of Baseball Teams.* Wilmington, DE: Sports Media Publishing, 2005.

Diamond, Dan, James Duplacey, Ralph Dinger, Igor Kuperman and Eric Zweig. *Total Hockey: The Official Encyclopedia of the National Hockey League.* Kansas City, MO: Andrews McMeel Publishing, 1998.

Dickson, Paul. *The New Dickson Baseball Dictionary.* New York: Harcourt Brace, 1999.

DiSalvatore, Bryan. *A Clever Base-Ballist: The Life and Times of John Montgomery Ward.* New York: Patheon Books, 1999.

Dixon, Phil and Patrick J. Hannigan. *The Negro Leagues: A Photographic History.* New York: Amereon House, 1992.

Durocher, Leo and Ed Linn. *Nice Guys Finish Last*. New York: Pocket Books, 1976.

Fiffer, Steve. *Speed: Baseball in High Gear*. Alexandria, VA: Redefinition, 1990.

Figueredo, Jorge S. *Who's Who in Cuban Baseball, 1878–1961*. Jefferson, NC: McFarland, 2003.

Filichia, Peter. *Professional Baseball Franchises: From the Abbeville Athletics to the Zanesville Indians*. New York: Facts On File, 1993.

Finnan, Jane. *Dominionball: Baseball Above the 49th*. Cleveland, OH: Society for American Baseball Research, 2005.

Fitts, Robert K. *Remembering Japanese Baseball: An Oral History of the Game*. Carbondale, IL: Southern Illinois University Press, 2005.

Friend, Luke and Don Zminda. *The Best Book of Baseball Facts and STATS Ever*. Great Britain: Carlton Books, 2001.

Frost, Mark. *The Greatest Game Ever Played: Harry Vardon, Francis Ouimet, and the Birth of Modern Golf*. New York: Good Comma Ink, 2002.

Gerlach, Larry. *Death on the Diamond: The Cal Drummond Story* from *The National Pastime: A Review of Baseball History, Number 24*. Cleveland, OH: Society for American Baseball Research, 2004.

Giglio, James N. *Musial: From Stash to Stan The Man*. Columbia and London: University of Missouri Press, 2001.

Gill, Bob. *Not Only the Ball Was Brown: Blacks in Minors*. Coffin Corner, 1989, Volume 11, Number 5.

Ginsburg, Daniel E. *The Fix Is In: A History of Baseball Gambling and Game-Fixing Scandals*. Jefferson, NC, and London: McFarland, 1995.

Golf Magazine. *GOLF Magazine's Encyclopedia of Golf: The Complete Reference, Second Edition*. New York: HarperCollins, 1993.

Goldstein, William. *A History of Early Baseball*. New York: Barnes and Noble, 2000.

Golenbock, Peter and Greg Fielden. *The Stock Car Racing Encyclopedia: The Complete Record of America's Most Popular Sport*. New York: MacMillan, 1997.

Golenbock, Peter. *Wrigleyville: A Magical History Tour of the Chicago Cubs*. New York: St. Martin's Griffin, 1999.

Gonzalez Echevarria, Roberto. *The Pride of Havana: A History of Cuban Baseball*. New York: Oxford University Press, 1999.

Green, Ben. *Spinning the Globe: The Rise, Fall, and Return to Greatness of the Harlem Globetrotters*. New York: HarperCollins, 2005.

Gregorich, Barbara. *Women at Play: The Story of Women in Baseball*. San Diego: Harcourt Brace, 1993.

Grosshandler, Stanley. "The Grosshandler Lists" from *The Coffin Corner Newsletter*. North Huntingdon, PA: Professional Football Researchers Association, Volume 27, Number 5, 2005.

Gutman, Dan. *It Ain't Cheating if You Don't Get Caught*. New York: Penguin Books, 1990.

Halberstam, David. Read by Edwin Newman. *October 1964*. New York: Random House Audio Books, 1994.

Hanks, Stephen. *150 Years of Baseball*. Lincolnwood, IL: Publications International, 1989.

Hardy, James D., Jr. *The New York Giants Base Ball Club: The Growth of a Team and a Sport, 1870–1900*. Jefferson, NC: McFarland, 1996.

Higbe, Kirby and Martin Quigley. *The High Hard One*. Lincoln and London: University of Nebraska Press, 1967.

Holtzman, Jerome. *The Commissioners: Baseball's Midlife Crisis*. New York: Total Sports, 1998.

Holway, John B. *Blackball Stars: Negro League Stars*. Westport, CT: Meckler Books, 1988.

———. *Black Diamonds: Life in the Negro Leagues from the Men Who Lived It*. Westport, CT: Meckler Books, 1989.

————. *The Complete Book of Baseball's Negro Leagues: The Other Half of Baseball History.* Fern Park, FL: Hastings House Publishers, 2001.

Humber, William. *Diamonds of the North: A Concise History of Baseball in Canada.* Toronto: Oxford University Press, 1995.

Ivor-Campbell, Frederick, Robert L. Tiemann and Mark Rucker. *Baseball's First Stars.* Cleveland, OH: The Society for American Baseball Research, 1996.

Isaacs, Neil D. *Vintage NBA: The Pioneer Era, 1946–1956.* Indianapolis, IN: Masters Press, 1996.

Isenberg, Michael T. *John L. Sullivan and His America.* Urbana and Chicago: University of Illinois Press, 1988.

Jackson, Mannie. *Harlem Globetrotters World Tour 2000 Program.* Harlem Globetrotters, 2000.

James, Bill. *The Bill James' Historical Baseball Abstract.* New York: Villard Books, 1986.

————. *The New Bill James Historical Baseball Abstract.* New York: The Free Press, 2001.

James, Bill, John Dewan, Don Zminda, Jim Callis and Neil Munro. *STATS Inc. All-Time Major League Handbook: Second Edition.* Morton Grove, IL: STATS Publishing, 2000.

Johnson, Daniel E. *Japanese Baseball: A Statistical Handbook.* Jefferson, NC: McFarland, 1999.

Johnson, Lloyd. *The Minor League Register.* Durham, NC: Baseball America, 1994.

Johnson, Lloyd and Miles Wolff. *The Encyclopedia of Minor League Baseball, Second Edition.* Durham, NC: Baseball America, 1997.

Kahn, Roger. *A Flame of Pure Fire: Jack Dempsey and the Roaring '20s.* New York: Harcourt Brace, 1999.

Kaiser, Ken and David Fisher. *Planet of the Umps: A Baseball Life from Behind the Plate.* New York: St. Martin's Press, 2003.

Kaplan, Jim. *The Fielders: The Game's Greatest Gloves.* Alexandria, VA: Redefinition, 1989.

Kelley, Brent. *The Negro Leagues Revisited: Conversations with 66 More Baseball Heroes.* Jefferson, NC: McFarland, 2000.

Kirsch, George B. *Baseball in Blue and Gray: The National Pastime during the Civil War.* Princeton, NJ: Princeton University Press, 2003.

Knisley, Michael. "Follow That Star." *The Sporting News,* March 19, 2001.

Koppett, Leonard. *Koppett's Concise History of Major League Baseball.* Philadelphia: Temple University Press, 1998.

————. *The Thinking Fan's Guide to Baseball.* New York: Total/Sports Illustrated, 2001.

Kriegel, Mark. *Namath: A Biography.* New York: Viking Penguin, 2004.

Lawrenson, Derek. *The Complete Encyclopedia of Golf.* London: Carlton Books, 1999.

Leavy, Jane. *Sandy Koufax: A Lefty's Legacy.* New York: HarperCollins, 2002.

Leckie, Robert. *The Story of Football: A Lavishly Illustrated History of America's Exciting Gridiron Sport.* New York: Random House, 1965.

Lee, Bill. *The Baseball Necrology: The Post-Baseball Lives of Over 7,600 Major League Players and Others.* Jefferson, NC: McFarland, 2003.

Leonard, Buck and James A. Riley. *Buck Leonard: The Black Lou Gehrig, An Autobiography.* New York: Carroll and Graf Publishers, 1995.

Levinson, David and Karen Christensen. *Encyclopedia of World Sport.* New York and Oxford: Oxford University Press, 1999.

Lewis, Michael. *Moneyball: The Art of Winning an Unfair Game.* New York: W. W. Norton, 2003.

Light, Jonathan Fraser. *The Cultural Encyclopedia of Baseball.* Jefferson, NC: McFarland, 1997.

Lomax, Michael E. *Black Baseball Entrepreneurs, 1860–1901: Operating by Any Means Necessary.* Syracuse, NY: Syracuse University Press, 2003.

MacCambridge, Michael. *America's Game: The Epic Story of How Pro Football Captured a Nation.* New York: Random House, 2004.

MacMillan. *The Baseball Encyclopedia: Eighth Edition.* New York: MacMillan, 1990.

Madden, W. C. *The Women of the All-American Girls Professional Baseball League: A Biographical Dictionary.* Jefferson, NC: McFarland, 1997.

———. *The All-American Girls Professional Baseball League Record Book: Comprehensive Hitting, Fielding and Pitching Statistics.* Jefferson, NC: McFarland, 2000.

Maher, Tod and Bob Gill. *The Pro Football Encyclopedia.* New York: Macmillan, 1997.

Malloy, Jerry. *Sol White's History of Colored Base Ball with Other Documents on the Early Black Game 1886–1936.* Nebraska: University of Nebraska Press, 1995.

Markel, Robert, Susan Waggoner and Marcella Smith. *The Women's Sports Encyclopedia: The Comprehensive Guide to Women's Sports, Women Athletes, and their Records.* New York: Henry Holt, 1997.

Masur, Louis P. *Autumn Glory: Baseball's First World Series.* New York: Hill and Wang, 2003.

Maltin, Leonard. *Leonard Maltin's 1999 Movie and Video Guide.* New York: Signet Books, 1998.

Mathewson, Christy. *Pitching in a Pinch: Baseball from the Inside.* Lincoln and London: University of Nebraska Press, 1994.

McDermott, Mickey and Howard Eisenberg. *A Funny Thing Happened on the Way to Cooperstown.* Chicago: Triumph Books, 2003.

McGraw, John. *My Thirty Years in Baseball.* Lincoln, NE: University of Nebraska Press, 1923.

McGuire, Mark and Michael Sean Gormley. *Moments in the Sun: Baseball's Briefly Famous.* Jefferson, NC and London: McFarland, 1999.

McKissack, Patricia C. *Jesse Jackson: A Biography.* New York: Scholastic, 1989.

McKissack, Patricia C. and Frederick McKissack, Jr. *Black Diamond: The Story of the Negro Baseball Leagues.* New York: Scholastic, 1994.

McLaurin, Jim. *NASCAR's Most Wanted.* Dulles, VA: Brassey's, 2001.

McNeil, William F. *Baseball's Other All-Stars.* Jefferson, NC: McFarland, 2000.

Mead, William B. *Low and Outside: Baseball in the Depression, 1930–1939.* Alexandria, VA: Redefinition, 1990.

———. *The Inside Game: Baseball's Master Strategists.* Alexandria, VA: Redefinition, 1991.

———. *Baseball Goes to War: Stars Don Khaki, 4-Fs Vie for Pennant.* Washington, DC: Broadcast Interview Source, 1998.

Mead, William B. and Paul Dickson. *Baseball: The Presidents' Game.* New York: Walker and Company, 1997.

Menzer, Joe. *The Wildest Ride: A History of NASCAR.* New York: Simon & Shuster, 2001.

Miller, Marvin. *A Whole Different Ballgame: The Sport and Business of Baseball.* New York: Carol, 1991.

Murdock, Eugene C. *Ban Johnson: Czar of Baseball.* Westport, CT: Greenwood Press, 1982.

Nadel, Eric and Craig R. Wright. *The Man Who Stole First Base: Tales from Baseball's Past.* Dallas, TX: Taylor, 1989.

National Football League. *NFL 2000 Record & Fact Book.* New York: Workman, 2000.

———. *NFL 2005 Record & Fact Book.* New York: Time Home Entertainment, 2005.

Nemec, David. *The Beer and Whiskey League: The Illustrated History of the American Association— Baseball's Renegade Major League.* New York: Lyons and Burford, 1994.

———. *The Great Encyclopedia of 19th Century Major League Baseball.* New York: Donald I. Fine Books, 1997.

———. *Great Baseball Feats, Facts and Firsts.* New York: New American Library, 2000.

Nemec, David and Pete Palmer. *Fascinating Baseball Facts.* Lincolnwood, IL: Publications International, 1994.

Obojski, Robert. *Bush League: A History of Minor League Baseball.* New York: Macmillan, 1975.

————. *Baseball's Strangest Moments*. New York: Sterling, 1988.

Okkonen, Marc. *The Federal League of 1914–15: Baseball's Third Major League*. Garrett Park, MD: Society for American Baseball Research, 1989.

Okrent, Daniel and Steve Wulf. *Baseball Anecdotes*. New York: Harper Perennial, 1989.

O'Neal, Bill. *The Texas League 1888–1987: A Century of Baseball*. Austin, TX: Eakin Press, 1987.

————. *The Pacific Coast League: 1903–1988*. Austin, TX: Eakin Press, 1990.

————. *The International League: A Baseball History, 1884–1991*. Austin, TX: Eakin Press, 1992.

————. *The Southern League: Baseball in Dixie, 1885–1994*. Austin, TX: Eakin Press, 1994.

Overmyer, James. *Queen of the Negro Leagues: Effa Manley and the Newark Eagles*. Lanham, MD: Scarecrow Press, 1998.

Patterson, Pat. *Football in Baltimore: History and Memorabilia*. Baltimore: The Johns Hopkins University Press, 2000.

Pepe, Phil. *Talkin' Baseball: An Oral History of Baseball in the 1970s*. New York: Ballantine, 1998.

Peterson, Robert. *Only the Ball was White: A History of Legendary Black Players and All-Black Professional Teams Before Black Men Played in the Major Leagues*. New York: McGraw-Hill, 1970.

————. *Cages to Jump Shots: Pro Basketball's Early Years*. New York: Oxford University Press, 1990.

————. *Pigskin: The Early Years of Pro Football*. New York: Oxford University Press, 1997.

Pietrusza, David. *Judge and Jury: The Life and Times of Judge Kenesaw Mountain Landis*. South Bend, IN: Diamond Communications, Inc., 1998.

————. *Rothstein: The Life, Times, and Murder of the Criminal Genius Who Fixed the 1919 World Series*. New York: Carroll & Graf, 2003.

Pietrusza, David, Matthew Silverman, and Michael Gershman. *Baseball: The Biographical Encyclopedia*. New York: Total/Sports Illustrated, 2000.

Porter, David L. *Biographical Dictionary of American Sports: Baseball*. New York: Greenwood Press, 1987.

————. *Biographical Dictionary of American Sports: Football*. New York: Greenwood Press, 1987.

————. *Biographical Dictionary of American Sports: Outdoor Sports*. New York: Greenwood Press, 1988.

————. *Biographical Dictionary of American Sports: Basketball and Other Indoor Sports*. New York: Greenwood Press, 1989.

Rader, Benjamin G. *Baseball: A History of America's Game*. Urbana and Chicago: University of Illinois Press, 1992.

Reaves, Joseph A. *Taking in a Game: A History of Baseball in Asia*. Lincoln, NE: University of Nebraska Press, 2002.

Ribowsky, Mark. *A Complete History of the Negro Leagues 1884–1955*. New York: Citadel Press Books, 2002.

Riley, James A. *The Biographical Encyclopedia of the Negro Baseball Leagues*. New York: Carroll and Graf, 1994.

Robbins, Mike. *Ninety Feet from Fame: Close Calls with Baseball Immortality*. New York: Carroll & Graf, 2004.

Roberts, James B. and Alexander G. Skutt. *The Boxing Register: International Boxing Hall of Fame Official Record Book*. Ithaca, New York: McBooks Press, 2002.

Rogosin, Donn. *Invisible Men: Life in Baseball's Negro Leagues*. New York: MacMillan, 1983.

Russo, Frank and Gene Racz. *Bury My Heart at Cooperstown: Salacious, Sad, and Surreal Deaths in the History of Baseball*. Chicago: Triumph Books, 2006.

Ryczek, William J. *Blackguards and Red Stockings: A History of Baseball's National Association, 1871–1875*. Wallingford, Connecticut: Colebrook Press, 1992.

————. *When Johnny Came Sliding Home: The Post-Civil War Baseball Boom, 1865–1870*. Jefferson, NC: McFarland, 1998.

Sachare, Alex. *The Official NBA Basketball Encyclopedia, Second Edition*. New York: Villard Books, 1994.

Salin, Tony. *Baseball's Forgotten Heroes: One Fan's Search for the Game's Most Interesting Overlooked Players*. Lincolnwood, IL: NTC/Contemporary Publishing Group, 1999.

Schlossberg, Dan. *The New Baseball Catalog*. New York: Jonathan David, 1998.

Schwarz, Alan. *The Numbers Game: Baseball's Lifelong Fascination with Statistics*. New York: St. Martin's Press, 2004.

Seymour, Harold. *Baseball: The Early Years*. New York: Oxford University Press, 1960.

———. *Baseball: The People's Game*. New York: Oxford University Press, 1990.

Shatzkin, Mike and Jim Carlton. *The Ballplayers: Baseball's Ultimate Biographical Reference*. New York: Arbor House, 1990.

Shouler, Ken, Bob Ryan, Sam Smith, Leonard Koppett and Bob Bellotti. *Total Basketball: The Ultimate Basketball Encyclopedia*. Toronto, ON, Canada: Sport Media Publishing, 2003.

Smith, H. Allen and Ira L. Smith. *Low and Inside: A Book of Baseball Anecdotes, Oddities and Curiosities*. Halcottsville, NY: Breakaway Books, 2000.

Solomon, Burt. *Where They Ain't: The Fabled Life and Untimely Death of the Original Baltimore Orioles. The Team that Gave Birth to Modern Baseball*. New York: Doubleday Books, 1999.

———. *The Baseball Timeline*. New York: DK Publishing, 2001.

Spalding, Albert G. *America's National Game*. Lincoln and London: University of Nebraska Press, 1992.

Sports Illustrated. *Sports Illustrated 2000 Sports Almanac*. New York: Time, 1999.

Steadman, John F. *From Colts to Ravens: A Behind-The-Scenes Look at Baltimore Professional Football*. Centreville, MD: Tidewater, 1997.

Stevens, David. *Baseball's Radical for All Seasons: A Biography of John Montgomery Ward*. Lanham, MD, and London: Scarecrow Press, 1998.

Sullivan, Neil J. *The Minors: The Struggles and the Triumph of Baseball's Poor Relation From 1876 to the Present*. New York: St. Martin's Press, 1990.

Thorn, John and Pete Palmer. *Total Baseball*. New York: Warner Books, 1989.

Thorn, John, Pete Palmer and Michael Gershman and David Pietrusza. *Total Baseball: The Official Encyclopedia of Major League Baseball, Sixth Edition*. New York: Total Sports, 1999.

Thorn, John, Pete Palmer, Michael Gershman. *Total Baseball: The Official Encyclopedia of Major League Baseball, Seventh Edition*. New York: Total Sports, 2001.

Thorn, John, Phil Birnbaum, Bill Deane, Rob Neyer, Alan Schwarz, Donald Dewey, Nicholas Acocella and Peter Wayner. *Total Baseball: The Ultimate Baseball Encyclopedia, Eighth Edition*. Wilmington, DE: Sport Classic Books, 2004.

Turner, Frederick. *When the Boys Came Back: Baseball and 1946*. New York: Henry Holt, 1996.

Tygiel, Jules. *Past Time: Baseball as History*. Oxford: Oxford University Press, 2000.

Veeck, Bill and Ed Linn. *Veeck as in Wreck*. New York: G. P. Putnam's Sons, 1965.

Voight, David Quentin. *American Baseball: Volume One*. University Park and London: The Pennsylvania State University Press, 1983.

Warfield, Don. *The Roaring Redhead: Larry MacPhail, Baseball's Great Innovator*. South Bend, IN: Diamond Communications, 1987.

Whiting, Robert. *The Chrysanthemum and the Bat: The Game Japanese Play*. Tokyo, Japan: The Permanent Press, 1977.

———. *The Samurai Way of Baseball: The Impact of Ichiro and the New Wave from Japan*. New York: Time Warner Book Group, 2004.

Whittingham, Richard. *What a Game They Played: An Inside Look at the Golden Era of Pro Football*. New York: Simon & Schuster, 1984.

Newspapers

Baltimore Sun
Chicago Tribune
Los Angeles Times
The Sporting News

Boston Globe
Dallas Morning Star
New York Times
Washington Post

Web Sites

apbr.com
baseballguru.com
baseballlibrary.combase
baseball1.com
cfl.com
databasefootball.com
etaiwannews.com
geocities.com
homeofheroes.com
japanesebaseball.com
minorleaguebaseball.com
pro-football-reference.com
sabr.org/bioproj
thebaseballcube.com
wikipedia.com

baseball-almanac.com
baseballhalloffame.org
ball-reference.com
boxrec.com
cubanball.com
decadesofracing.net
execpc.com
hhof.com
imdb.com
japanbaseballdaily.com
politicalgraveyard.com
proquest.umi.com
soccerhall.org
thedeadballera.com

Index

~

About the Author

Brian McKenna is a retail manager living in Baltimore County, Maryland, surrounded by his two fun-loving children, Brian and Rachel. He is currently working on a biography of Hall of Fame pitcher, manager, and executive Clark Griffith.